HIGHER

D1312827

GEOGRAPHY
PHYSICAL AND HUMAN ENVIRONMENTS

SECOND EDITION

Calum Campbell
Ian Geddes

HODDER
GIBSON
AN HACHETTE UK COMPANY

The publishers would like to thank the following individuals, institutions and companies for permission to reproduce copyright material:

Photo credits: Earth image used on chapter opener pages and in Task boxes throughout the book © leonello – iStock via Thinkstock/Getty Images; **p.6** © Drivepix – Fotolia; **p.13** © KeystoneUSA-ZUMA/REX; **p.15** © European Space Agency; **p.29** © Robert Garrigus/Alamy Stock Photo; **p.31** © Photodisc/Getty Images/World Landmarks & Travel V60; **p.32** (t) © Patrick Laux , (b) © Mamadou Toure BEHAN/AFP/GettyImages; **p.33** (l) © Greenshoots Communications/Alamy Stock Photo, (t/r) Courtesy of Hohum via Wikipedia Commons (http://creativecommons.org/licenses/by/2.0), (b/r) Courtesy of Marco Schmidt via Wikipedia Commons (http://creativecommons.org/licenses/by-sa/2.5/); **p.35** (t/l) © Martin Norris Travel Photography/Alamy Stock Photo, (t/r) © Elizabeth Whiting & Associates/Alamy Stock Photo; **p.36** © BOULENGER Xavier/Shutterstock; **p.44** (a) © vichie81 – iStock via Thinkstock/Getty Images, (b & c) © Ian Geddes; **p.52** © Anna Durinikova/Shutterstock.com; **p.54** © iweta0077/Shutterstock.com; **p.57** © David Dennis/Shutterstock.com; **p.59** © Goran Šafarek/Alamy Stock Photo; **p.65** (t) © CAISII MAO/AFP/Getty Images, (b) © Matt Cardy/Getty Images; **p.66** © ARCTIC IMAGES/Alamy Stock Photo; **p.68** © fraser band/Alamy Stock Photo; **p.69** South West Images Scotland/Alamy Stock Photo; **p.74** © 2019 Google DigitalGlobe; **p.75** © Photofusion/Shutterstock; **p.78** Calum Campbell; **p.81** (l/b)© NASA, (t/r) © All Canada Photos/Alamy Stock Photo, (b/r), © Stocktrek Images – Thinkstock/Getty Images; **p.82** (t/l) © Cavan Images/Alamy Stock Photo, (b/l) © staphy – Fotolia , (b/r) © Ion Alcoba Beitia/PhotoMedia/Don Paulson Photography – Superstock; **p.83** © Zoonar GmbH/Alamy Stock Photo; **p.89** © Peter Barritt/Alamy Stock Photo; **p.90** © SamStyles - iStock via Thinkstock/Getty Images; **p.92** (t) © Collpicto/Alamy Stock Photo; **p.93** (t/l) © Kevin George - iStock via Thinkstock/Getty Images, (t/r) © Bernhard Richter – iStock via Thinkstock/Getty Images; **p.94** © DEREKMcDOUGALL – iStock via Thinkstock/Getty Imgaes; **p.96** © Copyright N Chadwick and licensed for reuse under this Creative Commons Licence; **p.97** © Gary Tognoni – iStock via Thinkstock/Getty Images; **p.101** © Paul Heinrich/Alamy Stock Photo; **p.103** © SAM FRIED/SCIENCE PHOTO LIBRARY; **p.104** © Tom Bean/Alamy Stock Photo; **p.111** © a-plus image bank/Alamy Stock Photo; **p.113** © Copyright David Hawgood and licensed for reuse under http://creativecommons.org/licenses/by-sa/2.0/; **p.114** (t/l) © Calum Campbell, (t/r) © ChrisPole - iStock via Thinkstock/Getty Images; **p.117** © Miguel Ortega-Sánchez. Associate Professor. University of Granada; **p.121** © 2019 Google DigitalGlobe; **p.124** (t–b) © Copyright Andrew Smith and licensed for reuse under http://creativecommons.org/licenses/by-sa/2.0/, © milosz_g – Fotolia, © Ian Geddes; **p.125** © Apollo 17 Crew, NASA; **p.130** © Denis and Yulia Pogostins/Fotolia; **p.132** © Ian Geddes; **p.136** (l –r) Courtesy of Richard Hartnup via Wikipedia Commons (Public Domain), Courtesy of HolgerK via Wikipedia Commons (Public Domain), Courtesy of Soil Science via Flickr (https://www.flickr.com/photos/soilscience/5140652884); **p.142** (l) © AlbertoLoyo - iStock via Thinkstock/Getty Images, (r) © Ian Geddes; **p.143** © DanielPrudek - iStock via Thinkstock/Getty Images; **p.144** © zhudifeng - iStock via Thinkstock/Getty Images; **p.145** (t) © VCG/VCG via Getty Images, (b) © The Asahi Shimbun via Getty Images; **p.152** © Ian Geddes; **p.161** (l) © Wu Hong/EPA/Shutterstock, (r) © MANPREET ROMANA/AFP/Getty Images; **p.168** (t/r) © Stephen Bures/Alamy Stock Photo, (t/l) © MANPREET ROMANA/AFP/Getty Images, (m/l) © Servais Mont/Getty Images, (b/l) © HAP/Quirky China News/REX/Shutterstock; **p.171** © Ian Geddes; **p.173** © KHALIL MAZRAAWI/AFP/Getty Images; **p.176** (t) © REUTERS/Chaiwat Subprasom, (b) © Ian Geddes; **p.177** © Johnny Lye - iStock via Thinkstock/Getty Images; **p.178** (t) © luoman - iStock via Thinkstock/Getty Images, (b) © Goodshoot via Thinkstock/Getty Images, (r) © ANTONIO SCORZA/AFP/Getty Images; **p.180** © SEBASTIAN CASTAÑEDA/AFP/Getty Images; **p.183** © EVARISTO SA/AFP/Getty Images; **p.186** © Sipa Press/REX/Shutterstock; **p.192** © Bkamprath - iStock via Thinkstock/Getty Images; **p.200** © JordiDelgado - iStock via Thinkstock/Getty Images; **p.201** (t) © RGB Ventures/SuperStock/Alamy, (b) © Bo Rader/Wichita EagleMCT via Getty Images; **p.205** © Tim Graham/Alamy Stock Photo; **p.214** © 2019 Google DigitalGlobe; **p.215** (t/l) © I_Longworth – iStock via Thinkstoc/Getty Images, (r) © ColsTravel/Alamy Stock Photo; **p.223** (t/l) © Jon Sparks/Alamy Stock Photo, (t/r) © Vincent Lowe/Alamy Stock Photo; **p.225** © Brian Jannsen/Alamy Stock Photo; **p.226** (l) © Joe Gough – iStock via Thinkstock/Getty Images, (r) © aquasolid – iStock via Thinkstock/Getty Images; **p.229** © korhil65 – iStock via Thinkstock/Getty Images; **p.232** © Dimitry111 – Fotolia; **p.233** © robertharding/Alamy Stock Photo; **p.236** © Greg Balfour Evans/Alamy Stock Photo; **p.238** (left t–b) © aartstudio – Fotolia, © tomek_emigrant – Fotolia, © Copyright Stephen Sweeney and licensed for reuse under this license (http://creativecommons.org/licenses/by-sa/2.0/), © Copyright Billy McCrorie and licensed for reuse under this license (http://creativecommons.org/licenses/by-sa/2.0/), (right t–b) © Angus Forbes - iStock iva Thinkstock/Getty Images, © Trinity Mirror/Mirrorpix/Alamy Stock Photo; **p.241** © aerialarchives.com/Alamy Stock Photos; **p.242** © Celso Pupo rodrigues - Hemera via Thinkstock/Getty Images; **p.244** © Xiao Lu Chu/Getty Images; **p.246** (l) © KHALED DESOUKI/AFP/Getty Images, (r) © hxdbzxy - iStock via Thinkstock/Getty Images; **p.247** © chuyu - iStock via Thinkstock/Getty Images; **p.250** (t) © hris1johnson/Seidenstud via Wikipedia Commons (https://creativecommons.org/licenses/by/2.0/deed.en), (b) © Agencia Estado via AP Images; **p.252** (b/l) © imageBROKER/Alamy, (t/r) © SAJJAD HUSSAIN/AFP/Getty Images; **p.259** (l) © Monty Fresco/Stringer/Hulton Archive/Getty Images, (r) © Rolls Press/Popperfoto/Getty Images; **p.264** (t/l) © sandy young/Alamy, (b/l) © Carol McCabe/REX/Shutterstock, (t/r) © Topfoto.

Every effort has been made to trace all copyright holders, but if any have been inadvertently overlooked the Publishers will be pleased to make the necessary arrangements at the first opportunity.

Although every effort has been made to ensure that website addresses are correct at time of going to press, Hodder Gibson cannot be held responsible for the content of any website mentioned in this book. It is sometimes possible to find a relocated web page by typing in the address of the home page for a website in the URL window of your browser.

Hachette UK's policy is to use papers that are natural, renewable and recyclable products and made from wood grown in well-managed forests and other controlled sources. The logging and manufacturing processes are expected to conform to the environmental regulations of the country of origin.

Orders: please contact Hachette UK Distribution, Hely Hutchinson Centre, Milton Road, Didcot, Oxfordshire, OX11 7HH. Telephone: +44 (0)1235 827827. Email education@hachette.co.uk Lines are open from 9 a.m. to 5 p.m., Monday to Friday. You can also order through our website: www.hoddereducation.co.uk. If you have queries or questions that aren't about an order, you can contact us at hoddergibson@hodder.co.uk

We are an approved supplier on the Scotland Excel framework.

Schools can find us on their procurement system as: **Hodder & Stoughton Limited t/a Hodder Gibson.**

Cover photo © ldanupong - stock.adobe.com
Illustrations by Integra Software Services Pvt. Ltd., Pondicherry, India
Typeset by Integra Software Services Pvt. Ltd., Pondicherry, India
Printed in India

A catalogue record for this title is available from the British Library
ISBN: 978 1 5104 5776 8

MIX
Paper from responsible sources
FSC™ C104740
www.fsc.org

Contents

PHYSICAL ENVIRONMENTS

HUMAN ENVIRONMENTS

Introduction to Higher Geography

How to use this book

This book is one of two core text books and has been written to help you prepare for the SQA Higher Grade Geography examination. The focus of this core book is Physical and Human Environments and contains background information, course content, reflections and questions about each of the seven topics.

- Atmosphere
- Hydrosphere
- Lithosphere
- Biosphere
- Population
- Rural
- Urban

▲ **Figure 0.1** The 'big day' finally arrives!

The seven physical and human issues in this book have been broken down into a number of smaller descriptive topics. These are outlined in the table below.

Atmosphere	
	• Global heat budget
	• Redistribution of energy by atmospheric and oceanic circulation
	• Cause, characteristics and impact of the intertropical convergence zone

Hydrosphere	
	• Hydrological cycle within a drainage basin
	• Interpretation of hydrographs
	• Formation of erosional and depositional features in river landscapes:
	• V-shaped valley
	• waterfall
	• meander
	• oxbow lake

Lithosphere	
	• Formation of erosional and depositional features in glaciated landscapes:
	• corrie
	• arête
	• pyramidal peak
	• U-shaped valley
	• hanging valley
	• ribbon lake
	• drumlin
	• esker
	• terminal moraine
	• Formation of erosional and depositional features in coastal landscapes:
	• wave-cut platform
	• headland and bay
	• cave
	• arch
	• stack
	• spit
	• bar
	• tombolo

Biosphere	
	• Properties and formation of podzol, brown earth and gley soils

Population	
	• Methods and problems of data collection
	• Consequences of population structure
	• Causes and impacts of forced and voluntary migration

Rural	
	• Impact and management of rural land degradation related to a rainforest or semi-arid area
	• Rural land use conflicts and their management related to either a glaciated or coastal landscape

Urban	
	• The need for management of recent urban change (housing and transport) in a developed and in a developing world city
	• Management strategies employed
	• Impact of the management strategies

Aims of the Higher Geography course

The Higher Geography course develops learners' understanding of our changing world and its human and physical processes in local, national, international and global study contexts.

In our fast-changing and increasingly complex world, an underlying theme throughout this book is to encourage learners to interact with their environment.

This book will enable you to develop:

- a wider range of geographical skills and techniques
- an understanding of the complexity of ways in which people and the environment interact in response to physical and human processes at the local, national, international and global scales
- an understanding of spatial relationships and of the complexity of the changing world, in a balanced, critical and sympathetic way
- a geographical perspective on environmental and social issues and their significance
- an interest in, understanding of and concern for the environment and sustainable development.

We hope that you agree with the significance and importance of these aims.

Structure of Higher Geography Physical and Human Environments

Each chapter in this book shares a broadly similar format and contains the following features:

- Subject content
- Background content considered to be relevant to full understanding of each theme
- Key case studies
- Tasks to test knowledge, understanding and application of skills
- Opportunities for reflection
- Opportunities for further research.

A glossary of key terms is also provided at the end of the book.

To pass the Geography course you are expected to have acquired a range of skills and be able to interpret and analyse a range of resources including maps, photographs, field sketches, cross sections, transects, statistical/tabular data and graphs. SQA, in the question papers, also expect you to be able to apply these skills to geographical contexts with which you may be familiar or unfamiliar. In addition to all of this, over the course you will become skilled at developing and applying factual knowledge, interactions and theoretical knowledge and understanding:

- at local, national and global scales
- within a range of urban and rural environments
- within both developed and developing societies.

Throughout this book there is a focus on words such as causes, consequences, interpretation, impact, management and strategies.

Examination structure

The source of the information contained in this section is the Scottish Qualifications Authority – www.sqa.org.uk. You are strongly recommended to obtain a copy of the specification for the course and to refer to the website regularly for updates and information.

The SQA Higher Geography course contains three mandatory sections:

- Geography: Physical Environments
- Geography: Human Environments
- Geography: Global Issues

However, within this you have some scope for choice. As stated earlier, there are two books in this series. The other book, *Global Issues*, contains the following key topics:

- River Basin Management
- Development and Health
- Global Climate Change

These are the three most popular topics selected by the majority of schools to study. A fourth topic, 'Energy' is not covered in the Global Issues Book.

The four global topics have been broken down into a number of smaller descriptive topic areas:

River Basin Management	• Physical characteristics of a selected river basin • Need for water management • Selection and development of sites • Consequences of water control projects
Development and Health	• Validity of development indicators • Differences in levels of development between developing countries • A water-related disease: causes, impact, management • Primary health care strategies
Global Climate Change	• Physical and human causes • Local and global effects • Management strategies and their limitations
Energy	• Global distribution of energy resources • Reasons for increase in demand for energy in both developed and developing countries • Effectiveness of renewable and non-renewable approaches to meeting energy demands and their sustainability within different countries

How is Higher Geography assessed?

The course is assessed by three components:

- Component 1: Question paper 1, Physical and human environments (100 marks*)
- Component 2: Question paper 2, Global and geographical skills (60 marks*)
- Component 3: Assignment (30 marks)

Total marks available 190*

* An explanation: SQA has chosen to scale the question paper marks. This means that while Question paper 1 is marked out of 100 and Question paper 2 is marked out of 60, there is a statistical process that will reduce the overall value of each paper to 50 and 30 marks.

The course assessment is graded A–D. Your grade is determined on the basis of your total mark for the three course components added together.

Components 1 and 2: Question papers (160 marks)

The examination is set and marked by SQA and appointed specialist teachers of Geography. There are two question papers. You are required to answer in an 'extended-response' manner (i.e. you must write in sentences, not lists or bullet points) using knowledge, understanding and the skills you have acquired during the course.

This book covers in detail the content for Question paper 1.

Question paper 1: Physical and human environments (100 marks)

Question paper 1 has two sections:

- Section 1 Physical environments
- Section 2 Human environments

Each section is worth 50 marks and consists of extended-response questions. You should answer all the questions in each section.

You have 1 hour and 50 minutes to complete this question paper.

The content for Question paper 2 is covered in the accompanying book, *Global Issues*.

Question paper 2: Global issues and geographical skills (60 marks)

Question paper 2 also has two sections:

- Section 1 Global issues (40 marks)
  This section consists of extended-response questions. You should choose two from the four questions. Each question is worth 20 marks.
- Section 2 Application of geographical skills (20 marks)
  This section consists of a mandatory extended-response question. You should apply geographical skills acquired during the course. The skills assessed in this section include the use of mapping, numerical and graphical information.

You have 1 hour and 10 minutes to complete this question paper

Your teachers will guide you regarding standards, structure, requirements and marking. The SQA web will publish 'Specimen question papers' with marking instructions.

Component 3: Assignment (30 marks)

Geography is not only about reading from textbooks. It is also about researching, thinking for yourself and applying all that you have covered in the classroom in a practical setting. The assignment is your opportunity to demonstrate the application of these skills, knowledge and understanding within the context of a geographical topic or issue. The time allocated for the writing up the assignment under 'exam conditions' is 1 hour and 30 minutes.

While this book includes ideas for assignments, the Hodder book *How to Pass National 5 and Higher Assignments: Geography* by Susan Clarke covers the skills in considerable detail.

The assignment allows you to show your skills, knowledge and understanding by:

- identifying a geographical topic or issue
- carrying out research, which should include fieldwork where appropriate
- demonstrating knowledge of the suitability of the methods and/or reliability of the sources used
- processing and using a range of information gathered
- drawing on detailed knowledge and understanding of the topic or issue
- analysing information from a range of sources
- reaching a conclusion supported by a range of evidence on a geographical topic or issue
- communicating information.

Examination techniques

The Higher examination set by SQA is fair and is based on a clear specification. The paper is designed to fit the allocated time. SQA has a long history of delivering quality examination standards. A Higher Geography pass is recognised as a useful and worthwhile qualification, so it is worth time and effort to develop your skills and knowledge to ensure you achieve a pass.

Figure 0.2 shows the examination jigsaw – recognise the six parts required to be put together so that you pass.

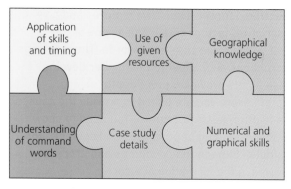

▲ **Figure 0.2** Examination jigsaw

 ## Reflection

Take a moment and jot down what you have to do to fail your Higher Geography examination! Take a moment and jot down why you deserve to pass.

You probably felt it strange to consider what you need to do to fail but hopefully you have come up with some of these suggestions:

- failure to revise
- failure to manage your time
- failure to turn up for the exam on the right day or time
- failure to follow the task that you are set.

All of this is under your control!

Command words

In the Geography examination there are seven possible 'command words' (or instructions that tell you how to answer a question). The SQA course assessment notes say that you have an opportunity to demonstrate your knowledge and competency by:

- using a wide range of geographical skills and techniques
- **describing**, **explaining**, **evaluating** and **analysing** complex geographical issues using knowledge and understanding which is factual and theoretical, of the physical and human processes and interactions at work within geographical contexts on a local, regional and global scale.

Be aware that there is overlap between the key command words highlighted on page 10.

1 **Describe**: Identify distinctive features and give descriptive, factual detail. This is one of the most widely used command words. The marking instructions also allow you to further develop these points providing more depth.

2 **Explain**: Here you are asked to provide the causes of a feature, issue or pattern. You need to show an understanding of processes and sources. For example, 'Explain the conditions and processes involved in the formation of a corrie.'

3 **Evaluate**: Weigh up several options or arguments and then **come to a conclusion** with regard to the importance, success or impact. Your judgement is important. Provide an insight into your thinking, leading to the decision or conclusion you reached. For example, 'Evaluate the effectiveness of various methods used to control the spread of malaria.'

4 **Analyse**: You need to be able to break down the content into its constituent parts in order to provide an **in-depth account**. These questions involve relationships between and within a topic, and recognise implications, links, variety of views and consequences. For example, 'Analyse the impact of migration on either the donor country or the receiving country.'

5 **Account for**: In this style of question you are asked to give reasons for trends, issues, decisions and alternative actions. Account questions, like many geographical tasks, are often based on issues which can be tested or may be subject to different views.

6 **Discuss**: The key idea here is to allow you to explore different ideas about a project or about impact or even change. Once again, you are expected to be able to review alternative scenarios. Although you can express your own views, you must also show an awareness of other contrasting views. For example, 'Discuss the possible impact of global warming throughout the world.'

7 **To what extent**: Here you are asked to consider the impact of a plan, strategy or programme and to form a view on the success or failure of that programme. In Geography, there is seldom 100 per cent agreement about the outcome. Your awareness of the competing interests and values is important. For example, 'To what extent has the Colorado River Management Project achieved its aims of flood control and power generation?'

The process model

Geographers have a way of going about their business. Geography is a social science or a social subject and as such it has a logical and sequential way of looking at the world and the human and physical interactions. Figure 0.3 shows the process model that illustrates the way geographers approach issues.

The marker's perspective

What do markers look for? They look for relevance – so if it is not asked for, then do not include it in your answer. Markers love detail, so work really hard at your case studies. Higher Geography is only marked in full marks, there are no half marks. You need to write in sentences. If you look at a set of markers' instructions (see www.sqa.org.uk) you will see how marks are awarded. For one mark you need to provide a developed (detailed) point, so get into the habit of writing sentences that show this.

Markers love to see that students have attempted diagrams to illustrate an answer. They will first mark all the writing and only then give additional marks for new information in and around the diagram. (Be aware though that if a question asks you specifically to draw a diagram you must do so as this forms part of the answer that will gain marks.)

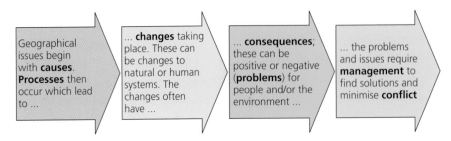

Geographical issues begin with **causes**. **Processes** then occur which lead to ...

... **changes** taking place. These can be changes to natural or human systems. The changes often have ...

... **consequences**; these can be positive or negative (**problems**) for people and/or the environment ...

... the problems and issues require **management** to find solutions and minimise **conflict**

▲ **Figure 0.3** The geographical way of doing things

Markers are fair and want you to do well. They like an answer that has a clear structure and can be easily read. Do not repeat yourself and get into the habit of using words such as, 'this is because ...' or 'an example of this is ...' Remember: you cannot lose marks, you only gain them.

To summarise, marks are awarded when your answers are:

- relevant to the issue in the question
- developed responses (by providing additional detail, reasons or evidence)
- used to respond to the command words/demands of the question (e.g. evaluate/explain/analyse).

Revision strategies

There are many good revision books and websites and your teachers will give you advice. Here are our top ten tips:

1 Create your own personal study space.
2 Get organised: cards, pens, folders, highlighter pens, notes ...
3 Use relaxation techniques to get you into the mood for revision.
4 Actively read and write notes.
5 Use your notes and past papers.
6 Be creative in your revision, for example try using mind maps.
7 Leave your study space organised for the next session.
8 Take breaks and time out and reflect on your revision session.
9 Put in plenty of quality revision time.
10 Get support from family and friends.

Bonus tip: Consider whether you need your phone/tablet in the same room as you when you revise!

You can either use technology to assist you with your revision to gain knowledge and skills OR it can be a distraction!

Examination techniques

- On the day of the exam, be organised and arrive at the exam hall in plenty of time, with all the equipment needed.
- Make sure that you have eaten and have brought water to drink.
- Follow all the instructions and answer the correct number of questions from each section.
- Remember relaxation techniques.
- Remember that you have done the work so do not panic, read the question again and stay calm.
- Keep your answers legible.
- Make sure the length of each answer you write is appropriate to the number of marks on offer.
- Be aware of time and manage it to maximum effect.
- At the end, check all your answers and add details.

Figure 0.5 provides a helpful summary of the ideal approach to the exam.

▲ **Figure 0.4** 'I got an A!'

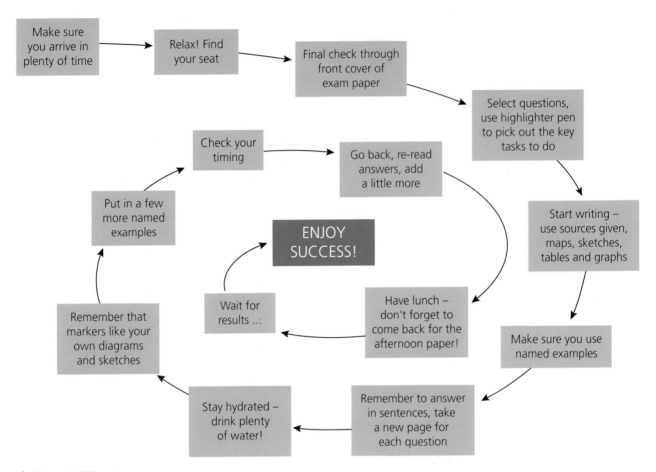

Make sure you arrive in plenty of time → Relax! Find your seat → Final check through front cover of exam paper → Select questions, use highlighter pen to pick out the key tasks to do → Start writing – use sources given, maps, sketches, tables and graphs → Make sure you use named examples → Remember to answer in sentences, take a new page for each question → Stay hydrated – drink plenty of water! → Remember that markers like your own diagrams and sketches → Put in a few more named examples → Check your timing → Go back, re-read answers, add a little more → Have lunch – don't forget to come back for the afternoon paper! → Wait for results ..: → ENJOY SUCCESS!

▲ **Figure 0.5** Tips to ensure success

Acknowledgements

I'd like to thank all the people and groups who have encouraged and supported me through the writing of this book:

- My wife Wendy and daughter Laurin
- Nancy and George Davidson
- Ian Geddes, my co-author and friend, and all of those at Hodder
- My former colleagues Jim Knox, Alan Johnstone, Bob Reid, Christine Campbell, Brady Robertson and Laura Kerr
- All the 'Byristas' (including Al Lee-Bourke, Martyn Olesen, Julian Pye, 'Jofus' Lumsden), Eddie and (the much missed) Evelyn Carden for your kindness and friendship.
- All my friends and their families
- Never forgetting Jim, Muriel, Charlie and Jane.

Calum Campbell

Writing this book has been a pleasure. I am delighted to acknowledge the support and encouragement from my wife, Susan, and daughters Amelia and Susan. Over the years I have been privileged to teach many students of geography and it is for them that this book has been written. Thanks also to my grandchildren Lucy, Katie, Blair and Donny, the future generation of geographers! Thanks to my co-author, Calum, it's been fun, especially your encouragement to partake in afternoon scones! The support and advice from the staff at Hodder Gibson in Glasgow has been immense. Thank you all.

Ian Geddes

Chapter 1 Atmosphere

Introduction

After working through this chapter you should be able to apply geographic skills alongside knowledge and understanding of the processes and interactions at work within the **atmosphere**. These should be applied on a local, regional and global scale. In particular you should have a detailed understanding of the **global heat budget**, redistribution of energy by atmosphere and ocean circulation, and the causes, characteristics and impacts of the **intertropical convergence zone (ITCZ)**.

1.1 What is the atmosphere?

The atmosphere is a blanket of gases surrounding our planet, held in place by the force of gravity. The atmosphere has numerous functions, not least being that in its current state life as we know it is supported and has flourished. It provides us with the correct balance of gases at lower altitudes to allow us to breathe and acts as a filter to remove harmful amounts of **solar radiation** which would otherwise wipe out life.

In addition, the atmosphere helps to:

- retain heat that would otherwise radiate back into space, leaving the planet frozen and lifeless
- move heat around the planet so that the lower latitudes are not too hot and the higher latitudes too cold
- reduce possible temperature extremes between day and night (**diurnal temperature variation**).

▲ **Figure 1.1** Felix Baumgartner prepares to jump to Earth from an altitude of 39 km (in the stratosphere) in 2012.

The atmosphere is a system that creates a balance of temperatures allowing life on Earth to exist.

Research opportunity

Take a few minutes to search online for these topics:

- How did our atmosphere form?
- How has our atmosphere changed since it first formed?

Next, research the following topics:
global warming; climate change; greenhouse effect; ozone depletion; ozone; sunshine and skin cancer. Think about how much discussion and debate is going on in this area (and how much material you could source for your assignment). You will find there is a lot of information. For a Geography student, a knowledge of the changes in our atmosphere over time and what caused them is helpful if you are considering these topics for your assignment.

Composition and structure of the atmosphere

The Earth's atmosphere is made up of many different gases: nitrogen (78.084 per cent), oxygen (20.946 per cent), argon (0.934 per cent), with the remainder being made up of small amounts of other gases, including carbon dioxide and water vapour (Figure 1.2).

Of the additional gases, water vapour (lower atmosphere), **ozone** (O_3) (upper atmosphere) and carbon dioxide play a greater role than their tiny amounts would suggest. Ozone helps to protect life on the planet by filtering out most of the harmful incoming **ultraviolet (UV) radiation** from the Sun. If Earth was not protected in such a way from the radiation, animal/human flesh would be exposed to extreme burning, eye damage, damaged immune systems, genetic damage, skin cancers and eventually death. Vegetation would mutate, suffer cell damage and also die.

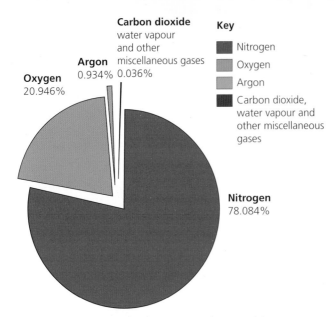

▲ **Figure 1.2** Present atmospheric gas composition

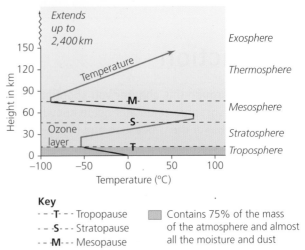

▲ **Figure 1.3** Structure of the atmosphere and temperatures within layers

Water vapour and carbon dioxide are two important **greenhouse gases** that help the atmosphere to trap some of the heat (infra-red radiation) trying to escape the planet and back into space. If the natural greenhouse gases did not do this, the Earth's temperature would fall by around 33°C and life would be impossible.

In addition to naturally occurring constituents we need to be aware that human-created pollutants such as sulphur dioxide, nitrogen oxide and methane from industry, power stations and car exhausts enter our atmosphere. This knowledge will allow further engagement with the topics noted earlier for background and research opportunities. The amounts of these gases are only at trace levels but are believed to have the potential to alter our atmosphere and its life sustaining properties.

The atmosphere is not the same from the surface of the planet to its boundary with space. **Atmospheric pressure** decreases with height but temperature changes are more complex and help us to identify different vertical zones. Five separate zones have been recognised within the atmosphere and these are (from the surface upwards) the **troposphere**, **stratosphere**, **mesosphere**, **thermosphere** and **exosphere** (see Figure 1.3). Each of these has its own specific composition and characteristics. The boundary between each zone is called a 'pause' and is named after the lower of the two

that meet. This means that the meeting point of the troposphere and the stratosphere is called the tropopause.

For the purposes of Higher Geography the focus of study will mostly be on the troposphere and the stratosphere.

In the troposphere we find most of the atmospheric moisture, 75 per cent of all the atmosphere's air and also dust. Due to human activity the majority of all atmospheric pollution is also found here. This is the layer where most **weather** and **climate** phenomena take place. Temperatures in the troposphere drop by 6.4°C for every 1,000 metres increase in height. This happens due to the surface of the planet being warmed by heat from the Sun, which in turn heats the air nearest to it and so the further above the surface the colder the air will be. Air pressure also decreases with height as the effect of gravity lessens.

Above the troposphere, the stratosphere is dry but marked by a steady increase in temperature. This is caused by a concentration of ozone (O_3) that absorbs high energy UV radiation from the Sun. As mentioned earlier, the **ozone layer** also helps protect life on the planet from the harmful rays.

The boundary between the troposphere and the stratosphere (tropopause) varies in height due to latitude and season. At the equator it can reach up to 16 km but by the poles it is only 8 km.

Task

1 Explain what the atmosphere is and why it is invaluable to life on our planet.
2 What is the composition of the atmosphere at present?
3 Explain the important role of greenhouse gases in the atmosphere.
4 How does the concentration of O_3 in the stratosphere help to protect life?

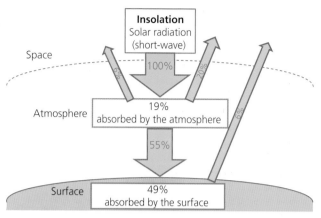

▲ **Figure 1.5** Solar radiation and energy exchange

1.2 Global heat budget

The global heat budget is the usable energy maintained by the Earth as a balance between energy received by the planet (input) and that which is radiated back out into space (output). This balance of energy powers the atmospheric system, ocean currents and climates which allow life to be sustained within the biosphere.

For the Earth, the Sun is the prime source of energy. The Sun is our closest star and, although the exact distance varies according to the position of the Earth in its orbit, it is approximately 150 million km away. The Sun is mostly made up of a hot plasma of hydrogen and helium gases and creates energy by thermonuclear fusion at its core. This energy is then radiated out from the core and into the solar system as heat and light (see Figure 1.4). Earth only intercepts a very small amount of this energy but it is vital for sustenance of life.

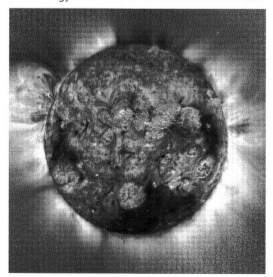

▲ **Figure 1.4** Temperature map of the Sun's corona photographed by the SOHO spacecraft

Earth receives its energy as incoming short-wave solar (Sun) radiation. This is also known as insolation (a good way to remember this is by thinking of it as **IN**coming **SOL**ar radi**ATION**). This moves downward through the atmosphere, interacting with each of the layers and their components, reducing the final energy amount that reaches the surface and filtering out harmful rays (Figures 1.5 and 1.6).

Some 32 per cent of the insolation is reflected or scattered back into space. This is known as the albedo (the intensity of light reflected from an object, such as a planet). The albedo of the Earth is caused by reflection from clouds and the planet's surface and scattering by gas particles in the atmosphere. In addition to this, another 19 per cent of solar radiation is absorbed by clouds' water vapour and dust (Figure 1.5).

From these figures it can be seen that only around 55 per cent of incoming solar radiation reaches the Earth's surface following absorption, scattering and reflection as it is passed through the atmosphere. Of this, only 49 per cent is absorbed by the surface (Figure 1.6).

The output from this system is mostly in the form of infra-red (long-wave) radiation. As it is coming from the Earth, this is referred to as terrestrial radiation (Figure 1.7). The incoming solar radiation was generated as short-wave due to the extreme heat of the Sun (approximately 5,505°C at its surface and 15 million °C at its core) while terrestrial radiation is mostly long-wave as it is *nowhere* near as warm. Of this long-wave energy, 6 per cent goes directly

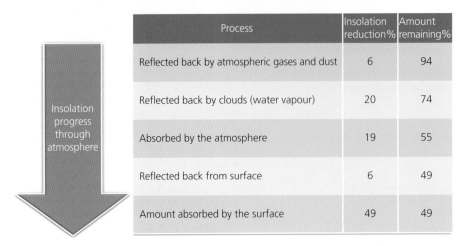

Process	Insolation reduction%	Amount remaining%
Reflected back by atmospheric gases and dust	6	94
Reflected back by clouds (water vapour)	20	74
Absorbed by the atmosphere	19	55
Reflected back from surface	6	49
Amount absorbed by the surface	49	49

▲ **Figure 1.6** Insolation's progress through the atmosphere

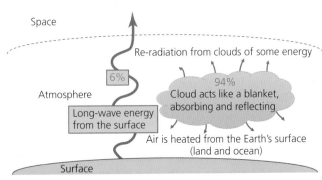

▲ **Figure 1.7** Terrestrial radiation

into space with the remaining 94 per cent absorbed by clouds, water vapour and carbon dioxide in the atmosphere. This remaining 94 per cent is not permanently trapped and will eventually be released back into space.

The amount of insolation absorbed or reflected by the Earth's surface is not a constant. It can be affected by the angle of the rays hitting the surface, due to its distance from the equator, and the Earth's tilt at different times of the year. The composition of the surface, colour, rock type or coverage (soil, vegetation, ice or water) also has an effect. Lighter-toned surfaces have higher albedos (for example glaciated landscapes) and as such reflect more energy. Darker soils and even coniferous forests reflect much less. Areas of water (lakes, seas and oceans) are more problematic and rely heavily on the angle at which the Sun's rays approach (Figure 1.8). When the Sun is

higher in the sky (more directly overhead), water can absorb over 95 per cent of insolation, but at a steeper angle reflection increases.

Natural surface type	Additional details	Albedo
Soil	Dark	0.40 to 0.50
	Light	
Sand	Dry, tropical desert	0.15 to 0.4
Grass	Long	0.16 to 0.26
	Short	
Forests	Deciduous (broad leafed with seasonal leaf loss)	0.15 to 0.25
	Coniferous (mostly needle-leaved or scale-leaved, evergreen and cone-bearing)	0.5 to 0.16
Agricultural crops	Seasonal variation in height and colour	0.18 to 0.27
Water	Sun high in sky	0.10 to 1.00
	Sun at steep angle	0.03 to 0.10
Ice	Sea	0.30 to 0.44
	Glacial	0.20 to 0.40
Snow	Old	0.40 to 0.95
	Fresh	
Tundra	Seasonal variation in colour, vegetation and wetness (ice covered in winter; lakes and swamps in summer)	0.18 to 0.25

Albedo is expressed on a scale of 0 to 1:
0 shows no reflectivity
1 shows that all light energy is reflected

▲ **Figure 1.8** Surface reflectivity

Artificial surfaces can also have an effect, especially in built-up areas with concrete (buildings and paved areas) reflecting up to 55 per cent and tarred (asphalt) surfaces (roads and car parks) 3 per cent when newly laid and 11 per cent when worn.

As mentioned earlier, water vapour, carbon dioxide and other greenhouse gases slow down the escape of terrestrial radiation from the atmosphere. This greenhouse effect acts as a blanket, retaining some of the heat and preventing the planet from becoming too cold.

It should be noted that much of the heating of the atmosphere comes from the energy being returned from the Earth's surface (long-wave terrestrial radiation) and through latent heat given out when water evaporates, rises from the surface and condenses.

Energy receipt

The amount of energy received from the Sun varies very little and is known as the solar constant. This is the amount of radiation received without the effect of the Earth's atmosphere. This figure is worked out to represent how much energy would be received at the surface of the Earth perpendicular (at right angles) to the Sun's rays at a time when the Earth is at its mean distance (the average of the greatest and least distances) from the Sun. The amount is generally accepted as approximately 1366 joules per second per square metre (J/s·m²).

This does not mean that every place on the surface of planet Earth receives this amount. The previous section showed that there is a vertical reduction in radiation as it travels through the atmosphere, but figures indicate that there is also an imbalance of energy receipt on different locations on the planet's surface. A simplified general rule would be that the further north or south travelled from the Tropics (towards higher or lower latitude) there is less energy being received at the surface per square metre.

Looking in greater detail, Figure 1.9 shows that:

- between approximately 35° North and 35° South there is an energy surplus (more than is required) because insolation is greater than outgoing radiation
- towards their respective Poles from 35° North and 35° South there is a deficit of energy (less than is required) as outgoing radiation exceeds insolation.

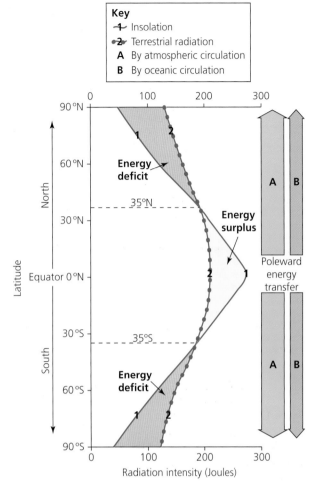

▲ **Figure 1.9** Energy balance and transfer

In addition to this, more energy is absorbed by the surface between 35° North and 35° South than in the rest of the surface area of the planet.

This pattern of temperature reduction from the intensely heated Tropics to the extremely cold polar regions is known as the latitudinal or global temperature gradient.

As can be seen in Figure 1.10, this global temperature gradient appears to be due to a number of factors:

- Between the Tropics the Sun's rays are more concentrated (focused on a smaller area) than further north or south, due to the curvature of the Earth. Moving away from the equator the surface of the planet slopes away from the Sun, causing rays of insolation to spread out further. These rays entering the atmosphere would have equal energy but by being forced to spread out as the surface curves away they are distributed over a much larger area. (From the Earth's surface the

Sun appears almost overhead in the Tropics but at higher latitudes it is lower in the sky.)

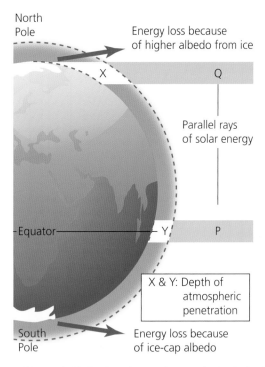

▲ **Figure 1.10** Equinox insolation receipt by latitude

- Again due to the curvature of the Earth, a ray will pass through less of the atmosphere near to the Equator than it will further north or south. This means that there will be more scattering and absorption of insolation in the higher latitudes resulting in less energy being received at the surface.
- In addition to this, at the polar regions large amounts of ice and snow increase the albedo effect and much more incoming solar radiation is reflected back towards space than from dense vegetation around the equator.

While the tropical latitudes have almost equal lengths of day and night throughout the year the higher latitudes do not have this constancy of insolation amounts.

- Earth orbits the Sun and because the planet is tilted on its **axis** parts of the Earth get more heat and light at different times of the year. During the northern hemisphere's spring and summer this area is tilted towards the Sun and gains more insolation and the length of daylight increases (Figure 1.11). At that same time the southern hemisphere is tilted away from the Sun giving it its autumn and winter with less insolation and shorter

daylight hours. This **axial tilt** (**axial obliquity**) has created the seasons and when the northern hemisphere is experiencing its autumn and winter (tilting away from the Sun) it will be spring and summer in the southern hemisphere. At two points in the year the Earth is in an up-right position in relation to the Sun giving equal lengths of night and day and insolation to both northern and southern hemispheres. These dates are known as the **vernal equinox** (March in the northern hemisphere and September in the southern hemisphere) and **autumnal equinox** (September in the northern hemisphere and March in the southern hemisphere) and Figure 1.11 shows this balance of insolation.

What is clear is that if these conditions were the only thing that affected energy receipt and temperatures then the tropical areas would become hotter and hotter while those further north and south would become much colder. This would severely limit the chances of life surviving on the planet. Fortunately the Earth has developed systems through which thermal (heat) energy is transferred from areas of surplus to areas of deficit.

Task

1   What is the global heat budget?
2   Explain the terms insolation and albedo.
3   Explain why only around 55 per cent of incoming solar radiation reaches the Earth's surface.
4   What is terrestrial radiation and how does it affect the atmosphere?
5   What is the solar constant?
6   Explain why not all areas of the surface of the Earth receive the same amount of energy from the Sun.

1.3 Energy transfer

Preventing the build-up of increasing latitudinal extremes in temperature is the interlinked redistribution of energy by **atmospheric circulation** and **oceanic circulation**. In simple terms, the energy is transferred from areas of surplus to areas of deficit by movement within the atmosphere and the oceans. It is believed that around 75 per cent of thermal energy is redistributed around the planet by atmospheric

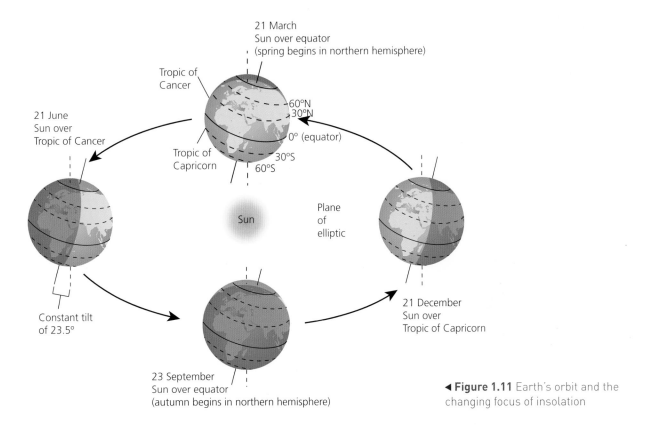

21 March
Sun over equator
(spring begins in northern hemisphere)

Tropic of Cancer

21 June
Sun over
Tropic of Cancer

60°N
30°N
0° (equator)

Tropic of Cancer

Tropic of Capricorn

30°S
60°S

Sun

Plane of elliptic

Constant tilt of 23.5°

21 December
Sun over
Tropic of Capricorn

23 September
Sun over equator
(autumn begins in northern hemisphere)

◀ **Figure 1.11** Earth's orbit and the changing focus of insolation

circulation and 25 per cent by ocean currents. These processes help to create and maintain the world's climatic zones as we know them.

These processes are complex, interdependent and can be influenced/skewed by local conditions. However, general models have been developed to allow for the understanding of the basic principles.

Energy transfer through atmospheric circulation: three cell model

This model of atmospheric circulation is the one which *most often features in examination papers*. It

was first put forward in the mid-nineteenth century and modern scientific studies have identified flaws within it. However, an understanding of the three cell model is an excellent starting point in the discussion of atmospheric circulation and energy transfer (Figure 1.12).

The model also takes into consideration the spinning action of the Earth as it rotates around its axis to explain the movement of winds.

The Coriolis effect (or Coriolis force) gives a reason for the pathways of the major winds at the Earth's surface. The Earth rotates from west to east, so in the northern hemisphere winds are deflected to the right,

Key

↗ Surface winds   🌀 Circulation cells

Winds

Cell A Hadley cell   1 North-east trade winds
Cell B Ferrel cell   2 Mid-latitude westerlies
Cell C Polar cell   3 Polar easterlies
                          4 South-east trade winds

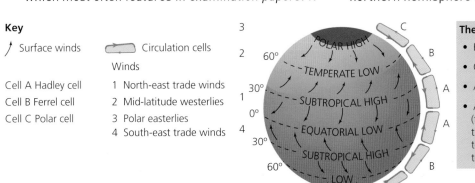

3   C
2   60° POLAR HIGH   B
          TEMPERATE LOW
     30°   A
1   SUBTROPICAL HIGH
     0°
4   EQUATORIAL LOW   A
     30° SUBTROPICAL HIGH
     60°   B
          LOW
                             C

The key principles:

- Hot air rises giving low pressure.

- Cold air sinks giving high pressure.

- Air moves from high pressure to low pressure.

- Air is deflected by the spinning of the Earth (the Coriolis force), which means that in the northern hemisphere winds are deflected to the right and in the southern hemisphere to the left.

▲ **Figure 1.12** Three cell model of atmospheric circulation, pressure belts and winds

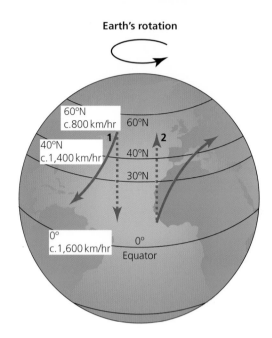

Earth's rotation

60°N
c.800 km/hr   60°N

40°N
c.1,400 km/hr   40°N

30°N

0°
c.1,600 km/hr   0°
Equator

The Coriolis effect

The Earth spins around on its axis from west to east.

- Because the Earth is a sphere and bulges around the equator this means that points nearer to the poles have a shorter distance to travel and therefore move at a slower speed than points at the equator with a larger distance to travel.

In the northern hemisphere:

- Winds coming from further south maintain the momentum caused by this increased speed and divert towards the right.
- As the land to the south has moved on at a faster rate, winds coming from the north also appear to move to their right.

In the southern hemisphere:

- The same principles result in the deflection of the winds to the left, mirroring the northern hemisphere.

◄ **Figure 1.13** Coriolis effect in the northern hemisphere

while in the southern hemisphere they are deflected to the left (Figure 1.13).

The three cell model suggests that there are two sets of three interlocking atmospheric cells (**convection cells**) redistributing thermal energy. One *set* of three is active in the northern hemisphere and the other in the southern hemisphere. These sets of cells mirror each other with identical processes on either side of the equator (see Figure 1.16 on page 22):

1 Hadley convection cells
2 Polar cells
3 Ferrel cells.

These atmospheric cells redistribute thermal energy in the following ways.

Hadley convection cells

These cells are powered by the effects of surface heating and are known as **thermally direct cells**. They are located between 30° North and 30° South of the equator. In this model the equator is seen as the warmest place on the Earth. The intensity of the solar energy causes the Earth's surface to heat up and in turn warm the air directly above it. The warmed air expands, becomes less dense, rises and creates an area of low pressure. This air climbs until it reaches the tropopause and spreads out along it towards the north and south (Figure 1.14).

The air becomes cooler and denser with altitude and its movement away from the intense heat source at the equator increases this process. This causes the air to sink around the subtropics about 30° North and 30° South of the equator (the **Horse latitudes**). By sinking down towards the surface the air creates high pressure areas. This descending air splits and travels in two directions across the surface of the Earth. Some is drawn by the low pressure back in the direction of the equator, completing the **Hadley cell**, while the remainder moves towards higher latitudes to become part of the **Ferrel cell**. The air that is returned to the equator becomes heated again and the cycle of air movement within the Hadley cell continues.

The air that was returned towards the equator in the final leg of the Hadley cell creates surface winds known as the **trade winds**. Due to the Coriolis effect, in the northern hemisphere, the trade winds blow from the north-east giving them the name the north-east trade winds; in the southern hemisphere, the winds blow from the south-east and are called the south-east trade winds. These winds meet at an area known as the intertropical convergence zone (ITCZ).

The ITCZ is responsible for the delivery of **precipitation** to tropical West Africa which sustains life in that region. It is also one of the key areas of study for Higher Geography. We will look more closely

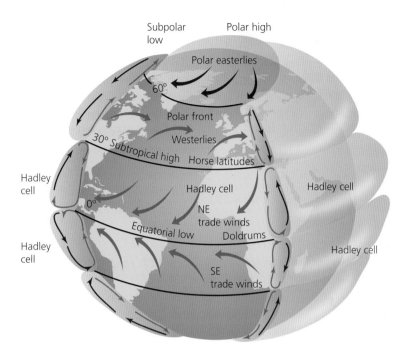

▲ **Figure 1.14** Hadley convection cell

at the ITCZ later in this book, so a good understanding of how the Hadley cell works and all of its component parts is vital. When convection causes the heated air to rise near the equator it takes with it a great deal of moisture and, as it cools and condenses at altitude, it can form massive and towering cumulonimbus clouds that produce thunderstorms.

As the air spreads north and south it releases the moisture it was carrying, providing much needed rain to the areas below. By the time the air sinks (about 30° North and South of the equator) it has lost most of its moisture. Where this dry air sinks to the planet's surface we find arid regions and some of the world's greatest deserts (e.g. Sahara, Kalahari, Australian and Atacama). Making these areas even drier is the heating effect of the land over which the air passes as it makes its way back towards the equator. As the air heats, it begins to suck up moisture from the land over which it travels, making these areas even drier.

Polar cells

Although a Ferrel cell lies between a Hadley cell and a Polar cell on the model, it is interlinked to both of these. An understanding of the actions at the Polar cells is important to the understanding of the creation of Ferrel cells and so we will look at the Polar cells first.

Polar cells are the smallest and weakest of the cells within the model. Like Hadley cells, Polar cells are thermally direct cells, relying as they do on surface heating to help power the system. Cold, dense air descends over the poles creating high pressure, then moves outwards along the surface towards the lower and warmer latitudes as polar easterlies. At around 60° North and South this air is warmed up and begins to ascend. As it rises it creates a zone of low pressure. The heating of the air at this point powers the cell. Air that ascended now moves back poleward to cool and drop down towards the surface, maintaining the cycle.

Ferrel cells

As you can see in Figure 1.16, the Ferrel cells are placed between the Hadley cells and the Polar cells. Unlike the other two types of cells, Ferrel cells are known as thermally indirect cells because they have a thermally indirect circulation which is dependent on the motion within the Hadley and Polar cells in between which they are found. The Ferrel cell moves in the opposite direction to the two other cells, being forced to rotate like a free spinning cog being turned by two powered cogs (see Figures 1.15 and 1.16).

As mentioned above, some of the air from the descending leg of the Hadley cell moves at ground

Powered cog   Free-spinning cog   Powered cog

▲ **Figure 1.15** Three cog model of interrelated air circulation

level towards the higher latitudes rather than returning to the equator. When this air meets the Polar cell air moving to lower latitudes (around 60° North and South), it assists in the warming and ascent of the air within the Polar cell while being forced upwards itself. As some air moves northwards to complete the Polar cell, the remainder moves towards the south at altitude to complete the Ferrel cell.

The Ferrel cells allow for the transfer of warm air from the Hadley cell to the higher latitudes while also moving cold air to lower latitudes to be re-warmed.

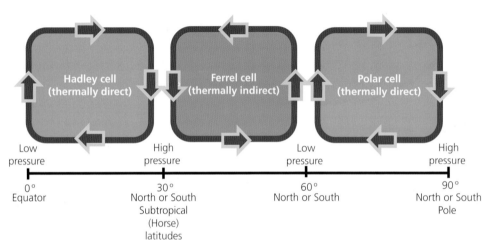

◄ **Figure 1.16** Three cell model of atmospheric circulation

Research opportunity

If you are interested in the Coriolis effect and the way that it seems to bend winds the following experiment is a fun way to demonstrate this. Be sure that you do this safely.

1. Begin by selecting a football (soccer style) and at least two more people.
2. Go to a play park where there is an old-fashioned style roundabout (not at an angle but flat).
3. One person sits on the outside of the roundabout's floor (make sure this person is sitting safely and is solidly balanced). A second person should sit in the middle of the roundabout, facing the person sitting at the edge. The person in the middle should have the football.

4. The third person now spins the roundabout.
5. Once the roundabout is up to speed the person in the middle should hold the ball as if to push it forward towards the person on the outside, then gently throw it straight at that person (the idea is not to make it easy or difficult or to hit the person on the edge but just to gently throw it towards him so that he could catch the ball comfortably).
6. Note what happens to the ball. Repeat a number of times to confirm what happens.

If you want to research this further, try a web search on 'Coriolis force' and/or 'conservation of angular momentum'.

1.4 Modern thinking on atmospheric circulation

Modern thinking on atmospheric circulation has been heavily influenced by the ability to check or challenge models through the use of large amounts of accurate and detailed data. Modern models are starting to include both local and global elements, surface types, land height, particles and pollutants, and be tempered by the growing realisation that the system is not a fixed one. The recognition that the system reacts to altering conditions has even influenced research into climate change.

So where do we stand at present? While being aware that the systems are actually more complex than previously believed, there is a tacit acceptance of a new three-part model. This model retains the Hadley and Polar cells but replaces, or greatly changes, the Ferrel cell with elements suggested from recent scientific observations:

1 There are alternate areas of high and low pressure which travel at relatively low levels.
2 Associated with these are a series of high-level wavelike motions known as Rossby (planetary) waves which travel around the globe from west to east (westerlies). Within these are found jet streams, narrow bands of fast-moving air (normally 160–320 km/h but which can reach speeds as high as 480 km/h. Jet streams assist with the rapid transfer of energy around the world (see 'Jet streams' section below).
3 These new observations acknowledge that the transfer of thermal energy is not only south to north or north to south but includes elements that are *roughly* horizontal to the lines of latitude.

Rossby waves

Rossby waves are long, variable velocity, east-to-west-moving waves (undulations) of air, found in the mid and upper troposphere, which travel around the globe. They can have a major influence on the weather. Rossby waves are created by:

● variations in the temperatures of surfaces over which air travels (e.g. oceans/land)

● lower altitude wind movements being forced to rise and drop when flowing over mountains (topographic forcing)
● amplification by the Coriolis effect. In the northern hemisphere, air that is forced to rise turns to the right and, as it falls, it turns to the left, creating a peak and trough (up and down) pattern.

Rossby waves follow meandering paths around the globe and the number of meanders vary with the seasons with the highest number in summer (probably between four and six in the summer and three in the winter).

Figure 1.17 (on the next page) shows the northern hemisphere and demonstrates that the meanders formed by Rossby waves play an important role allowing energy transfer in this new model:

● by looping southwards, cold polar air is moved/transferred further south (lower latitudes)
● similarly, when the wave loops northward warmer air is moved/transferred further north (higher latitudes).

Some of these meanders can become very pronounced as they loop further south or further north, leaving a narrow neck. Much like its river counterpart in the formation of an oxbow lake, the neck of these meanders can be broken through and the meander detached. The Rossby wave now continues on a less meandering path but leaves behind a mass of:

● cold air (southern loop)
● warm air (northern loop).

This results in isolated pools of warm air in the higher latitudes or cold air in the low latitudes. These are often slow in dissipating or moving and can result in abnormal weather conditions in those latitudes where they have been left behind.

Jet streams

Jet streams form due to a combination of the Coriolis force and proximity to the boundaries of neighbouring air masses with significant differences in temperature (Figure 1.18). On the Earth such marked temperature gradients exist between a) cold polar air and subtropical air and b) equatorial air and subtropical air and this is

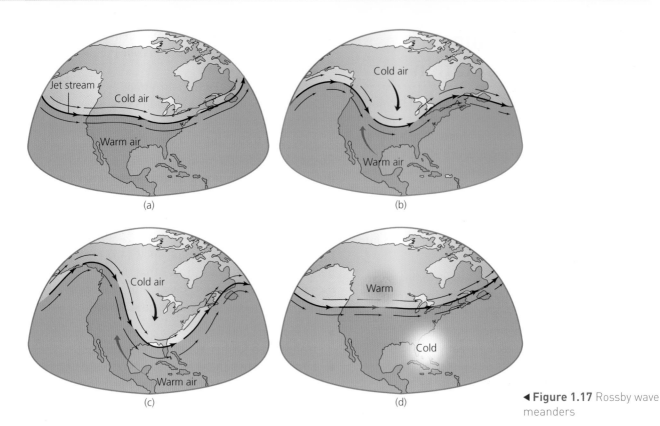

(a)

(b)

(c)

(d)

◀ **Figure 1.17** Rossby wave meanders

where the two main jet streams are found. The polar jet stream is the faster of the two, being generated at a boundary between two air masses where the differences in temperatures are much larger.

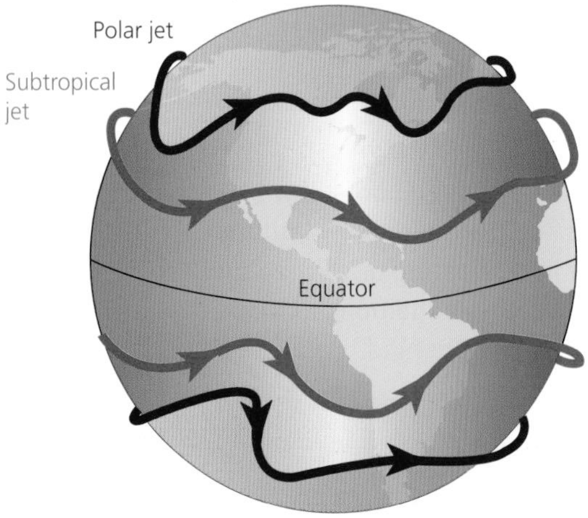

Figure 1.18 Jet stream locations

Polar jet

Subtropical jet

Equator

▲ **Figure 1.18** Jet stream locations

Both hemispheres have polar jet streams (at 7–12 km) and subtropical jet streams (at 10–16 km). The polar jet streams are located between 40–60° North and

South and the subtropical jet streams around 25–30° North and South. In the northern hemisphere the polar jet stream passes over the middle to northern latitudes of North America, Europe and Asia and the oceans between, while the southern hemisphere polar jet stream mostly circles Antarctica.

Rossby waves and jet streams are directly linked to surface high and low pressure systems.

The relationships between surface convergence and divergence and upper air flows are illustrated in Figure 1.19 and described below.

As a Rossby wave bends northwards towards the pole:

1 The air increases in speed.
2 The air spreads out (upper troposphere divergence) and as a result of this air is sucked up in an anticlockwise direction from below.
3 The air/wind is drawn inwards at the surface (surface convergence).
4 This upward movement of air creates an area of low pressure (cyclone/depression).

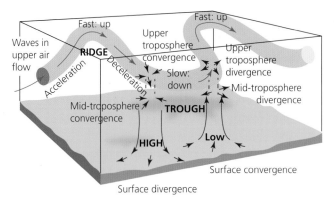

▲ **Figure 1.19** Convergence and divergence

As a Rossby wave swings southwards:

1   The air slows down.
2   The air piles up together (upper troposphere convergence).
3   Some of this air is forced to sink and does so in a clockwise direction.
4   This downward movement of air creates an area of high pressure at the surface (anticyclone).
5   Air/wind spreads outwards at the surface (surface divergence).

Rossby waves with their jet streams are very important for mid-latitude weather development. Not only do they help with the movement of the boundaries of warmer and cooler air, and assist in the development of high and low pressure areas, but they help to drive weather systems from west to east.

A large proportion of everyday weather conditions are the result of the movement of depressions and anticyclones (see Figure 1.21 on page 26).

Scotland's weather is affected by jet streams. In the autumn and winter months the polar jet stream is dragged further southwards due to the Sun's position and the focus of its heating being at a more southerly latitude (Figure 1.20). As a result of its southward movement, this jet stream now passes over Scotland and directs a series of depressions towards it, bringing wet and windy weather. During the summer months it is usual for the polar jet stream to have moved northwards due to the Sun's return to the northern hemisphere (Figure 1.20). This takes the path of the jet stream to higher latitudes much further north than Scotland. Due to this the usually unpleasant weather associated with depressions bypasses Scotland. If for some reason the path of the polar jet stream stays further south, Scotland can experience some very unseasonable weather during the summer months.

It should be recognised that the position of the Rossby waves and jet streams are not fixed (they move around quite a bit) and movements of warm air from the south or cold air from the north can buckle their path and direct weather systems to areas that would not normally experience them. Some climate change models suggest that there could be large-scale changes to the paths of the Rossby waves and jet streams if the planet continues to warm.

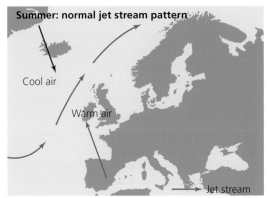

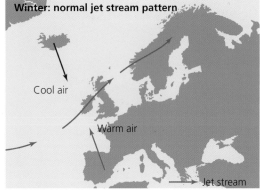

▲ **Figure 1.20** Passage of a jet stream across the North Atlantic (summer and winter)

Research opportunity

As atmospheric circulation depends on an understanding of the movement of thermal energy and air, this would be a good place to look online for animations of the processes. Try searching for animations of:

- three cell model of atmospheric circulation
- Rossby waves
- jet streams
- Rossby waves, jet streams and surface weather.

You may find it helpful and interesting to research the following:

- First World War Zeppelins being blown off course at very high speeds. Was this due to jet streams?
- Flying from North America to Scotland can be much quicker than the return journey. Could this be due to the jet streams?

- Wasaburo Ooishi, a Japanese meteorologist, used weather balloons to track upper level winds as they ascended into the Earth's atmosphere near Mount Fuji. Did he discover jet streams in the 1920s?
- The Japanese use of the jet stream to enable their Fu-Go (hydrogen balloon bombs) to attack North America during the Second World War.
- On Saturday, 20 March 1999, the Breitling Orbiter 3 balloon, piloted by Brian Jones and Bertrand Piccard, became the first balloon to fly nonstop around the world. How was the jet stream used to assist in this flight?
- Are jet streams possible sources of clean energy in the fight against climate change?

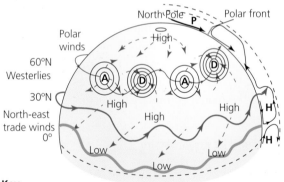

Key

- ITCZ (intertropical convergence zone)
- → Rossby waves
- → Subtropical jet stream
- **A** Anticyclone **D** Depression
- - - Tropopause
- **H** Hadley cell
- **P** Polar cell
- ↘ Winds

▲ **Figure 1.21** Atmospheric circulation in the northern hemisphere

Task

1 Why does surplus energy need to be transferred between low and high latitudes?
2 Which systems redistribute the energy and for how much is each responsible?
3 With the use of diagrams, explain the workings of the three cell model of atmospheric circulation. Make sure that you show the differences between *thermally direct* and *thermally indirect* cells.
4 Detail what would be a more modern understanding of atmospheric circulation (newer or adapted models).
5 What are Rossby waves and jet streams?
6 What part do Rossby waves and jet streams play in the transference of energy in the atmosphere?
7 How is Scotland's weather affected by the movement of the polar jet stream?
8 What is the difference between *convergence* and *divergence* of winds?

1.5 Global wind patterns

Wind patterns have become established as part of atmospheric circulation and the redistribution of thermal energy. A very simple model of these global surface winds (Figure 1.22) has developed in line with the three cell model (including the effects of Coriolis force) described earlier.

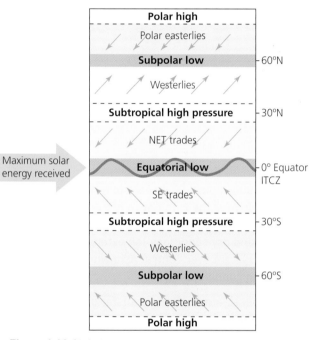

Maximum solar energy received

▲ **Figure 1.22** Global surface winds

A general rule for winds is that they blow from areas of high pressure to areas of low pressure. From the three cell model we have identified latitudinal pressure belts between which the winds travel. These are, working from the equator both north and south, an equatorial low (intertropical convergence zone (ITCZ)), subtropical highs, subpolar lows and polar highs (Figure 1.22). The location and the winds can be identified as:

- from approximately 30° North and South the trade winds converge on the equator. Around the equator there is an area of calm often referred to as the Doldrums
- from approximately 30° to 60° North and South the mid-latitude westerlies blow poleward
- from the Arctic and the Antarctic the polar easterlies travel to around 60° North and South.

Problems with the global surface winds model

As this model was based on the three cell model (see pages 19–22), it suffered from the same problems of age and flaws. Improved meteorological understanding and information gathering has shown that the positions of these winds are not locked into permanent bands but instead move with the apparent position of the Sun in the sky throughout the year.

Movement of the ITCZ

As described earlier in this chapter, the focus of the Sun is not always on the equator. Instead, as the Sun 'migrates' across the sky, the belt of maximum surface heating also moves. This belt is known as the thermal (heat) equator. Due to this the ITCZ moves north and south with the Sun and so do the pressure belts and trade wind systems (Figure 1.23).

Mid-latitude westerlies

These are more variable than suggested. In the northern hemisphere this may be linked to the effect of the alternating series of high pressure and low pressure areas created and moved by Rossby waves and the jet stream. Because there are fewer landmasses to block or deflect the winds, westerlies and their associated depressions in the southern hemisphere have stronger winds and may last for longer periods.

Polar easterlies

Some meteorologists point out that the polar easterlies do not appear to be regular. To some, this brings into doubt the existence of a Polar cell and suggests that these winds, when they do appear, should be seen as a result of mid-latitude depressions.

Anomalies in Asia

The model of global surface winds, and the three cell model on which it is based, would suggest that in summer a high-pressure area should be present over southern Asia. In reality there is low pressure that brings in monsoon conditions (high rainfall resulting

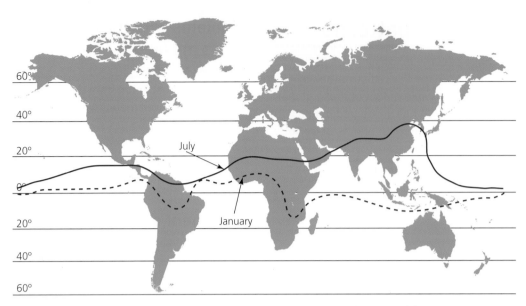

▲ **Figure 1.23** Location of the intertropical convergence zone at maximum positions

in 80 per cent of southern Asia's annual rainfall). Unlike the northern hemisphere where the oceans and land masses are aligned north to south, here the Asian continent lies to the north and the Indian Ocean to the south. The southern hemisphere has significantly more ocean than land (a ratio of 4 to 1 as compared to 1.5 to 1 in the northern hemisphere) and this has an effect on the weather systems. This is mainly due to water heating up and cooling down more slowly than land.

Towards summertime, as the thermal equator and the ITCZ move northwards, there is increased heating of southern Asia. This forms a cyclonic monsoon cell which is, for a time, held to the south by the position of the subtropical jet stream. In the summer months the subtropical jet stream moves northward over the Himalayas into central Asia and this allows the monsoon cell to move further northward while being fed with moisture and warmth from the Indian Ocean (Figure 1.24). The additional heat helps to power the monsoon even further and the additional moisture increases its potential for rainfall. As this mass of wet and warm air moves towards the Himalayas it rises, is cooled and condensed and so creates the strong monsoon rainfall.

As the surface temperatures cool on the Himalayan (Tibetan) Plateau this creates the conditions that allow the subtropical jet stream to move back southwards over the Himalayan mountains, bringing with it cool air that sinks and encourages high pressure and dry conditions (an extension of the high pressure system over central Asia which is also due to the cooling conditions).

So, in general, atmospheric transfer of thermal energy is carried out through a complex system involving pressure cells and global winds which move energy from areas of surplus to those of deficit. For exams you need to know the simple three cell and global surface winds models (and the principles behind them) as well as being aware of and able to comment on more modern viewpoints and why the simple models can be criticised.

 Task

1　Describe the location of the three main wind groups, referring to their latitude and relation to areas of high and low pressure.

2　Explain the problems with this simple model of global surface winds which only describes the three main wind groups.

Indian subcontinent: Summer

Himalayan (Tibetan) Plateau

Mawsynram

Low pressure

Mumbai •

Arabian Sea

Summer ITCZ

Bay of Bengal

Indian Ocean

Equator

→ Winds blowing inland bringing moisture and warmth from the Indian Ocean

░ Position of the ITCZ and its accompanying area of low pressure due to the movement of the thermal equator

Note

Mawsynram (a small village in Meghalaya state in north-eastern India) claims the highest annual rainfall in the world. Mawsynram receives 11,872 mm (nearly 12 m) of rain in an average year, the vast majority falling during the summer monsoon.

▲ **Figure 1.24** Indian subcontinent monsoon

Indian subcontinent: Winter

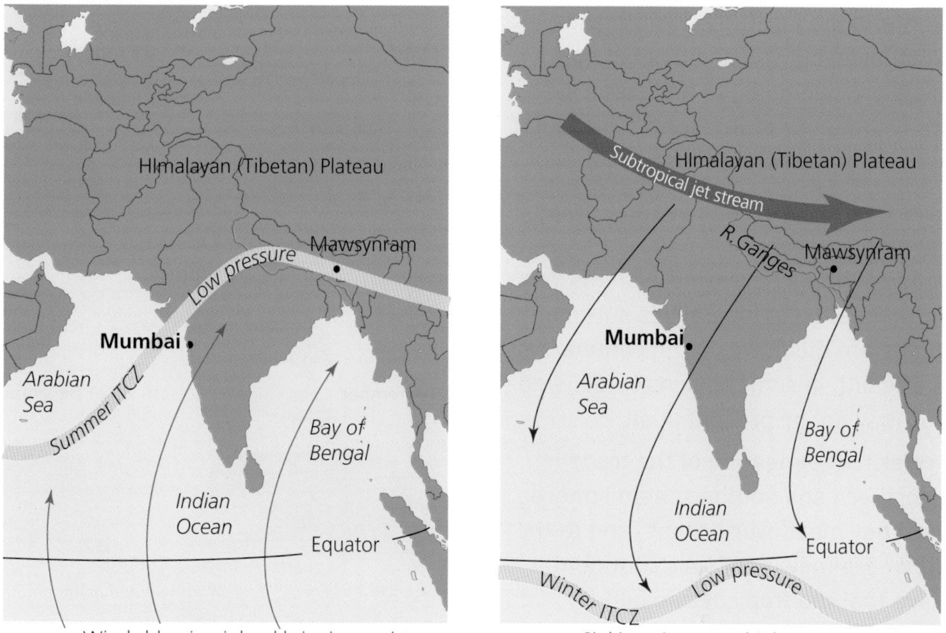

Subtropical jet stream

Himalayan (Tibetan) Plateau

R. Ganges

Mawsynram

Mumbai •

Arabian Sea

Bay of Bengal

Indian Ocean

Equator

Winter ITCZ

Low pressure

→ Sinking air creates high pressure and cool winds blow from inland (dry)

░ Position of the ITCZ and its accompanying area of low pressure due to the movement of the thermal equator

➤ Winter subtropical jet stream

1.6 Intertropical convergence zone (ITCZ)

Earlier when discussing Hadley cells the intertropical convergence zone was briefly mentioned. Its simple definition states that the ITCZ is where the trade winds from the northern and southern hemispheres meet. This forms a line that can be traced around the world.

Certainly the ITCZ got its name simply as a description of where the trade winds met but recent studies have shown that it is more complex and that the location of a low pressure zone is a vital element of its description.

A zone of low pressure at the thermal equator is on average a few hundred kilometres wide where, theoretically, winds move inwards and then rise through convection. This convection causes heavy rainfall and thunderstorms (Figure 1.25).

▲ **Figure 1.25** ITCZ storm clouds

At this stage it is helpful to think of the ITCZ as being the same around the Earth. This will make it easier for your studies, but you should also note that meteorologists are beginning to find some weaknesses in the global use of this term. They point out that their analysis of data shows that:

- trade winds are mainly an oceanic feature driven by subtropical high pressure
- continental tropical areas have wind systems driven by uneven heating of the Earth's surface
- subtropical highs are much weaker in continental areas and as a result, in some regions trade winds do not meet or may not be present at all.

Meteorologists refer to the meeting of the trade winds from the northern and southern hemispheres as the ITCZ where they meet over oceans, and to the tropical rain belt where they meet over continental areas. They believe that the tropical rain belts have much more to do with the low pressure and convection created at the thermal equator. For the present, however, we will look at these as a single phenomenon.

Knowledge of the workings of a Hadley cell is important to an understanding of the ITCZ and its effects (look back to page 20 of this chapter if you are unsure). What is certain is that the procession throughout the year of the Sun's location relative to the Earth's surface changes the point where the maximum heat is received (the thermal equator). This results in the movement of the position of convection and the Hadley cell northward and southward with the Sun (Figure 1.26). The position of the ITCZ may lag behind that of the thermal equator by two to three weeks.

Due to this movement of the ITCZ, tropical regions would normally experience a wet and a dry season every year.

The intense rainfall associated with the low-pressure area created by rising air at the position of maximum convection therefore moves north and south at the same time. In some areas, such as the Sahel in Africa (a semi-arid region bordering the southern edge of the Sahara Desert and running from Senegal to Chad), the northerly movement of the ITCZ is the slender lifeline that makes the difference between survival, famine and death.

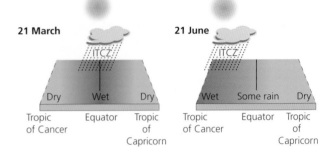

▲ **Figure 1.26** Annual movement of the intertropical convergence zone

Although our case study is focused on Africa, the ITCZ (see Figure 1.23 on page 28) has an effect on areas all around the world and even slight variations in its timing or rainfall amount can cause wide-scale problems:

- When the ITCZ has remained for longer than expected, Central America suffers from landslides that have killed thousands. Crops rot in the fields due to too much rainfall leading to food shortages, famine and resultant epidemic disease.
- The United States experiences intensified hurricane events due to a slight positional change of the ITCZ in relation to the hurricane breeding grounds.
- Recent studies suggest that the ITCZ pushes in front of it areas of higher air pollution while the precipitation from the convectional rainfall helps to cleanse the atmosphere of aerosols.

Case study: Africa and the intertropical convergence zone

What creates the particular qualities of the ITCZ in Africa?

We already know about the effects of the Sun's heating and the ITCZ's movement but we must also be aware of the air masses and trade winds that move towards this low-pressure area and help create some of its climatic qualities.

Winds from two air masses converge over Africa:

1 The south-west trade winds from the **Tropical Maritime (mT) air mass**
This air mass originates over the Atlantic Ocean within 30° of latitude of the equator. Having developed over water it has a high level of humidity of around 65–82 per cent. Its development in the tropics results in the area being hot. Unstable weather conditions are associated with this air mass. The winds developing from the mT air mass are known as the **South-Western Monsoon** (Figure 1.27).

2 The north-east trade winds from the **Tropical Continental (cT) air mass**
The Tropical Continental (cT) air mass has its origin over the Sahara Desert in the north of Africa (Figures 1.27 and 1.28). Travelling over these dry and hot regions results in the air mass developing similar qualities. It is hot with low relative humidity of around 10 to 18 per cent, bringing with it stable and monotonously predictable weather conditions, though these can be accompanied by poor visibility due to dusts picked up and carried by the wind. The winds developing from the cT air mass are known as the **Harmattan (North-East trades)**.

On its own, the convection created by the Sun's heat on the line of the ITCZ would not necessarily bring heavy

▲ **Figure 1.28** Sahara Desert

rainfall if it were not for the addition of the humidity brought to it by the Tropical Maritime air mass:

- The low air pressure associated with the ITCZ draws in the air and winds from the Tropical Maritime air mass and this feeds the system with the moisture gathered from the Atlantic Ocean and the Bay of Guinea over which it has travelled.
- This not only helps bring moisture to the line of the ITCZ but provides rainfall to the area behind it.
- As the two air masses meet they are forced to rise rapidly, creating turbulent conditions and forcing the air to cool and condense as it rises. This creates massive thunderstorms and heavy precipitation around the line of the ITCZ.

January

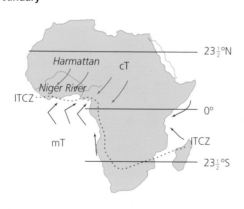

July

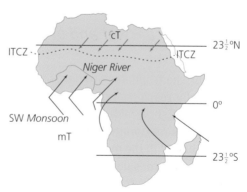

Key

······ ITCZ Intertropical convergence zone
cT → Tropical Continental
mT → Tropical Maritime

0 2,000 4,000
km

NB The SE Trades become the SW Monsoon as they cross the equator and are deflected to the east

▲ **Figure 1.27** Features and seasonal locations of the tropical air masses

In front (to the north) of the ITCZ, conditions are very different. Under the influence of the continental tropical air and winds this area experiences very hot and dry weather. Living conditions are extremely difficult.

Areas towards the northerly limit of the ITCZ are dependent on its arrival for survival. The rain that it brings may be all that is experienced within a year and is needed to enable crops or natural vegetation to grow or to replenish what little water supplies there are.

▲ **Figure 1.29** Countries of West Africa

Focus on West Africa – wet and dry seasons

- **July**: The northern hemisphere summer sees the thermal equator reaching its most northerly position (summer solstice, mid-June). As such, the ITCZ is also at its maximum northerly location (~20° North) by July. With the movement of the ITCZ northwards an increasing area experiences its wet season. Moist air is drawn in from the Atlantic across West Africa (South-Easterlies from the Indian Ocean on the east coast) to create a wet season with its heavy rainfall (Figure 1.30). It should be noted that as the ITCZ moves further over land

moisture is being lost and there is less available for rainfall at the northerly limits (Figure 1.27).

▲ **Figure 1.30** Wet season rains in east-central Ghana

- **January**: The ITCZ migrates southwards to the Tropic of Capricorn and reaches its maximum southerly position by January following the Sun's arrival (winter solstice, mid-December). Due to the larger landmass in the northern half of Africa, the ITCZ still affects the southern part of western Africa (from 5° to 8° North) near the coast but the majority of the landmass experiences a dry season (Figure 1.31). With the Tropical Continental air mass pushing south, rainfall is rare, temperatures are hot and the north-easterly Harmattan brings dust collected from its travels across desert regions (Figure 1.27).

▲ **Figure 1.31** Dry season in the Sahel (Mali)

An overview of the annual rainfall patterns for the area of West Africa affected by the ITCZ shows that the further north:

- the greater the concentration of rainfall within the summer months (wet season), with this being the only rainfall for those at the more northerly extremes
- the lower the mean annual rainfall
- the less reliable the rainfall, deviating greatly from the annual mean.

Life and the ITCZ

It is no exaggeration to say that for many people in West Africa the ITCZ is the key factor in their quality of life, creating the conditions that allow for basic survival for some, and for others a variety of sources of food and a substantial water supply.

Figure 1.35 shows the changing conditions in West Africa, from Ghana in the south northward through Burkina Faso and into Mali, due to the influence of the ITCZ. In general, moving northwards:

1 Temperatures *rise*.
2 Rainfall amounts *decrease*.
3 The length of the wet season *decreases*.
4 The length of the dry season *increases*.
5 Vegetation height, density, complexity and amount *decrease*.
6 There are distinct zones from rainforest and mangrove, through Guinea savanna, Sudan savanna, into the Sahel region and finally tropical desert (Figures 1.32, 1.33, 1.34 and 1.36).
7 Living conditions become *more difficult*.

▲ **Figure 1.32** Rainforest, southern Ghana

▲ **Figure 1.33** Guinea savanna in Ghana

▲ **Figure 1.34** Sudan savanna, Burkina Faso (wet season)

Vegetation and human activity are reliant on the rain provided by the ITCZ. Where rainfall amounts are higher there is a greater abundance of plant life. In the south this has resulted in the development of a complex and dense rainforest environment, while in the north the savanna lands die back leaving heat-resistant and direct sun-resistant **xerophytes** as the dominant plant life (Figure 1.36).

Even though Ghana has lost vast amounts of its rainforest through commercial exploitation, what remains is believed to have over 4,500 different types of vegetation, while the Sahara Desert is estimated to include only 500 species over its vast 9,400,000 km² area.

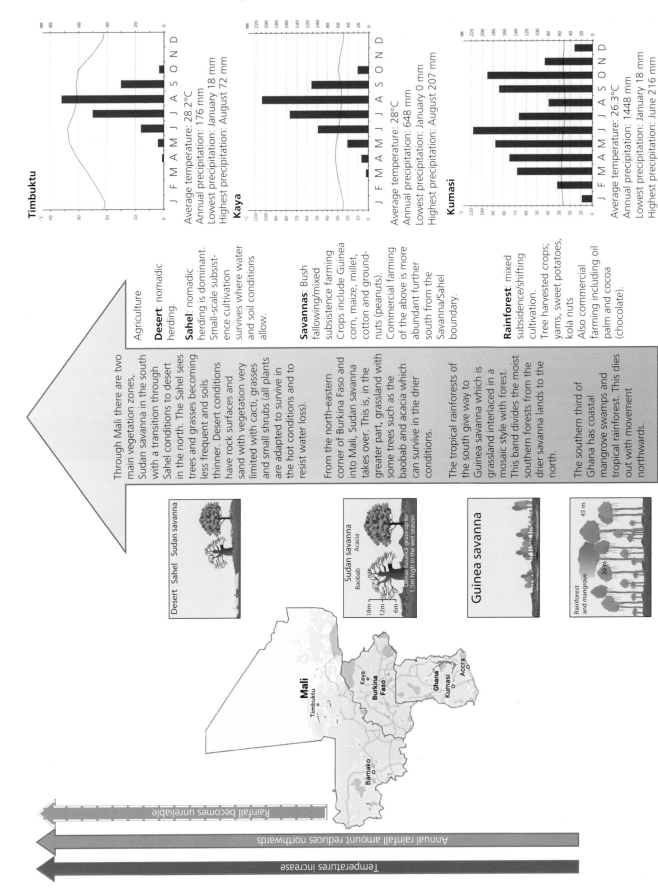

Timbuktu

J F M A M J J A S O N D

Average temperature: 28.2°C
Annual precipitation: 176 mm
Lowest precipitation: January 18 mm
Highest precipitation: August 72 mm

Kaya

J F M A M J J A S O N D

Average temperature: 28°C
Annual precipitation: 648 mm
Lowest precipitation: January 0 mm
Highest precipitation: August 207 mm

Kumasi

J F M A M J J A S O N D

Average temperature: 26.3°C
Annual precipitation: 1448 mm
Lowest precipitation: January 18 mm
Highest precipitation: June 216 mm

Agriculture

Desert: nomadic herding.

Sahel: nomadic herding is dominant. Small-scale subsistence cultivation survives where water and soil conditions allow.

Savannas: Bush fallowing/mixed subsistence farming Crops include Guinea corn, maize, millet, cotton and ground-nuts (peanuts). Commercial farming of the above is more abundant further south from the Savanna/Sahel boundary.

Rainforest: mixed subsidence/shifting cultivation. Tree harvested crops; yams, sweet potatoes, kola nuts Also commercial farming including oil palm and cocoa (chocolate).

Through Mali there are two main vegetation zones, Sudan savanna in the south with a transition through Sahel conditions to desert in the north. The Sahel sees trees and grasses becoming less frequent and soils thinner. Desert conditions have rock surfaces and sand with vegetation very limited with cacti, grasses and small shrubs (all plants are adapted to survive in the hot conditions and to resist water loss).

From the north-eastern corner of Burkina Faso and into Mali, Sudan savanna takes over. This is, in the greater part, grassland with some trees such as the baobab and acacia which can survive in the drier conditions.

The tropical rainforests of the south give way to Guinea savanna which is grassland interlaced in a mosaic style with forest. This band divides the moist southern forests from the drier savanna lands to the north.

The southern third of Ghana has coastal mangrove swamps and tropical rainforest. This dies out with movement northwards.

Desert   Sahel   Sudan savanna

Sudan savanna   Acacia
Baobab
18m   12m   6m
Dense tussock grass up to 1.5m high in the wet season

Guinea savanna

Rainforest and mangrove
45 m
30 m

Rainfall becomes unreliable

Annual rainfall amount reduces northwards

Temperatures increase

Mali
Timbuktu
Bamako
Kaya
Burkina Faso
Ghana
Kumasi
Accra

▲ **Figure 1.35** West Africa and the ITCZ

The Niger is a West African river which has both its source (the Guinean Plateau) and mouth (Nigeria) outside our case study area, but it flows through Mali providing a source of water to the Sudan Savanna lands, the Sahel and even the desert around Timbuktu (Figure 1.37). This is not a constant volume of water but it is indispensable where rainfall is unreliable. The river reflects the seasonal changes and rainfall patterns of the areas through which it flows but is fed in its initial stages by the annual 1,500 mm of precipitation found near its source.

▲ **Figure 1.36** Sahara Desert. After a small amount of rainfall, dormant seeds sprout quickly and attempt to complete their growing cycle before the ground dries out

▲ **Figure 1.37** Banks of the River Niger near Timbuktu

The savanna lands provide a broad zone of agriculture (both arable and livestock) before dissipating as they merge with the Sahel. Rain-fed agriculture is not only reliant on the amount of rainfall but by the available growing season (the period of warmth and rainfall), together with the ability of the soil to maintain moisture for sufficient time to sustain the full growth of plants.

Although the movement of the ITCZ is fairly predictable because it is related to the movement of the Sun, there are variations in its *rate* of movement. Unexpected climate conditions can hold it in place or slow it down, and in recent years its unpredictability has increased. If the movement of the ITCZ north or south is delayed there may be less than average rainfall, or rain may arrive at a time which limits the growing season, potentially resulting in poor yields or even crop failure.

The availability of suitable growing seasons decline with movement northwards from the Gulf of Guinea to the Sahara and agriculture of any kind becomes more dependent on **groundwater** or rivers.

Farmers in both the Sudan Savanna and Sahel have adapted to low rainfall conditions in a variety of ways:

● Sudan Savanna (annual rainfall 600–1,000 mm) During the wet season rainfall sustains crop growth but dry season shortages necessitate alternative water sources. Groundwater from wells and rivers (such as the Niger) are used as sources of water for irrigation. Multiple cropping is also practised to reduce the chance of food shortages as a result of disease affecting particular types of crops.

● Sahel (annual rainfall in northern Mali 203 mm) The extremely low levels of rainfall mean that agriculture relies on groundwater and accessibility to water from rivers (such as the Niger). Irrigation is exploited when rivers allow (rivers may run dry due to lack of rainfall or overuse). Where rivers or seasonal rainfall flood land the moistened soils are utilised for planting, or pastoralists will bring their animals to feed on grasses and herbs that grow as the floodwaters recede. These **floodplains** provide invaluable grazing land during the dry season.

Task

1 What is the thermal equator and why does it move?
2 Define the term 'intertropical convergence zone'.
3 Explain how the Hadley cell forms an important part of our understanding of the ITCZ.
4 Explain the weather conditions linked to the ITCZ (refer to the air masses and winds involved and their qualities).
5 Describe and explain the movement of the ITCZ over the course of a year.
6 In detail, describe the wet and dry seasons of West Africa.

7 Analyse the three climate graphs in Figure 1.35 and explain the pattern of rainfall shown (remember to compare totals and months within this).
8 Using West Africa as an example, explain the effects of the ITCZ and its movement on the weather, seasons and agriculture.
9 Prepare a learning resource (e.g. a booklet, large poster, PowerPoint presentation, animation, webpage or other multimedia resource) to explain the workings and effects of the ITCZ to your classmates or other students studying at Higher level.

It is fair to say that life in the Sahel is becoming more and more extreme as the ITCZ fails to deliver enough rainfall and is unreliable (Figure 1.38). Adding to this problem is the poor management of the land, mostly because of an increase in population. Trees have been felled to provide building materials and fuel for small industry, cooking and heating. Felling of trees has removed:

- root structures which hold the delicate and valuable soils in place
- shade which helps to preserve soil moisture
- shelter which acts as a windbreak to prevent soils from being blown away.

The removal of soil makes this land even less able to support humans, flora and fauna. With all these alterations the Sahara Desert is moving southward to replace the former Sahel savanna.

▲ **Figure 1.38** Northern Senegal, erosion of the dry, sandy soils.

1.7 Energy transfer through oceanic circulation

Ocean currents also assist in the redistribution of energy around the planet. Warm currents heat the atmosphere as they move poleward. Around 25 per cent of the movement of global heat budget energy is by oceanic currents.

This circulation of oceanic water can be divided into two parts: surface current circulation and thermohaline circulation.

Surface current circulation

The top few hundred metres of oceanic water are driven by the force and friction of atmospheric winds interacting at the ocean surface–atmosphere interface. Ocean currents are set in motion and in general direction by this interaction with the prevailing winds.

The pattern of *surface* ocean currents is shown in Figure 1.39. In general they form large circular loops known as **gyres** deflected and contained by the continental landmasses. Currents moving away from the equator are known as warm currents while those moving towards it are cold. These are relative terms and jumping into a warm current would not necessarily make you feel warm – remember that the **North Atlantic Drift** brings a so-called warm current to Scotland, but jumping into the sea at Oban may not bring you the experience you might have expected!

The Niger is a West African river which has both its source (the Guinean Plateau) and mouth (Nigeria) outside our case study area, but it flows through Mali providing a source of water to the Sudan Savanna lands, the Sahel and even the desert around Timbuktu (Figure 1.37). This is not a constant volume of water but it is indispensable where rainfall is unreliable. The river reflects the seasonal changes and rainfall patterns of the areas through which it flows but is fed in its initial stages by the annual 1,500 mm of precipitation found near its source.

▲ **Figure 1.36** Sahara Desert. After a small amount of rainfall, dormant seeds sprout quickly and attempt to complete their growing cycle before the ground dries out

▲ **Figure 1.37** Banks of the River Niger near Timbuktu

The savanna lands provide a broad zone of agriculture (both arable and livestock) before dissipating as they merge with the Sahel. Rain-fed agriculture is not only reliant on the amount of rainfall but by the available growing season (the period of warmth and rainfall), together with the ability of the soil to maintain moisture for sufficient time to sustain the full growth of plants.

Although the movement of the ITCZ is fairly predictable because it is related to the movement of the Sun, there are variations in its *rate* of movement. Unexpected climate conditions can hold it in place or slow it down, and in recent years its unpredictability has increased. If the movement of the ITCZ north or south is delayed there may be less than average rainfall, or rain may arrive at a time which limits the growing season, potentially resulting in poor yields or even crop failure.

The availability of suitable growing seasons decline with movement northwards from the Gulf of Guinea to the Sahara and agriculture of any kind becomes more dependent on **groundwater** or rivers.

Farmers in both the Sudan Savanna and Sahel have adapted to low rainfall conditions in a variety of ways:

- Sudan Savanna (annual rainfall 600–1,000 mm) During the wet season rainfall sustains crop growth but dry season shortages necessitate alternative water sources. Groundwater from wells and rivers (such as the Niger) are used as sources of water for irrigation. Multiple cropping is also practised to reduce the chance of food shortages as a result of disease affecting particular types of crops.
- Sahel (annual rainfall in northern Mali 203 mm) The extremely low levels of rainfall mean that agriculture relies on groundwater and accessibility to water from rivers (such as the Niger). Irrigation is exploited when rivers allow (rivers may run dry due to lack of rainfall or overuse). Where rivers or seasonal rainfall flood land the moistened soils are utilised for planting, or pastoralists will bring their animals to feed on grasses and herbs that grow as the floodwaters recede. These **floodplains** provide invaluable grazing land during the dry season.

Task

1 What is the thermal equator and why does it move?
2 Define the term 'intertropical convergence zone'.
3 Explain how the Hadley cell forms an important part of our understanding of the ITCZ.
4 Explain the weather conditions linked to the ITCZ (refer to the air masses and winds involved and their qualities).
5 Describe and explain the movement of the ITCZ over the course of a year.
6 In detail, describe the wet and dry seasons of West Africa.
7 Analyse the three climate graphs in Figure 1.35 and explain the pattern of rainfall shown (remember to compare totals and months within this).
8 Using West Africa as an example, explain the effects of the ITCZ and its movement on the weather, seasons and agriculture.
9 Prepare a learning resource (e.g. a booklet, large poster, PowerPoint presentation, animation, webpage or other multimedia resource) to explain the workings and effects of the ITCZ to your classmates or other students studying at Higher level.

It is fair to say that life in the Sahel is becoming more and more extreme as the ITCZ fails to deliver enough rainfall and is unreliable (Figure 1.38). Adding to this problem is the poor management of the land, mostly because of an increase in population. Trees have been felled to provide building materials and fuel for small industry, cooking and heating. Felling of trees has removed:

● root structures which hold the delicate and valuable soils in place
● shade which helps to preserve soil moisture
● shelter which acts as a windbreak to prevent soils from being blown away.

The removal of soil makes this land even less able to support humans, flora and fauna. With all these alterations the Sahara Desert is moving southward to replace the former Sahel savanna.

▲ **Figure 1.38** Northern Senegal, erosion of the dry, sandy soils.

1.7 Energy transfer through oceanic circulation

Ocean currents also assist in the redistribution of energy around the planet. Warm currents heat the atmosphere as they move poleward. Around 25 per cent of the movement of global heat budget energy is by oceanic currents.

This circulation of oceanic water can be divided into two parts: surface current circulation and thermohaline circulation.

Surface current circulation

The top few hundred metres of oceanic water are driven by the force and friction of atmospheric winds interacting at the ocean surface–atmosphere interface. Ocean currents are set in motion and in general direction by this interaction with the prevailing winds.

The pattern of *surface* ocean currents is shown in Figure 1.39. In general they form large circular loops known as gyres deflected and contained by the continental landmasses. Currents moving away from the equator are known as warm currents while those moving towards it are cold. These are relative terms and jumping into a warm current would not necessarily make you feel warm – remember that the North Atlantic Drift brings a so-called warm current to Scotland, but jumping into the sea at Oban may not bring you the experience you might have expected!

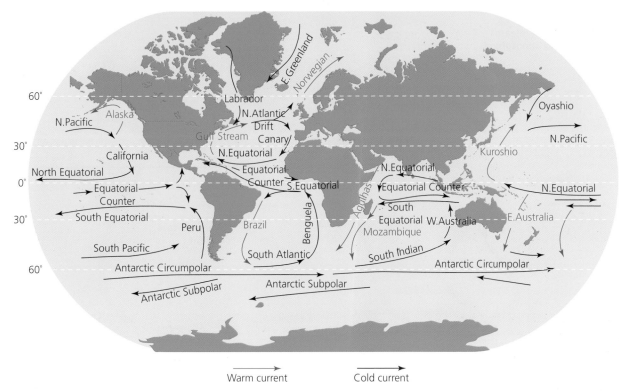

Warm current   Cold current

▲ **Figure 1.39** Ocean currents and their patterns

The direction of currents around a gyre is clockwise in the northern hemisphere and anticlockwise in the southern hemisphere. Coriolis force, which, as we have already learned, deflects the movement of air in the atmosphere and bends its path in relation to the surface, has the same effect on ocean currents and assists in creating the clockwise and anticlockwise patterns in each hemisphere.

The average speed of circulating water at the extremities of a gyre is around 5 km/h but at its centre its movement may be very slow and difficult to determine.

The gyres in both the Atlantic and the Pacific are restricted by being contained between continental masses, while the **Antarctic Circumpolar Current (West Wind Drift)** has no such obstructions and circulates unimpeded around the globe in a west to east direction.

Examples of prevailing winds driving these currents can be identified as:

● Atlantic westerlies move the North Atlantic Drift north-eastwards across the Atlantic Ocean to north-western Europe, bringing warmer waters which assist in giving the area a milder climate. This protects north-western Europe (including Scotland) from experiencing the extreme cold winters of continental central and eastern Europe.

● The trade winds, which blow from the north-east towards the south-west in the northern hemisphere and from the south-east to the north-west in the southern hemisphere, guide both the North and South equatorial currents towards the west.

● The Antarctic Circumpolar Current is powered by a westerly wind more obviously suggested in its alternative name, the West Wind Drift.

Thermohaline circulation

Deeper waters are driven by temperature, salinity and density change. The word thermohaline is derived from 'thermo' meaning temperature and 'haline' relating to the degree of saltiness.

Thermohaline circulation forms the major part of the movement of energy around the globe. It moves around 10^{15} W of heat energy towards the poles and influences climate significantly. This circulation also

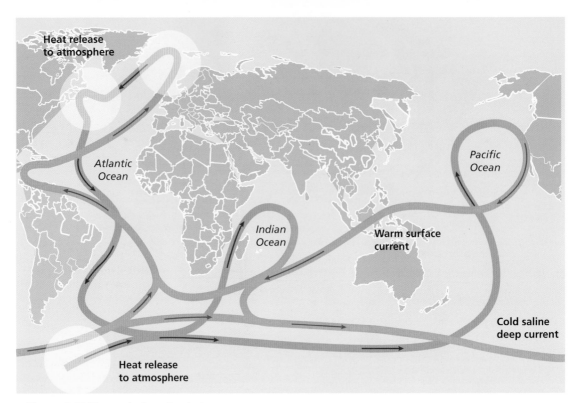

Heat release to atmosphere

Atlantic Ocean

Indian Ocean

Pacific Ocean

Warm surface current

Cold saline deep current

Heat release to atmosphere

▲ **Figure 1.40** Thermohaline circulation

turns over and remixes all the planet's deep water in approximately 700 to 1,000 years (Figure 1.40).

Thermohaline currents are driven by salinity and temperature change. When water is warm it expands and reduces in density. Adding salt to water makes it denser due to the spaces between the water molecules being occupied by the salt. Water in an ocean will organise itself according to density. Denser water sinks lower than less dense water and this movement downwards helps to drive the system around the planet.

The main drivers of this circulatory pattern result from high-density water sinking. This critical part of the thermohaline circulation occurs when warmer surface waters travel poleward and meet colder, denser and more saline waters from the polar regions. These denser waters sink down to the floor of the ocean and move towards lower latitudes. The warm water moving polewards is cooled at higher latitudes and also sinks to join the submarine current.

The heat released by this cooling warms the surrounding atmosphere. This sinking of these waters powers the circulatory process of the closed system. The cooler waters will eventually mix with warmer waters and rise to the surface in either the Indian Ocean or the Pacific to become part of the warm moving current. Not only does this circulation transport heat but as it sinks it carries oxygenated water and dissolved surface level carbon dioxide deep into the oceans.

El Niño and La Niña

The interrelationship of atmospheric and oceanic conditions can be exemplified during two specific sets of conditions found in the Pacific Ocean: El Niño and La Niña (Figure 1.41).

To understand these changes is important to first understand the concept of **Walker circulation** and **Walker cells**. Walker circulation is a theoretical model of how air moves in the troposphere in tropical

Previously only thought to affect climate and weather conditions in the Pacific region, It is now believed that El Niño and La Niña have a global influence. In Africa dry conditions are experienced from December to February with higher rainfall from March to May while El Niño is the dominant force in the Pacific. The opposite is found when La Niña is dominant.

Pacific 'neutral' conditions:

- Trade winds blow east to west
- Trade winds bring moist warm air and warm surface water to the west
- Heavy rains through thunderstorms in the west due to convection and moisture
- Drier air returned eastward at high altitude
- Central and eastern Pacific cool
- Cooler waters bring nutrients to the surface in the east and fish flourish

El Niño and La Niña are regular and natural events within the climate system. Episodes usually last between nine months and a year to 2 years (although prolonged events may remain for a number of years). Both are regular events usually reappearing after 2 to 7 years. Recently the regularity and intensity of El Niño has become the most dominant factor. Climatologists believe that this is linked to the increased heating of the Pacific Ocean due to global warming. This could have a great effect on those who rely on the pattern of rainfall or fish stocks to survive. This particularly affects the less developed nations in the regions influenced by the events.

Both El Niño and La Niña are formed due to variations in air pressure in the tropical western Pacific and temperatures in the central and eastern Pacific.

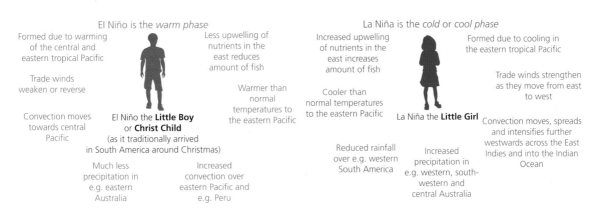

El Niño is the *warm phase*

Formed due to warming of the central and eastern tropical Pacific

Trade winds weaken or reverse

Convection moves towards central Pacific

El Niño the **Little Boy** or **Christ Child** (as it traditionally arrived in South America around Christmas)

Much less precipitation in e.g. eastern Australia

Increased convection over eastern Pacific and e.g. Peru

Less upwelling of nutrients in the east reduces amount of fish

Warmer than normal temperatures to the eastern Pacific

La Niña is the *cold* or *cool phase*

Increased upwelling of nutrients in the east increases amount of fish

Cooler than normal temperatures to the eastern Pacific

La Niña the **Little Girl**

Reduced rainfall over e.g. western South America

Increased precipitation in e.g. western, south-western and central Australia

Formed due to cooling in the eastern tropical Pacific

Trade winds strengthen as they move from east to west

Convection moves, spreads and intensifies further westwards across the East Indies and into the Indian Ocean

El Niño and La Niña events are a natural part of the global climate system.

▲ **Figure 1.41** El Niño and La Niña key points

regions. It suggests that the air circulates within a cell (Walker cell) which is self-contained (Figure 1.42). The lower part of the circulation of air flows east to west across the tropics near the surface:

- Air rises in the west.
- At higher altitudes the upper part of the circulation flows in the opposite direction, west to east.
- In the east the air sinks and reconnects with the lower part of the circulation and the cycle continues.

Due to the predictability of a closed cell, the location of particular weather conditions can be anticipated. If conditions change and the cell moves these weather conditions also move with the cell.

El Niño and La Niña are formed due to variations in both air pressure in the tropical western Pacific and temperatures in the central and eastern Pacific. These variations trigger movements of the Walker cell

in the Pacific and so move the positions of its climate characteristics.

Pacific neutral conditions

In what is described as 'neutral' conditions within the Pacific (Figure 1.42) (i.e. the area is not experiencing either El Niño or La Niña), conditions would be expected to be as follows:

- Trade winds blowing east to west.
- Trade winds bringing moist warm air and warm surface water to the west.
- Heavy rains through to thunderstorms to the west of the Pacific due to convection and moisture.
- Drier air returned eastward at high altitude.
- Central and eastern Pacific *relatively* cool (i.e. not excessively hot).
- Cooler waters bring nutrients to the surface in the east and fish flourish through being supplied with a food source.

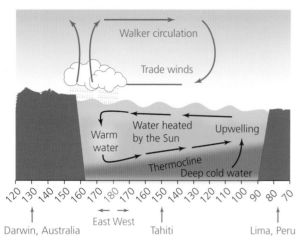

▲ **Figure 1.42** Pacific neutral conditions

El Niño

El Niño (Figure 1.43) is formed because of a warming of the central and eastern tropical Pacific and a warm phase. During an El Niño period the conditions change:

- Trade winds weaken or reverse in direction, blowing west to east.
- **Convection currents** move towards the central Pacific, creating heavy rainfall in this location but reducing the rainfall on the Asian side of the Pacific and, for example, eastern Australia.
- Increased convection may reach the eastern Pacific, for example, Peru.
- Upwelling of nutrients to the ocean surface in the east is reduced and results in a reduced number of fish in those waters.

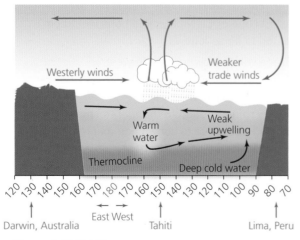

▲ **Figure 1.43** El Niño

La Niña

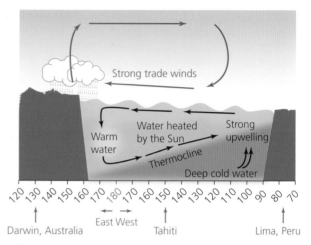

▲ **Figure 1.44** La Niña

La Niña (Figure 1.44) is the counterpart to El Niño and is the cool phase. It is formed due to a cooling in the eastern tropical Pacific and has an opposite effect to El Niño. La Niña results in the following:

- A strengthening of the trade winds as they move from east to west.
- The point of convection is moved further west than the Pacific neutral conditions, across the East Indies and into the Indian Ocean.
- Precipitation levels increase in, for example, western, south-western and central Australia.
- Western South America, in particular, receives much reduced rainfall.
- The eastern Pacific experiences lower than normal temperatures.
- Ocean upwelling increases in the eastern Pacific along with the amounts of nutrients and fish occupying these waters.

El Niño and La Niña are regular events, usually reappearing after around two to seven years. Episodes usually last between nine months and a year to two years (although some prolonged events may remain for a number of years). Recently a possible change in pattern has been observed by **climatologists** who have noted that an increase in regularity and intensity of El Niño has become the most dominant factor. This may be related to increased sea temperatures due to **global warming**.

Both El Niño and La Niña were previously only thought to affect climate and weather conditions in the Pacific, but it is now believed that they have a global influence. Some of their influences are described below.

Impact of El Niño

- Increased convection leads to heavy rainfall and flooding in the eastern Pacific (e.g. Peru and California, USA), resulting in flash floods and **debris** flows.
- A reduction in convection in the western Pacific (Indonesia, Malaysia and northern Australia).
- A reduction of upwelling nutrients to the ocean surface in the eastern Pacific which causes a decrease in the number of fish caught. This reduces food supply, especially for those who rely on fish as a staple in their diet. This can have a disastrous economic effect on communities who rely on fish to process and sell.
- Extreme temperatures lead to conditions where bush and forest fires create extremely hazardous and deadly situations in Australia, Malaysia, Borneo and other East Indies regions.
- Disruption of the monsoon across South Asia and into the Indian Ocean upsets traditional farming practices and can lead to hunger and starvation as well as economic difficulties.
- In Africa a correlation has been seen between droughts in the Sahel region and a dominant or long-term El Niño pattern.
- Tropical cyclone activity in the North Atlantic is reduced during strong El Niño conditions. Hurricanes are seen to reduce by 60 per cent and the intensity of cyclonic systems is reduced. This probably results from stronger than normal westerly winds experienced in El Niño periods.
- Mild, wet and windy weather occurs in the British Isles and north-west Europe.

Impact of La Niña

Generally these are typically opposite to those associated with El Niño.

- Reduced convection in the eastern Pacific, producing less than expected precipitation levels.
- An increase in convection in the western Pacific (Indonesia, Malaysia and northern Australia), resulting in increased rainfall. This has led to an increase in number and severity of **tropical storms** as far apart as Australia, Bangladesh and Mozambique.
- A rise in the upwelling of nutrients in the east of the Pacific, causing an increase in fish stocks and therefore food supply, and employment/economic benefits for the fishing industry.
- Wetter than normal conditions are found outwith the Pacific over south-eastern Africa and north-eastern Brazil.
- During the northern hemisphere summer, rainfall is increased during the Indian monsoon, especially in north-west India.

Task

1 What percentage of the movement of global heat budget energy is through the action of ocean currents?
2 Explain the differences between surface current circulation and thermohaline circulation.
3 What is a gyre?
4 Describe and explain the circulation patterns of gyres in:
   a) the northern hemisphere
   b) the southern hemisphere.
5 Explain the concept of Walker circulation.
6 Explain the formation of El Niño.
7 What weather conditions would be expected during an El Niño event:
   a) to the west of the Pacific Ocean?
   b) in the middle of the Pacific?
   c) to the east of the Pacific?
8 During El Niño what would the effects be:
   a) on fishing communities in Peru?
   b) on people in the outback (bush) of eastern Australia?
9 Explain the formation of La Niña.
10 What type of weather conditions would be expected during a La Niña event:
   a) to the west of the Pacific Ocean?
   b) in the middle of the Pacific?
   c) to the east of the Pacific?
11 Detail at least three global impacts each of El Niño and La Niña.

- The African Sahel region receives increased amounts of rainfall (in an area where water supply is at a critical, life-threatening level).
- Tropical cyclones and hurricanes increase in number and intensity in the North Atlantic, particularly affecting the Caribbean and the USA.
- An increase in storms and snow moving in from the Atlantic affecting the British Isles.

Reflection

Take some time to think and make notes about the following:

- In discussing El Niño and La Niña, this chapter has focused on the physical changes and weather patterns they cause. How much does poverty make coping with the effects of El Niño and La Niña worse?
- How might richer nations deal with the problems of the wet and dry seasons experienced in relation to the ITCZ if they happened in their countries?
- Would rich countries have become rich if they had had to experience these conditions?

Summary

You have now completed this chapter and should be able to answer questions, discuss and explain and apply knowledge and understanding of the key factors and interactions of atmospheric and oceanic processes in the elements required by SQA for Higher Geography:

- global heat budget
- redistribution of energy by atmosphere and oceanic circulation
- cause, characteristics and impact of the intertropical convergence zone.

In addition to this you should be able to make reference to the material in the case study as an exemplar to show greater understanding of the facts and processes as they relate to real people and places locally, regionally and globally.

Hopefully your own research (and additional teacher examples) will have given you a wider understanding of the topic, not just for your exam, but for your own geographical development.

SQA examination-style questions

Below are some examples of possible exam questions. These are by no means the only questions that could be asked but they give you an idea of what to expect. Some questions may be accompanied by maps or graphs from which you can gather extra information to assist with your answer. However, you should be able to answer these questions without looking at maps or graphs, although we have given you a suggestion of what to look for in the final question.

1   Explain why the Earth's surface absorbs only 49 per cent of the solar energy received at the edge of the atmosphere. You should refer to conditions both in the Earth's atmosphere and at the Earth's surface.
2   Explain how the atmosphere transfers energy from the tropical latitudes towards the poles.
3   Explain how ocean currents assist in transferring energy around the globe.
4   With the aid of an annotated diagram or diagrams, explain why there is a surplus of solar energy in the tropical latitudes and a deficit of solar energy towards the poles.
5   Describe the origin and characteristics of the Maritime Tropical and Continental Tropical air masses.
6   Explain the variation in rainfall within West Africa (look at the map and three climate graphs in Figure 1.35, page 34).

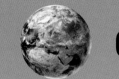

Chapter 2 Hydrosphere

Introduction

What could be more important than a study of planet Earth and its people? The **hydrosphere** is one of four Physical Environment themes in the Higher Geography SQA course.

For the examination you may be given a question based on one or more of the following broad topics:

- the **hydrological cycle** within a **drainage basin**
- interpretation of **hydrographs**
- formation of erosional and depositional features in river landscapes:
  - V-shaped valley
  - waterfall
  - meander
  - oxbow lake.

There is an overlap in some of the content, knowledge, and skills in this chapter on the hydrosphere with the Global Issues section on River Basin Management.

In order to fully understand these three broad topics, this chapter includes some additional background information.

2.1 The hydrosphere

Water is found in the air, on the land, trapped as ice, between rocks and in every living thing. Water is the compound H_2O and, in its purest form, is made up of 2 hydrogen atoms bonded to 1 oxygen atom. 'Hydro' comes from the Greek word for water. The hydrosphere is the liquid water component of the Earth. It includes the oceans, seas, lakes, ponds, rivers and streams. The hydrosphere covers about 70 per cent of the surface of the Earth and is the home for many plants and animals. Hydrology is the study of water and anything linked to water is part of the hydrosphere.

Water is an unevenly distributed but essential resource. The amount (volume) of water in our planet is fixed. It does not enter into or leave planet Earth. This is recognised as a system. What does change is the property of that water, i.e. whether it is a gas, a liquid or a solid. While the total amount of water is fixed, there is concern over the competing demands for its use, availability and quality. Water is a **sustainable resource**. That means that with recycling and with management, water can be used again and again. Unfortunately there is human interference in the cycle, which can result in environmental **degradation**, conflict and waste.

Since 1900 the population of the planet has increased by 400 per cent, while the demand for water in the same period has increased by 700 per cent and the amount of water on the planet has increased by 0 per cent.

2.2 Global hydrological cycle

In order to understand the workings of the hydrosphere, you need to understand the global hydrological cycle. This cycle describes the movement and circulation of water (as a liquid, solid or vapour) between the oceans, **atmosphere**, vegetation and land.

It is the power from the Sun (solar energy) that heats the surface of the Earth, oceans, lakes, rivers and atmosphere.

Figure 2.1 is a very significant diagram. You may be expected to describe and explain the movements and flows and you may also be asked to draw your own version of the hydrological cycle. So where do you start? The amount of water in our planet does not alter. The key idea behind the cycle is that water transfers from the oceans into the atmosphere over the land before returning to the oceans. Of course we need to add some detail to this.

Flows and transfers within the hydrological cycle

The flows or transfers involved are:

- evaporation
- transpiration
- evapotranspiration
- condensation
- precipitation
- overland flow or run-off
- infiltration and percolation
- throughflow and groundwater flow.

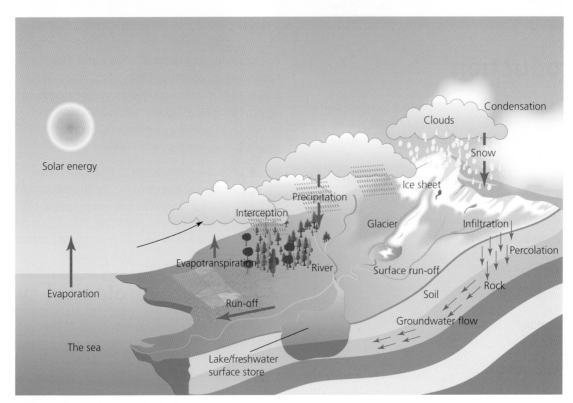

▲ **Figure 2.1** Global hydrological cycle

▲ **Figure 2.2** Water in its three forms: ice, water and vapour.
a) Ice: Vatnajökull Glacier, Iceland; b) Water: Red Sea, Egypt; c) Vapour: Clouds over Atlas Mountains, Morocco

Storage stages within the hydrological cycle

The storage stages (see Figure 2.3) are:

- oceans
- rivers
- lakes
- ice caps and glaciers
- vegetation
- the atmosphere
- soil and the ground.

Processes of the hydrological cycle

By heating the oceans, lakes, rivers, glaciers and the Earth's surface, water is evaporated into the atmosphere. In addition, water is lost through the leaves of plants and trees (transpiration) to the atmosphere. The combined action of evaporation and transpiration is known as evapotranspiration. All this water vapour/moisture is contained in the atmosphere and is transferred or moved by global winds, until cooling takes place (condensation), when the vapour returns to liquid form and precipitation will occur (rain, sleet, snow and hail).

Most of this precipitation will return to the oceans and Earth's surface. The return can be rapid when the precipitation falls over the oceans but longer when returned via rivers or glacial melting, in some cases years or even thousands of years. This is the simple process of a closed system and an example of a cycle. As a result of climate change it is suggested that some glaciers are melting at an advanced rate and water which may have been locked into glaciers for thousands of years is being released into rivers and oceans at an accelerated pace. However, in the past there have been periods of cooling (possibly resulting in numerous ice ages) when large quantities of water have been locked up or stored in glaciers and ice sheets.

Water returns to the sea via other routes. Water may fall directly into rivers and lakes and return as surface water or run-off. When we consider the mighty rivers of the world (for example, the Nile, Yangtze, Mekong, Amazon and Mississippi) and the uncountable number of more modest-sized rivers, you may be surprised how small this transfer is in terms of significance to the cycle.

Also, water returns to the oceans when water infiltrates into the soil and ground. It can be stored within the layers of the rocks (groundwater) or more slowly through the soil and ground (groundwater flow) to emerge as springs or to feed rivers (throughflow) which flow back to the sea.

In any question relating to the hydrological cycle, you need to know and understand the processes, flows, storage and overall system. Table 2.1 provides a summary of the main flows or transfers that make up the hydrological cycle and a drainage basin cycle (see page 46).

Global water storage

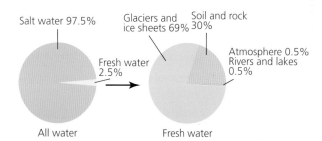

▲ **Figure 2.3** Global water storage

Task

Look at the information in Figure 2.1.

1. Describe, with the aid of a diagram, the hydrological cycle.
2. Explain how a balance is maintained within the hydrological cycle.
3. Analyse why water is regarded as a sustainable resource and explain the importance of maintaining water quality.
4. Describe the pattern of global water storage.

▼ **Table 2.1** Summary of key flows or transfers of a hydrological cycle and a drainage basin cycle

Keyword	Explanation
Baseflow	The **baseflow** is the groundwater flow that feeds into rivers through river banks and river beds.
Channel flow	**Channel flow** is the water flowing in a river; it is also known as the river **discharge**.
Condensation	The change in the atmosphere when droplets of water vapour cool and change back into liquid water. This liquid takes the form of water droplets or clouds.
Evaporation	The process by which liquid water is transformed into water vapour. Considerable solar energy is required for this change. Evaporation rates vary with temperature, wind speed, humidity, hours of sunshine and seasonality.
Evapotranspiration	The two components of evaporation and transpiration.
Groundwater	Water stored within rocks, rock pores and joints.
Groundwater flow	Water flowing slowly below the **water table** through **permeable rock**.
Infiltration	Water soaks into and moves through the soil; this process of infiltration is influenced by the permeability and porosity of the soil. Once the soil is saturated, then further infiltration is blocked.
Interception	The process by which raindrops are prevented from directly reaching the soil surface. Vegetation (e.g. leaves) is capable of breaking up the fall of precipitation. This is more noticeable in the summer months when deciduous trees are in full leaf cover.
Percolation	As the water moves through and seeps down the soil it may continue to move deeper (percolate) into the rocks and settle down to the water table.
Precipitation	The main input. The variables include type or form of precipitation (e.g. rain or snow), the total amount, seasonality and the intensity.
Run-off or overland flow	The total of all the water that flows over the surface of the river basin, mainly flowing away within rivers.
Stem flow	**Stem flow** is water running down a plant stem or tree trunk.
Throughfall	Water dripping from one leaf or plant to another is known as **throughfall**.
Throughflow	Water that continues to move downhill through the soil and ground and which may emerge into rivers, lakes or streams.
Transpiration	A biological process by which water is lost from a plant through the minute pores (stomata) in the leaves. Transpiration rates depend on the time of year (season), type and amount of vegetation.

2.3 River landscapes

For SQA Higher Geography, you are expected to be able to explain how a selection of erosional and depositional features are formed in river landscapes. SQA has listed four features that could come up in examinations: V-shaped valleys, waterfalls, meanders, and oxbow lakes. You have to be able to create annotated diagrams to show the stages in the formation of the named features.

To clearly explain the formation of these features, you must be able to describe in detail how rivers alter the landscape, and the fluvial **processes** involved.

This section requires prior knowledge and a general understanding of the key **denudation** processes:

- weathering
- erosion
- transportation
- deposition.

Energy within a river system

For fluvial processes to be effective, they depend on the amount of energy within the river. The larger the amount of energy, the larger amount of change the river can create. In general, the steeper the gradient and the greater the volume of the river, the more energy the river will have. In the river model (see page 51) the river's energy varies from one section to another due to the different conditions experienced, for example:

- the upper course has a steep gradient and its height above sea level gives it the greatest amount of gravitational potential energy, which can be turned into kinetic energy further along the river's course
- in the middle course the gradient has reduced, and the gravitational potential energy turns into kinetic energy
- by the lower course, the river's gradient is very much reduced and it has very little gravitational potential energy but has the highest level of kinetic energy.

The greatest amount of energy in a river is used simply to keep it flowing as it overcomes the friction between the river and its wetted perimeter (bed and internal sides of the river channel). The rougher the bed of the channel, the greater the amount of energy that is used to overcome the friction created. Bends in a river also increase friction with riverbanks, increasing the energy used. If the volume of water in the river is reduced, the river must use more of its energy to overcome the friction of its wetted perimeter, and less is available for erosion or transportation of material.

Stream flow

River water does not move as one solid, unified mass but has various component movements within it. The way that water flows within a river (streamlines) can influence the amount and type of erosion, and deposition by a river:

- **Laminar**
  This kind of movement is the simplest of the three and has the least effect on the landscape. The streamlines are straight or gently curved horizontal sheets running parallel to each other (Figure 2.4). These do not mix or cross but instead 'slide' over each other. Laminar flow is unable to support load in **suspension**.

Laminar flow

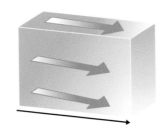

Direction of river movement

▲ **Figure 2.4** Laminar flow

- **Turbulent**
  Most rivers experience turbulent stream flow. 'Turbulent' is used to describe something that is experiencing disorder, confusion, or is not stable or calm. For a river this is a good description where the water experiences irregular fluctuations in its velocity, and where there is a continual mixing of the streamlines (Figure 2.5). This creates a complex pattern of movement within a river, forming twists, swirls, and **eddies**. The level of turbulence increases at higher velocity, where the river channel meanders, or the river bed is rough. Turbulence is closely associated with **hydraulic action**, assisting in the development of meanders, and hollows (**potholes**) on the river bed.

Turbulent flow

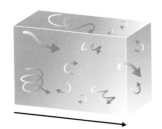

Direction of river movement

▲ **Figure 2.5** Turbulent flow

- **Helicoidal**
  Helicoidal flow is a horizontal element of turbulence that moves in a corkscrew motion (Figure 2.6). This is typically generated in areas where the channel bed is undulating with alternating pools (deeper) and riffles (shallower). The water is slowed down as it crosses the riffles but speeds up through the pools and this

causes the corkscrew motion to be produced. This corkscrew motion moves downstream but also slews back and forth across the river. This movement is key to the creation and development of meanders.

Helicoidal flow

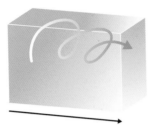

Direction of river movement

▲ **Figure 2.6** Helicoidal flow

Fluvial processes (river processes)

These are the processes through which rivers can shape and alter their channels and valleys, and also create new land features. These processes assist with:

- erosion
- transportation
- deposition.

Fluvial erosion

Fluvial erosion is the wearing away of the land by rivers. Four main processes are involved. The first three of the processes assist in the alteration of the river channel's shape, depth and width, the final one alters the shape and size of materials within the river:

- **Hydraulic action**
  Here, the movement of water creates pressure or force against the sides and bed of the river channel. The direct force of this moving water dislodges or breaks off material from the river channel. Hydraulic action also includes cavitation whereby air bubbles get trapped into cracks and other spaces in the river's bed and banks, and then are compressed by the moving water. The increase

of pressure caused by this compression causes the voids (spaces) to implode and can generate an intense shock wave, with the previously compressed air and jets of water firing out. These can damage even solid rock, breaking off pieces. Cavitation is an important process in the development of rapids and waterfalls, usually in conjunction with abrasion. In the upper course of a river, hydraulic action is mostly responsible for vertical erosion and, in the lower course, lateral erosion.

- **Abrasion** (corrasion)
  This is the eroding of the river channel by the river's load (e.g. sand, stones, pebbles, rocks). This load may have resulted from earlier erosion by the river or from material that has fallen into the channel because of weathering or mass movement. As the river moves (transports) its load, debris can scrape, scratch or hit against the channel's bed and banks and so wears them away. Abrasion is responsible for both vertical and horizontal erosion.

- **Solution** (corrosion)
  This is chemical erosion by the river. In simple terms, the water dissolves minerals in the rocks over which it is flowing (a reaction between the chemicals in the water and those in the rocks).

- **Attrition**
  This affects a river's load. As the load materials (e.g. stones, pebbles, rocks) are being carried downstream by the river, they hit or rub against each other and the river's bed and banks. These collisions break off sharp edges and eventually make the load smoother and more rounded.

Along with fluvial erosion, the processes of weathering and mass movement also assist in breaking down and changing the landscape in river valleys.

Fluvial transportation

Fluvial transportation is how a river carries and moves its load. The river gains its load from its own fluvial erosion plus other materials which may have fallen into it through weathering and mass

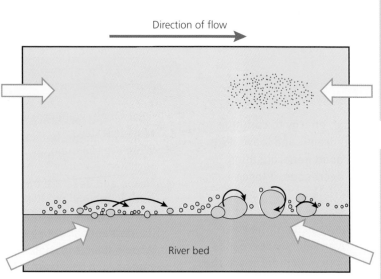

Solution
Minerals are dissolved in the water. They may be in the water following chemical weathering of the land around the river or from solution (corrosion) creating a chemical reaction between the river and its wetted perimeter. Material transported dissolved in the water is known as solute load.

Saltation
Smaller rocks, pebbles, and stones are bounced in a hopping-like action along the river bed. The river has enough energy to lift the smaller particles for short distances but not enough to carry them for long distances. Materials moved this way are part of the bed load.

Suspension
Fine, light, and small particles are carried by the water. The river has the energy to lift these, hold them within the river's flow, and transport the particles for long distances. This is known as suspended load.

Traction
The force of the water in the river rolls drags or slides boulders and rocks along the river bed. These are moved in this way because the river doesn't have enough energy to carry them or even bounce them. This is most commonly found in the upper course of a river. Materials moved along the river bed in this way are part of the bed load.

Direction of flow

River bed

▲ **Figure 2.7** Fluvial transportation processes

movement. As the load is being transported it assists in the processes of fluvial erosion (abrasion and **attrition**).

There are four main processes involved in fluvial transportation (Figure 2.7). And these depend on the amount of energy the river has available and the size of the load:

- **Traction**
  The force of the water in the river rolls, drags, or slides boulders and rocks along the river bed. These are moved in this way because the river doesn't have enough energy to carry them or even bounce them. This is most commonly found in the upper course of a river. Materials moved along the river bed in this way are part of the bed load.
- **Saltation**
  Smaller rocks, pebbles, and stones are bounced in a hopping-like action along the river bed. The river has enough energy to lift the smaller

particles for short distances but not enough to carry them for long distances. This is most commonly found in the upper and middle courses of a river. Materials moved in this way also form part of the river's bed load.

- **Suspension**
  Fine, light, and small particles (e.g. clay, silt and sand) are carried by the water. The river has the energy to lift these, hold them within the river's flow, and transport the particles for long distances. This process can happen throughout the whole course of the river, increasing as it nears the river's end at its mouth. Materials moved in this way are known as suspended load.
- **Solution**
  In 'fluvial erosion' above, we saw that in the process of solution (corrosion) river water dissolves minerals in the rocks over which it is flowing (a reaction between the chemicals in the water and those in the rocks). In 'fluvial

transportation, 'solution' is the dissolved state in which the minerals are moved. This process mostly happens in the middle and lower course of the river. Materials moved in this way are known as solute load.

Fluvial deposition

If a river doesn't have enough energy to continue to transport material, it will drop it and leave it in place. This is deposition. A good generalisation is that, as a river's velocity decreases, it loses the ability to transport materials and they are deposited. The greater the size or mass of the load particle, the greater the velocity of the river needed to transport it. As river velocity decreases, the larger and heavier items (e.g. boulders) are the first to be deposited and the smallest particles are the last. This explains why, in the upper course of a river, where the river may be nothing more than a mountain stream, there are boulders and larger rocks on the river's bed, while near the mouth there is only fine silt.

There are different possible reasons for a river's velocity to decrease:

- when the river is forced to slow down by meeting a slower flowing area of water, such as at its mouth where it may enter an ocean/sea, loch/lake or another less powerful river. The sudden reduction in speed may result in materials being dumped in the river's channel and into the body of water it has entered, forming a delta
- on the inside of a bend (here, the river's velocity is slower), such as at a meander
- when the river slows due to a sudden reduction in gradient
- when the river overflows its banks. As the water slows on the river banks, a build-up of material results, creating levees (embankments) and more deposition as it spreads out over the shallow floodplain

- when there is a decrease in discharge in the river, e.g. during a drought or after a flood as the river returns to its normal discharge level.

Task

1 Describe the differences between laminar and turbulent flow.
2 What are the main characteristics of the type of turbulence known as helicoidal flow?
3 Name and describe the four main processes of fluvial erosion.
4 Name and describe the four main processes of fluvial transportation.
5 What happens to material that is being transported by a river (its load) when the river's velocity and energy decreases? Mention the effects on different sizes of load.

River long profile

This is a model showing how a perfect river's gradient changes as it flows from its source to its mouth (Figure 2.8). It is possible to split the river into three sections within its journey. These sections are the:

- upper course
- middle course
- lower course.

Each of these three sections of a river can be defined by a change in gradient, dominant fluvial processes and the landforms found within each one. Within the model, we can also see the cross sections of a river valley as expected during the upper, middle, and lower courses.

It is interesting to notice that the contours on a map bend (point like an arrowhead) upstream towards the river's source (Figure 2.9).

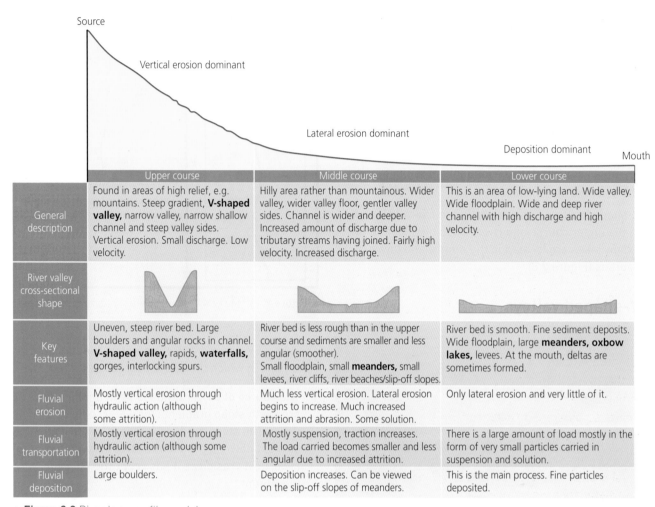

▲ Figure 2.8 River long profile model

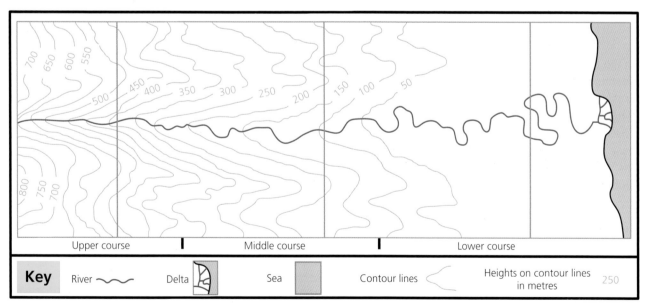

▲ Figure 2.9 Map showing contour patterns in the three stages of a river

2.4 Four landforms for the SQA Higher examination

As noted earlier, for the SQA Higher examination you are expected to be able to explain how V-shaped valleys, waterfalls, meanders, and oxbow lakes are formed in river landscapes. Now that you are aware of the circumstances and processes involved in the creation of such landforms, this section will focus on the selected landforms.

V-shaped valleys and waterfalls are typically found in the upper course of a river, while meanders and oxbow lakes are located in the middle and lower courses (Figure 2.8).

V-shaped valleys

▲ **Figure 2.10** V-shaped valley Landmannalaugar rainbow mountains in Iceland

In the upper course of a river, the river valley can be seen to be V-shaped in cross section (Figure 2.10). The cross section of the river valley changes as it moves into the middle and lower courses, losing the V-shape. The valley sides become more gently sloped and the base of the valley gets flatter and wider. By the time the river reaches the lower course, it is difficult to identify a valley at all (Figure 2.8 and Figure 2.9).

A helpful tip for looking at maps was mentioned earlier: contours point like arrowheads (V-shapes) towards the river's source. This is most noticeable in the V-shaped area of the upper course (Figure 2.11).

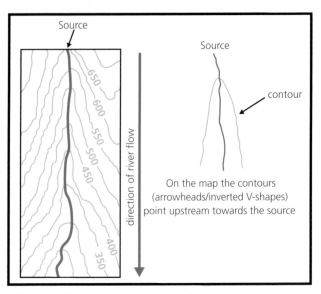

▲ **Figure 2.11** Map of a V-shaped valley in a river's upper course

The typical V-shaped valley is created due to the conditions in which the upper course is situated.

1   The source of a river tends to be in an upland area with steep gradients for water to flow down. The steep gradient forces water to flow straight downslope, and the stream is limited to vertical erosion as it has very little lateral movement.
2   The vertical erosion is mostly in the form of hydraulic action, abrasion, and solution.
3   This vertical erosion exposes the sides of the steep valley it creates to weathering and mass movement. The rock forming the valley sides is broken down by **chemical weathering** and **mechanical weathering**, such as **freeze–thaw**. The now destabilised rock falls into the river (sometimes as landslides) and is transported further downstream. As the material is transported, it assists in the process of abrasion and increases erosion.
4   Over time, as the process continues, the characteristic steep-sided V-shaped cross section of an upper course valley is formed. Due to more resistant rocks being found in upland areas, valley sides are not widened greatly and their slopes remain steep (Figure 2.12).

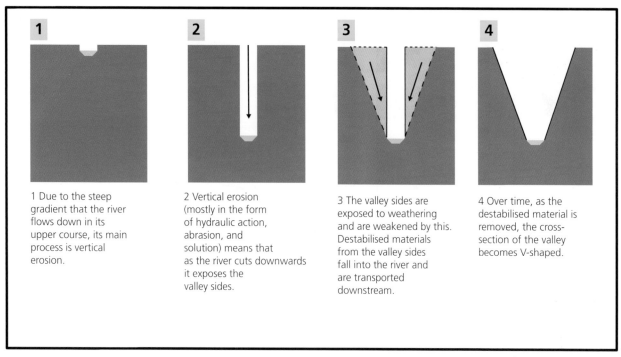

▲ **Figure 2.12** Formation of a V-shaped valley

When the river meets obstacles of hard, resistant rock it winds around these and takes the path of least resistance. This winding leaves narrow necks of high land (spurs) that extend into the river valley on either side. The river occupies almost all of the valley floor and spurs stick into the river valley from both sides (Figure 2.13).

The spurs appear to overlap as the river winds from one side to the other around them. The spurs appear to interlock like the teeth of a zip and these are known as **interlocking spurs** (Figure 2.14).

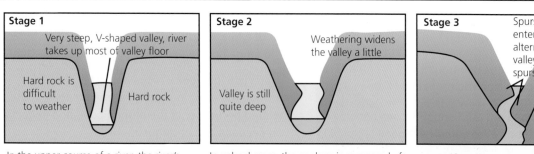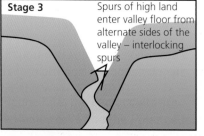

Stage 1	**Stage 2**	**Stage 3**
Very steep, V-shaped valley, river takes up most of valley floor. Hard rock is difficult to weather. Hard rock	Weathering widens the valley a little. Valley is still quite deep	Spurs of high land enter valley floor from alternate sides of the valley – interlocking spurs
In the upper course of a river, the river's water volume and discharge are low. The river uses most of its energy overcoming friction with its channel. What energy it has left over is used by hydraulic action, abrasion, and solution to deepen the channel (vertical erosion).	In upland areas, the geology is composed of hard, resistant rock such as granite or slate. Weathering (such as freeze–thaw) slowly widens the valley. Due to the hard and resistant rocks, the valley sides are not widened greatly and their slopes remain steep. This gives the valley its steep-sided V–shape. Repeated weathering weakens the rock so that fragments break loose and tumble down the hillside into the river, which transports the material downstream.	The winding path taken by the river is due to obstacles of hard, resistant rock in its path. The river takes the path of least resistance as it flows downstream. This results in projections of high land that slope into the valley from either side. These projections of sloping land are called spurs.

▲ **Figure 2.13** The formation of interlocking spurs

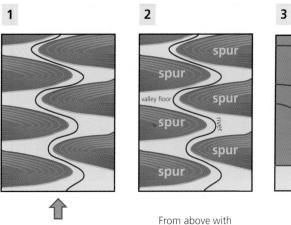

| 1 | 2 | 3 |

The upper course of a river valley with spurs sloping down and pointing into the valley from both sides.

From this position the spurs seem to overlap and link together. These are known as interlocking spurs.

From above

From above with annotation

Looking up-valley from the position of the blue arrow in 1

▲ **Figure 2.14** Interlocking spurs

Waterfalls

Waterfalls (Figure 2.15) are most likely to be found in the upper course of a river. As the name suggests, a waterfall is a place where the water in a river falls down a steep or vertical drop (often from a considerable height). These are typically found where the **bedrock** over which the river flows is made up of rock types that have different levels of resistance. These rocks will, therefore, erode at different rates. Those with less resistance will erode quicker than those with greater resistance.

A typical waterfall in the upper course of a river is formed in the following way (Figure 2.16):

1   Where a river, travelling over the surface of a resistant rock type (e.g. **basalt** or dolerite) moves onto a layer of less resistant rock

▲ **Figure 2.15** Falls of Kirkaig, Inverkirkaig, Scotland

(e.g. sandstone or limestone) it begins to erode downwards quicker than it had on the resistant rock (**differential erosion**). This creates a 'step down' downstream of the junction point where the more resistant rock meets the less resistant rock.

2   Over time, the processes of fluvial erosion (hydraulic action, abrasion and solution) continues to cut down into the less resistant rock and the 'step down' becomes larger and larger, meaning that the water has to fall further.

3   As the river continues to fall, the turbulent, plunging water (carrying boulders, rocks and other materials) physically impacts the less resistant rock, while also increasing hydraulic action and abrasion at the base of the fall. This erodes a deep depression at the base of the fall known as a **plunge pool**.

4   The turbulent water swirls the transported materials (boulders, rocks and other debris) around the pool, increasing abrasion against the wetted perimeter of the plunge pool, and in doing so deepens and enlarges it.

5   The swirling action of the water also assists the river in eroding the cliff face that forms the backing to the waterfall, **undercutting** (eroding underneath) the resistant rock above. This leaves part of the resistant rock, with no support below it, overhanging the plunge pool.

Waterfalls may develop in different ways, under different circumstances or conditions, and within other sections of a river's course, but for the SQA examination you are expected to be able to describe

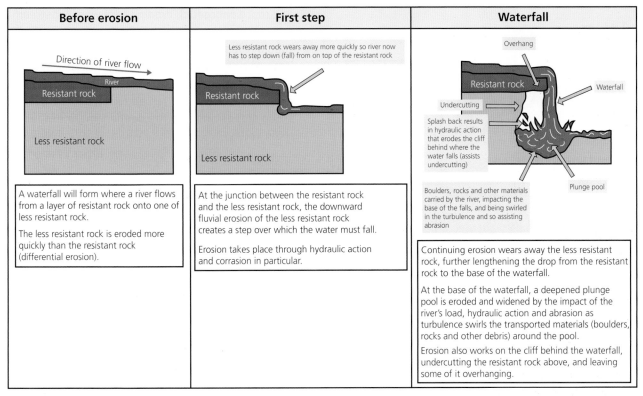

Before erosion	First step	Waterfall

Before erosion

Direction of river flow

River

Resistant rock

Less resistant rock

A waterfall will form where a river flows from a layer of resistant rock onto one of less resistant rock.

The less resistant rock is eroded more quickly than the resistant rock (differential erosion).

First step

Less resistant rock wears away more quickly so river now has to step down (fall) from on top of the resistant rock

Resistant rock

Less resistant rock

At the junction between the resistant rock and the less resistant rock, the downward fluvial erosion of the less resistant rock creates a step over which the water must fall.

Erosion takes place through hydraulic action and corrasion in particular.

Waterfall

Overhang

Resistant rock

Waterfall

Undercutting

Splash back results in hydraulic action that erodes the cliff behind where the water falls (assists undercutting)

Plunge pool

Boulders, rocks and other materials carried by the river, impacting the base of the falls, and being swirled in the turbulence and so assisting abrasion

Continuing erosion wears away the less resistant rock, further lengthening the drop from the resistant rock to the base of the waterfall.

At the base of the waterfall, a deepened plunge pool is eroded and widened by the impact of the river's load, hydraulic action and abrasion as turbulence swirls the transported materials (boulders, rocks and other debris) around the pool.

Erosion also works on the cliff behind the waterfall, undercutting the resistant rock above, and leaving some of it overhanging.

▲ **Figure 2.16** Formation of a waterfall

and explain the formation of a waterfall as described here, and to draw diagrams showing that process.

The continued erosion of a waterfall can lead to the formation of a feature known as a **gorge**. This is formed in the following manner (Figure 2.17):

- As the undercutting continues, the more resistant rock overhanging the plunge pool is unable to support its own weight and collapses. In fact, that piece of the river bed collapses downwards to the base of the waterfall.
- The position of the waterfall moves further upstream (seems to have moved backwards).
- The collapsed material that falls into the plunge pool now assists in the erosional processes through impact and then by being moved by the turbulent, swirling action of the river against the bed and banks (abrasion).
- The backward erosion (wearing away the cliff face behind the falling water) continues and again undercuts the **cap stone** and another overhang is formed.
- A and B repeat themselves and the waterfall appears to have moved further upstream.
- The process continues to repeat over time

(hundreds or thousands of years) and the waterfall's position moves further and further upstream.

- As the position of the waterfall has 'moved' upstream, erosion has carved a narrow and steep-sided valley with bare rocky walls through the landscape with the river at the base of it. This is a gorge.

This type of gorge is known as a **gorge of recession**, simply meaning that it is a gorge created by a receding waterfall (eroding backwards and upstream) (Figure 2.18).

How waterfalls form under different conditions

There are other reasons for a waterfall to form. Over time, a river creates a smooth concave long profile (Figure 2.8) from source to mouth. This is the point of balance (equilibrium) and the river always attempts to achieve and maintain this shape. If something disrupts this balance, the river will vertically (downward) erode to re-establish the concave long profile. The balance can be disrupted by, for example:

- Tectonic movement causing land to rise, or a fall in sea level due to **eustatic change** or **isostatic**

1

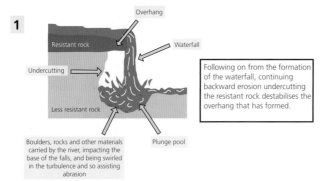

Following on from the formation of the waterfall, continuing backward erosion undercutting the resistant rock destabilises the overhang that has formed.

2

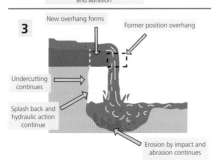

The overhang eventually fails to support its own weight and collapses into the plunge pool.

With the collapse, the position of the waterfall has moved further upstream.

The collapsed overhang's resistant rock increases the erosional ability of the turbulent currents within the plunge pool to abrade.

Backward erosion continues.

3

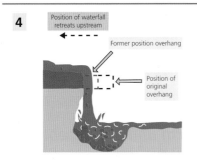

The continuing backward erosion creates another overhang and the process repeats itself.

4

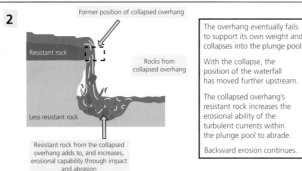

The process continues to repeat over time (hundreds or thousands of years) and the waterfall's position moves further and further upstream.

As the position of the waterfall has moved upstream the erosion has carved a narrow steep-sided valley through the surrounding the rocks with the river at the base of it. This is a gorge.

▲ **Figure 2.17** Formation of a gorge

adjustment. The point where the concave slope of the long profile is broken by these changes is known as the **knickpoint**. Where upstream land is higher, the river must now drop down to the lower downstream section and so forms a waterfall. The river gains more potential energy as the downstream base of the river falls and the river experiences **rejuvenation** (it becomes 'younger'

and more energetic), eroding backward (upstream) to regain a concave long profile.

- Glacial erosion (Chapter 3) wears away the base of river valleys and steepens their sides. Tributary valleys are not deepened as far and rivers from these are forced to fall down the steep slopes and into the deeper, more eroded, main valley.

> ## Research opportunity
>
> There are different shapes and types of waterfalls. Take some time to make an internet search for the following terms which describe the different appearances of waterfalls. Then draw diagrams and describe what each looks like:
>
> plunge waterfall, horsetail waterfall, cataract waterfall, fan waterfall, tiered waterfall, block waterfall, cascade waterfall, punchbowl waterfall, segmented waterfall.

Meanders and oxbow lakes

Meanders and oxbow lakes are the final two river features that may be included within the SQA Higher examination. Both features are normally located in the middle and/or lower course of a river, with a greater number and larger more developed examples found in the lower course. They form more easily on gentle slopes, where the valley floor is also wider and composed of unconsolidated (loose, not compact or dense) sediments or less resistant rock. Oxbow lakes develop from meanders.

Conditions change as the river moves out of its upper course. The river is no longer in mountainous terrain, its height and gradient have decreased, the base of the valley has widened, a floodplain has developed and the sides of the valley are also less steep. Due to these changes, erosion moves from a vertical focus to both vertical and lateral (horizontal) action; vertical erosion decreases while lateral erosion increases. Although the river's gradient has reduced, its velocity is maintained because its channel has become smoother and deeper, so reducing friction with the river's wetted perimeter. Discharge also increases

Before	During	After
Below shows the position of a waterfall 1 .	Backward erosion and undercutting undermine the resistant rock on which the river flows, creating an overhang. In time and being so far undercut that the overhang cannot support itself, the overhang collapses into the river. The position of the waterfall is now further upstream, 2 . As this happens a high, steep-sided, narrow valley is left downstream of the waterfall. This is the start of a 'gorge of recession'.	With continued backward erosion, undercutting and overhang collapse, the waterfall position recedes, moving further and further upstream, 3 . Downstream of the waterfall the 'gorge of recession' has become much longer.

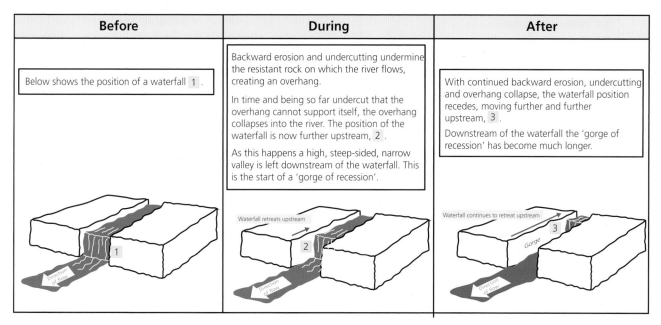

▲ **Figure 2.18** Development of a gorge of recession

as many tributaries join the main channel, resulting in an increased volume of water. Due to variations in the channel's cross-sectional depth (deep and shallow areas) and its twisting course, the river can lose energy as it slows, and materials are deposited (Figure 2.8).

Meanders

Meanders are large bends formed by the river (Figure 2.19). These bends can vary in size and the channel of the river follows a sinuous course (winding like a snake) downstream.

As we have already seen (page 56), interaction between the river and its wetted perimeter can have a great influence on the river's amount and type of erosion and deposition, resulting from its stream flow and the effects of turbulence. Pools (deeper areas with faster flowing water) and riffles (shallow areas where water slows and is agitated in contact with the river bed) in the river's channel are believed to instigate the formation of meanders. As a pool and riffle pattern forms, the path of the flowing water starts to move from side to side (Figure 2.20).

▲ **Figure 2.19** Cuckmere River meandering, East Sussex, England

The pools and riffles disrupt the movement of the river and, as a pool and riffle pattern forms, the path of the flowing water moves from side to side, while also generating turbulence and helicoidal flow (Figure 2.6 and Figure 2.21) that corkscrews from bank to bank through the water. The river now moves from side to side as it flows downstream and, once this movement has started, the processes of fluvial

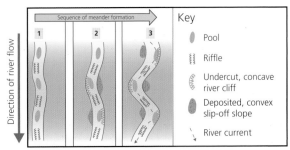

Notes

1 A sequence of pools and riffles has formed in the river and the water in the river starts to move from side to side.

2 The water begins to erode (undercut) the outer bank and deposit on the inner bank. This accentuates the bends in the river. Alternate pools migrate to opposite sides of the channel while the riffles locate on the straighter sections between curves.

3 The erosion on the outside of the bends and the deposition on the inside creates the sinuous pattern of meanders, with the associated lateral movement of their positions.

▲ **Figure 2.20** Formation of a meander from pools and riffles

erosion and deposition begin to create the more pronounced shape of a meander.

On the outside of the river bend, the velocity of the water is higher. The water is pushed towards its outer bank and this increases lateral erosion through hydraulic action and abrasion. This causes the outer

bank to be undercut and destabilised, and later to collapse, allowing the river channel to move further in that direction. This collapse leaves behind a steep-sided bank known as a **river cliff**. The fast flow of the water also deepens the channel on the outside of the bend through vertical erosion (Figure 2.21).

On the inside of the river bend, the water is slow-moving and lacking energy, and so deposits material here (mostly sand, silt, **gravel**, and pebbles). These deposits build up to form a gentle slope known as a **slip-off slope** or **point bar** (Figure 2.20 and Figure 2.21).

Helicoidal flow plays a vital part in erosion, transportation and deposition within the formation of a meander. A helicoidal flow's corkscrew motion impacts the upper part of the outside bend before assisting in the transportation of eroded materials as it corkscrews downwards. The eroded materials are deposited by the river on the inside of the next bend where friction caused by the water on the shallower bed reduces the river's energy and ability to continue to carry as much load.

The shape of meanders become more pronounced over time as erosion wears away the outside bank

On the outside of the river bend, the velocity of the water is higher. The water is pushed towards its outer bank and this increases lateral erosion through hydraulic action and abrasion. This causes the outer bank to be undercut and destabilised, and later to collapse, allowing the river channel to move further in that direction. This collapse leaves behind a steep-sided bank known as a river cliff. The fast flow of the water also deepens the channel on the outside of the bend through vertical erosion.

On the inside of the river bend, the water is slow-moving and lacking energy, and so deposits material here (mostly sand, silt, gravel and pebbles). These deposits build up to form a gentle slope known as a slip-off-slope or point bar.

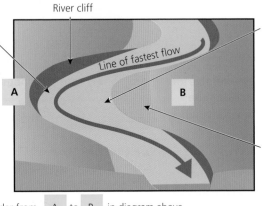

Slip-off slope (point bar)

Cross section across meander from A to B in diagram above

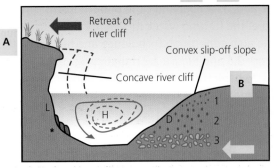

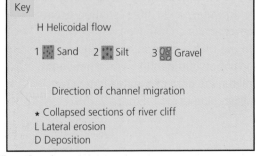

▲ **Figure 2.21** Formation of a meander

and deposition builds up on the inner bank. Meanders also appear to move their position (migrate) on a floodplain (from side to side and downstream) because of this continual erosion and deposition.

The continued erosion and deposition can also lead to the creation of oxbow lakes which develop from meanders.

Oxbow lakes

Oxbow lakes are curved lakes which are formed from abandoned meanders (Figure 2.23). Being formed from former meanders, they are found close to a river (Figure 2.22 and Figure 2.24).

With the continuing processes of erosion and deposition, a meander may form an extreme loop shape. The neck of land between the start of an individual meander and its end becomes narrower as the sites of erosion, on the outsides of the bends at

▲ **Figure 2.22** Oxbow lake near the Sava River, the Balkans

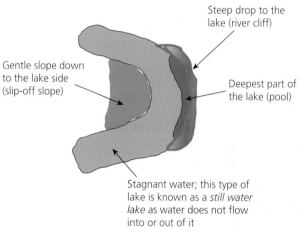

▲ **Figure 2.23** Elements of a meander

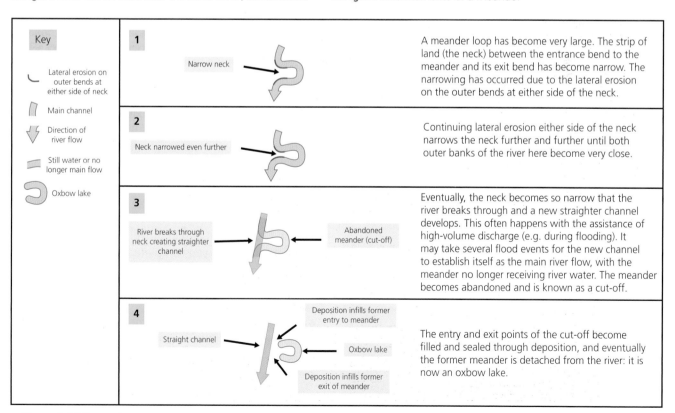

▲ **Figure 2.24** Formation of an oxbow lake

these points, work towards each other. Eventually, the neck becomes so narrow that the river breaks through and a new straighter channel develops. This often happens with the assistance of high-volume discharge (e.g. during flooding). It may take several flood events for the new channel to establish itself as the main river flow. The meander becomes abandoned and is known as a **cut-off**. The entry and exit points of the cut-off become filled and sealed through deposition and eventually the former meander is detached from the river: it is now an oxbow lake.

The oxbow lake loses its main source of water (the river) and over time begins to dry out, the water in the lake slowly evaporating (often becoming a swamp, bog or marsh during the process) (Figure 2.24).

When the oxbow lake has fully dried out, it becomes a curved indentation on the floodplain. It is not unusual for heavy rain to temporarily refill the former oxbow lake.

 Task

This task may be best suited working in groups or pairs.

1   There are four SQA selected features for examination: V-shaped valleys, waterfalls, meanders and oxbow lakes. Consider dividing the four features among the groups, so that all four are covered. Create a learning resource (e.g. booklet, large poster, PowerPoint presentation, animation, webpage, or other multimedia resource) to explain to other students how the four features were created.

2   The class may have only one final product or more than one! You may need to form groups, negotiate and debate the best way to complete the task, what tasks each person will do and what form the final presentation will take.

3   The presentation should locate where each feature is within a river model, the conditions needed for formation, the fluvial processes involved and explanations of how the features form. Why not add examples and pictures?

4   Finally, the groups should make their presentations to their class, or teacher, ask for positive feedback and make any changes necessary to create a perfect class resource.

2.5 SQA examination-style questions

Below are some examples of possible exam questions on river landscape landforms. These are by no means the only questions that could be asked but they give you an idea of what to expect in the exam. Look at the notes below the questions and then attempt to answer the questions. Once you have done this, attempt to answer the questions again but this time for the remaining two features, a V-shaped valley and a meander.

1   Explain with the aid of an annotated diagram or diagrams how a waterfall is formed.

2   Explain the formation of an oxbow lake. You may wish to use an annotated diagram or diagrams.

Treat these as 10-mark questions:

● Be prepared to detail the stages of development of the feature.

● Know the names and explain the fluvial processes involved in each stage of the development of the feature, and where and how they help to form the landform.

● Don't forget to say what the feature actually is and what it looks like.

● If the question asks you about one particular feature, do not waste time by including details, explanations and diagrams about something that develops from it. For example, don't detail the development of an oxbow lake when you are only asked about a meander.

● If the question suggests a diagram, do it! Prepare (and memorise) diagrams showing the stages of development of the four features that could come up in examinations: V-shaped valleys, waterfalls, meanders and oxbow lakes. Take time to draw and redraw (edit and improve) these until you have ones which you can complete in the time allocated for the question.

● Diagrams should include detailed annotation that describes and explains.

● Make sure that your diagrams are accurate, clear, tidy and of sufficient size so that the marker can easily work out what you are trying to show and explain.

Make it easy for yourself by creating perfect answers (including diagrams) for these types of questions for each of the four features that could come up in examinations: V-shaped valleys, waterfalls, meanders and oxbow lakes. If you become familiar with your answers it should take some stress from you at exam time and allow you to achieve good marks.

2.6 Drainage basins

Any small river joining the main one is called a **tributary**. The place where two rivers join is called the confluence. Where the river flows into a sea or sometimes a lake this feature is known as the mouth. The route through which a river flows is called the river channel. The collection of channels that make up the paths of all the streams flowing into a drainage basin is called the channel network. Some drainage basins are huge (such as the Amazon, which covers about a third of the South American continent), while others are more modest in size.

What is the relationship between the (global) hydrological cycle and the hydrological cycle within a drainage or river basin? The global hydrological cycle is an example of a closed system. That means that there is a continuous circulation of water (as a liquid, solid or vapour) between the oceans, the atmosphere, vegetation and the land. The total amount of water is fixed and cannot be altered in amount. The total amount of water is the same with no water added to or lost from the cycle; water simply moves from one storage type to another.

You are now going to look at the water cycle within a river or drainage basin. A drainage basin is an area drained by a river and all of its tributaries. Clearly there is overlap in terminology and ideas between the global hydrological cycle and a drainage basin. The boundary of a drainage basin is marked by a line or ridge of high land. This line separates one basin from another and is called the watershed. The watershed determines which direction and into which river system precipitation will eventually run. A drainage basin is an example of an open system, because the amount of water within the system varies. It is only one small part of the very large global hydrological system.

Most of the flows and stores in a drainage basin are broadly the same as in the hydrological cycle.

Case study: River Clyde

Figures 2.25 and 2.26 show the location and extent of the River Clyde drainage basin. Although only the third longest river in Scotland, some people would argue that it is the most important (apologies to the folk who live along the Tay or Spey or Forth or even the awesome River Irvine!). The river flows over 170 km and drops in elevation 600 m on its passage to the sea.

The river has an incredible story to tell: its history and the growth of Glasgow, trading across the Atlantic, shipbuilding and industrial growth, decline and redevelopment, tourism, **flood** control, centre of culture, animal and bird habitats and so on.

Research opportunity
You may be interested in studying aspects of the River Clyde for your assignment. A web search will reveal many relevant sources that could be used to back up your fieldwork. A good starting point is www.clydewaterfront.com

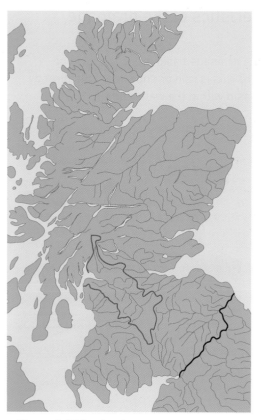
▲ **Figure 2.25** Scotland and the River Clyde Basin

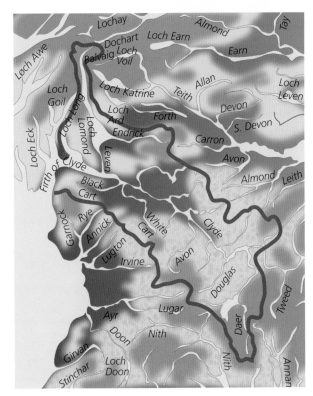

▲ **Figure 2.26** River Cycle drainage basin

Characteristics of the drainage basin

Inputs to the drainage basin are in the form of precipitation. This is rain or snow that falls directly above the basin within the watershed.

Water is lost as outputs from the drainage basin either by the river and its tributaries carrying it out into the sea, or through evapotranspiration (the loss of water directly from vegetation, water surfaces and from the ground).

The drainage basin has two further features:

- water storage in lakes, rocks and the soil
- a process of water movement, flow or transfer through infiltration, percolation, surface run-off or throughflow.

An alternative way to show this information is by drawing a flow diagram (Figure 2.28).

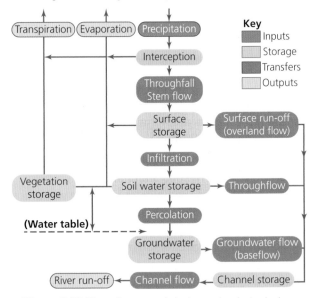

▲ **Figure 2.28** Flow diagram of drainage basin hydrology

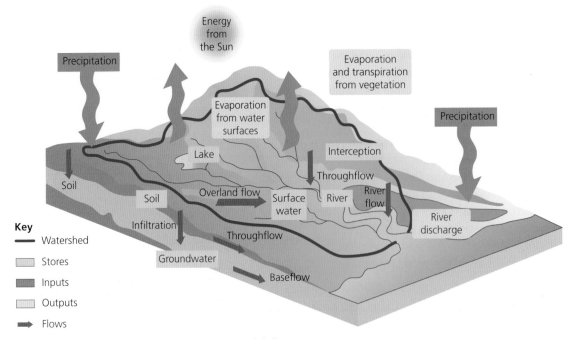

▲ **Figure 2.27** Drainage basin as a systems model diagram

Drainage basin measurements

All drainage basins are different, so how can we describe them and compare them? What do we want to know about rivers? Is it the river length, the area of the basin or river discharge? During the 1930s and 1940s various geographers (e.g. Horton and then Strahler) attempted to measure river basins and their river systems. This information is important because the more we know about rivers the easier we can manage them, especially with regard to flood control. There are two key measurements:

- drainage density
- stream order.

Drainage density

Drainage density (DD) is the total length of all the streams and rivers in a drainage basin divided by the total area of the drainage basin. It is a measure of how well or how poorly a watershed is drained by stream channels.

Drainage density = sum of length of all the rivers ÷ area of drainage basin (measured in km per km^2)

DD depends on both climate and the physical characteristics of the drainage basin. Soil and underlying rock type will affect the run-off in a watershed, with **impermeable** rocks in the ground assisting a rapid surface run-off and therefore leading to more frequent streams or greater density within the basin. Rugged regions or those with high relief will also have a higher drainage density than other drainage basins if the other characteristics of the basin are the same.

DD can affect the shape of a river's hydrograph during a rain storm. High densities can also indicate a greater flood risk.

In the UK most drainage densities are between 2 and 4 km per km^2. However there are variations. In south-east England, where there is chalk, limestone and sandy rocks, drainage densities may be less than 1. In the impermeable **granite** rocks found in the mountains of Scotland and Wales the drainage density could be over 5 km per km^2.

Other contributory factors in determining DD:

- **Land use**: DD is greater in areas with little vegetation.
- **Time**: DD tends to decrease over time. Systems that are old and stable tend to have lower DD.
- **Relief**: the steeper the gradient then the greater the DD.
- **Precipitation**: the greater the intensity, duration and amount, the greater the DD.

There is also a causal link between higher drainage density and the risk of flooding. Why do you think this is so?

Stream order

- A first order stream has no joining tributaries and is part of the source.
- A second order stream occurs when two or more first order streams meet and merge.
- A third order stream forms when two or more second order streams merge.
- A fourth order stream occurs when two or more third order streams emerge, and so on.

So, for example, a five order river system is made up of first, second, third, fourth and fifth order streams.

My research indicates that a river such as the Tay is a five order river system and that of the Mississippi is a ten order river system. This gives some idea of the size of the Mississippi system.

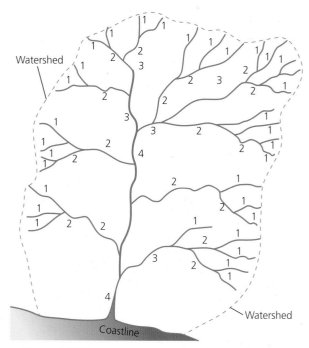

▲ **Figure 2.29** Stream ordering: a fourth order drainage basin

Task

1 Explain the difference between stream order and drainage density.
2 Consider your house and your domestic water supply. Describe the following parts of the system:
    a) The input of water and the source.
    b) How the water is stored and transferred within the house.
    c) How the water is used.
    d) How the water will leave the house (output).
3 Now compare your findings with the basics of the river drainage basin.

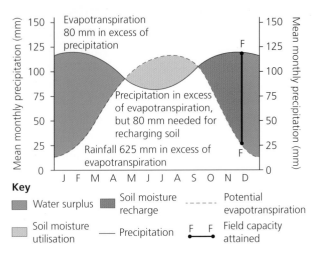

▲ **Figure 2.30** Water balance in a seasonal zone such as the UK

Water balance

Water balance is worked out from inputs (precipitation) and outputs (basin discharge and evapotranspiration).

The water balance affects how much water is stored in the river basin. In the UK the general water balance shows a seasonal imbalance. The water balance of a basin/country can be studied using a water budget graph (Figure 2.30) which illustrates the relationship between temperature, precipitation and evaporation rates over a year.

The water balance can be shown using the formula:

$$P = Q + E + / - S$$

precipitation (P) = streamflow (Q) + evapotranspiration (E) +/− changes in storage (S)

In order to interpret the graph shown in Figure 2.30, you need to:

- note the annual precipitation line
- note the evapotranspiration line
- understand that when precipitation is greater than evapotranspiration then there is a water surplus
- understand that when precipitation is less than evapotranspiration then there is a water deficit.

In wet months/seasons, precipitation exceeds evapotranspiration, thereby creating a water surplus. At first the pores of the soil are refilled with water. The ground stores become saturated with water, resulting in more surface run-off and higher

discharge. This means that river levels rise. Overall there is a water surplus during this period.

In drier months/seasons, precipitation is lower than evapotranspiration. Ground stores are depleted as some water is used (by plants, vegetation and humans), some flows into rivers and there is evaporation back into the atmosphere. Overall there is a water deficit in the ground during this period, which will be replaced during the next wet/surplus period.

In the autumn precipitation again starts to exceed evapotranspiration and the first of the surplus water is used to recharge the soil. When this happens the soil reaches its field capacity.

 Task

Look at Figure 2.30.

1 In which months is there a water surplus?
2 In which months is there a water deficit?
3 Why is there soil moisture recharge in October?
4 When is field capacity attained?

2.7 Hydrographs

The discharge of a river can be measured over a long period of time – a year or many years – and the river's flow over a period of time can be shown in a graph, known as a hydrograph. The monthly or yearly flow of a river is known as its **regime**.

You may be asked a question about your interpretation of hydrographs, so some additional background information is necessary.

In this section the following key points will be covered:

- Rivers – their discharge and significance and how hydrographs can help water engineers manage rivers
- Hydrographs and their interpretation
- Physical factors affecting hydrographs
- Human factors affecting hydrographs
- Main influences affecting hydrographs
- Flooding and its impact and management

You will also look at several case studies relating to hydrographs.

River discharge

This section is about river discharge (also known as river run-off) – the volume of water passing a point/station in a river in a given time. It is measured in cubic metres per second (**cumecs**). Sometimes, for examination purposes, discharge is given as the depth of the river in metres.

There is a basic relationship between the river drainage basin, discharge or run-off, amount of precipitation, evapotranspiration and storage. For example, after heavy rain the level and amount of water in a river will rise and following a period of drought the river will run low or even dry up. Of course, as you will see below, it is often not as simple as that and other factors will intervene.

Diagrams such as Figure 2.31 tell us the average monthly discharge and the times of expected highest and lowest discharge. River basins need to be managed at both local and national levels. Understanding the regime of a river is vital when water engineers need to decide what river management needs to be in place and at what time of the year flood prevention strategies are more likely to be required, for example, when to release water from a dam, installing flood barriers or even evacuating homes at risk of flooding.

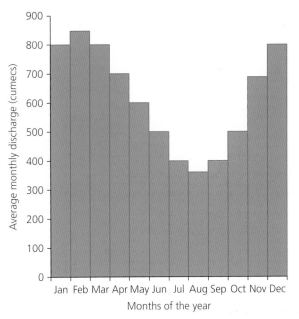

▲ **Figure 2.31** Hydrograph showing River Severn regime

No two rivers are the same and even rivers within the same river basin have different discharge patterns.

▲ **Figure 2.32** Flooding in northern India

▲ **Figure 2.33** Flooding in south-west England, 2014

▲ **Figure 2.34** Floodwater destroys a road in Iceland following volcanic eruption, 2010

 Task

Look at Figures 2.32, 2.33 and 2.34 and for each image describe and assess the impact of the damage shown.

Rivers play a vital role in our lives, as the list below shows. Rivers:

- are part of a system that drains the land and carries water through an area
- provide power (hydroelectric power)
- provide water to irrigate the land
- transport people and goods up and down their length
- are used to penetrate far inland to 'open up an area'
- are used by industry for cooling, discharging waste and as a raw material
- are used for recreational purposes
- can be barriers that divide and separate regions and people
- supply us with food (fish) and drinking water
- can flood and cause misery: when measured in terms of human lives lost and damage to property, flooding is by far the largest natural disaster/hazard
- may be contaminated and polluted with industrial, agricultural and human waste.

From this list it is clear that an understanding of rivers and their flow is essential, as this enables us to then manage the river and the basin. In order to maximise the use and minimalise the risks associated with rivers we need to be able to measure, record, use and control river systems. A hydrograph is an important measurement used in the management and control of water.

Hydrographs and their interpretation

How do we measure water flow in a river? The principle is the same whether you are conducting your own research in a small river that you know or measuring the stream flow of the mighty River Nile. Information is needed on the speed of the water and the cross-section area of the river at the point at which the measurement is to be made. We then take the cross section and multiply it by the speed of the river at that point. The final figure is measured as cubic metres per second, known as cumecs.

Now imagine this: You are standing at the side of a river. Picture 600 fridges (typical size) passing in front of you over 1 second. That's about 600 cumecs!

Discharge can be expressed as:

$D = A \times V$

Where:

- D = discharge
- A = cross-section area
- V = velocity

Hydrographs can be used to show and describe discharge – it may be an annual discharge pattern of flow or discharge over a day, week or whatever period of time is chosen. Hydrographs can be used to compare different rivers.

Figure 2.35 is a very simple hydrograph that shows a monthly river discharge over one year. Measurement is taken daily, averaged out for the month and then plotted on the graph. It is possible to do this for many years in order to see the long-term pattern. Variations from year to year can also be recorded.

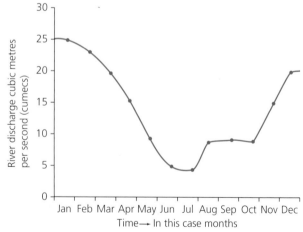

▲ **Figure 2.35** Hydrograph showing the yearly regime and discharge of the model 'River Geo'

Task

Look at Figure 2.35.

1 Describe the general monthly pattern of discharge over the year.
2 Identify the times when the river is at its lowest discharge.
3 Identify when the river is likely to experience the highest level of discharge.

Storm hydrographs

Along a river such as the Clyde or the Colorado there are many gauging stations where discharge data is collected and used to construct short-period (storm) hydrographs. These graphs show in detail how a river or part of a river basin responds to heavy rain.

Over the short term a flood or storm hydrograph can be used to show short-term variations. They cover a relatively short time period, usually hours or days rather than weeks or months. Storm hydrographs allow us to investigate the relationship between a rainfall event and discharge.

You may well be asked to interpret a storm hydrograph.

Case study: Storm hydrograph of the River Irvine

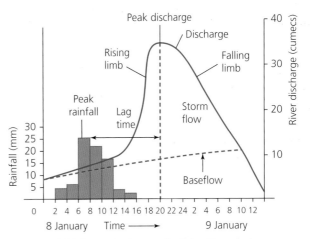

▲ **Figure 2.36** Storm hydrograph of the River Irvine

The key elements of a hydrograph such as that shown in Figure 2.36 are described in Table 2.2.

The crucial set of figures is to compare the peak discharge with the bankfull discharge. When the peak discharge is greater than the bankfull discharge, the river will overflow the channel and flooding will occur.

▼ **Table 2.2** Key elements of a hydrograph

X axis	Showing time, usually by hour/day.
Y axis	Showing precipitation (measured in mm) and discharge (measured in cumecs).
Base flow	The discharge of the water pre-storm. Most rivers have a certain amount of water flowing in the river; this is the usual pattern of surface run-off. The base flow tends to be fairly constant. After the flood discharge has passed rivers return to their base flow.
Discharge line	The solid line on a hydrograph which shows (usually hourly) the discharge over the complete study period.
Rising limb	The steepness of the **rising limb** reflects how rapidly the water reaches the river channel. There are many human and physical factors (see later in this chapter) that affect the speed at which the discharge increases.
Peak discharge	**Peak discharge** is the highest point on the discharge line. It shows the time of discharge and the discharge in cumecs at the peak of the flow.
Peak rainfall	**Peak rainfall** is the time and amount of the highest period of precipitation.
Reclining or falling limb	The **reclining limb** (or **falling limb**) measures not only the time but the speed at which river discharge starts to decline after the surge.
Lag time	The gap or time between maximum precipitation and the time that the river discharge increases. In particular the difference between the peak rainfall and peak discharge. Depending on the size and character of the river and its basin, the **lag time** can be minutes, hours or days.
Storm flow	**Storm flow** is the gap between the river discharge and the base flow.
Bankfull discharge	**Bankfull discharge** occurs when a river's water level reaches the top of its channel. When this happens the river will overflow its channel and flood the surrounding land.

Analysis of the River Irvine storm hydrograph

The hydrograph shown in Figure 2.36 covers a period of 36 hours (8–9 January 2015) on the River Irvine close to Kilmarnock, East Ayrshire. During this period there was a period of light rain followed by heavier rain. The rainfall is measured (in mm) in 2-hour blocks as is river discharge (in cumecs). This period followed two weeks with very little precipitation. It started to rain around 02.00 and continued to rain for 14 hours. Precipitation reached a peak between 06.00 and 08.00 with 25 mm falling. During the period covered by the hydrograph approximately 75 mm of rain fell.

River discharge was also recorded over the same period. The discharge line shows the changes throughout the study period. The line shows a low initial discharge of around 5 cumecs (this is the base flow). After 4 hours of rain (06.00) the discharge of the river had increased slightly. At the time of peak rainfall the discharge was still low. By 14.00 hours the river discharge was increasing (rising limb), rapidly reaching a peak discharge at 20.00 hours of 35 cumecs. The gap between the peak rainfall and discharge (known as the lag time) is 16 hours. Although the rain had ceased over 8 hours before, the discharge continued to rise. After 22.00 the level

▲ **Figure 2.37** Flooding in Perth

and discharge of the river fell (shown as the falling limb) until it almost reached the pre-flood base level at 12.00 on day 2. The area between the base flow and the discharge level is known as the storm flow. The greatest risk of flooding and damage to property was the hours either side of 22.00.

In Higher Geography you are expected to be able to interpret hydrographs, so what does this mean?

You may be asked to:

- **Describe**: inform the marker what you see. You can mention the basics, as well as more detailed information. You can describe a photo, text, a

---

 Task

Study Table 2.3 and answer the questions below.

▼ **Table 2.3** River discharge over a 24-hour period

Time	Precipitation (mm)	River discharge (cumecs)	Time	Precipitation (mm)	River discharge (cumecs)
00.00	0	8	14.00	25	31
02.00	0	8	16.00	31	27
04.00	23	10	18.00	11	12
06.00	35	15	20.00	0	8
08.00	14	18	22.00	0	69
10.00	5	59	24.00	0	56
12.00	2	57			

1 Construct your own hydrograph using the information in the table.

2 In general terms describe the pattern of precipitation over the 24-hour period.

3 In general terms describe the pattern of river discharge over the 24-hour period.

4 Calculate the lag time from peaks 1 and 2.

5 Estimate the base flow level.

▲ **Figure 2.38** Flooding in Dumfries

diagram, a table or graph. With a describe question you do not go into an explanation or give reasons.

- **Explain**: suggest reasons for the cause or impact of something and identify relationships.
- **Analyse**: identify different parts and relationships and consider their impact and implications.
- **Evaluate**: make a judgement of the impact (negative and positive).
- **Account for**: give reasons for or explain.
- **Discuss**: explore ideas about the issue, taking into consideration a variety of views.
- **To what extent**: questions will cover impact or strategy or alternatives. You will also be expected to come to a conclusion based on the evidence given.

Physical factors affecting storm hydrographs

Drainage basins have a variety of unique characteristics that influence river discharge and the hydrograph. These factors can be either physical or human, but we will begin by examining the physical influences (Figure 2.39).

A range of physical factors affect the shape of a storm hydrograph. These are described below.

Size of basin, shape and relief

Large drainage basins catch more precipitation so have a higher peak discharge compared to smaller basins. Smaller basins generally have shorter lag times because water does not have as far to travel. The shape of the drainage basin also affects run-off and discharge. Drainage basins that are more circular in shape lead to shorter lag times and a higher peak discharge than those that are long and thin, because water has a shorter distance to travel to reach a river. Drainage basins with steep sides tend to have shorter lag times than shallower basins. This is because water flows more quickly on the steep slopes down to the river.

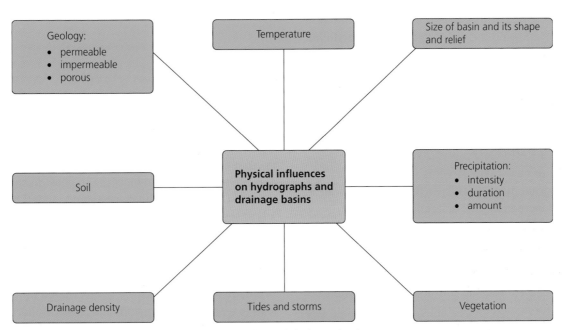

▲ **Figure 2.39** Physical influences on hydrographs and drainage basins

Precipitation

The amount of precipitation can have an effect on the storm hydrograph. Heavy storms result in more water entering the drainage basin which results in a higher discharge, while the type of precipitation can also have an impact. The lag time is likely to be greater if the precipitation is snow rather than rain. This is because snow takes time to melt before the water enters the river channel. When there is rapid melting of snow the peak discharge could be high. When the precipitation is prolonged then the land and soil will become waterlogged and saturated and once maximum saturation has been reached then the drainage into the river will be fast. If the drainage basin is already saturated, then surface run-off increases due to the reduction in infiltration. Rainwater enters the river quicker, reducing lag times, as surface run-off is faster than base flow or throughflow. Heavy rain falling on saturated soil will produce a steeply rising limb. Spring snowmelt over frozen ground means that the water will reach the river channel even faster with increased river discharge.

Geology

Rocks can vary both within and between basins. Rocks can be permeable (allowing water to flow through) or impermeable (not allowing water to pass or flow through). Rocks can also be porous, allowing the water to soak through and be stored within (e.g. chalk), or allowing the water to run along 'bedding planes' (e.g. limestone). Impermeable rocks permit faster surface run-off and flow into the river system. Permeable and porous rocks absorb water, slowing down run-off and increasing lag time.

Drainage density

Basins that have many streams (high drainage density) drain more quickly, so have a shorter lag time and increased risk of flooding.

Temperature

When the temperature is low, water may be stored as snow or ice, reducing run-off. However, when temperatures increase during the spring, melting and therefore run-off will increase. Higher temperatures increase evaporation/evapotranspiration and reduce run-off. If the ground has been baked hard by the heat of the summer, or if it is frozen, then the effect is similar to that of impermeable rock.

Soil

Soils vary in their ability to absorb water. Larger pore spaces are found in sandy soils, allowing greater water storage and reducing the risk of flooding. A clay soil has little in the way of storage space and precipitation will have faster discharge, increasing the risk of flooding.

Vegetation

If the drainage basin has a significant amount of vegetation (crop cover, woodland) then this will have a major effect on the storm hydrograph. Vegetation intercepts precipitation and slows the movement of water into river channels, which increases lag time. Water is also lost due to evaporation and transpiration from the vegetation, reducing the peak discharge of a river. Evidence suggests that a tropical rainforest intercepts 75 per cent of precipitation compared to only 10 per cent interception over arable land.

Human factors affecting storm hydrographs

A range of human factors affect the shape of a storm hydrograph (see Figure 2.40). These are considered below.

Urbanisation

Areas that have been urbanised result in an increase in the use of impermeable building materials such as asphalt. Urbanisation results in houses, factories and roads covering the land. This means infiltration levels decrease and surface run-off increases. This leads to a short lag time and an increase in peak discharge. If topsoil is removed the compacted land left behind increases run-off. When roads are constructed there is an increase in the impermeable surface area, which means a reduction in the amount of water that returns to ground and soil storage.

Drainage systems that have been created by humans lead to a short lag time and high peak discharge as water cannot evaporate or infiltrate into the soil.

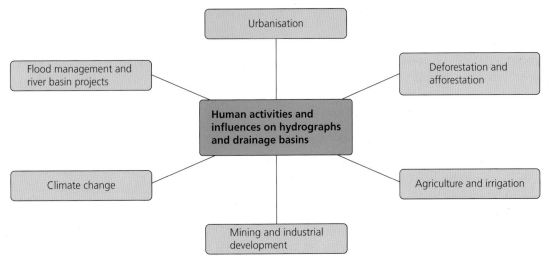

▲ **Figure 2.40** Human influences on hydrographs and drainage basins

Drainage ditches and storm channels all increase the speed at which water is removed from the fields and enters the river channel. When a river is straightened, such as when a navigation canal is built, then discharge increases, with the risk of accelerated discharge and flooding downstream.

Deforestation

Deforestation results in increased run-off, although this may be matched by increased afforestation (the establishment of trees on previously non-forest land). Areas of mature woodland are able to reduce the impact of precipitation. However, when trees are cleared, even moorlands and grassy areas are less effective in delaying rapid run-off and discharge. **Soil erosion** may also increase, with the loose soil carried to the river, reducing channel capacity and resulting in less water being required before flooding takes place. Plant roots, especially those of trees, reduce through-flow by taking up water from the soil.

Overgrazing

Overgrazing and ploughing leave areas with less vegetation, resulting in a similar outcome as deforestation.

Climate change

This can cause an alteration in river discharge. Climatologists suggest that there will be an increase in rainfall with more storms in some areas and increased flooding.

Mining

Opencast mining/quarrying often results in the displacement of water courses and rivers. Silting-up of lakes, reservoirs and rivers reduces their storage capacity, increasing run-off and discharge. Opencast quarrying reduces vegetation cover and increases evaporation. Some people believe (although this is contested) that cloud formation patterns will be altered, thereby affecting precipitation.

Irrigation

When you take water from a river or from the ground (using a well) you may reduce river discharge. Water will also be more exposed to evaporation from open canals, ditches and channels. Irrigation has an impact on the hydrological cycle since it alters flow and storage.

Flood management and river basin projects

These types of projects, for example the construction of dams, alter discharge levels. Although such projects are intended to reduce the likelihood and impact of flooding, they alter river regimes too. There are also several examples of dam failure which resulted in massive flooding.

● Reflection

Think about a new-build area near where you stay, which was previously fields or countryside, and compare it now with how it was when nothing was built there.

1 Identify where and how water is prevented from entering the ground layer or the previous topsoil.
2 Identify all the methods by which water falling on the new surfaces is removed from the area.
3 How will the changes alter the rate in which water reaches the river channel?
4 How would it be possible to redesign an area such as this to:
   a) reduce increased run-off that is created by the newly built-up area
   b) minimise any increase in the rate in which water reaches the river channel.
5 Look over the answers you came up with for question 4 and discuss them with others in your class. Through this discussion, you could identify any problems with your solutions, find common ground, or even identify solutions to some of the issues that architects, builders, and environmentalists have been trying to solve.

Main influences affecting hydrographs: a summary

As has been shown above, there are many factors that influence run-off, discharge and lag time. Often there are several factors involved at any one time. We can understand this further if we consider the main influences separately, as described below, and then look at Figures 2.41 to 2.44 which illustrate each of these influences.

1 **Gradient**: If the valley side is gentle then the discharge will be lower and slower when compared with a steep slope.
2 **Area**: Large basins receive greater amounts of precipitation than smaller basins. As a consequence, larger basins will have a larger run-off and a longer lag time since all the distances involved are greater.
3 **Land use**: We need to consider how the land is used. If the area is forested then the trees will intercept the falling precipitation, some of which will be stored and absorbed, thereby reducing the discharge and lag time. However, in a landscape that is mainly urban (roads and houses), the water will be channelled quickly and flow much faster into the river.
4 **Geology of the area**: If the rock type is permeable then the precipitation is more likely to be absorbed into the ground, slowing down the time it takes to reach the river. If the rock type is impermeable then the run-off will be fast, the lag time short and the discharge greater.

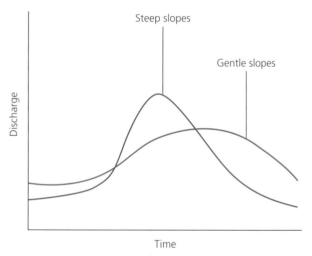

▲ **Figure 2.41** Hydrograph showing gradient, discharge and lag time

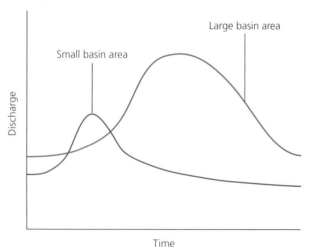

▲ **Figure 2.42** Hydrograph showing area of drainage basin, discharge and lag time

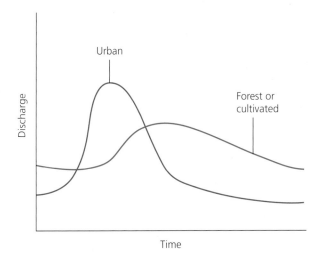

▲ **Figure 2.43** Hydrograph showing land use, discharge and lag time

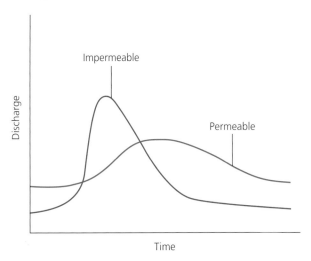

▲ **Figure 2.44** Hydrograph showing geology/rock type, discharge and lag time

Task

1   Identify three physical factors and explain why they may increase the risk of flooding.
2   Why is prolonged rainfall a major cause of flooding?
3   Name and then explain three human activities that increase the risk of flooding.

Case study: River Nile hydrograph

Records exist going back many years for most of the major rivers. This means it is possible to measure discharge before and after major events, such as the building of the Aswan Dam across the River Nile.

The River Nile brought life to Egypt. This mighty river flows for some 6,400 km from the mountains of equatorial Africa (Blue Nile) and Lake Victoria (White Nile) before it discharges into the Mediterranean Sea.

The River Nile used to flood, completely changing the scenery around the Nile and destroying fields and villages and causing human suffering and loss of life. Of course, a positive feature of this flooding was that the annual flood water left behind a layer of rich and fertile sediment that enriched the fertility of the soil.

Since the construction of the Aswan Dam in the 1960s, the River Nile does not flood downstream from the dam. The highest threat to flooding on the River Nile was in the months of August, September and October, when river discharge was at its greatest. Flooding does still take place in the upper stretches of the Nile, for example, in the mountains of Ethiopia.

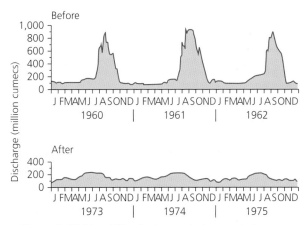

▲ **Figure 2.45** River Nile discharge: before and after construction of the Aswan Dam

Task

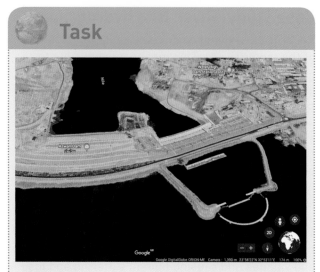

▲ **Figure 2.46** Aswan Dam, Egypt

1 Describe the flood hydrographs for the River Nile before and after the construction of the Aswan Dam (see Figure 2.45).
2 Explain the hydrograph after the construction.
3 Assess the likely human and physical impact of the change in discharge.

Impact of flooding

Measured in terms of human, economic and environmental costs, floods are the greatest cause of natural hazard chaos. As we have seen, flooding occurs when the amount of water moving down a river exceeds the capacity of the river's

channel. The excess water will flow over the bank and spread over the floodplain. Flooding is linked to river discharge and our management of the resulting flood. The more we know and understand about rivers then the more we can do to control flood risk and limit damage to a minimum. We have considered what happens when there is a period of exceptionally high precipitation and the impact of this water reaching the river channel (the shorter the time lag, the greater the impact). We also know that following a period of persistent rain, the land becomes saturated and not only will the surplus water flow into the river channels, but it will also accumulate in hollows and areas with little outward drainage.

By keeping records over a long period of time it is possible to build up a river profile of 'flood frequency'. Some flooding is very unproblematic. For example, snowmelt from the Himalayas will swell the River Brahmaputra and flooding will happen. Since this is expected, people will avoid the most vulnerable locations, or have flood management strategies in place. It is the unexpected that creates the greatest potential for disaster. Strategies to deal with flooding usually involve putting flood defences in place and details of such **hard engineering** and **soft engineering strategies** can be found in the companion book, *Global Issues*, in the section on river basin management. Another factor is global climate change, again considered in more detail in *Global Issues*.

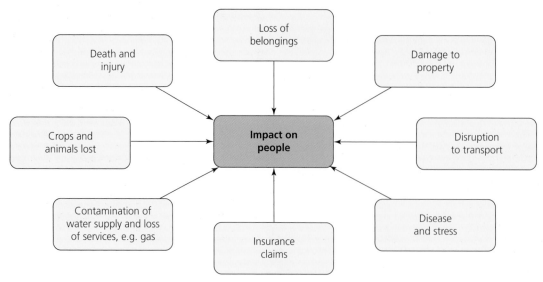

▲ **Figure 2.47** Model diagram for the impact of flooding on people

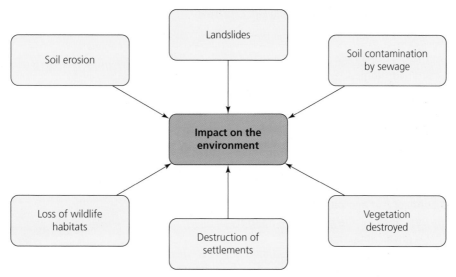

▲ **Figure 2.48** Model diagram for the impact of flooding on the environment

Task

1 Look at Figures 2.47 and 2.48 and select three of the effects or impacts shown. Describe in detail the possible damage that could be caused.
2 Suggest strategies that could be taken to reduce that impact.

Summary

Water is constantly being recycled as it moves through a system known as the hydrological cycle (an example of a global closed system or model). The model demonstrates the importance of flows or transfers, and storage phases.

The action of rivers creates features of erosion and deposition in the landscape and transports materials

Research opportunity

Carlisle flood, January 2005

▲ **Figure 2.49** Carlisle flood, January 2005

You are required to complete a case study analysis of the Carlisle flood. An internet search will provide you with plenty of information, including images, videos, PowerPoint presentations and news articles.

Your report should include details on the following:

• A general history of flooding in the area
• Investigation of the local rivers
• Weather
• Hydrograph of the flood
• Causes, damage and human and environmental impact
• Local response at the time
• Long-term strategies and management
• Final comments and analysis

downstream. The materials being transported also add to the erosional potential of a river.

Every stream or river is part of a river basin system which has its own mini hydrological cycle (drainage basin cycle). A drainage basin has its own inputs and outputs and, since the amount of water in a river basin can vary, this shows that it is part of an open system.

To fully understand rivers and their uses, control, conflicts and risks, we need to be aware of the connection between the physical and human environment. This study of the hydrosphere has shown that water is essential for life on Earth and that its action can alter the physical landscape.

You should now be able to understand these topics and answer questions relating to:

- the formation of erosional and depositional features in river landscapes
- the fluvial processes involved
- the hydrological cycle within a drainage basin
- the interpretation of hydrographs.

SQA examination-style questions

Below are some examples of possible exam questions. These are by no means the only questions that could be asked but they give you an idea of what to expect. Some questions may be accompanied by diagrams, maps or graphs from which you can gather extra information to assist with your answer.

1   Explain how the following human factors can have an impact on the hydrological cycle:
- Urbanisation
- Mining and industry
- Farming
- Reservoirs/dams
- Deforestation.

2   Study Figure 2.50. Explain the movements of water in the hydrological cycle.

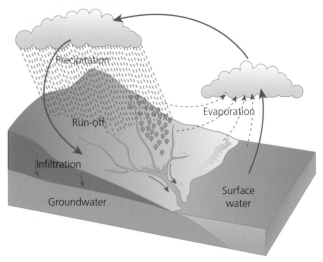

▲ **Figure 2.50** Hydrological cycle

3   Study Figure 2.51.
- Explain the changes in discharge level of the River Wyre (days 1 and 2).
    or
- Evaluate three human factors that can influence the rate of run-off from any river system.
    or
- Evaluate three physical factors that can influence the rate of run-off from any river system.

4   With reference to Figure 2.51, comment on the relationship between the amount and timing of the precipitation and the amount and timing of discharge.

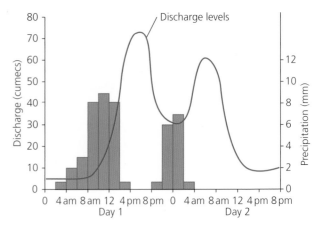

▲ **Figure 2.51** Discharge levels of the River Wyre, February 2014

Chapter 3 Lithosphere

Introduction

The lithosphere refers to the physical landscape of the Earth. Derived from the word 'lithos' (meaning rock), it is essentially the Earth's crust and upper mantle. Over millions of years, the Earth's surface has interacted with the atmosphere and the hydrosphere and these interactions have produced distinct landforms.

For the SQA exam you are required to describe and explain the stages and processes in the formation of specified erosional and depositional landforms. You are expected to show a detailed understanding of the factors responsible for glacial and coastal erosion and deposition in your answers.

SQA suggest that you should have prior knowledge and understanding of the following:

- The Earth's structure (its internal layers and properties).
- The key denudation processes of **weathering**, erosion, transportation and deposition.
- The three main rock types – **igneous**, **metamorphic** and **sedimentary** – and be aware that a landscape's speed of change may be determined by the differing rates of erosion of different types of rocks.
- Isostacy. **Lithospheric plates** float on the denser **asthenosphere** below. The plates sink, rise, bend or deform to keep the natural balance between gravity and buoyancy obtained from the asthenosphere. This is known as isostasy (from the Greek *ísos* meaning 'equal' and *stásis* 'standstill'). Plates sink if load is added (e.g. through formation of volcanoes, sediment deposition, glaciation, an increase in sea level flooding previous land areas, new large-scale lakes). If load is removed (e.g. via weathering and erosion of landforms such as mountains, erosion creating valleys, the removal of ice masses following glaciation, lowering of sea level removing water coverage, lakes and other large bodies of water drying up) the lithosphere rises up again (**isostatic rebound or uplift**) in a process known as **isostatic recovery**. Movement of

the lithosphere (down or up) due to changing load is known as **isostatic adjustment**.
- Changing sea level. Isostatic change is a local sea level change, where the sea level position appears to move upward (as the land moves downwards) or downwards (as the land moves upwards) due to isostatic adjustment. This does not mean that there is a change in the volume of water in the oceans.
- Eustatic change, which is a term given to a global change in sea level. This can happen for several reasons.
  a) The volume of water changes as:

    - Increasing water temperature causes water to expand (often in conjunction with an atmospheric temperature increase) and so sea level rises.
    - Increasing glaciation traps water in ice caps and glaciers and reduces precipitation, causing less water to be available in liquid form for the oceans. Sea level reduces.
    - Melting ice caps and glaciers return stored water to the hydrological cycle and the oceans (sea levels are around 130 m higher at present than they were during the last ice age).
  b) The shape (geometry) of an ocean basin changes. This results from **tectonic plate** movement, over millions of years, changing the position of continental landmasses and altering the shape and depth of ocean basins.
- Classification of coastlines and landforms due to sea level change. Different types of **coastlines** and landforms can appear because of changing sea level and can be placed into the following categories:
  a) **Emergent coastlines** – these have appeared from the sea (either due to the land rising through isostatic recovery or through the sea level dropping), for example **raised beaches** (Figures 3.1 and 3.2).
  b) **Submergent coastlines** – this is where the sea has flooded a coastal area, for example **rias** and **fjords** (fiords) (Figure 3.2).

▲ **Figure 3.1** Raised beach, between Bennane Head and Ballantrae, South Ayrshire, Scotland

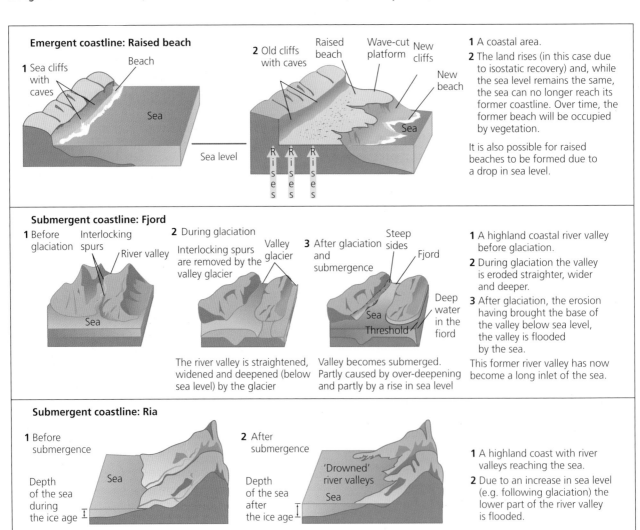

▲ **Figure 3.2** Raised beaches, fjords and rias

Time

The world is complex. Tectonics, climate, specific local conditions, weathering, erosion, transportation and deposition interact to differing degrees and rates over vast periods of time to alter the lithosphere. We can witness some of these changes happening in front of our eyes. Others take place over geologic time, which is much slower than humans can recognise, but the alterations are massive. We need to be aware of short-, medium- and long-term changes to the lithosphere.

3.1 Influence of glaciation

Glaciation has had a massive influence on the landscapes that we see today, both in Scotland and in large areas of the world. For the last 2.5 million years (Quaternary Period) Earth has experienced global temperatures that have fluctuated from extreme cold to relative warmth. This has resulted in a cycle of glaciation, with each ice age lasting for around 100,000 years followed by interglacials of approximately 10,000 years. So for the majority of the last 2.5 million years the Scottish landscape has been subject to weathering, erosion, transportation and deposition during glacial conditions.

Many of the glacial features identified in Scotland may be a result of not just one glacial period but numerous ones.

The last glacial period ended between 15,000 and 20,000 BP (before present) although about 13,000 BP there was a short period of roughly 1,000 years which saw a return to colder conditions.

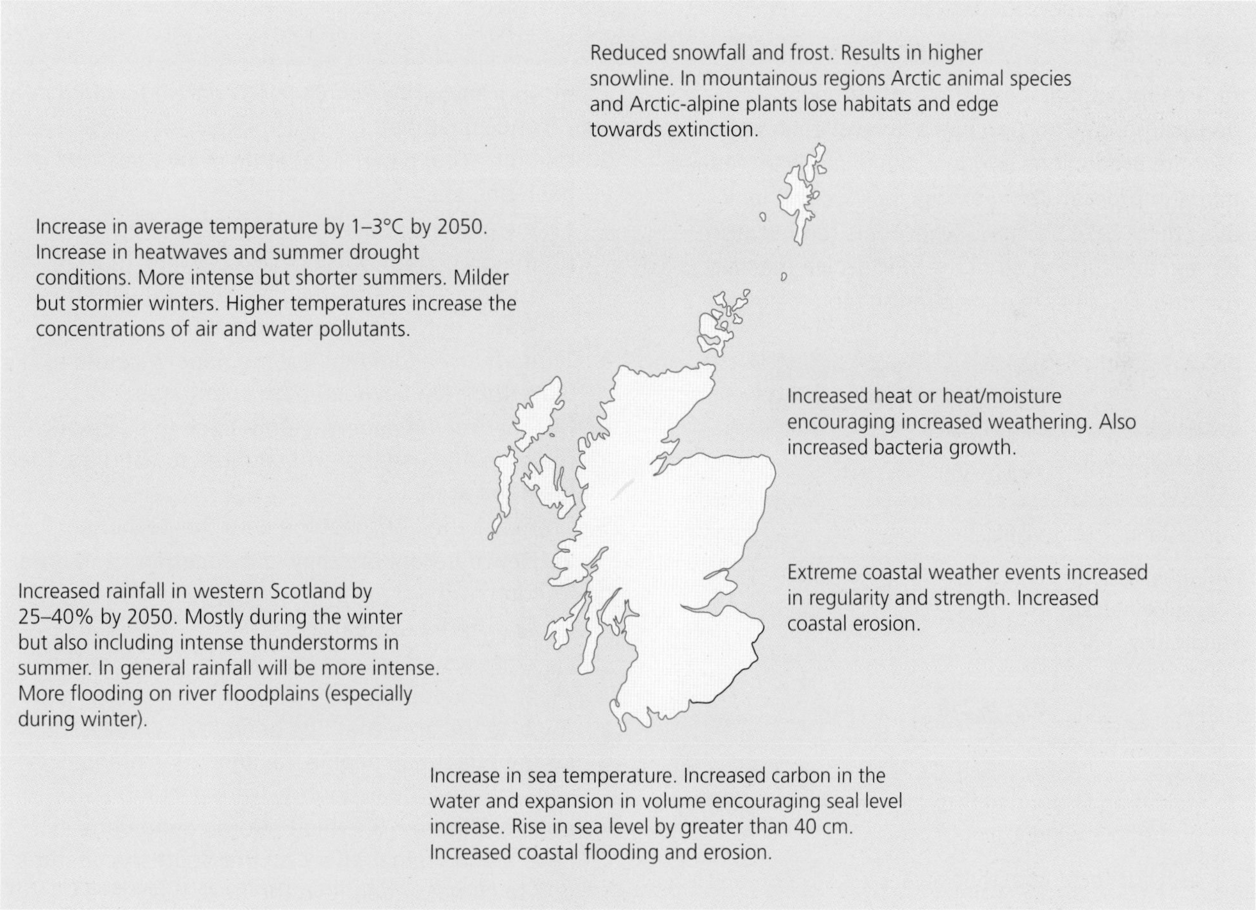

Reduced snowfall and frost. Results in higher snowline. In mountainous regions Arctic animal species and Arctic-alpine plants lose habitats and edge towards extinction.

Increase in average temperature by 1–3°C by 2050. Increase in heatwaves and summer drought conditions. More intense but shorter summers. Milder but stormier winters. Higher temperatures increase the concentrations of air and water pollutants.

Increased heat or heat/moisture encouraging increased weathering. Also increased bacteria growth.

Increased rainfall in western Scotland by 25–40% by 2050. Mostly during the winter but also including intense thunderstorms in summer. In general rainfall will be more intense. More flooding on river floodplains (especially during winter).

Extreme coastal weather events increased in regularity and strength. Increased coastal erosion.

Increase in sea temperature. Increased carbon in the water and expansion in volume encouraging seal level increase. Rise in sea level by greater than 40 cm. Increased coastal flooding and erosion.

▲ **Figure 3.3** Scotland: projected climate change, 2050–75

Research opportunity

While the Higher exam focuses on the formation of glacial features, SQA suggest that you need:

- an understanding of the cyclical nature of climate changes over the last 2 million years or so (the Quaternary Period), so that you appreciate how glacial landforms can take several periods of glaciation to form
- an awareness of the eustatic and isostatic sea level changes in the Quaternary Period to develop an understanding of potential and predicted changes and the rate of change in sea level, e.g. due to climate change.

To begin an internet search about the Quaternary Period, try the following keywords and phrases: *Quaternary glaciations in the northern hemisphere; quaternary glaciation in Scotland; Loch Lomond stadial; Loch Lomond readvance; glaciation in the British Isles; glaciation in Scotland, Quaternary sea level changes.*

Next, think about the following question: Why has the Quaternary Period had such an effect on the landscape and coastline of Scotland?

Task

At present, global ice melt is resulting in approximately 2 mm rise in sea level each year. Climate predictions suggest significantly increased global temperatures. For this task we will look at a worst case scenario where this temperature increase results in all of the world's ice masses melting. Details are shown in the table below.

Location	Volume of ice (km³)	Predicted sea level rise (m)
Antarctic ice sheets	29,528,300	74
Greenland	2,850,000	7
All other ice caps, ice fields, and valley glaciers	180,000	0.5
Total	32,638,300	81.5

1 Select an Ordnance Survey map showing either of the following:
   a) your local coastline
   b) your favourite British Isles coastal town/city and coastline.
2 Using tracing paper or acetate draw the positions of:
   a) the present coastline
   b) the predicted 'worst case' coastline (use contours and spot heights to assist with this). Watch out for any new islands!
3 Trim off any additional tracing paper/acetate to leave the area between both coastlines.
4 Put the tracing paper/acetate back in place on the map and use the grid squares to estimate the lost land area.
5 Compare the old coastline with the new one.
   a) How different are they (e.g. location, land area lost)?
   b) Are there new features?
   c) What would we see that was different in the new coastline?
6 Analyse the area that has been lost. What would be the effects on people, facilities, farmland, urban areas, the economy, transportation?
7 Look at Figure 3.3. Which altered conditions will have an additional effect on the Scottish coastline due to climate change in the next 100 years?

3.2 Formation of erosional and depositional features in glaciated landscapes

Glacial ice covers around 10 per cent of the Earth's surface, its distribution being in areas where sub-zero temperatures are regularly experienced, at high altitudes and high latitudes. At present the British Isles does not experience glaciation but it has in the past and evidence of this glaciation (both erosional and depositional) can be identified. Only a very short time ago (by geological standards), say 15,000 years, Scotland was beneath around 1,000 m of glacial ice (at its thickest, in the west around the Firth of Lorne in Argyll, it reached ~1,600 m).

Glacial ice mass types

Glacial ice masses can be categorised as three main types.

1 Ice sheet and ice caps

Slow-moving, continuous sheets or layers of ice that cover extensive areas over a large period of time (e.g. those which cover Antarctica and Greenland at present – see Figure 3.4) are also referred to as continental glaciers. Where smaller areas are covered these are referred to as ice caps. They are typically less than 500,000 km² but may be much smaller at around 1,000 km² (Figure 3.5).

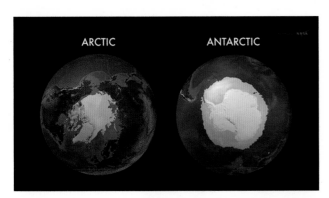

▲ **Figure 3.4** Polar ice sheets

▲ **Figure 3.5** Ice cap, Canadian Arctic

2 Mountain or valley glaciers

A mountain or **valley glacier** is held (restricted) within, for example, a valley, which directs the general movement of the ice (Figure 3.6).

▲ **Figure 3.6** Valley glacier

3 Piedmont glaciers and ice shelves

Glaciers which on reaching the foot of a glacial region spread out onto flat ground are known as **piedmont glaciers** (Figure 3.7). When, in a similar circumstance, the glacier spreads out onto the ocean it is known as an **ice shelf** (Figure 3.8).

▲ **Figure 3.7** Commonwealth glacier, Antarctica, a piedmont glacier

▲ **Figure 3.8** Ice shelf, Antarctica

Conditions needed for glaciation

For glacial ice to build up and for glaciers to expand it has been observed that at present most are found in regions where there are winter conditions with low temperatures and heavy snowfall, and low summer temperatures. These conditions ensure that snow which accumulates in the winter is not fully removed (melted) by warm summer temperatures. To allow for continued survival, growth and expansion, glacial ice relies on regular supplies of snow (either directly as precipitation, from avalanches or wind drifted). Small amounts of additional snow to create ice may maintain a glacier or allow it to move very slowly. Where the amount of snow does not match snow loss because of evaporation (sublimation) the ice may disappear.

Formation of glacial ice

Glacial ice is formed from compacted layers of snow and other forms of solid precipitation. The accumulation of snow leads to its recrystallisation

as it is buried and, through a number of stages, metamorphoses into glacial ice (Figures 3.9 and 3.11).

It is likely that in the early stages of glaciation this would take part in upland areas (above the snow line) with a northerly aspect (facing away from the Sun).

Stage 1: Snow falls and begins to accumulate. Snow has an ice crystal lattice structure and spaces mainly filled with air, giving a 'fluffy' texture at this stage.

Stage 2: Over a short period the snow becomes partly melted (due to ablation). Meltwater seeps downwards then refreezes at a deeper level. The snow compacts moderately due to its crystals collapsing and expelling air due to their own weight and that of any more snow landing above. The layer now has a granular appearance and is known as névé.

Stage 3: Névé that lasts a full season and becomes buried beneath the new season's snowpack is given the name firn (from German and literally meaning 'last years'). Firn is found below the level where ablation occurs in névé. With additional weight from above because of added snowfall the firn continues to be compacted and more air is squeezed out. This makes it slightly denser than névé while maintaining its granular consistency in a manner often described as looking like wet sugar.

Stage 4: Throughout this repeating process, increasing compression due to additional layers of snow above causes the snow/névé/firn crystals to metamorphose under pressure through different forms until they are squeezed into a solid (glacial ice) (Figures 3.10 and 3.11).

▲ **Figure 3.9** Sub-glacier ice

▲ **Figure 3.10** Development of glacial ice: layers of snowfall and compaction

When is ice classified as a glacier?

For ice to be classified as a glacier, it must:

- have been formed in the method described above, by the accumulation of snow, resulting in its re-crystallisation into ice
- have formed over land
- move across the Earth's surface due to **internal flow** (**creep**) or **basal sliding** (see later in this chapter) as a result of the influence of gravity.

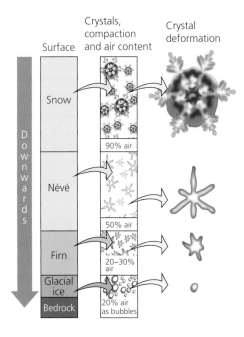

At warmer times during the season the ice crystals at or near the surface may partially melt and this water can travel downwards to refreeze. This is known as melt-freeze metamorphism.

The snow's ice crystals are very delicate and any movement can snap off the crystals' arms. This also happens when under pressure from the layers above when buried. The crystals then melt together and over time they become rounded.

The process of change to the crystals due to the weight of the layers above is known as pressure metamorphism.

◀ **Figure 3.11** Changes in snow during the formation of glacial ice

Glacial ice and glaciation as a system

A glacier can be looked on as a system with **inputs**, **storage** and **outputs** (Figure 3.12). The majority of inputs are found within the **zone of accumulation**, the area where the glacier builds up and the accumulation of ice is higher than ablation. Storage is predominantly the ice itself, although snow, meltwater (within, above and below), rock **debris** and any other material *carried* or *held within* the glacier is included. The majority of the output of the glacier takes place in the **zone of ablation**, where ablation is greater than the amount of accumulation. This includes any meltwater *leaving* the glacier, evaporation or the **calving** of **icebergs** at the terminus (snout).

Glacial ice movement

Glaciers may advance (move further downhill) or retreat (melting from the snout giving the appearance of going backwards, although in reality just shortening). Whether a glacier advances or retreats is dependent on the **glacial budget** (the balance between accumulation and ablation). If within the whole glacier system:

- the levels of accumulation and ablation are equal, the glacier will maintain its position
- the level of accumulation is higher than ablation (**positive regime** – a positive mass balance) the glacier will grow and advance
- the level of ablation is higher than accumulation (**negative regime** – a negative mass balance) the glacier will retreat.

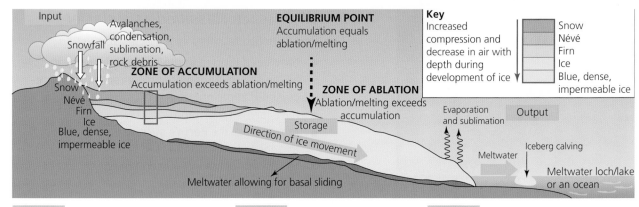

Input

1 Snow (precipitation).
2 Snow from avalanches or blown from surrounding area.
3 Condensation of atmospheric water vapour which freezes.
4 Sublimation of atmospheric water vapour to ice crystals.
5 Rock collected by glacial movement (e.g. plucking) carving the landscape.
6 Rocks and rock fragments that fall onto the glacier from above (e.g. as part of avalanches or due to weathering and erosion).

Storage

1 The ice that forms the body of the glacier.
2 Meltwater on the surface, sides, base and within the glacier.
3 Rock debris moved/carried by the glacier (e.g. sand, gravel, rock (of numerous sizes)) and any other material that is carried on the surface, sides, base or within the glacier.

Output

1 Ice melt (meltwater).
2 Ice and snow sublimating to water vapour.
3 Surface snowmelt or evaporation.
4 Surface snow blown off the glacier.
5 The calving of icebergs if the snout of the glacier extrudes into water (ocean, sea, loch/lake).
6 Rock debris (e.g. sand, gravel, rock (of numerous sizes)) deposited by meltwater.
7 Rock debris deposited as the glacier retreats (moraine).

▲ **Figure 3.12** A glacier as a system

If glacial ice were static there would be very little alteration to the land beneath it. Glacial ice moves under the power of its own weight and gravity, and this movement allows erosion, transportation, and deposition to occur. Over the long periods of time that glaciation occurs this can create wide-scale and massive changes to the pre-glacial landscape.

A number of factors can influence the rate of movement of a glacier:

- Steepness of slope: the steeper the slope the greater the influence of gravity.
- Climate conditions: those which cause a positive regime and/or where there is regular meltwater produced will lubricate the ice flow.
- Temperature/conditions at the base of the glacier: if the base of the glacier can melt the meltwater will act as a lubricant, allowing the ice to slide and move more easily.

Gravitational forces generated by the weight of glaciers allow glaciers to move. Three major processes allow for this movement: internal flow, basal sliding and **bed deformation**.

Internal deformation

This type of movement (also known as **internal flow**) is created because of the weight and pressure of the ice which causes the ice crystals to distort and realign in the direction of the movement of ice. This allows the ice crystals to slide past each other and the glacier to move downhill. Movement can continue even if the lower layers are stuck to the underlying rock (think of a pack of cards: you can slide the ones above forward even though the card at the bottom is stuck to the table). As the glacier's weight becomes too heavy to maintain the shape of the glacier it starts to move, with ice layers slipping forward within the glacier. This type of movement is the *only* type that occurs in polar glaciers, but it also occurs in temperate glaciers.

Basal sliding

Here the glacier slides over its rocky bed and this can be accomplished in three ways:

1 **Basal slip** where water builds up between the ice and the underlying rock. This lubricates the interface between the two and so allows the ice to slide downhill.

2 **Enhanced basal creep** where the lowest layer of ice is pushed against obstacles larger than one metre wide and the pressure causes the ice to plastically deform/bend around the obstacle.

3 **Regelation** where the increased pressure found on the uphill side of a small object (less than one metre in width) causes the ice to melt, flow around the object as water and then refreeze on the downhill side where the pressure is less.

In general the sliding of a glacier is not fully constant but takes place in a jerky fashion with movements of a few centimetres. This is often described as 'stick and slip' due to a sudden slip of small patches of the ice followed by refreezing or reattachment.

Bed deformation is where movement is accomplished due to the deformation of the rock material that underlies the base of the glacier. This tends to happen when the underlying rock is a weak rock or soft sediment. It is similar to the processes found in internal flow because the pressure of the ice deforms the structures of the underlying rocks so that they will also move forward/downhill and the ice moves with them.

The condition at the base of the glacier is very important to the movement of the ice and has resulted in two types of glaciers being identified in relation to this:

1 Cold based
2 Warm based

Such glaciers are classified by the temperature at the base of the glacier. **Cold-based glaciers** have temperatures below freezing (throughout) and so experience very little (if any) melting to provide lubrication. The base of the glacier is attached to the valley and its movement is severely restricted by this. Cold-based glaciers are the norm in polar regions because of low temperatures and a lack of moisture to create precipitation, with a lack of even surface melting to lubricate any part of the glacier. With these glaciers remaining static or moving very slowly the processes of erosion and transportation take place at exceptionally slow rates, if at all. Any movement is through internal flow.

Warm-based glaciers experience conditions where the base of the glacier is above the melting point of ice (due to the pressure it of being under large amounts of ice this temperature is actually

lower than 0°C, its surface melting point). There may be a number of reasons for the temperature here being warmer but it is mostly due to friction caused by the glacier's movement or in some locations geothermal heating. The melting of the ice at the base of the glacier increases lubrication between the glacier and the rock beneath allowing the glacier to move more easily. If surface melting is also involved the meltwater will pass through the ice to assist with lubrication throughout the glacier and also increase the speed of movement. Warm-based glaciers result in faster erosion and transportation.

3.3 Glacial erosion processes

Pure ice is softer than most rock and moves very slowly. Initially ice may seem an unlikely or at least inefficient agent of erosion. A second look is necessary to understand why scientists believe that, partly due to its enormous erosional properties, ice has changed our landscape dramatically.

We have already mentioned that gravity and the movement of ice plays a major part in erosion but on its own ice would have relatively little effect if it simply slipped downhill. Two major processes turn this relatively neutral action into one that can drastically wear away and change the landscape.

Plucking

Simply put, plucking is the action of the glacier, as it moves downslope, ripping/pulling and detaching rocks from the underlying rock. The rock removed may be minuscule or more than 3 m in size (some texts will describe the largest as being the size of a house!) and it will become embedded within the ice as it moves onwards. This movement of the ice itself erodes the valley base and sides while also providing much of the rock debris material that will assist in the effectiveness of the second process, abrasion.

The most effective plucking will take place on rock surfaces where the underlying rock is of a less resistant type and/or there are weaknesses due either to the rock type, previous weathering (e.g. freeze–thaw, Figure 3.13) or pressure put on it by the glacial ice.

Task

1 What are the conditions needed for glaciation to occur?
2 Explain how glacial ice is formed.
3 What features must ice possess to become classified as a glacier?

4 Using Figure 3.12 and the section headed 'Glacial ice and glaciation as a system' (page 83) create your own learning resource which combines the text and diagram. Explain all of the key features mentioned.

Diagram (a)

Top of Ice freezes first

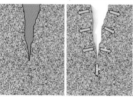

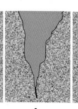
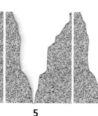

Scree (talus)

1
Water collects in rock fractures.

2
Temperature drops below 0°C and the water in the fracture freezes. Water at the top of the fracture freezes first forming a stopper. Freezing moves downwards with the water expanding by around 9%. Trapped by the stopper this expanding ice puts pressure on the sides of the fracture forcing it to expand (see diagram (b)).

3
After thawing, the original amount of water contained does not fully fill the now expanded fracture.

4
Additional water from thawing ice or precipitation can now fill the remainder of the fracture.

5
The increased volume of water allows for the next freezing event to continue to widen the fracture in the same manner as it had done before.

6
Repeated freezing and thawing will eventually split the rock apart. The sharp broken-off fragments are known as scree or talus and often build up at the base of cliffs and steep slopes.

Diagram (b)

The way that freezing water puts pressure against the sides of the rock fracture is similar to how we use wedges hammered into fractures by sledgehammers to split rocks.

Because the ice freezes from the top down it puts pressure on the sides of the rock in the same way that the metal wedge does as it is forced further into the fracture.

▲ **Figure 3.13** Freeze–thaw

Pre-existing fractures and joint patterns in the bedrock initially assist in the plucking process then, after the original surface has been stripped away, the underlying rock experiences **pressure release**. This pressure release causes the bedrock to expand and fracture allowing for plucking to continue and so intensifying the vertical and lateral erosion caused by the glacier.

There are a number of theories as to how this plucking takes place and it may be that there is *not* just one process in action. However, the primary mechanism is thought to be due to the patterns of melting and freezing which we have already identified as part of basal flow:

1 Ice flowing over a bump or step in the bedrock experiences higher pressure on the uphill side of the object and this creates melting. This water flows to the downhill side and refreezes (regelation), attaching itself to the bump or step. As the glacier moves onwards the rock (or part of it) is pulled out and incorporated within the ice at the base of the glacier (Figure 3.14).

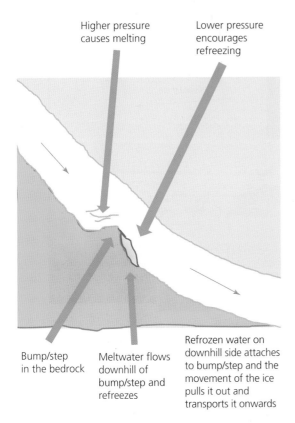

Higher pressure causes melting

Lower pressure encourages refreezing

Bump/step in the bedrock

Meltwater flows downhill of bump/step and refreezes

Refrozen water on downhill side attaches to bump/step and the movement of the ice pulls it out and transports it onwards

▲ **Figure 3.14** Pressure change and regelation

2 In places where conditions at the base of the glacier change from melting to freezing of subglacial water, rocks and sediments become incorporated within the ice and are removed from the bed as the glacier continues to move downhill. This can take place over a large spatial area (Figure 3.15).

3 An additional theory is that hydraulic pressure due to meltwater flow *assists* in the breaking up and removal of part of the bedrock. This rock is moved and eventually located at a position where it is wedged within the ice or it becomes incorporated in the glacier as conditions change and the meltwater freezes (Figure 3.16).

Glacial abrasion

Plucking, along with rock falling down into the sides of the glacier (due to mechanical (physical) weathering, such as freeze–thaw, undercutting or avalanches) gives ice the ability to carry out large-scale erosion, known as glacial abrasion. The rock debris embedded in or being moved along with the base and sides of the glacier scours, scrapes and grinds against the valley sides and floor. This has been described as being reminiscent either of sand papering or of rasp file filing (Figure 3.17). In general this greatly wears away and smoothes the underlying rock.

Larger rocks and more resistant rocks being moved by the glacier cut into and make grooves on the floor and sides of the valley. These can be from a few centimetres to over a metre in depth and are called striations.

The abrasive action also provides additional rock material to assist in the continuation and intensification of the process. The grinding of the underlying rock produces a supply of powdered

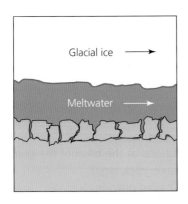

Glacial ice →

Meltwater →

Conditions at the base of the glacier allow meltwater to flow.

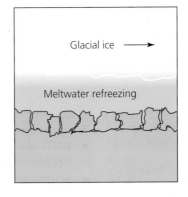

Glacial ice →

Meltwater refreezing

Conditions at the base of the glacier change and the meltwater refreezes attaching the ice to the bedrock and into faults in the rock.

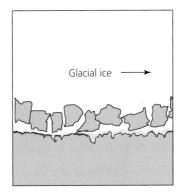

Glacial ice →

As the glacier continues to move, rock fragments are pulled out and moved downhill, embedded within the ice.

▲ **Figure 3.15** Change in base of glacier temperature

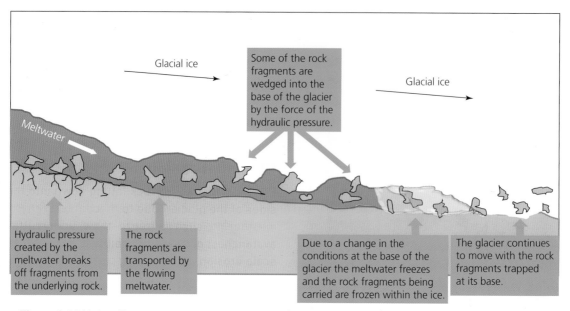

▲ **Figure 3.16** Hydraulic pressure assisting in plucking (**glacial quarrying**)

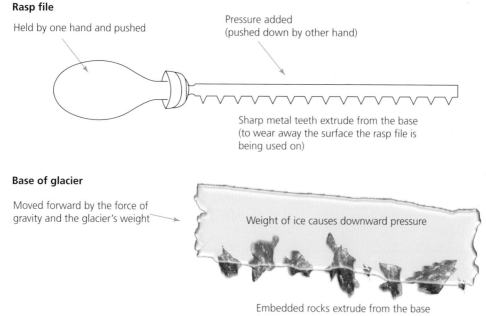

▲ **Figure 3.17** Comparison of a rasp file to the base of a glacier

rock (**rock flour**) which also becomes embedded in the ice and adds to its abrasive and polishing capabilities.

The effectiveness of these glacial erosion processes depends on numerous factors and their interaction, including:

- amount of ice contained within the glacier
- rate of accumulation of ice and the regime of the glacier
- gradient (steepness of slope) of the land being eroded
- speed of the glacier
- particular conditions at the base of the glacier (frozen, meltwater, rock type)
- warm- or cold-based glacier
- degree of resistance from the bedrock
- amount of additional rock added to the sides of the glacier from weathering, undercutting and avalanches
- amount of pre-glacial weathering.

It is said that under perfect conditions a glacier of just over 100 m wide has the potential to rip up, crush and move millions of tonnes of bedrock in a single year!

The name given to the unsorted rock waste carried and eventually deposited by glacial ice is moraine (Figure 3.18 and Figure 3.37 on page 100).

▲ **Figure 3.18** Moraine

 Task

1 Evaluate the following statement:

   'Meltwater plays an important role in both the movement of, and erosion by, glaciers.'

2 Explain the processes of:
   a) plucking   b) abrasion.
3 Explain how plucking assists the process of abrasion.
4 Using a diagram/diagrams explain the processes involved in *freeze–thaw* physical weathering.

3.4 Landscape features created by glaciers

So far we have been looking at background information to help you to understand glaciation in general. In the SQA Higher examination you are expected to be able to:

- explain how landscape features created by glaciers are formed
- explain and show the processes involved in the formation of these features and link these to an annotated diagram or diagrams

- explain and use the correct technical terms in your explanations (e.g. plucking and abrasion)
- identify features from maps, photographs or diagrams
- use mapping skills (e.g. six-figure references, identification of heights, measuring sizes and distances)
- evaluate the circumstances that have led to the creation of features that you have identified from maps, photographs or diagrams.

The features of glacial deposition selected by SQA to appear in the examination are corries, arêtes, pyramidal peaks, U-shaped valleys, hanging valleys and ribbon lakes.

Corries, cirque or cwm

These concave amphitheatre-like hollows (ranging from relatively small in size up to around a square kilometre) form at the heads of valley glaciers (Figure 3.19). Each, in their native languages, describes how the feature looks:

- Corrie from the Scots Gaelic 'coire' meaning a cooking pot or cauldron.
- The French cirque is derived from the Latin for circle and refers to its rounded back and bowl-like appearance.
- Cwm (pronounced 'coom') is Welsh for valley.

Put together these describe the feature well – a 'round-backed, bowl- or cauldron-shaped valley'. On maps it is often helpful to look out for these words as part of the names of places in the mountains to help you to identify them. In Scotland the inclusion of 'coire' or 'choire' is often helpful.

Although the term cirque has been adopted for international use, due to the Scottish nature of this course, we will refer to these features as corries.

Corries are formed by glacial erosion and regularly act as the birthplace/source of valley glaciers. Corries are initially formed where snow builds up in hollows high up on the sides of mountains. Although during major periods of glaciation this snow build-up can happen on any sloping face of a mountain and lead to the formation of a corrie, greater accumulation is likely where the conditions are more favourable:

- protected from the majority of the Sun's energy which could discourage snow from amassing (north to north-east facing slopes in the northern hemisphere)

Reflection

Obviously good old-fashioned studying and learning is important so that you become comfortable with the key terms and the processes involved. Next, you have to 'think smart'. Prepare for assessment and examination questions by creating your own clear, concise and easy to reproduce explanation and diagram answers. You may find it helpful to remember the following acronym:

What might you **NEED** for your answer?

Name the feature

Explain the processes of creation

Example of the feature

Diagram(s)

Remember:

- Avoid giving over-complex and wordy explanations; include all the key points clearly.
- Make sure your explanation follows the process in a logical manner. One of the easiest ways to do this is to state the conditions *before*, *during* and *after* and draw diagrams to illustrate this.
- Look at specimen or past exam papers and work out what's expected and how much time you'll have to answer such a question. Then make sure that your answer fits with this.
- Don't always rely on the first version that you create.
- As you gain more understanding and confidence, regularly return to your prepared answer and edit and alter it until you are happy with it.

Once you have your perfect explanation, learn how to reproduce it, regularly try it out and be ready to walk into your examination with extra confidence.

Before you begin the next section, you may find it helpful to look over the Hydrosphere section (pages 43–76), and especially rivers and valley landforms. To begin an internet search you could try the following keywords and phrases:

rivers; river processes; river erosion; river transportation; river deposition; river valley features.

▲ **Figure 3.19** Cwm Cau, Snowdonia

- sheltered from the prevailing wind which could blow snow out of the hollows (in Scotland this would be on the north-east facing slopes).

We have already looked at the processes involved for snow to become glacial ice and these will take place in these hollows if there is an accumulation and regular supply of snow.

Formation of a corrie

The formation of a corrie will take place over a number of stages (Figure 3.20):

- After accumulation in the hollow the snow begins its process of compression into glacial ice.
- Any period of thawing (e.g. during spring or summer) releases meltwater into any cracks

Beginning	During active glaciation	After glaciation
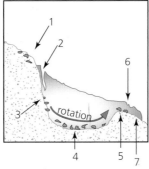	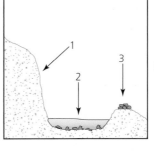	Long section view

Snow accumulation in hollow high on mountain slope under favourable conditions.

1 Snow.
2 Névé/firn.
3 Meltwater enters base and allows for freeze–thaw.
4 Meltwater during thaws (spring/summer) removes frost-shattered debris.

Deepening of hollow due to rotational movement of occupying ice (resulting from pressure due to accumulation of snow and ice on upper area or rear of hollow). Abrasion utilising plucked material and additional rock from freeze–thaw. Meltwater entering through bergschrund and due to friction assists in lubrication.

1 Freeze–thaw with scree formed falling into the ice.
2 Bergschrund forming access for rock and meltwater.
3 Headwall being plucked and abraded (meltwater assists lubrication for ice movement).
4 Plucking and abrasion (meltwater assists lubrication for ice movement) deepens.
5 Upward movement of rotational ice reduces erosion and leaves rock lip.
6 Crevasses as ice readjusts to movement downslope into valley.
7 Ice being pushed out and down valley.

1 Steep headwall (may also have scree slopes).
2 Corrie lochan (cirque lake or tarn) may occupy the deepened hollow.
3 Rock lip often accentuated by deposited moraine.

◄ **Figure 3.20** Corrie formation

or fractures of exposed rock and mechanical weathering in the form of freeze–thaw takes place. Any loose disintegrated material is removed by meltwater streams, enlarging the hollow and forming a steep backwall (headwall).

- The meltwater also enters cracks or fractures in the bedrock at the base of the hollow, preparing for refreezing and attachment to the ice and so creating conditions for future plucking and abrasion on the movement of the ice.

- Movement of the ice within the hollow is triggered by the continued accumulation of snow and ice. Increasing weight at the top edge of the hollow leads this to slip downwards and around the hollow. During this rotational sliding, rock is plucked from both the backwall and the base,

becomes embedded within the ice, and abrades and deepens the hollow. This process repeats over time with the enlarging of the hollow allowing for greater ice accumulation and intensified erosion.

- Additional rock debris from freeze–thaw action on the back wall falls down the bergschrund (a crevasse formed at the back of a corrie glacier between the ice attached to the headwall and the moving glacial ice) and supplies extra load to be utilised in abrasion. The bergschrund also acts as a pathway for meltwater to reach the underside of the ice and act as a lubricant for movement.

- The 'bowl shape' of the corrie is created by the rotational movement of the ice within the hollow.

As it exits the hollow on its downward edge, the ice is moving upwards within its rotation and so has reduced erosional power. This results in a rock mound (lip) at the entrance to the rest of the valley (this may also have moraine deposited on it, accentuating the mound).

During glaciation continued ice accumulation and rotational movement of the ice will not only continue to erode the hollow but will also push ice out of the hollow and over its lip. This ice will form the beginning of a valley glacier (mountain glacier), the ice being pushed further and further down the valley.

After glaciation the bowl shape of a corrie may provide a collection point for water (meltwater or run-off). This creates small deep lakes (corrie lochans/lochs or, in England, tarns) although not every corrie will have one (Figure 3.19). Continued freeze–thaw also results in scree slopes at the base of the headwall.

Figure 3.21 gives some hints on how to identify corries on an Ordnance Survey map.

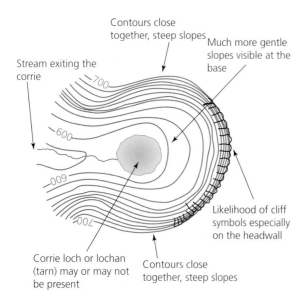

General points
1 Overall contour shape like a horseshoe.
2 Lower contours towards the middle with the highest to the outside.
3 A corrie may be identified by the use of terms associated with it:
  (i)   Coire or choire is the name in Scotland.
  (ii) Combe or cove in the Lake District.
  (iii) Cwm in Wales.
  (iv) Lochan within this shape referring to the lake in Scotland.
  (v)   Tarn in the Lake District.

▲ **Figure 3.21** Corrie: basic identification features on maps

Arête

An arête is a thin (often described as 'knife-edged') ridge of rock formed between two adjacent or parallel glacially eroded valleys as the valley walls are worn towards each other (Figure 3.22). They are also formed when two corrie headwalls erode towards each other backwards until they meet, leaving a narrow and steep-sided rock ridge (Figures 3.25 and 3.26). The ridges are further sharpened by the actions of freeze–thaw with scree developing on the lower slopes. Remember that in an assessment or an exam you may need to describe the processes related to glacial troughs or corrie erosion to enable you to get maximum marks.

▲ **Figure 3.22** Carn Mor Dearg arête (Ben Nevis)

Pyramidal peak

A pyramidal peak (Figure 3.23) (also known in its most extreme form as a glacial horn – see Figure 3.24) is an angular and pointed mountain peak somewhat reminiscent of the shape of a pyramid (Figure 3.30). These are formed when three or more corries surround a mountain and erode backwards into it. This carves the pyramid shape with a peak and steep walls (faces). The number of faces depends on how many corries have been involved in the formation of the peak.

Radiating out from the peak and forming the dividing points between corries are arêtes but with enough time and continued erosion these will also be worn away leaving the more extreme horn shape with the steep faces fully exposed (Figure 3.24).

Again, to achieve maximum marks in an assessment or exam response you may need to detail the process of corrie (and maybe even arête) formation when you are explaining the formation of a pyramidal peak.

Task

1 Draw a diagram of a pyramidal peak and annotate its key features.

2 Explain in detail how the key features of a pyramidal peak are formed.

▲ **Figure 3.23** Goat Fell (a pyramidal peak), Arran

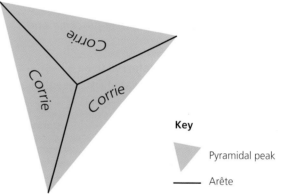

▲ **Figure 3.24** The Matterhorn (a glacial horn), Switzerland

At least one more corrie on the other side

Arête

Arête

Arête

Corrie

Corrie

▲ **Figure 3.25** Pyramidal peak

Simple diagram from above

Corrie

Corrie

Corrie

Key

Pyramidal peak

Arête

Look at Figure 3.26 for some hints on how to identify a pyramidal peak on an Ordnance Survey map.

Possible contour pattern

Possible contour pattern with key point annotation

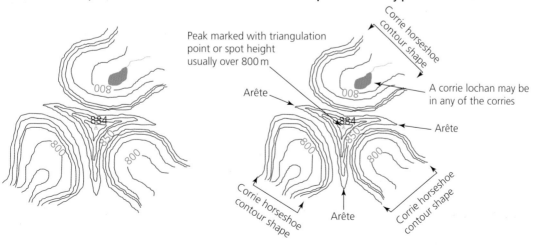

Peak marked with triangulation point or spot height usually over 800 m

Corrie horseshoe contour shape

A corrie lochan may be in any of the corries

Arête

Arête

Corrie horseshoe contour shape

Arête

Corrie horseshoe contour shape

▲ **Figure 3.26** Pyramidal peak: basic identification features on maps

Glacial troughs (U-shaped valleys)

After moving out from their corrie birthplace, mountain glaciers occupy and move down pre-existing river valleys and proceed to reshape them, removing both overlying rock waste and eroding the bedrock both laterally and vertically. Glacial troughs vary in depth and width due to the:

- underlying rock type and its qualities
- size of the glacier
- gradient of the glacier
- climatic conditions at the time of glacial action
- type of glacier (e.g. cold-based or warm-based).

The pre-glaciation river valley will typically have a V-shaped cross section. Following glacial erosion (and the glacier's final retreat) the valley will be straighter, steep sided, deeper, wider and broad floored. The creation of this glacial valley involves the pushing away of overlying rock material by the glacier's snout (Figure 3.37 on page 100) and the processes of *plucking* and *abrasion* (Figure 3.28).

The glacial trough is often referred to as a **U-shaped valley**, in reference to its excavated cross-sectional

▲ **Figure 3.27** Glencoe glacial trough

shape (Figure 3.28). In fact many of these glacial troughs develop a parabolic cross-sectional shape that is due to the addition of glacial deposition, especially **lateral moraines**, and also screes and **alluvium** (Figures 3.27 and 3.29).

Simply looking at a river's valley as an empty V-shape makes it easy to see its cross-sectional change, but if we look up a river valley towards its source we can see additional features which would have been in the way of the glacier. Rivers tend to wind between pieces of land which slope down into the valley. With the **spurs**

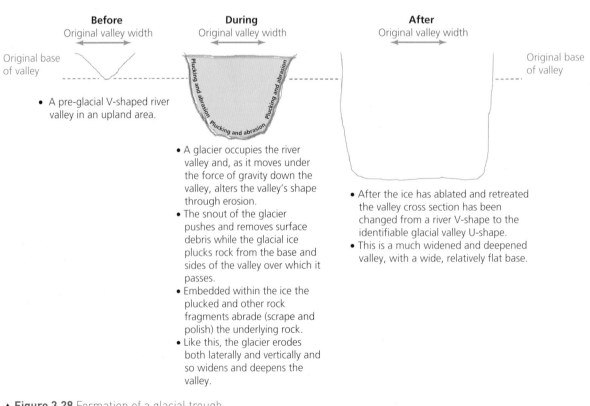

Before
Original valley width

Original base of valley

- A pre-glacial V-shaped river valley in an upland area.

During
Original valley width

Plucking and abrasion

- A glacier occupies the river valley and, as it moves under the force of gravity down the valley, alters the valley's shape through erosion.
- The snout of the glacier pushes and removes surface debris while the glacial ice plucks rock from the base and sides of the valley over which it passes.
- Embedded within the ice the plucked and other rock fragments abrade (scrape and polish) the underlying rock.
- Like this, the glacier erodes both laterally and vertically and so widens and deepens the valley.

After
Original valley width

Original base of valley

- After the ice has ablated and retreated the valley cross section has been changed from a river V-shape to the identifiable glacial valley U-shape.
- This is a much widened and deepened valley, with a wide, relatively flat base.

▲ **Figure 3.28** Formation of a glacial trough

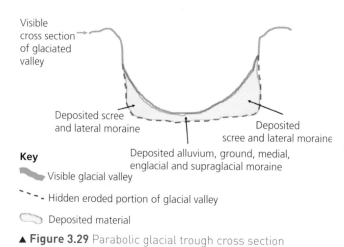

Visible cross section of glaciated valley

Deposited scree and lateral moraine

Deposited scree and lateral moraine

Deposited alluvium, ground, medial, englacial and supraglacial moraine

Key

Visible glacial valley

Hidden eroded portion of glacial valley

Deposited material

▲ **Figure 3.29** Parabolic glacial trough cross section

on alternating sides of the river valley, they appear to link or lock together like a zip (Figure 3.30), giving them the name interlocking spurs.

A glacier is not as easy to deflect from its path as a stream/river and because of its erosional force it wears away the parts of the spurs which stick out. This straightens the valley by 'chopping off' the

sections which slope in from the valley sides and leaves steep cliff faces on the valley walls which are known as truncated spurs (Figure 3.30). Truncated means 'to shorten by cutting off the head or the end'.

The rivers which now occupy (or re-occupy) the glacial troughs appear to be small in comparison to the troughs. The valley size is larger than that which would have been predicted to be eroded by a river of its size; from this observation such rivers were given the name misfit stream because, quite simply, they didn't fit. It wasn't until the processes of glaciation were understood that these post-glacial features were able to be placed within the context of their natural surroundings.

In long section glacial valleys do not exhibit an equal slope from start to finish but instead show an irregularity dependent on the conditions within the valley. The amount and location of abrasion along the valley floor may be dependent on a number of factors, such as:

- the location of differing bedrock types with varying amounts of resistance

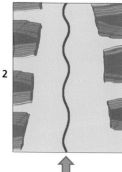

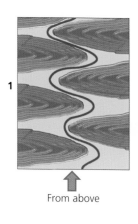
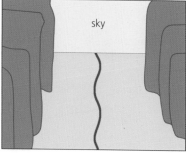
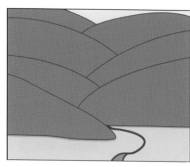
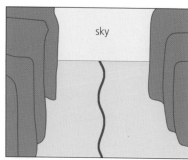

From above

From above with annotation

Looking **up-valley** from the position of the blue arrow

Before glaciation
An upland river valley prior to glaciation with spurs pointing into the valley and appearing to interlock.

After glaciation
The glacier has moved down through the river valley and, being more powerful and less flexible than flowing water, created a straightened path through erosion (pushing, plucking and abrading).

TS = truncated spur

▲ **Figure 3.30** Formation of truncated spurs

- zones of weaknesses along fault lines
- the location at the base of the glacier where particularly large or resistant rocks (or sections of rock) are attached
- the amount of contact, or contact pressure, between the base of the glacier and the bedrock (conditions can cause a glacier to move by rotational sliding, giving the effect of a wave action first being pushed down against the bedrock then lifted up. This gives points of intense, followed by reduced, abrasion over varying distances)
- the addition of extra power and abrasive materials, such as when a **tributary glacier** merges with the main valley glacier
- when the glacier passes between particularly resistant rock that narrows the valley, forcing much of its erosive power downwards.

This selective over-deepening results in varying depths and lengths of elongated rock basins on the glacial valley floor. During and following glacial retreat these rock basins may become filled with water, creating ribbon lakes (ribbon lochs) – long and relatively narrow, finger-shaped lakes (Figures 3.31 and 3.32). Ribbon lakes may also be formed where deposited moraine blocks a valley and traps water behind it.

▲ **Figure 3.31** Ribbon lake: Wastwater, in Cumbria

A glacial trough that reaches the coastline, having brought the base of the valley below sea level, will become flooded following glacial retreat. Where previously there was a river valley, now there will be a long, narrow, steep sided and deep inlet of the sea. This is known as a fjord (Figure 3.2).

There are many fjord coastlines around the world. The name itself was originally used to describe the features of western Norway, but also refers to Iceland, Greenland, Alaska, Chile, New Zealand and the sea lochs of western Scotland.

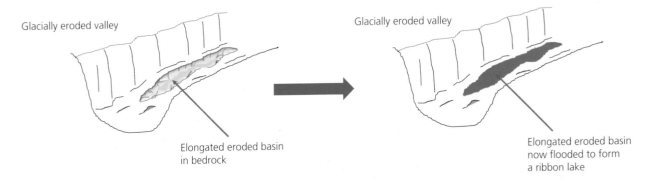

Glacially eroded valley

Elongated eroded basin in bedrock

Glacially eroded valley

Elongated eroded basin now flooded to form a ribbon lake

Selective erosion due to the bedrock type and resistance, along with the intensity and location of abrasion, results in places where elongated basins are worn.

During glacial retreat the eroded basins flood to form ribbon lakes: long, relatively narrow, often very deep, finger-shaped lakes.

▲ **Figure 3.32** Formation of a ribbon lake (post-glacial feature)

Hanging valley

A hanging valley is a glacial trough/valley whose mouth is found high above the floor of the main glacial trough. When standing on the main trough floor one can look up and see a valley which ends higher up the valley wall. But why do they not match in depth?

The pre-glacial river system would have had a main river fed by smaller tributary rivers which eroded their own smaller valleys that sloped down to the main valley bottom. Glaciers occupied the valleys of the river system and duplicated their patterns, with the main glacier fed by smaller tributary glaciers. Whereas rivers eroded so that the bases of their valleys sloped down into each other, glaciers eroded in a different manner.

While the tops of the glaciers may have been at the same levels their erosional abilities were linked to their size. The smaller tributary glaciers had less erosional power and could not erode vertically to the same extent as the main valley glacier. Simply put, the tributary glacier was not digging down as far. After ablation and glacial retreat the base of the tributary valley was no longer at the same level as that of the main glacial trough (Figures 3.33 and 3.34).

All the processes we have discussed so far with regard to the creation of a glacial trough apply to a hanging valley. It is a glacially eroded valley after all, but what makes it special is that it ends up with its mouth high up on the side of the main glacial trough.

▲ **Figure 3.34** Hanging valley and waterfall, Yosemite Valley, USA

Two additional post-glacial features that may appear due to the particular location of a hanging valley are **waterfalls** and **alluvial fans**. When a misfit stream that occupies a hanging valley reaches its mouth it is forced to fall down the valley wall of the main trough, creating a waterfall, which can be quite spectacular in glacial valleys. When the falling water reaches ground level its sudden change from the steep gradient to a flatter one means it loses its transporting power and the material that it has been carrying is deposited. These sediments build up to form a three-dimensional fan shape spreading out from the valley wall onto its base.

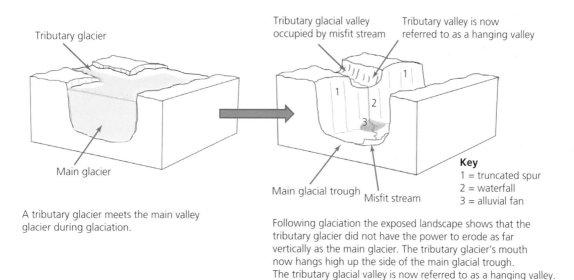

A tributary glacier meets the main valley glacier during glaciation.

Following glaciation the exposed landscape shows that the tributary glacier did not have the power to erode as far vertically as the main glacier. The tributary glacier's mouth now hangs high up the side of the main glacial trough. The tributary glacial valley is now referred to as a hanging valley.

Key
1 = truncated spur
2 = waterfall
3 = alluvial fan

▲ **Figure 3.33** Hanging valley, waterfall and alluvial fan

Reflection

So far you have looked at glacial troughs and some of the features found within them but now you need to link this to your map analysis skills.

- What would a glacial trough look like on a map?
- Would every glacial trough look exactly the same? Why?
- How would a map show the steep slopes of the valley sides?
- How would the relatively flat and wide valley bottom be shown?

- How would a waterfall be shown?
- What would an alluvial fan contour pattern look like?
- Are there any other symbols which might be found to show the landscape in these areas?

Always remember to check the conventional symbols (key) for the map you are using as these may give you extra hints or suggestions as to what is on the map.

Figure 3.35 gives some suggestions of what may be identifiable on a map.

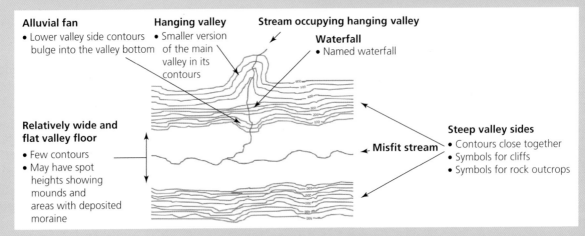

▲ **Figure 3.35** Glacial trough basic identification features on maps

 # Task

1 Why is the term 'glacial trough' usually better than 'U-shaped valley' when describing a glacially eroded valley?

2 Working in a team or pair, create a learning aid (e.g. report, pamphlet, poster, webpage or PowerPoint) that explains the processes which form a glacial trough. Your work should:
   a) include annotated or animated diagrams, photographs or video to enhance your explanation
   b) discuss the conditions and processes before, during and after glaciation
   c) explain the conditions that lead to the formation of glacial ice
   d) explain the different processes which assist in the erosion of the trough
   e) explain any technical terms used.

3 When you present your final results to others, make sure:
   a) your work achieves what it is trying to do (i.e. helps people to learn about the processes which create a glacial trough)
   b) you can answer questions and use your knowledge to expand on or clarify your points
   c) you consider your presentation skills and the quality of the presentation materials themselves.

4 Explain the location of a hanging valley's mouth high up the wall of a main glacial trough.

5 Identify three types of water feature found in a glacial trough following the retreat of the ice and explain how each of these features is formed.

Reflection

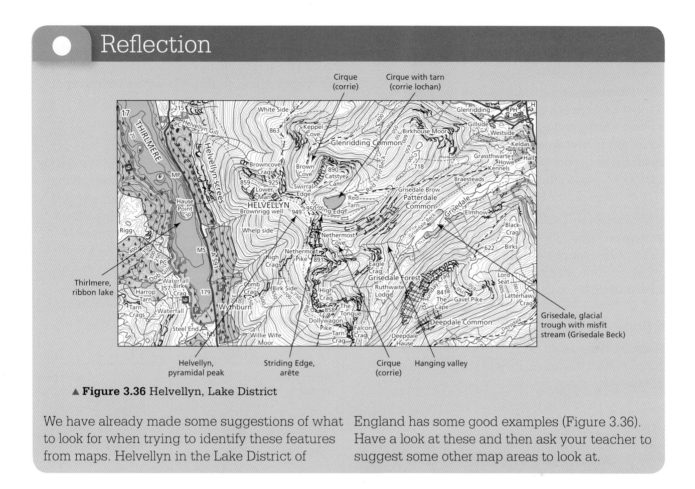

Cirque (corrie)

Cirque with tarn (corrie lochan)

Thirlmere, ribbon lake

Grisedale, glacial trough with misfit stream (Grisedale Beck)

Helvellyn, pyramidal peak

Striding Edge, arête

Cirque (corrie)

Hanging valley

▲ **Figure 3.36** Helvellyn, Lake District

We have already made some suggestions of what to look for when trying to identify these features from maps. Helvellyn in the Lake District of England has some good examples (Figure 3.36). Have a look at these and then ask your teacher to suggest some other map areas to look at.

3.5 Features of glacial deposition

The features of glacial deposition selected by SQA to appear in the examination are drumlins, eskers, and terminal moraines. It is, however, important that you understand a bit more about moraine in general as it features widely in the stages of development of depositional landforms.

Moraine

Moraine is the term used to describe all of the accumulated unconsolidated material e.g. silt, clay, sand, gravel, stones, rocks, boulders (see Figure 3.18 on page 89) picked up, moved and finally deposited by glacial ice. Moraines do not show layering or progression of grain size in their deposits, which are unsorted. The load carried by a glacier includes all of the accumulated unconsolidated material, e.g. silt, clay, sand, gravel, stones, rocks, boulders (see Figure 3.18) picked up, moved and finally deposited by glacial ice. It includes rock/sediment plucked from the underlying bedrock along with that which has fallen on the glacier's surface from the valley walls. When the glacier retreats this moraine is deposited on the valley floor in positions relating to where it was carried by the ice.

There are several types of moraine, classified by the position in which they were carried by the glacier (e.g. at its base, sides, snout, surface or internally) or deposited (e.g. laid down (smeared) beneath the ice or released during ablation) relative to the glacier. Figures 3.37 and 3.38 show the six main locations of the different types of moraine described below.

1 Lateral moraine

Lateral moraine forms along the sides of the glacier and consists of plucked material and that which has fallen from the valley sides. After retreat these will form mounds running along the base of the valley walls.

2 Medial moraine

Where two glaciers merge a **medial moraine** is formed where two of their lateral moraines have joined together. These result in dark lines running along the centre of a glacier and after retreat forms a ridge running along the centre of the valley. If numerous glaciers meet there may be multiple dark bands in the middle of the glacier and a similar number of ridges after retreat.

3 Ground moraine

Ground moraine collects by the base of the glacier. This material may be deposited where it was when the glacier retreated or transported by meltwaters further down the valley and beyond.

4 Englacial moraine

Englacial moraine refers to any material that is found trapped within the body of the ice. This includes material that has fallen down crevasses from the surface.

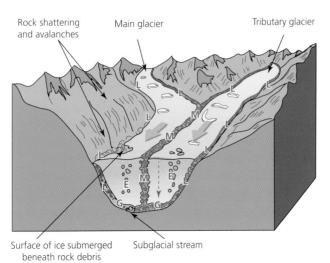

Rock shattering and avalanches
Main glacier
Tributary glacier
Surface of ice submerged beneath rock debris
Subglacial stream

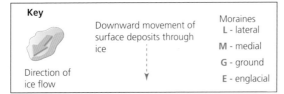

Key

Direction of ice flow

Downward movement of surface deposits through ice

Moraines
L - lateral
M - medial
G - ground
E - englacial

▲ **Figure 3.37** Moraine types

5 Supraglacial moraine

Supraglacial moraine can be found anywhere on the surface of the glacier. This term can be used to describe lateral and medial moraine that has not reached beneath the surface of the ice, moraine which falls from the valley sides to cover areas of the surface (e.g. rock falls and avalanches), as well as any rock debris or dust that settles on the top of the glacier.

6 Terminal moraine

Terminal moraine marks the end point of the glacier at its furthest extent. Rock, sediments and soil that have accumulated from plucking and abrasion and the push effect of the snout of the glacier build up to form a mound or hill running from one side of the valley to another. The term **end moraine** is often used and simply means the moraine at the end of a glacier and not necessarily that of the furthest extent of this erosion. It may have retreated and then re-advanced but not as far as its previous maximum distance.

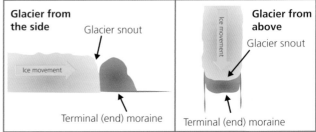

Glacier from the side
Glacier snout
Ice movement
Terminal (end) moraine

Glacier from above
ice movement
Glacier snout
Terminal (end) moraine

▲ **Figure 3.38** Position of a terminal (end) moraine

Drift or **glacial drift** is the name for all material deposited by glacial ice. This can be divided into two groups:

1 Moraine deposited directly by the ice in an un-stratified (not layered) and unsorted manner. This is known as till.
2 Moraine transported by meltwater, stratified, sorted and then deposited. These are called **fluvioglacial** deposits.

Till deposits and landscape features

Till is an unsorted and unstratified accumulation of glacial deposits. These sediments range in size from the smallest sediments to boulders the size of houses. The rock fragments are usually angular though some may be slightly polished or striated from abrasion while embedded in the glacier. They are not, however, rounded like those of a river bed.

There are two types of till, although it is difficult to distinguish between the two:

1   Basal till (lodgement till): This is a material carried (lodged within) the base of the glacier and deposited beneath the ice due to pressure, partial melting and friction as the ice moved. It is often described as being smeared on the underlying ground surface.
2   Ablation till: This is moraine carried on the glacier's surface (supraglacial) or within the body of the ice (englacial) and released, let down and deposited as the ice melted. This forms a coating of unsorted material on top of exposed bedrock or basal till deposits.

We will focus here on a till feature formed by basal till (subglacial) – drumlins.

Drumlins

Drumlins get their name from their description in Irish Gaelic ('droimnín' – smallest ridge) and Scottish Gaelic ('druim' – mound). These are elongated, oval ridges sculpted and streamlined from basal till by the action of moving ice (Figure 3.39). Drumlins have often been compared to the shape of upturned canoes or halved eggs. They have a steeper end (stoss, facing the direction from where the ice came) and a longer, gentler sloping lee slope (facing the direction the ice moved towards) (Figure 3.40). The long axis of a drumlin is parallel to the direction in which the ice has been flowing. Drumlins can be of different sizes but some may be up to a few kilometres long and 50 m in height.

Drumlins tend to be found in tightly packed clusters known as drumlin swarms rather than being isolated individual features. When looked at from above, they look like eggs packed together on their sides and this has given this type of landscape the name 'basket of eggs topography' (Figure 3.40).

There are a variety of theories as to how a drumlin is formed:

● fluvioglacial deposition beneath the ice
● fluvioglacial deposition, which is then compressed, deposited on and reshaped by the moving glacier
● similar to the above, with large subglacial floods (beneath the ice) eroding giant drumlin-shaped hollows in the base of the ice, which are then infilled with sediment as the floodwaters slow and reduce. The ice then presses down onto the bed below, imprinting the drumlin and further deposits as it moves
● fluvioglacial erosion and shaping of basal moraine by channels of water
● changes in pressure and movement within the ice, resulting in a wave motion of the basal ice and the deposition of drumlins during the upward movement and a smoothing of deposits as the ice moves downwards again
● bedrock deflection of basal flow (e.g. a mound of bedrock creates an upward followed by downward ice movement, similar to the above) and deposition around the core of rock. However, the majority of drumlins have no evidence of bedrock cores.

There may be some aspects of truth in all the above but there is no one, single accepted theory or model.

Recent studies of an active drumlin field at the margins of the Múlajökull glacier in Iceland (Figure 3.42) have provided previously inaccessible evidence and a greater understanding of the processes involved there (Figure 3.41). This study suggests:

▲ **Figure 3.39** Drumlin

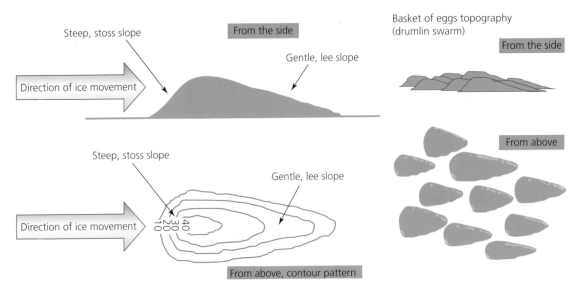

▲ **Figure 3.40** Formation of drumlins

- There is a progressive layer-by-layer build-up of deposited material under the moving ice over time.
- The initial deposition encourages the moving ice to move upwards and slowly, depositing more layers, and over time the shape and size becomes exaggerated.

- The final shaping of the drumlin takes place during a glacial surge (increased forward movement). This carves and smoothes the final shape.

Why the initial deposit is made still has not been fully explained but may be linked to the earlier theories described. It may be as simple as the

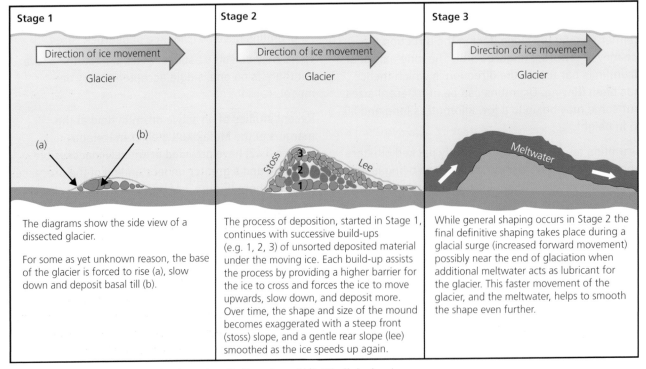

▲ **Figure 3.41** Drumlin formation based on findings from Múlajökull, Iceland

bedrock being less than flat or a stuttering forward movement of the ice due to changing circumstances (possibly nearing the end of its lifespan). The final surge may be due to increased meltwater acting as a lubricant for movement during climate change.

Fluvioglacial landscape features

These are landforms associated with meltwater from glaciers or ice sheets. Meltwater streams may be found during active ablation, at the end of glaciation (de-glaciation), or prolonged periods when the ice remains still and does not advance (ice stagnation).

Near the end of glaciation vast amounts of meltwater are released, often under pressure and at high velocity. This discharge of meltwater can be at different locations in relation to the glacier:

- on the surface (supraglacial)
- within the ice (englacial)
- beneath the ice (subglacial)
- emitting from the snout.

When trapped within tunnels in or under the ice, or in subglacial valleys, pressure builds up due to the large amount of meltwater flowing downstream through the restricted spaces. Under pressure the water moves at high speed and in a turbulent manner with an energy that enables it to transport large amounts of material. The high pressure within the tunnels can also allow some of this water to be pushed upwards on the sides of the valleys, resulting in water-deposited features in a direction that would not be expected.

When the volume of water drops, the pressure also drops and the energy to transport material becomes much reduced. This results in deposition and the formation of fluvioglacial landscape features.

Fluvioglacial deposition is different from till in that it is sorted and stratified due to it being transported by water (often over long distances). Movement by water also alters the basic shape of deposited materials through attrition (rocks smashing against each other as they are being moved), resulting in them being broken into smoother and rounder shapes.

▲ **Figure 3.42** Meltwater from the snout of the glacier at Múlajökull, Iceland

Eskers

Eskers are long, narrow and steep-sided, winding ridges of stratified (layered) sand and gravel that are found within areas of till on which they have been deposited (Figure 3.43).

They may be several kilometres in length (in the USA and other locations some reach hundreds of kilometres) and around 5 to 10 m in height (although they may reach 20 to 30 m).

Eskers run in the same direction as the flow of the glacier and are often described as looking like railway embankments that wind lengthways down valleys.

They may form long continuous mounds, have gaps along their lengths, and/or form part of a system with other eskers branching off.

Most eskers form:

- near the glacier's terminus (snout)
- where the glacier reached its final position and is stagnant or in retreat. Here the glacier is relatively thin and not moving quickly or forward (so there is no moving ice to destroy the landform)

▲ **Figure 3.43** Esker in Manitoba, Canada

- mostly inside tunnels, either beneath (subglacial) or within (englacial) the glacial ice (Figure 3.44). Some may also be formed in supraglacial channels (above the ice) or in crevasses and, like the englacial stream deposits, are lowered to ground level during the melting phase.

This is a simple step-by-step description of how an esker forms within, or under a glacier (Figure 3.45).

1   For an esker to form there must be a large amount of sediment and meltwater, and this fits with the conditions around the time of glacial retreat.

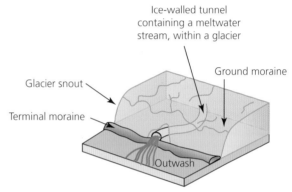

▲ **Figure 3.44** Ice-walled tunnel, with a meltwater stream, near glacier's terminus

Stage 1   Meltwater entering the glacier through moulin (vertical shafts) and other cracks in the ice, allowing surface water to reach the internal ice-walled tunnels

Glacier

Ice-walled tunnel with stream

Ice-walled tunnel with stream

Ground moraine

Stratified (layered) sediment deposited by stream

Stage 2

The stream has dried up in the ice-walled\tunnel

The stream has dried up leaving stratified (layered) sediment deposited by the stream

Increased amount of stratified (layered) sediment deposited by the stream over time and as hydrostratic pressure reduced and the water slowed

Stage 3

As the glacier melts and the tunnel walls are removed the deposited sediment is further deposited on the valley floor, forming an esker

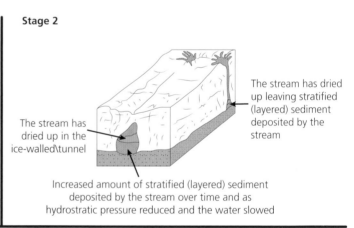

Ground moraine

Stratified (layered) sediment (sand and gravel)

▲ **Figure 3.45** Formation of an esker

2   Meltwater collects and flows as streams or rivers through ice-walled tunnels within or at the base of the ice. This water often carries vast amounts of debris released during melting of the glacier and from the surroundings.

3   Meltwater may descend into the glacier from surface cracks in the ice or through well-like vertical shafts called **moulins**.

4   The large volume of water flowing through and being restricted by the ice walls of the tunnel creates a considerable amount of hydrostatic pressure, enabling great quantities of sediment and other debris to be carried. Hydrostatic pressure also explains why some eskers run uphill for short distances: the water is pushed upslope under the pressure.

5   When the pressure and speed of the water are reduced, or the river/stream dries up, material previously being carried by the water is deposited within the tunnels.

6   As the glacier melts away and the tunnel walls are removed, the deposited debris is further deposited on the valley floor, forming an esker.

Research opportunity

The glacial landforms selected by SQA to appear in the examination are arêtes, pyramidal peaks, U-shaped valleys, hanging valleys, ribbon lakes, drumlins, terminal moraines and eskers. Using internet searches, textbooks, libraries or other resources look up these features and:

1   identify (and note down) good examples of each landform

2   find photographs or videos of the locations you have identified and become familiar with how each landform looks

3   be prepared to use this information to add detail to exam answers.

3.6 Formation of erosional and depositional features in coastal landscapes

The term 'coast' is commonly defined as the interface or transition between the land and sea, or more simply the land beside the sea. Coastlines are very important to people in Scotland as they are part of the lives of most people in the country: the furthest on land you can be away from the coastline is only 80 km (less than an hour's drive). To put that into perspective, at 46° 17′ N, 86° 40′ E is the Gurbantünggüt (Dzoosotoyn Elisen) Desert in China which is 2,648 km from the nearest coastline on the Yellow Sea. This is the furthest distance from the coast on the planet.

Quiz questions regularly ask about the lengths of coastlines, but these are very difficult to work out and estimates may vary considerably depending on the source of the measurement. A map with greater detail will usually result in a larger figure than those calculated from a smaller scale map. As such, the figures given below should only be seen as rough estimates:

- Scotland: 16,500 km including islands (9,910 km for the mainland only)
- British Isles: 36,000 km
- World: 356,000 km.

Task

1   Explain what is meant by the term moraine.

2   Explain the locations of the six main types of moraine associated with a valley glacier.

3   What are the differences between basal till and ablation till?

4   How would you be able to distinguish between moraine and fluvioglacial deposits?

5   Create your own diagram with annotations showing the main features of a drumlin.

6   What have the studies at the Múlajökull glacier in Iceland told us about how drumlins are formed?

7   Explain how meltwater assists in the formation of fluvioglacial landscape features.

8   Draw annotated diagrams to show how each of the following features are formed:
   a) terminal moraine
   b) an esker.

When looking at the figure for the world it is thought-provoking to realise that the average distance from planet Earth to the Moon is 384,400 km.

The figures given above show that there is a very large distance of interaction between seas/oceans and land throughout the world. These large distances mean that coastlines are subject to very changing circumstances because of climate, weather conditions, rock types and the different mixtures of all of these and their effect on processes. Looking at the coastlines of the British Isles we can see a wide variety of landforms and coastal types over short distances on this little island group alone.

In the SQA Higher examination you are expected to be able to:

- explain how coastline landscape features are formed
- explain and show the processes involved in the formation of these features and link these to an annotated diagram or diagrams
- explain and use the correct technical terms in your explanations (e.g. hydraulic action, corrasion, attrition, saltation and solution)
- identify coastal landscape features from maps, photographs or diagrams
- use mapping skills (e.g. six-figure references, identification of heights, measuring sizes and distances)
- evaluate the circumstances that have led to the creation of features that you have identified from maps, photographs or diagrams.

The features of coastal landforms selected by SQA to appear in the examination are:

1 erosional features: wave-cut platforms, headlands and bays, caves, arches and stacks
2 depositional features: spits, bars and tombolos.

To be able to describe the stages in the creation of these features, you should be aware of some other coastal landforms and the processes in action at the coastline.

Coasts as systems

Coastal landscapes are formed by a system of interactions between erosion, transportation and deposition processes, the *majority* of which are carried out by the action of waves with the assistance of the other denudation processes. These interactions are as follows:

- **Inputs**: Waves, tides, currents, rock types, rock structure, river sediments and eroded coastal sediments that have been transported along the shore into the area, sediments transported from offshore, climate and weather.
- **Processes**: Wave action, wave type, tidal movement, erosion, transportation, deposition and sub-aerial processes (see next page).
- **Outputs**: The products of the processes involved in terms of landforms created, for example *landforms of erosion* such as cliffs, caves, stacks, wave-cut platforms or *landforms of deposition* such as beaches, spits, bars and tombolos. In addition, outputs include sediments which have been washed out to sea or along the shore elsewhere.

Sub-aerial processes are a combination of land-based (above the high water mark) weathering and mass movement that assist in the alteration of the shape of the coastline. These processes include:

- freeze–thaw
- exfoliation
- biological weathering
- chemical weathering
- mass movement, for example:

  - rockfalls: these are due to freeze–thaw on cliffs or undercutting of a cliff face or hillside by wave action so that the rock simply falls down
  - landslides: after cliffs become soaked in water from precipitation or from the sea, the lubricating effect causes those cliffs made of softer rock to slip down
  - slumping: triggered through a similar process to that causing landslides but differs due to a resultant rotational sliding motion along a concave plane. A cliff formed from this will take on a crescent shape from top to bottom
  - soil creep: occurs on gentle slopes at a slow pace to produce a surface which is step-like and uneven in an undulating manner. This is a slow process where dampened soil moves downhill because of an increase in its mass from the additional water
  - mudflow: occurs on steep slopes where the soil has become saturated and there is little vegetation to help bind it in place. Because of the increased amount of water within the soil it becomes lubricated and increases in mass, encouraging it to move swiftly downhill.

Physical factors influencing coastal landscapes

Weather and climate conditions

For example, prevailing wind and regular or infrequent storms all influence the regularity and strength of waves approaching the coastline.

Lithology (rock type)

As mentioned earlier in this chapter, some types of rocks may be more resistant to erosion than others and those with weaknesses will be more susceptible to particular types of erosion.

Slope (dip) or geological structure

Some cliffs are formed in layers which slope in towards the land (Figure 3.46, top) while others slope towards the sea (Figure 3.46, bottom). Those which slope towards the sea have rocks which will easily fall into the sea following erosion.

Where there are layers of resistant and less resistant rocks, alternating mass movements (landslides) are likely as the less resistant rock will be worn away quicker leaving little support for the more resistant rocks above.

If the coastline has the same type of rock running parallel to the sea (along its length) this is known as concordant (Pacific-type). Because of this, erosion is maintained at similar rates and as such there are very few bays and headlands (Figure 3.47) in this type of coastline.

Discordant coastlines (Atlantic-type) are those where bands of different rock types run perpendicular (at right angles) to the coast. This means that there will be different types of rock as we move along the coastline. Due to differing rates of resistance and erosion this leads to coastlines with bays and headlands (Figure 3.47). The less resistant rocks wear away at a quicker rate forming bays, while the more resistant rock is left sticking out into the sea as a headland.

Cliff slopes towards land

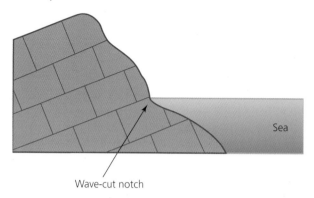

Cliff slopes towards sea

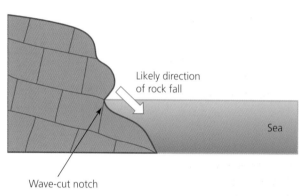

▲ **Figure 3.46** Cliff slope

From above

Concordant coastline   **Discordant coastline**

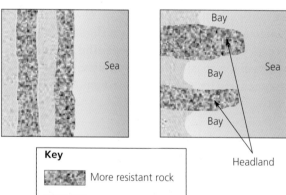

▲ **Figure 3.47** Concordant and discordant coastlines

Tides

Tides are formed as a result of the gravitational effect of the Moon and the Sun on the oceans on planet Earth. Tides depend on the position of the Moon and the Sun in relation to the oceans as the Earth rotates. The Moon's and Sun's gravity pulls the water beneath them until it forms mounds (higher water levels) which result in high tides. The Moon, being much closer to Earth, has a greater influence on tides. When the Moon and the Sun act together, pulling from the same side, tides become higher than normal and are known as **spring tides**. When the Moon and the Sun are on opposite sides their counteraction results in lower than usual high tides known as **neap tides**.

Tides act like massive waves around the planet, causing the alternate rising and falling of ocean/sea level and therefore the distance to which the ocean/sea will reach onto the coastline. The processes of the ocean/sea will therefore be against different positions on the coastlines depending on which tide is dominant.

In the British Isles the height difference between high and low tides is 3–7 m. The speed of movement of water as it changes in height between tides also affects the amount of erosion, transportation and deposition of material.

Sea level changes

In the introduction to this chapter, we saw the causes and effects of sea level changes which result in emergent or submergent coastlines. The changing positions of the coastline exposes different areas, landscapes and rock types to the actions and effects of the sea.

Waves

Winds blowing over the surface of an ocean or sea create waves. Energy is transferred from the wind to the water through friction between the air and water molecules at the air–water interface. Waves are a result of this energy passing through the water, causing it to move in a circular motion (Figure 3.48). This circular or orbital motion means that not only does the water create a mound on the surface but a column of water plunges downwards to about half of

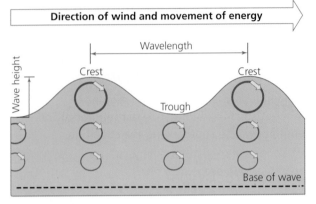

▲ **Figure 3.48** Wave shape and creation

the wave's wavelength beneath the surface. The water doesn't actually move forward much but the energy does, being transferred through the water in the same direction as the wind. It is this energy that powers the erosion and transportation attributed to waves.

The amount of energy being transferred is dependent on the wind speed creating the wave, the duration of the wind and the amount of distance over which that wind blows. The **fetch** is the maximum distance travelled by the wind over an area of water to create the waves. With a prevailing wind from the south west, the fetch approaching the British Isles is diagonally across the Atlantic Ocean (a distance of thousands of kilometres), allowing the generation of strong waves. The south-west of England and the west coasts of Ireland and Scotland receive more powerful waves than the eastern coast, where available fetches are only that of the width of the North Sea.

Stronger winds, their extended duration and/or a longer fetch increase the energy and height of waves. Storm conditions moving landward will increase the energy, strength and height of waves and increase their effects on the coastline.

Waves may also be created because of submarine volcanic eruptions, earthquakes or landslides which displace large amounts of water and transfer energy in the form of waves known as **tsunamis**.

As a wave approaches the shore the seabed becomes shallower, creating friction with the bottom of the wave. This causes the lower portion of the wave to slow down and compress while on the surface the wave crest rises in height, creating an elliptical motion rather than circular. This creates an imbalance and the wave breaks and collapses, its energy transferred in the direction of the remainder of the ellipse (Figure 3.49).

The water thrown onto the shore is known as **swash** while the draining of the water back down into the sea because of the coastal slope is known as **backwash**.

Types of waves

The shape and action of waves as they reach the coastline will determine whether they assist in the building of a coastline (**constructive waves**) or its wearing away (**destructive waves**).

Constructive waves deposit material and build beaches. They tend to occur where there is low frequency of waves (for example six to eight per minute) and are most effective where the seabed gently slopes towards the coastline, creating a gradual increase and friction with the base of the wave. This results in a steadily increasing elliptical shape slouching forward and developing into a low and long shape. This shape creates **spilling breakers** where the crest is thrown forward, pitching material which is being transported up the gentle gradient.

Due to there being few waves, following waves cannot interfere with the power of this swash action and the gentle slope means that the backwash is weak, so less material is drawn back towards the sea. This results in an accumulation of material on a beach (deposition) (Figure 3.49).

Destructive waves remove materials from the shore. They are higher, more frequent waves (at least 10 to 15 per minute) which approach the coastline. A rapid approach, especially up steeply sloping seabed coastlines, results in the friction at the base of the wave swiftly increasing. This causes a wave shape that is much steeper and creates a **plunging breaker** which results in a curling crest and a strong plunge that pulls backwards with little forward movement. It creates a weak swash and a strong backwash that drags material into the sea (Figure 3.49), leading to an erosional effect on a beach.

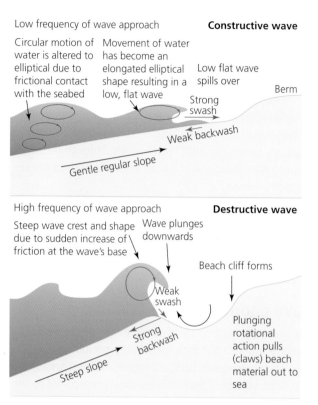

▲ **Figure 3.49** Constructive and destructive waves

🌍 Task: Summary questions

1. In what way can coastlines be described as systems?
2. What is a sub-aerial process?
3. Explain how physical factors can influence coastal landscapes.
4. How are waves formed?
5. Using the text and Figure 3.48 describe and explain the movement of:
   a) water within waves
   b) energy through waves.
6. List three factors that influence wave height and explain how they do this.
7. Explain why the south-west of the British Isles experiences stronger waves than the east coast.
8. What are the meanings of the following terms?
   a) swash   b) backwash
9. Using diagrams and annotations explain the following:
   a) constructive waves
   b) destructive waves.

3.7 Coastal erosion processes

As discussed above, coasts can be looked on as a system, with inputs, processes and outputs. The processes involved include those *above* the high water mark (land based), which we have already referred to as sub-aerial processes, and those which we will now focus on, *below* the high water mark. Note that the shaping of a coastline is a joint effort of both of these types of process.

Processes *below* the high water mark include:

- wave pounding
- hydraulic action
- corrasion (abrasion)
- attrition
- corrosion (solution).

Wave pounding

This term expresses the brute strength of the power of waves against the rock face. **Wave pounding** can exert shock waves of up to 30 tonnes/m² and smash off pieces of rock. This has often been compared to the action of a sledgehammer. It may be seen as a process in itself or as a sub-process of hydraulic action.

Wave pounding assists in the weakening of the rock face, creating openings for, and increasing the effectiveness of, hydraulic action while providing rock debris for corrasion (abrasion).

Hydraulic action

This process takes place as a result of waves breaking against a rock face. Any air which is trapped within cracks, faults, joints or bedding planes is compressed (squeezed) and put under pressure. When the wave retreats, the air expands again with explosive force, weakening the fissures and loosening or breaking off pieces of rock. This can be particularly effective in rock types which are well jointed or well bedded (such as limestone and sandstone) or which are loosely consolidated (such as clay) and will break apart relatively easily.

Increased energy within the waves, such as during storms, increases the effectiveness of hydraulic action. Pressure exerted by an average wave during a winter Atlantic storm is around 11,000 kg/m².

Corrasion (abrasion)

All forms of rock debris and sediment (sand, pebbles and shingle) are propelled against cliff faces by waves. This is an abrasive action which wears away the rock over time. Repetitive and long-term corrasion at the foot of a cliff can erode a **wave-cut notch** (an indentation at the base of the cliff) which undermines the cliff, creating an instability which may result in the collapse of the rock above.

Attrition

The eroded material produced by wave pounding, hydraulic action and corrasion is itself worn down through attrition. Wave action causes items of rock debris to bump into each other, scrape against each other and so break off and wear away their surfaces. Over time the debris becomes smaller, rounder and smoother. The reduction in size of this material makes it easier for waves to transport the rock debris away from the base of the cliff. With the material moved away, waves have more access to the cliff line and erosion becomes more effective. The worn down debris also becomes available for the creation of depositional features elsewhere.

Corrosion (solution)

Corrosion involves chemical weathering and refers to the breaking down of the coastal rock following a reaction to chemicals in the seawater. Reactions will depend on the rock types and the chemicals found in the sea. For example, carbon dioxide in the **atmosphere** becomes dissolved in seawater, creating a weak form of carbonic acid. Excretions from coastal organisms such as barnacles and limpets can also add to the acidity of the water. Calcareous rich rocks (e.g. limestone) react with the acid and are slowly dissolved. Salt from seawater can assist in the breakdown of rock through **salt crystallisation**. Corrosion can also take place above the high water line due to spray being blown there.

3.8 Features of coastal erosion

Cliffed coastlines

Figure 3.50 shows the actions of coastal erosion processes on what most people would recognise as a typical cliff face. However, it should be noted that there are a variety of cliff profiles; some appear to be almost vertical, while others have uniform gradients or convex or concave slopes (Figure 3.51).

To appreciate why there are different profiles it is necessary to remember the physical factors that influence coastal landscapes, some of which were mentioned in the section 'Coastal erosion processes' on page 110.

The *main* influences are:

- lithology (rock type) and its resistance
- slope (dip) or geological structure
- balance between erosion rate at the cliff base and of sub-aerial processes
- balance/change of general conditions.

Lithology (rock type) and its resistance

Rock types or deposits which are more susceptible to erosion (e.g. clay or moraines) are more

▲ **Figure 3.51** Sea cliffs, north of St Abb's Head, Scottish Borders

likely to experience undercutting. This results in the cliff slumping and the formation of convex sloping. By being less resistant to erosion, they are also more likely to change, sometimes very quickly. More resistant cliff faces (e.g. granite, Carboniferous limestone or sandstone) retain a relatively regular steep and at times almost vertical slope, often reaching great height (the island of Hirta in the St Kilda archipelago of the Outer Hebrides has the highest sea cliffs in Britain at 430 m).

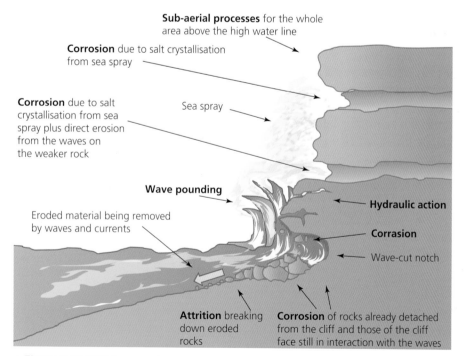

Sub-aerial processes for the whole area above the high water line

Corrosion due to salt crystallisation from sea spray

Corrosion due to salt crystallisation from sea spray plus direct erosion from the waves on the weaker rock

Sea spray

Wave pounding

Eroded material being removed by waves and currents

Hydraulic action

Corrasion

Wave-cut notch

Attrition breaking down eroded rocks

Corrosion of rocks already detached from the cliff and those of the cliff face still in interaction with the waves

▲ **Figure 3.50** Cliff face erosion

Not all cliffs are made of one single type of rock and this can result in different rates of erosion. Multiple layers of rock can lead to complex erosion patterns and shapes. A simple version is shown Figure 3.52 where a cliff is made from one rock type or two types of rock, one more resistant than the other.

Slope (dip) or geological structure

Where the rock strata is horizontal and the joints vertical there is a relatively uniform resistance, resulting in steep cliff faces. Figure 3.46 on page 107 shows that where the rock strata dips towards the land the cliff face will also slope in that direction. If the strata dips towards the sea an overhanging cliff will be created.

Balance between erosion rate at the cliff base and of sub-aerial processes

High energy wave action on a regular basis at the base of a cliff encourages erosion. Wave-cut notches develop (Figure 3.50), the cliff face collapses and with the assistance of the wave energy and coastal currents the rock debris is removed. This leaves the base of the cliff open to continued wave erosion and such conditions will result in steep cliffs. Remember that this can take place over a long period of time or relatively quickly depending on the rock type.

If for some reason the waves are not able to access the base of the cliff, or their power is reduced, the amount of erosion will decrease. This enables sub-aerial processes to become more dominant and they will shape the cliff from above.

The rate of removal of rock debris from the base of the cliff plays an important role in the effectiveness of wave erosion. A build-up of collapsed rock that is not removed may create an actual barrier between the waves and the new cliff face and block any continued erosion. In addition the rock debris may create shallow water for the waves to pass over and thus slow them down, reducing their energy and ability to erode. For erosion to be effective it is therefore important that the wave action and inshore currents are strong enough to remove collapsed cliff face debris.

Balance/change of general conditions

Changing conditions can have a major effect on cliff processes. An increase in sea level, a change in the regularity and severity of storms or altered current patterns will result in a different balance of erosional processes and the manner in which a cliff develops.

1 Less resistant rock at cliff base.

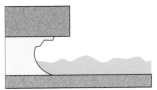

The less resistant rock at the base will erode away quicker resulting in undercutting and the collapse of the rock above. Compared with 2 and 3 this will result in a quicker erosion of the cliff face under the wave erosion conditions.

2 More resistant rock at cliff base.

Undercutting will still take place here on the more resistant rock but it will be at a much slower pace. The less resistant rock on top will remain in place but will experience more sub-aerial erosion and shape change.

3 Uniform resistance for full height of cliff.

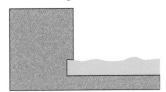

Uniform resistance should result in a relatively uniform cliff retreat. With a less resistant rock this will be much quicker than with a more resistant rock. Even with resistant rock the pattern will still involve some level of undercutting nearer the base where the waves regularly hit the rock face.

▲ **Figure 3.52** Different rock resistance in cliff face

Wave-cut platforms

Wave-cut platforms are also known as **coastal platforms** or shoreline platforms.

When looking at the erosion of harder rock cliffs, it was highlighted that the action of the waves creates wave-cut notches near the base of the cliff face. As the notch enlarges, the cliff face becomes unstable and the weight above cannot be supported, causing the rock above the notch to collapse and the cliff to retreat. Attrition, retreating waves and coastal currents then clear away the rock debris that has fallen to the base of the cliff.

Over time and because of these repeated actions, the cliff retreats farther and farther away from where it was initially and a wave-cut platform (a flat platform or terrace with an incline of less than 5°) replaces where the base of the cliff was (Figures 3.53 and 3.54).The wave-cut platform becomes exposed at low tide. Even at times when the waves reach the cliff they have to travel across a wide area of shallow water which reduces their energy and ability to erode. This reduction of base erosion slows or stops cliff retreat and sub-aerial processes become the predominant factor. This dominance of sub-aerial processes results in the development of a gentler cliff.

Wave-cut notch

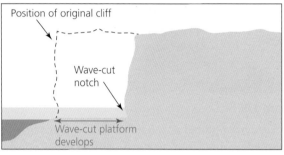

Position of original cliff

Wave-cut notch

Wave-cut platform develops

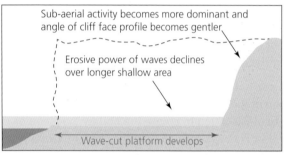

Sub-aerial activity becomes more dominant and angle of cliff face profile becomes gentler

Erosive power of waves declines over longer shallow area

Wave-cut platform develops

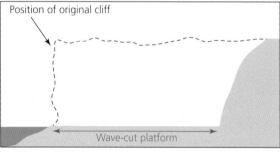

Position of original cliff

Wave-cut platform

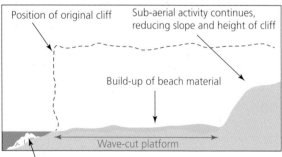

Position of original cliff

Sub-aerial activity continues, reducing slope and height of cliff

Build-up of beach material

Wave-cut platform

An additional feature may develop here throughout the process in the shape of an extended terrace formed from rock debris cleared off the wave-cut platform

▲ **Figure 3.54** Wave-cut platform formation

▲ **Figure 3.53** Caunter Beach, Cornwall. Wave-cut platform viewed from cliff top

Sea caves

▲ **Figure 3.55** Sea caves, Culzean Castle, Ayrshire

Sea caves are defined as a natural hollow, passage or chamber eroded into rock (e.g. cliff faces) by wave action at the coast (Figure 3.55). They are also known as littoral caves as they are formed at the littoral zone of the coastline (the area above water at low tide and underwater at high tide).

For a sea cave to form there must be a non-uniform erosion of the rock face so that it erodes quicker in a particular section to create the hollow, passage or chamber. This section will take the form of a weak zone in the rock, a joining point between bedding planes of different hardness or simply a different type of rock within the cliff face.

All of the erosive processes of wave action work together to wear away and further weaken the flaws in the cliff face. As the hollow begins to appear hydraulic action becomes the predominant process with corrasion grinding within the hollow assisting with its deepening and widening. The confined space within the hollow intensifies the erosive action.

Hydraulic action smooths the lower portions of sea caves while the roofs may show a rougher, angular texture as the result of rock falls.

Arches, stacks, needles and stumps

These are features which form on hard rock coastlines with headlands and bays. For these features to form, erosion has to take place on a headland or promontory, so it is important to mention this in any assessment or exam answer.

▲ **Figure 3.56** Arch and stump. 'Green Bridge of Wales', Pembrokeshire Coast

This example shows the development of landform features from cave erosion to a stump. For the SQA exam, you only need to be able to describe, explain and draw annotated diagrams of the landform features from a cave to a stack (stages 1 to 4 in the description below). Remember that you will also need to be able to name and explain the processes of erosion involved, which are discussed earlier in this chapter.

The process of sea cave formation is the starting point in a series of developmental steps that lead through caves, arches, stacks, needles to stumps (Figures 3.56 and 3.57):

1 If a cave erodes from one side of a headland through to the other (or caves from either side meet), this passageway or tunnel is known as an arch. The roof of an arch is known as its keystone.
2 Continued wave erosion expands and enlarges the arch.
3 Removal of the rock below makes the keystone unstable and eventually this collapses.
4 The headland is now detached from the other side of the now collapsed arch which remains as a pillar of rock known as a stack.
5 Continued wave erosion and weathering *may* sharpen the stack to form a needle shape.
6 Wave erosion lower down the stack/needle between its low and high water marks narrows this area to a point where it is unable to support the rock above. This causes the stack/needle to collapse, leaving a small low-lying rock island called a stump. A stump is usually low enough to be submerged at high tide.

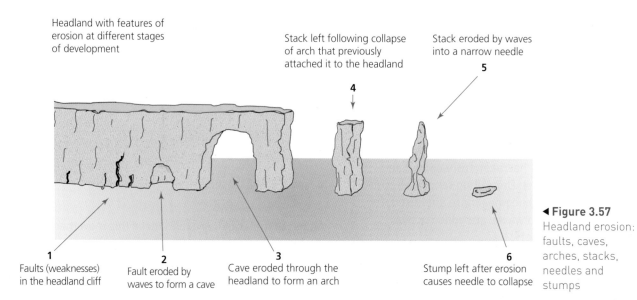

Headland with features of erosion at different stages of development

Stack left following collapse of arch that previously attached it to the headland
4

Stack eroded by waves into a narrow needle
5

1
Faults (weaknesses) in the headland cliff

2
Fault eroded by waves to form a cave

3
Cave eroded through the headland to form an arch

6
Stump left after erosion causes needle to collapse

◀ **Figure 3.57**
Headland erosion: faults, caves, arches, stacks, needles and stumps

🌍 Task

Note: In your answers always use the names of processes that are involved and make it clear that you know how these processes work.

1 Create your own table summarising the five main processes of coastal erosion below the high water mark.
2 Explain why cliffs may develop different profiles (shapes).
3 Create a series of three annotated diagrams showing the stages *before*, *during* and *after* the development of a wave-cut platform.
4 Copy the table below and complete the second column with a brief explanation of the features listed:

Feature	Explanation
Cliff	
Sea cave	

Wave-cut notch	
Wave-cut platform	
Arch	
Stack	
Needle	
Stump	

5 Explain the stages that start as a weakness in a headland cliff face and lead to the formation of a stump. You should:
   a) use and explain the technical terms for the erosion processes that take place
   b) describe and name the intermediary features formed
   c) use annotated diagrams to highlight your key points.

3.9 Features of coastal deposition

Earlier we looked at the effect that different types of waves (constructive or destructive) may have on the coastline. As you read about the features of coastal deposition you should keep in mind the actions of waves.

Waves and tidal currents transport the material that they will eventually deposit in four ways:

1 **Solution**: Minerals which have been dissolved in seawater are carried (invisibly) in solution.
2 **Suspension**: Small particles are carried along in the water, often making it cloudier or tinted. This is very visible during and after a storm when large amounts of sediment are transported.

3 **Saltation**: Larger particles are bounced along the seabed. These sediments are too large and heavy to be kept fully afloat and this results in the bouncing motion.

4 **Traction**: Traction refers to the bigger pieces of sediment, such as pebbles, being rolled along the seabed.

This section focuses on features created by previously eroded material that has been transported and deposited at the coast. Deposition tends to occur where the coastline becomes more sheltered, currents weaken and waves are constructive.

There are two types of coastline in relation to deposition:

1 Swash-aligned coasts are oriented parallel or roughly parallel to the direction of the prevailing waves. These are affected only by the action of the waves, either constructively or destructively, as a closed system.

2 Drift-aligned coasts are oriented at an angle to the prevailing waves. Constructive and destructive waves will have an effect but the system is open and heavily influenced by the direction of currents in the process of longshore drift (see below). Not only will beaches form but the movement of materials along the coastline will assist in the formation of spits, bars and tombolos for example.

While constructive and destructive waves relate to the movement up and down beaches, a second process central to the formation of drift-aligned coasts assists in the movement of material across a beach (parallel to the sea). This is longshore drift.

Longshore drift

Prevailing wave directions tend to be at an angle towards the coastline. This results in the swash of a wave propelling material *diagonally* up the beach. The backwash, however, does *not* return at an oblique angle but instead drains straight back down into the sea.

If we follow the progress of one grain of sand or pebble it will be thrown up the beach at an angle by the swash, be pulled straight down the beach by the backwash, caught by the next swash and thrown farther along the beach at an angle, then drain straight back down with the backwash. As time goes on this grain or pebble will move in a zigzag motion along the beach (Figure 3.58).

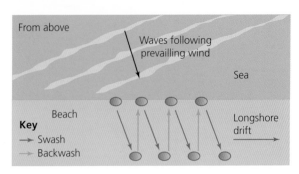

▲ **Figure 3.58** Longshore drift

All beach material has experienced this movement and the beach is therefore neither static nor a permanent feature. Material being carried further along the coast has the potential to form other features.

There will be a general movement in one direction – that of the prevailing wind, although every now and again a change in condition (seasonal wind direction) will cause an alteration in direction.

Beaches

The term 'beach' refers to the build-up of *wave* deposited material between the low water mark and the highest points reached by storm waves at the high water mark. Beaches are active zones, changing every second at a microscopic level and on a vast scale during storms.

When thinking of a beach, you may immediately think about a golden sandy holiday beach, but it is important to realise that they come in many forms, are made from different materials and are of different colours. Beaches can be made up of numerous materials including sand, gravel, pebbles, shingle, cobbles, rocks or shells. Colours include white, golden, red, tan, black and more. These differences are due to the properties of the source rocks or minerals that have been deposited by the waves.

Even the slope of the beach may be due to the type of material being deposited. Sand beaches with finer grain sizes usually result in flat or gentler slopes than those with larger grains. Much of this is as a result of the limited ability of finer grains to absorb water from the swash of the waves. This results in the backwash flattening out the beach material as it moves some sand backwards towards the sea. Coarser grained materials absorb more of the swash so a smaller amount of it becomes backwash, resulting in fewer grains being dragged back seaward. Through this process coarse grained materials pile up on the beach.

▲ **Figure 3.59** Trafalgar beach, Cádiz, Spain

Bayhead and lateral beaches

Bayhead beaches are ones which form from sediment deposited in bays between two headlands. They are typically crescent shaped. The headlands on either side restrict the lateral movement of sediments and there is a balance of retained beach materials as the vast majority of sediment is contained in the bay. This enables the beach to maintain its crescent shape.

Lateral beaches form on straight coastlines where sediments can be moved along their length by longshore drift. These beaches can usually stretch for some distance along the coastline. Unlike bayhead beaches, these are open, uncontained systems and they could disappear if a regular input of sediment was not available to replace that which is moved.

Spits, bay bars and tombolos

It is very important to understand the processes of longshore drift as spits, bay bars and tombolos (Figure 3.60) all form as a result of sediment and debris material being moved along the coastline. In an assignment, assessment or exam answer some explanation of longshore drift will assist in gaining marks when commenting on their formation.

Spits

These are common along indented coastlines where there are bays (e.g. discordant coastlines) or where there are river mouths and estuaries or rias. Spits are low, narrow ridges of pebbles and/or sand formed by deposition; they are joined to the land at one end and stick out into a body of water (the sea or an estuary) (Figure 3.60).

The chief process in the formation of a spit is longshore drift. When the coastline curves inwards and away from its previous direction, longshore drift continues on its original course. At the position of this change of direction, the longshore drift is forced to slow (possibly by meeting with river water moving from the inland side, a change in currents from the seaward side moving in towards the bay or estuary or just by meeting the slower or still water sheltered within a bay). This causes the longshore drift to lose its energy and begin to deposit material.

The first materials to be deposited due to this loss of energy are the larger pieces such as shingle/pebbles. Initially this will form a submerged mound but with continued deposition it will rise above the surface

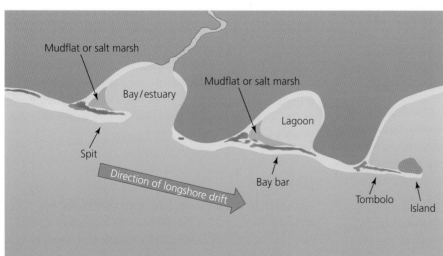

◀ **Figure 3.60** Spits, bay bars and tombolos

to become a short extension of beach material (a small low-lying spit) out into the sea or bay. Over time the spit will develop and in normal conditions the lighter sediments are dropped further out to build up, while the overall growth is contributed to in storm conditions by larger material being deposited above the high water mark.

Strong flows of water from rivers and out through the estuaries help to prevent extended development of a spit, by changing the direction of the main force of water, this time from the river out to sea. It is possible, however, for the spit to force the river into a diversion and alter the width and position of its mouth. Limitations on the spit's growth can also be experienced when it develops directly out to sea and the depth of water reduces the chance of materials building up above the surface or where coastal currents are stronger and continue to transport the material elsewhere.

Over time, and with a continued source of sediment, a spit can develop, change shape and become a more permanent fixture.

Many spits develop hooked or curved ends and there may be a number of reasons for this:

- Waves bend (refract) as they move around a headland and this drags materials into a curved shape, pointing inland.
- They may be a response to a change in the prevailing wind to coincide with the next most dominant wave direction.
- The effect of storm conditions where waves approach in a different direction to longshore drift and push sediment in an inland direction may assist with the deformation of a spit.

Spits may also develop multiple curved ends (**recurved spits**). They are formed due to lengthy periods where the wind direction has changed or during times when there has been a series of storms altering the direction of sediment transport and deposition.

Sands may also be blown by the wind to create **sand dunes** on a spit (bar or tombolo). This can become a more permanent structure if vegetation takes hold and stabilises the dunes. With sand dunes and vegetation colonising the spit, it becomes more resistant to wave erosion, even during storm conditions.

Throughout the creation of a spit an area of calm water develops behind it. The spit shelters the area,

acting as a barrier against incoming waves and wind. Material may be deposited here from either the low energy waves coming around the spit and into the sheltered area, or by waters exiting from the landward side (e.g. from a river or as a low tide that causes water to retreat to the sea). The waves become trapped, slowed down and reduced in their energy and ability to transport sediments, leading to the formation of **mudflats** (**tidal flats**) or **salt marshes** (**saltings**) from the deposits.

Mudflats are a build-up of a mixture of tidal sediments and alluvium which are covered at high tide but exposed during low tide. They can be particularly treacherous because they maintain a good deal of water within them. During low tide, water channels form as water drains from the sediments, or where streams and small rivers, which previously entered the estuary where the mudflat is now situated, continue their course towards the sea.

When conditions become possible for algae and vegetation (**halophytic** plants) to colonise the mudflats, salt marshes form. This marshland is intermittently flooded during high tides or storm conditions and sediments are not only simply deposited but trapped by the marsh vegetation. The plant root systems stabilise the silt and when the plants decompose the **organic** material builds up to form peat. Like mudflats, salt marshes are intersected by a complex network of water channels and retain pools of salt or brackish water (Figure 3.61).

Salt marshes can act as a natural coastal defence, trapping and stabilising sediments and creating shallows near the coast that slow down and remove the energy from incoming storm waves.

This development from a sheltered, shallow water area through mudflat to salt marsh is the early stage of this becoming a fully stabilised new area of land. Over time the build-up of wave-deposited alluvial and organic material will raise the height of the area above sea level and excess water will drain from it.

Bay bars

These occur where longshore drift continues in a straight line across a bay (Figure 3.60 on page 117). The process is the same as the creation of a spit but

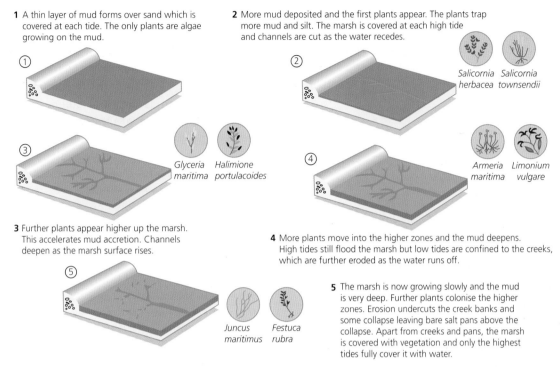

1 A thin layer of mud forms over sand which is covered at each tide. The only plants are algae growing on the mud.

2 More mud deposited and the first plants appear. The plants trap more mud and silt. The marsh is covered at each high tide and channels are cut as the water recedes.

Salicornia herbacea *Salicornia townsendii*

3 Further plants appear higher up the marsh. This accelerates mud accretion. Channels deepen as the marsh surface rises.

Glyceria maritima *Halimione portulacoides*

4 More plants move into the higher zones and the mud deepens. High tides still flood the marsh but low tides are confined to the creeks, which are further eroded as the water runs off.

Armeria maritima *Limonium vulgare*

5 The marsh is now growing slowly and the mud is very deep. Further plants colonise the higher zones. Erosion undercuts the creek banks and some collapse leaving bare salt pans above the collapse. Apart from creeks and pans, the marsh is covered with vegetation and only the highest tides fully cover it with water.

Juncus maritimus *Festuca rubra*

▲ **Figure 3.61** Salt marsh formation

this time the coastline bends inland, the spit builds up and, as long as beach material continues to be supplied, it continues until it joins the headland at the other side of the bay. This kind of bar is known as a bay bar. Bay bars can be formed of either sand or shingle. Simply put, a bar is a ridge of deposited material above sea level connected at both ends to the mainland.

As with a spit, bay bars can become stabilised and exhibit beach and dune structures. A bay bar will trap the waters of the bay behind it in what is termed a lagoon. Without breaches in the bay bar to supply new water, these lagoons may eventually dry out and become a land area. This development would see a similar process to that found behind spits where mudflats and salt marshes form before ultimately draining and drying out.

Tombolos

A bay bar links two parts of the mainland together. A tombolo links the mainland to an island. Again this is formed through the same process as the formation of a spit or bar. Longshore drift continues past the turning point of the coastline and deposits beach material until it reaches an offshore island and forms a link with it. In some places a tombolo can be formed between two islands.

Maps and coastlines

When using an Ordnance Survey (OS) map always try to identify the coastal features covered in this chapter and try to link them with the conventional symbols which may be shown. Make sure you are familiar with the symbols before your examination. During an examination a key or explanation of these symbols will usually be provided but it is possible you may be given a different type of map so having an understanding of OS map symbols is always an advantage.

Have a look at the OS map symbols for 1:25,000 maps and in particular those marked 'Water features', 'General features', 'Heights', 'Rock features or heights' and 'Natural features'.

Task

Note: In your answers always use the names of processes that are involved and make it clear that you know how these processes work.

1 Explain the processes by which waves and tides transport material.
2 With the help of an annotated diagram show and explain the main features of longshore drift.
3 What is a beach?
4 Explain the formation and development of the following:
   a) spit
   b) bay bar
   c) tombolo.
5 Explain the sequence of events that would lead to new land forming behind a spit or a bay bar.

Always be aware of contours and contour patterns and check what you see with the descriptions that you know of the features.

In the introduction to this chapter we noted that within the exam the 'necessary skills will include the ability to identify erosional and depositional features from maps', but you may find that you will have to interpret the coastline in relation to other SQA Higher units as well. This means a good understanding of the symbols for roadways, paths, tourist features, nature reserves and national parks is invaluable.

In assignments you might also find yourself having to describe what a coastline looks like with the assistance of a map. Below are some examples of things you could mention:

- *General direction of the coastline*: Use the points of the compass for this, for example, north to south or east to west or other points in between. If it turns and changes, state that this happens and where (giving grid references).
- *Shape of the coastline*: A good use of vocabulary can save you a lot of words. Is the coastline straight, curved, fretted, indented? There are other terms which you have learned that could

be used as description, such as concordant or discordant.
- *Height and steepness*: Again a good understanding of contours and contour patterns helps. Look for information and state the maximum and minimum height. Is the slope steep, concave or convex? If it is steep, are there cliff symbols? Is there a spot height near the cliff symbol to give the cliff height? Is the complete 'slope' vertical or stepped? Look for slope symbols suggesting where the surface has slipped.
- *Shore*: Look for symbols showing what type of beach material is present such as shingle, mud or sand. Look at the base of a cliff: are there symbols showing flat rock at the base of a cliff suggesting a wave-cut platform? Is a beach backed by sand dunes or are there signs of salt marsh or mudflats? If there is a long stretch of beach, how long is it? If the beach is particularly wide, how wide is it? Is it a bayhead beach or a lateral beach?
- *Distinctive landforms*: You have already been asked to look out for cliffs, beaches and even wave-cut platforms but there may be more. Look out for caves, arches, stacks and stumps on erosional coastlines and spits, bay bars, lagoons and tombolos on depositional coastlines.
- *Names*: Don't just look for patterns and symbols; straightforward names may state exactly what a feature is or at least hint towards it.

Remember: Don't just state that a feature is there, identify it with a six-figure grid reference. If it is a stretch of coastline give the grid references for the start and finish of the stretch you're describing.

Summary

Having completed this chapter, you should now be able to describe and explain the stages and processes in the formation of the SQA specified erosional and depositional landforms from glacial and coastal landscapes.

You should also be able to show a detailed understanding of the factors responsible for glacial and coastal erosion and deposition.

Research opportunity

▲ **Figure 3.62** Durdle Door

Figure 3.62 shows the location of Durdle Door on the Dorset coast. This is a very famous natural sea arch and a coastline of spectacular erosional features.

1 Undertake some research into Durdle Door and familiarise yourself with the surrounding coastline.

2 Using the map and referring to the section on 'Maps and coastlines' on pages 119–120, write a detailed description of this coastline.

3 Use the information you have obtained to create a presentation in which you describe the coastline of the area and explain how the main features were formed.

4 From what you have learned in this chapter and your own research, predict what will happen to Durdle Door in the future. Describe this new coastal feature.

SQA examination-style questions

In the SQA exam you may be required to explain the stages and processes in the formation of specified erosional and depositional landforms from glacial and coastal landscapes. The specified landforms which could come up in the exam are:

- **glacial** – corrie, arête, pyramidal peak, U-shaped valley (glacial troughs), hanging valley, ribbon lake, drumlin, esker, terminal moraine
- **coastal** – wave-cut platform, headland and bay, cave, arch, stack, spit, bar, tombolo.

You are expected to show a detailed understanding of the factors responsible for glacial and coastal erosion and deposition in your answers. It is also important to be able to name and describe the processes that help in the creation of these features.

Exam preparation

Being a geographer is not just about exams, but they are important. Take your time to work out what you need to do to revise properly and prepare yourself by answering the examination-style questions in this book.

You should have been checking your understanding throughout this chapter, but, in particular, do your best to be able to:

- name all the key glacial and coastal erosional and depositional features, and explain their formation in detail

- succinctly explain the processes which lead to the formation of these features
- use the correct names for the processes which help to form these features – remember that an understandable misspelling will be accepted, so just try your best
- give a named example of each feature whenever possible.

In addition to this you should work on your mapping skills to:

- become familiar with symbols and conventional signs (on Ordnance Survey maps in particular) for glacial and coastal landscapes
- be able to identify glacial and coastal features on maps
- be able to look at the surrounding areas and evaluate the possible outcomes of continued erosion or deposition.

Types of questions

In the SQA Higher examination, one question type asks you to 'identify' a single feature (landform) and to explain how this forms.

For an 'explain' question, such as 'explain how a corrie is formed' you must do more than just describe. You should refer to the processes involved – name them and say how they have created the feature. If you only 'describe', no more than half of the available marks can be awarded.

A well-annotated diagram with detailed labels (covering all the information you would give on the processes in a text-only answer) can gain full marks.

Explain questions tend to be worth 10 marks.

1   Now try example question 1. You can use your notes, this book or other resources to help you create the best possible answer.

Example question 1

Corries are landscape features that are present in glaciated areas.

Explain the conditions and processes involved in the formation of this feature.

You may wish to use an annotated diagram or diagrams in your answer.

(10 marks)

2   Next, copy out the following generic question:

Explain the conditions and processes involved in the formation of a [specified glacial or coastal landform feature].

You may wish to use an annotated diagram or diagrams in your answer.

3   Use the copied-out question as a template for a set of perfect answers for each of the key features in the glaciated and coastal landscapes lists above. For example, for a wave-cut platform the question would be:

Explain the conditions and processes involved in the formation of a wave-cut platform.

You may wish to use an annotated diagram or diagrams in your answer.

(10 marks)

4   Work in a pair (or small group) to discuss your responses. Suggest improvements to your own and your partner's answers.

5   To review your answers for each feature, reflect on these questions:

- Have you 'explained', not just 'described'?
- Have you named and described how processes create the feature?
- Would your answer for each feature gain full marks?
- Would you be able to recreate your answer for each feature in the time allowed in the exam?

Rework your answers until you can answer 'yes' to all these review questions. You may want to have a few goes at these answers until you get them perfect and have created a great revision resource.

A second type of question gives a diagram, picture or list and asks you to select one or more of the features shown, which could be glacial or coastline landforms, and explain how the feature(s) are formed. Again, this type of question is likely to be worth 10 marks.

Example question 2

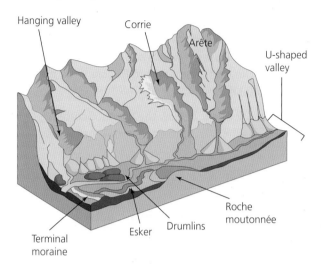

▲ **Figure 3.63** Upland glacial features

Select one erosional landform and one depositional landform from the diagram in Figure 3.63.

With the aid of annotated diagrams, explain the formation of each feature.

Example question 3

Look at Figure 3.64 and explain the processes and stages in the formation of a sea stack.

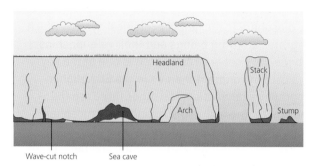

▲ **Figure 3.64** Coastal erosion features

Introduction

The biosphere is the global ecological system which integrates all living beings and their relationships with the physical environment. It is one of the key Physical Environment themes in the SQA Higher Geography examination; the other three are the lithosphere, the hydrosphere and the atmosphere. In this chapter we will concentrate on examining the biosphere through a study of the soil plus all the microbes, animals and plants found in this layer.

Before looking at the biosphere in detail, it is useful to first consider some facts about soil.

Soil influences many areas of our lives. It is an integral part of our ecosystem. The composition of the soil in an area has a direct effect on the plant and animal life there. It takes more than 500 years to form 2 cm of topsoil.

'A fully functional soil holds 3,750 tonnes of water per hectare, thus reducing the risk of floods. It holds pollutants to a certain extent. Soil stores around 10 per cent of the emissions of carbon dioxide. Just one gram of soil contains 5,000 to 7,000 different species of bacteria. A spoonful of soil can hold a substantial amount of living beings.

Seventy-five per cent of the Earth's crust is composed of silica and oxygen. Soil is a non-renewable natural resource. This should make us think of how much we value this resource. Damage to the soil can disturb nature's balance and prove a threat to life.

Scientists have found 10,000 types of soil in Europe and about 70,000 types of soil in the United States. (Fortunately we are going to have a look at only three soil types!)'

Adapted from: www.buzzle.com/articles/facts-about-the-soil.html

In order to fully understand the biosphere, this chapter includes some additional topics and general background information. The SQA question paper may include a question on the properties and formation processes of podzol, brown earth and gley soils.

Alternatively you may well be asked to draw an annotated diagram of a soil profile. The word 'podzol' comes from the Russian words *pod* = 'under' and *zola* = 'ash'. Gley also comes from Russian and means 'compact, bluish grey'.

Figures 4.1, 4.2 and 4.3 show the typical Scottish landscapes associates with each of the three soil

▲ **Figure 4.1** Podzol landscape

▲ **Figure 4.2** Brown earth landscape

▲ **Figure 4.3** Gley landscape

types that will be studied: podzols, brown earth and gley soils.

This chapter will consider the following:

- The biosphere and its importance
- Understanding soil
- Properties of soils
- Soil processes and formation
- Soil profiles
- Case studies of podzol, brown earth and gley soils, including their properties, location, creation processes, profiles and the human response

4.1 The biosphere and its importance

The biosphere really defines life on our planet. As geographers we use the word 'biosphere' to describe our living world. All microbes, animals and plants can be found in this layer. It extends from the upper areas of the atmosphere, where birds and insects can be found, down to the deep hidden caves in the ground or to the bottom of the oceans.

Every part of our planet, from the polar ice caps to the equator, features life of some form. We now know that microbes live deep beneath the Earth's land surface and that the total mass of such microbial life may well exceed all animal and plant life on the surface. The actual thickness of the biosphere on Earth measures several thousand metres in altitude, for example birds flying at 11,000 m down to the sludge at the bottom of the ocean tranches at a depth of 8,000 m.

No evidence of a biosphere has been detected beyond our planet (yet!).

The biosphere is believed to have evolved some 3.5 billion years ago. The origin of that life is a science worthy of study independently and involves biopoesis (life created naturally from non-living matter such as organic compounds) and biogenesis (life created from living matter). Geographers and geochemists define the biosphere as being the total sum of living organisms (biota or biomass).

Figure 4.4 shows the Earth as an example of a 'closed system', which in turn is made up of four 'open systems': the atmosphere, biosphere, hydrosphere and lithosphere. The arrows indicate flows between the systems.

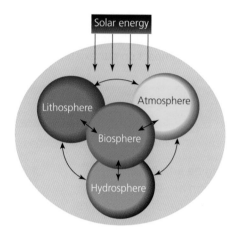
▲ Figure 4.4 Earth's systems

▲ Figure 4.5 Earth as seen from Apollo 17

Our biosphere is dependent on countless interactions of species and communities around the globe. The Earth is home to so many species and different kinds of biological communities because they have been able to adapt to almost every kind of environment – the darkness of the ocean depths, the cold conditions of Antarctica and the super-hot geothermal volcanic landscapes. It is this that gives our planet its greatest resource as well as its richness of plant and animal diversity. Our survival depends on our knowledge and skills to handle the increasing demands put on planet Earth. At this time of climate change, population growth and concern over the Earth's energy resources, the need to understand how the biosphere works has never been greater. We may well have altered the balance that once existed. Human activities are causing changes to the patterns and flows of energy and nutrient cycling, resulting in the extinction of animal and plant species. Evidence suggests that some 25,000 species are lost every year. How might this impact on our existence?

Task

David Suzuki, an environmentalist and scientist, says:

'I can't imagine anything more important than air, soil, water, energy and biodiversity. These are the things that keep us alive.'

1 What is the geographical background to this quotation? Do you agree?
2 How would you define biosphere?
3 Explain the difference between an 'open' and a 'closed' system.

4.2 Understanding soil

In Geography we study complex structures using models and a systems approach to try to simplify and help us explain what is happening.

Systems

Soils are part of what is called an open system, where materials and energy are gained and lost at its boundaries. The soil system has inputs, outputs, storage and recycling frames or loops. A system allows us to study and analyse relationships within the soil and all the variables. A soil system changes over time. A state of equilibrium means the **inputs** and outputs are in balance. If a soil is in balance then it is a **sustainable soil** and it is not being damaged in any way. However, if that balance is upset, due to either a change in the physical inputs, such as increased precipitation or drought, or a change in human inputs, such as increased farming demands, then there will be an imbalance and a loss of equilibrium. The system will no longer be sustainable. In addition to providing a stable base to support plant roots, soil stores water and nutrients required for plant growth. Fortunately, many farmers are choosing to use sustainable agricultural techniques such as conservation tillage, crop rotation and organic fertilisation in order to protect valuable soil resources.

Models

Peter Haggett's classic 1965 definition of a model still works really well today:

'A simplified version of reality, built in order to demonstrate the properties of reality.'

For example, we can create a laboratory model or a computer model showing a soil and subject it to change. We can vary the bedrock, precipitation and temperature, the slope and human activity and study

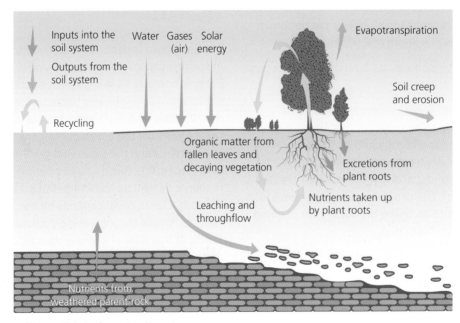

▲ **Figure 4.6** An 'open' soil system

the changes in the soil. Throughout your study of Higher Geography you will encounter models, for example relating to urban growth, population growth, rivers and valleys and development.

 Task

With reference to Figure 4.6, describe the inputs and outputs from the soil system.

You may have noticed some of the following:

Inputs:

- Water from the atmosphere or from rivers entering the system.
- Gases such as oxygen and nitrogen from the air.
- Energy and heat from the Sun (solar).
- Mineral nutrients from the bedrock.
- Respiration from soil animals and plants.
- Organic matter and nutrients from decaying plant and animal biota.

Outputs:

- Water lost back to the atmosphere through **evaporation** and **transpiration** (collectively known as evapotranspiration).
- Minerals and nutrients lost through downward **leaching** and out through the flow of water.
- Loss of soil and soil particles through soil creep and **erosion**.

Recycling (loops):

- Water in the biosphere is part of a wider system also known as the **hydrological cycle**.
- Organic matter and nutrients in autumn when the leaves are shed or when plants die and decompose due to the action and activity of micro-organisms.

4.3 Properties of soils

'To many people who do not live on the land, soil appears to be an inert, uniform, dark brown coloured, uninteresting material in which plants happen to grow. In fact little could be further from the truth.'

Brian Knapp, *Soil Processes* (1979)

'Essentially, all life depends upon the soil ... There can be no life without soil and no soil without life; they have evolved together.'

Charles E Kellogg

Soil can take thousands of years to form, yet can be destroyed by environmental change, abuse and carelessness in a matter of a few years. Soil can be created and destroyed by the weather, flooding or natural and man-made events in a few minutes.

The James Hutton Institute (www.hutton.ac.uk) give us a basic definition of soil as:

'... the solid material on the Earth's surface that results from the interaction of weathering, and biological activity on the soil parent material or underlying hard rock'.

The study of soils is called **pedology** (from the Greek word *pedon*, meaning soil or earth). Pedology regards soils as naturally occurring features and, in order to understand their properties and formation processes, we must look deeper at their characteristics, distribution, processes and methods of formation. The James Hutton Institute is a great source of information, with some superb posters showing the key UK soil types.

In this chapter three classic soil types will be explored in detail, namely podzol, brown earth and gley soils. On a global setting, thousands of different soil types can be recognised. The key variables are identified and described below.

While soil can be investigated by collecting samples from the surface, we need to consider a vertical cross section from the surface layer down to the solid rock underneath, also known as the bedrock. From this cross section it will be clear that distinct layers can be seen. These layers are known as **horizons** and the complete cross section is known as a soil profile.

A simple definition of soil emphasises the relationship and interaction of physical, chemical and biological processes, all of which vary according to different natural environments, climate, vegetation and relief.

What exactly is soil?

It is time to look down and grab a large handful of soil! Any soil from any part of the country will do. When the soil is separated you should be able to identify the following key components:

- weathered rock/mineral matter that is **inorganic** and which is based on broken-down bedrock, also known as **regolith**)
- water   • air
- soil biota, consisting of:
  - micro-organisms (bacteria, fungi and algae)
  - soil animals (protozoa, nematodes, mites, springtails, spiders, insects and earthworms)
  - plants living all or part of their lives in or on the soil
  - decayed organic matter (from leaves, roots, leaves, pine needles, dead vegetation).

The proportion of the components of a soil varies according to a combination of other influences. Table 4.1 and Figure 4.7 show the composition of three broad virtual soil categories:

- a 'typical' UK garden soil
- a desert sandy soil
- a wet clay marshy soil.

▼ **Table 4.1** Composition of soil (per cent by volume)

	UK garden soil (%)	Desert sandy soil (%)	Wet clay marshy soil (%)
Mineral matter (weathered parent rock)	45	84	40
Soil biota 1 (living and decayed organic matter)	10	5	10
Soil biota 2 (micro-organisms and soil animals)	5	1	2
Air	20	5	10
Water	20	5	38

▼ **Table 4.2** Summary: key features of three soil types

Soil type	Features
UK garden soil	A casual study of the soil in my back garden indicates a 'balanced' soil. Since it is of glacial moraine in origin there are many stones, pebbles and smaller particles. I can also see lots of fine minerals from the underlying sandstone. The soil is fairly heavy when I try to turn it with a spade, showing that it retains some moisture. This explains the higher percentage of water contained within it. Nevertheless, it has plenty of soil biota, with evidence of both animal, insect and organic matter. I can grow some excellent potatoes and the grass grows freely!
Desert sandy soil	Travel over the Atlas Mountains in Morocco and you will gradually find that the soil is influenced by desert and semi-desert conditions. A handful of the soil shows that it is very heavily influenced by the underlying weathered rocks. The small sand particles means that there is less space for air and the climate means that there is little water held in the soil. As a result of this there is little live or dead biota.
Wet clay marshy soil	As I travel towards Glasgow I pass over the Fenwick Moor near the Whitelee wind farm. If you explore the land and the soils here, the soil is wet and very sticky. The land is higher in elevation and the weather is more extreme. The land does not drain well. The soil contains more water with less air. This type of soil encourages hill peat to develop on the colder, waterlogged acidic soils.

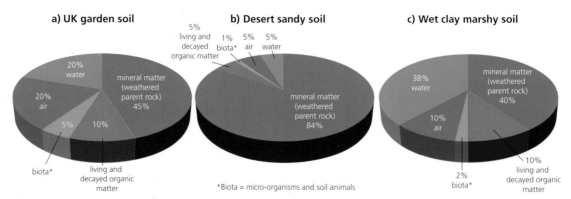

▲ **Figure 4.7** Soil type and percentage composition by volume: a) UK garden soil; b) Desert sandy soil; c) Wet clay marshy soil

Task

In your own words, describe what Table 4.1 and Table 4.2 show in terms of similarity and difference when analysing the soil composition of these three 'standard' soils.

Air and water exist in all soils. The percentage by volume can vary greatly from place to place and from time to time. Air and water occupy the voids (spaces) in all soils. The desert soil described in Table 4.2 has a low percentage of water (for obvious reasons) and the voids will be filled by atmospheric air. Consider the typical 'garden' soil described and how the soil may change from season to season. In the winter it may be very wet and even saturated. When spring comes round and as we move into summer the soil becomes drier. This is due to varying amounts of rain and the increasing rise in temperature which causes evaporation to take place from the soil. However, a dry, well aerated soil can quickly change and become saturated following heavy rain.

4.4 Soil processes and formation

We will now consider in detail the processes that influence the formation of soil. Certain factors will feature repeatedly (e.g. climate) but we also need to consider other interactions, such as the very strong relationship between soil and vegetation and biota.

Climate has a very strong influence on the vegetation found in an area. If we consider both temperature and precipitation then the correlation between these two factors is clear. A cool, wet climate supports vegetation that can grow in such a regime, for example coniferous trees. Alternatively, a warm and wet climatic regime will encourage tropical vegetation with diversity of trees, shrubs and plants. This in turn has a direct influence on the biota: live vegetation, insects and animals reflect the climate and the abundance or scarcity of vegetation. A rich array of biota, both alive and decayed, will be found in areas with positive features that encourage growth. Following on from this, the type of soil that occurs will reflect the climate, vegetation and biota of the area.

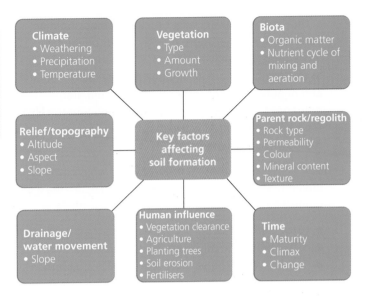

▲ Figure 4.8 Key factors affecting soil formation

Figure 4.8 illustrates the key factors that affect soil formation. As stated earlier, the SQA examination question will cover 'properties and formation processes of podzol, brown earth and gley soils', so make sure you understand and remember the information shown in Figure 4.8.

Formation process 1: Mineral matter from the parent rock/regolith

The solid bedrock is also known as the regolith. Often a soil develops from the minerals, colour and general characteristics of the underlying rock (also known as the parent rock) – this is known as residual soil. For example, in an area of sandstone the basic soil contains the particles, colour and features of the bedrock, while limestone or chalk produces soils that are alkaline, free draining and often light in colour. Rocks such as granite are rich in silica and are more likely to be acidic. Rocks such as basalt and gabbro are darker in colour and may have a reddish tinge due to the presence of iron oxides.

Since Scotland was heavily influenced by the action of glacial erosion, transportation and deposition, it has coverings of glacial moraine/glacial till throughout the country. The minerals, rocks and assorted debris contained within the soil may be local or may have been carried from a more distant source.

Minerals are affected by the rates and processes of weathering. Hard rocks such as granite or schist weather slowly and tend to result in what is called a 'thin soil'. However, softer rocks such as shale or sandstone weather more quickly and produce far more mineral particles. Bedrock material contributes to the depth, texture, drainage capacity (permeability) and quality (nutrient content) of a soil and also influences its colour. In most of Scotland and the UK, the bedrock material is the main factor in determining the general soil type.

Soils have a texture or a 'feel' to them which may be linked to the size of the soil mineral particles. As a guide we use the following terms:

- Clay – when the particle size is less than 0.002 mm
- Silt – when the particle size is 0.002–0.05 mm
- Sand – when the particle size is 0.05–2.00 mm.

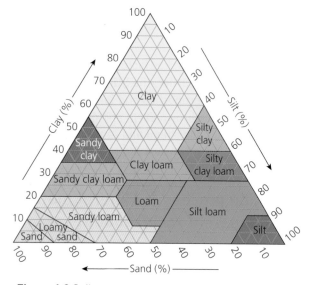

▲ **Figure 4.9** Soil texture

Task

1 The texture chart in Figure 4.9 shows 12 different soil types. Use this chart to identify the following soil types:

   a) Clay 60%; silt 20%; sand 20%
   b) Clay 20%; silt 40%; sand 40%

2 Explain how the parent material can influence the soil. You could mention:
   a) colour
   b) texture
   c) structure
   d) mineral composition
   e) permeability/drainage.

Formation process 2: Soil biota

Biota is what gives soil its life. One of my students described this as 'all the creepy and smelly things in the soil'. By that she meant soil bacteria, worms, plants, fungus, roots and insects. These organisms absorb nitrogen, mix and aerate the soil, hold the soil together and give it life. Decaying vegetation also provides the **humus** needed for the topsoil which is the most fertile zone of the soil. All the biota interact in what is described as the nutrient cycle. Plants take up mineral nutrients from the soil and return them to it after they die. Soil horizons are less distinct where there is much soil organism activity. Roots contribute dead roots to the soil, bind the soil particles together and redistribute and compress soil.

Human activity also affects soil and biota development through the addition of fertiliser, the breaking up of the surface of the soil by ploughing, draining and irrigating the land. Humans, through ignorance, also mistakenly may alter rates of soil erosion and degradation.

▲ **Figure 4.10** Healthy garden soil

Formation process 3: Climate

Climate determines the type of soil on a global scale. A study of the distribution of world soil types corresponds closely to patterns of climate and vegetation. Temperature and moisture affect weathering and leaching. Wind moves sand and other particles, especially in dry regions where there is limited plant cover. The type and amount of precipitation influence soil formation by affecting the movement of ions and particles through the soil, influencing the development of different soil profiles. Seasonal and daily temperature fluctuations affect the effectiveness of water in weathering parent rock material and affect soil dynamics. The cycle of freezing and thawing is an effective mechanism to break up rocks and other consolidated materials. Temperature and precipitation rates affect biological activity, rates of chemical reactions and types of vegetation cover. At low temperature soil formation is slower. Higher temperatures encourage decomposition.

Of major significance in the development of soils is the action of water moving vertically down and up through the soil. There are two processes to consider: leaching and capillary action.

When precipitation is greater than evapotranspiration then the movement of water in the soil is downwards. This is known as leaching – the removal of soluble minerals, salts and humus – which will be washed downwards from the soil and may accumulate in what is called the subsoil. In a country like Scotland, leaching is found in most of our soils. As water moves down through the soil, it carries away some of the nutrients that plants use, such as nitrates and sulphites. Under normal circumstances, minor levels of leaching occur with typical rainfall and the breakdown of organic materials on the surface resupplies the soil. In the case of excessive rainfall or irrigation, the effects of soil leaching can be more dramatic.

Alternatively when the rate of evapotranspiration is greater than precipitation then water and minerals in solution can be drawn upwards by the process of capillary movement. In a country with a strong seasonal variation in precipitation both processes can occur during a year.

Leaching impacts the soil because the dissolving and removal of soluble salts/bases reduces the agricultural output/yield of the soil. By adding chemical fertilisers, this problem can be overcome. When capillary action takes place the salts can be brought closer to and can be deposited on the surface of the soil. These salts can form an alkaline crust.

Once again, agricultural output will be reduced unless these salts are broken up and neutralised by the addition of other chemical fertilisers.

Associated with the climate is the impact of weathering. This refers to the breakdown and decomposition of rocks and minerals by the air, water, Sun and frost. Chemical weathering involves the alteration of the chemical composition of rock minerals, while physical weathering involves the breakdown of rocks into smaller and smaller particles.

Formation process 4: Time

Soils usually take a long time to be established. Research indicates that it can take some 2,500 to 10,000 years for a soil to reach maturity and at a depth to support farming. In Scotland it can take about 400 years for 10 mm of soil to develop. In Scotland the soils are relatively young since they are mainly post glacial. We know that soils tend to take on many of the features of the solid bedrock. However, over time changes take place as organic material will accumulate, there will be biotic activity and a reaction to the climate. Of course, there will always be exceptions to this time frame. Soils can quickly form and be fertile on newly deposited alluvium from a river or volcanic ash. Soils can also change over time.

Formation process 5: Relief/topography

Soils are certainly influenced by the land, the altitude, aspect and steepness of the slope. The most obvious variable is the height of the land above sea level. As altitude increases, the amount of precipitation, cloud cover, temperature, length of growing season and wind changes. The rate of soil accumulation will slow down. In Geography, 'aspect' refers to direction of slope. For example, in a country such as Scotland a south- facing slope tends to be warmer and drier than a slope that faces north. When the Sun is shining the heat will accumulate more on these south-facing slopes and the soils will be warmer. Settlement, farming and human activity generally favour such a slope direction.

Task

▲ **Figure 4.11** Rannoch Moor, Scotland

Suggest ways in which the relief and climate may affect soil formation in an area such as that shown in Figure 4.11.

A third factor of topography is the angle and steepness of a slope, which can have an impact on soil depth and drainage. Soils on steep gradients are likely to be thinner, less developed and drier than soils found on more gentle slopes. Also the greater the slope, the greater the water run-off and the greater the possibility of soil erosion. The more gentle the slope, the slower the movement of water down through the soil. Clearly there will be problems when the angle of slope is between 0 and 5 degrees and the soil is waterlogged.

Formation process 6: Drainage and water movement

Often relief and drainage will be considered together. Water not only flows down and across a slope but also moves vertically downwards through a soil. This movement of water has a significant effect on the soil through the processes of leaching and capillary action. For a soil to be living it needs to have a water flow. Stagnant water collecting in a badly drained zone will result in the development of gley and peaty soils. Figure 4.12 shows features of the relationship between slope and soil.

Water will move from an upper well-drained (shedding) site from which there will be surface water run-off and throughflow towards a lower receiving site where there will be an accumulation of water, minerals and organic deposits. A catena is where soils are related to the topography of the slope and is a sequence of soil types down the slope.

Formation process 7: Vegetation

Vegetation has a major influence on soil and it's important to remember its link with climate and biota activity. Vegetation can be natural (grass, trees, mosses and lichens) or planted (trees and crops). Generally the more vegetation there is, then the greater the influence on the soil development. More vegetation means more dead leaves, pines and roots (litter and humus).

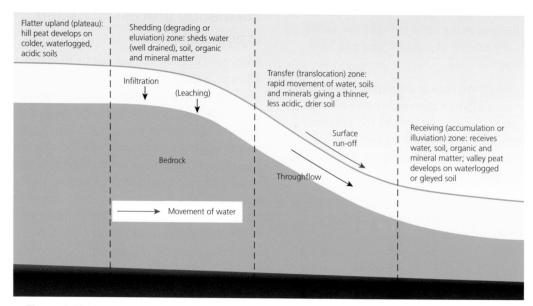

▲ **Figure 4.12** Model of the relationship between water movement, slope and soil

A surface which has little vegetation will contain less litter and humus and therefore less potential for the development of a soil. Soils are complex, but they have a logical sequence of development:

- **Decomposition**: the breakdown of plant materials into its basic organic components.
- Humification: the breakdown of plant remains leading to the formation of humus. In Scotland two forms of humus will be found:
  - mull humus: found under deciduous woodland (brown earth) where the plentiful plant matter is actively broken down by prolific soil biota
  - mor humus: found under coniferous woodland or heather moorland in cool, wet conditions. Breakdown is slow due to the limited activity of soil biota.

Formation process 8: Human influence and activity

People are increasingly able to hasten change to the landscape. If we start by considering Scotland then a survey will indicate that there are very few places where an 'original' landscape can be found, unaffected by human action. We clear forests, plough land, plant crops, create new forests, irrigate and drain land, create lakes, burn moors and fertilise the land. We cover the soil with roads, buildings and houses. It is in our interests to look after our soil and generally we do. Farmers are anxious not to over-cultivate the land or treat it so poorly that it loses its value, or damage it so that it becomes eroded or degraded. We must be careful not to allow chemical seepage or flooding to cause further degradation to the land.

Conclusion: soil formation processes

Soils develop and change over time. As has been shown earlier in this chapter, at any time up to eight different processes can be working to influence the development of a soil. To understand and appreciate how a soil can best be managed you need to be aware of these inter-relationships.

Although soils take thousands of years to develop they can be very quickly damaged by human action. We have seen that natural soil deterioration can be caused by leaching and erosion (by wind and water), but the balance of the soil is being upset further by human activities.

Although this section is not about soil erosion, it is useful to have a basic background to the main causes. It is easy to blame farmers, but there is a global increased demand for food because of ever-growing population numbers. Land is under pressure and farming is more intensive, with larger and more powerful machinery and more marginal land being cultivated.

As with many key resources we need to manage our soils. Soil erosion leads to a decline in output and productivity. As discussed earlier, soils vary in their capacity to retain fertility depending on climate, relief and drainage.

Task

1 Draw a model showing the key formation processes in the development of soils.
2 Climate is one of the key factors affecting soil formation. Explain the various processes involved.
3 Explain the difference between leaching and capillary action.
4 How do people influence the formation and sustainability of soils?

4.5 Soil profiles

Pick up any book on soils and you will see vertical cross-section diagrams. These are called soil profiles. A profile will contain different horizontal layers or horizons. Classic textbooks refer to three horizons. To that we need to add the surface layer of fresh vegetation and litter.

Before we consider in detail the three soils which form part of your Higher Geography study, it is necessary to consider what might be described as an idealised soil profile (Figure 4.13) so that you can recognise the key features of soil profiles (Table 4.3).

The soil profile model shown in Figure 4.13 consists of:

- the surface layer (sometimes referred to as the 'Ao' or 'O' horizon)
- the topsoil (A), subsoil (B) and regolith (C), with the underlying unaltered bedrock (sometimes referred to as the 'D' horizon).

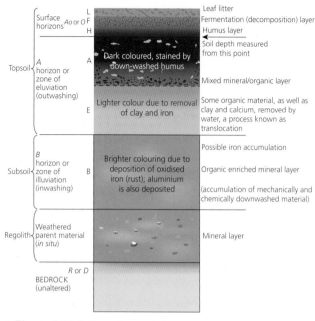

▲ **Figure 4.13** Soil profile model

Some words of caution. As this is a model you may never see a soil exactly like this one! However, it is a useful diagram because we can compare all soils against it and note similarities and differences. The following should be noted when comparing soils with the model in Figure 4.13:

● All horizons are not always present.
● The layers may not always be distinct.
● Soil will vary in depth.
● Bedrock characteristics vary from place to place.
● There may be human interference to change the horizons.
● Local conditions will greatly affect the profile, e.g. a seasonally frozen surface.
● Humus may be found mixed deeper in the soil.

It should be noted that all the categories that we recognise, the horizons we see and even the soil types shown on a global map, do not adequately reflect the complexity of the study of soils!

▼ **Table 4.3** Key features of the horizons contained in an idealised soil profile

Horizon	Key features
Ao or O horizon (surface horizon)	Surface layer of debris ('litter' of leaves, heather, pine needles and cones)
	Fermentation layer where organic material starts to decompose
	Humus (decomposed remnants of vegetation, bacteria and animals together with their waste products)
	Humification (decomposition of organic materials from worms, mites, bacteria and fungi)
	Can be acidic, with a pH of 4.0 to 5.0
	Live vegetation
A horizon (upper layer or topsoil)	Biological activity is at its maximum
	Humus and humification continues with accumulation
	Zone most affected by leaching and downward movement of soluble materials
	Zone of eluviation (the washing out of organic and mineral matter such as particles of clay)
	Rich in organic material
	Nutrient rich
	Fine textured
	Often described as the 'topsoil'
B horizon (subsoil)	Zone of accumulation or illuviation (in-washing), where clays, organic matter and minerals are washed from horizon A and re-deposited
	Less organic matter
	Coarser in texture
	Often darker brown/red in colour
	Often contains the 'iron pan', a layer that impedes drainage
	Horizons Ao, A and B make up what we consider to be the true soil
C horizon (regolith)	Recently weathered rock material (known as the regolith) from the bedrock
	Mineral layer or large and smaller particles lying on top of the underlying solid bedrock
	Lacking in nutrients, organic matter and 'life'

Translocation is the movement of material in solution or suspension from one horizon to another. The upper mineral horizon losing the material is the eluvial horizon, where leaching takes place (a process also known as eluviation). The lower horizon, where the accumulation of washed-down materials occurs, is the illuvial horizon.

 Task

1 What is a soil profile? Draw a model profile, clearly identifying the key layers.
2 How can people influence a soil to improve it? How is it possible for humans to cause a soil to degrade or be damaged?
3 Why is soil such an important resource?

Zonal and azonal soils

We have established that in a global context there is an enormous variety of soil types. This will not surprise you since there are a huge number of possible combinations of soil-forming factors.

Three broad soil groupings are recognised.

- Zonal soils: These mature soils reflect the development under some of the classic situations that have been introduced so far. They form under the influence of climate, vegetation and biota activity. Zonal soils have formed over a long period of time and have reached a stable state.
- Azonal soils: At the opposite end of the spectrum we have the azonal soils. These immature soils lack the development of a B horizon. They tend to be associated with recent glacial deposits, volcanic (tectonic) soils, scree slopes, sand dunes, salt marshes and even fresh river alluvium.
- Intrazonal soils: Intrazonal soils do not reflect climatic or vegetation standard influence. The associated soils may be very heavily influenced by one factor, such as the chalk soils found on escarpments in the south-east of England, or very poorly drained peat lands of the Scottish Highlands.

In SQA Higher Geography you are expected to have detailed knowledge of the properties and formation processes of podzol, brown earth and gley soils.

In the examination, for each of the three soil types, you should be able to complete the following tasks:

- Interpret a soil profile.
- Draw a simplified soil profile.
- Understand the properties and formation processes of each soil type.

This chapter includes additional background information on soils with regard to location, features of relief, drainage, climate, natural vegetation and the human response.

The James Hutton Institute (www.hutton.ac.uk) is an excellent source of information regarding soils in Scotland and in particular the data linked to characteristics and processes.

Case study: Key soil types – podzol, brown earth and gley

Refer to Table 4.5. It contains considerable detail about podzols, brown earth and gley soils. You need to study the table in relation to the previous section 'Soil processes and formation' (pages 129–133) and Figure 4.8 on page 129.

The soils in Scotland have all formed since the last glaciers melted around 11,000 years ago. Soils are always evolving by natural processes and by human activity. These interactions are responsible for the wide range of soils that exist in Scotland today. Due to the

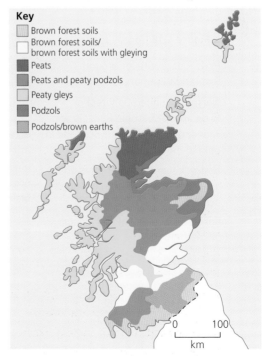

Key
- Brown forest soils
- Brown forest soils/ brown forest soils with gleying
- Peats
- Peats and peaty podzols
- Peaty gleys
- Podzols
- Podzols/brown earths

0   100
km

▲ **Figure 4.14** Generalised soil map of Scotland

▼ **Table 4.5** Summary and comparison of the three main soils

	Podzol soil	Brown earth soil	Gley soil
	 ▲ **Figure 4.15** Podzol profile 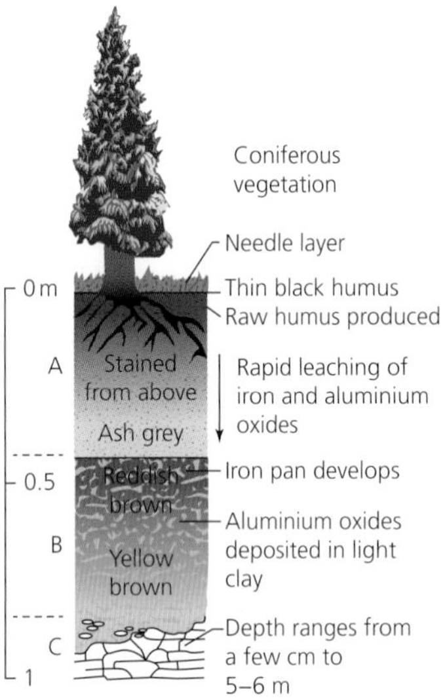 ▲ **Figure 4.18** Podzol profile	 ▲ **Figure 4.16** Brown earth profile 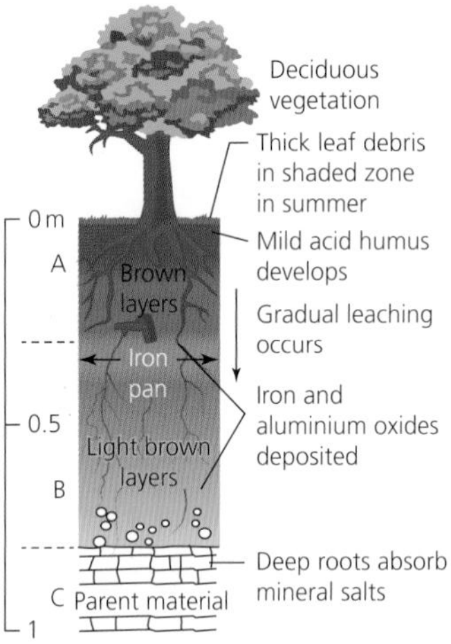 ▲ **Figure 4.19** Brown earth profile	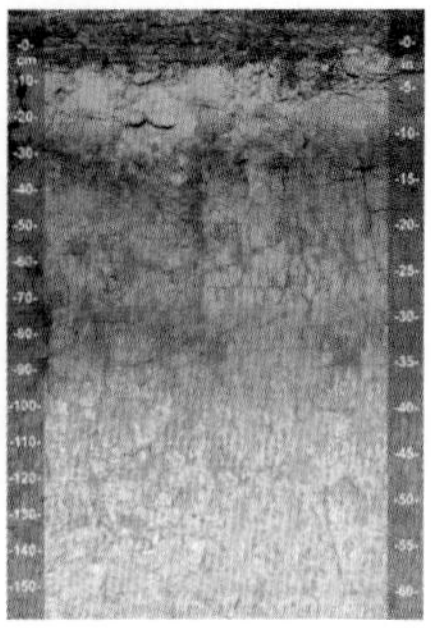 ▲ **Figure 4.17** Gley profile 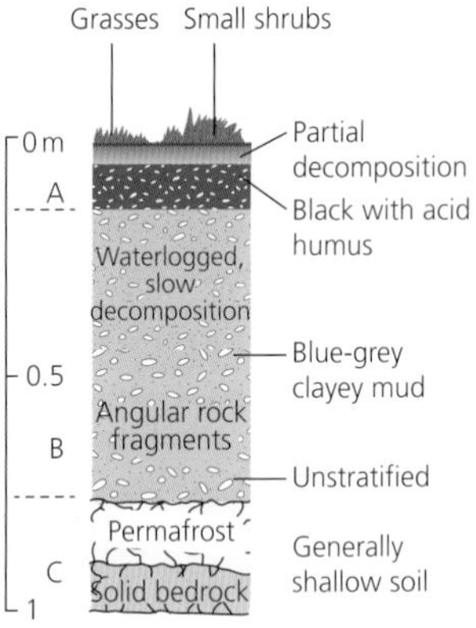 ▲ **Figure 4.20** Gley profile
% coverage	Podzol accounts for around 27% of Scotland's land areas.	Represents around 15% by area of soils in Scotland.	Covers around 34% of Scotland.
Location	Northern coniferous forest or taiga area of Europe. Podzols are widespread throughout Scotland in upland moorlands. Bedrock (parent material) is often acid rocks such as granite and schist. Formed since end of last ice age.	Temperate deciduous forest. In Scotland, their occurrence is restricted to the warmer, drier climate characteristic of eastern areas but they also occur in sheltered highland glens at lower elevations and on areas of base-rich parent materials. Formed since end of last ice age.	Gley soils are widespread in Scotland, linked to areas with impermeable subsoils and generally in areas with poor drainage, such as floodplains. Gleys are also found in the **permafrost** regions of northern Europe. Formed since end of last ice age.
Relief and drainage	Found at all elevations from sea level to the summit of the Cairngorms.	Often found in rolling land, hill sides, well drained low-lying areas.	Hollows and flat areas, wet and exposed areas, with poor drainage.

Figure 4.18 labels: Coniferous vegetation; Needle layer; Thin black humus; Raw humus produced; 0 m; A; Stained from above; Ash grey; Rapid leaching of iron and aluminium oxides; 0.5; Reddish brown; Iron pan develops; B; Yellow brown; Aluminium oxides deposited in light clay; C; 1; Depth ranges from a few cm to 5–6 m

Figure 4.19 labels: Deciduous vegetation; Thick leaf debris in shaded zone in summer; Mild acid humus develops; 0 m; A; Brown layers; Gradual leaching occurs; Iron pan; Iron and aluminium oxides deposited; 0.5; Light brown layers; B; Deep roots absorb mineral salts; C; Parent material; 1

Figure 4.20 labels: Grasses; Small shrubs; Partial decomposition; Black with acid humus; 0 m; A; Waterlogged, slow decomposition; Blue-grey clayey mud; 0.5; Angular rock fragments; B; Unstratified; Permafrost; Solid bedrock; C; Generally shallow soil; 1

▼ **Table 4.5** Summary and comparison of the three main soils *(continued)*

	Podzol soil	Brown earth soil	Gley soil
Climate	Long, cool or cold winters and short, mild to warm summers. Precipitation can be low to fairly heavy. Snow. Short and limited growing season.	Less extreme climatic conditions. Warmer conditions with lower precipitation, allowing more rapid decomposition. Favours vegetation growth.	Cold and wet. Although rainfall can be high with waterlogging, a gley soil can also form in lower rainfall areas where there is little warmth from the Sun and drainage is poor.
Natural vegetation	Associated coarse grassland, vegetation and coniferous woodland (pines, firs, spruce). The vegetation generally is tolerant of low-nutrient, low status soils. Litter based on needles.	Deciduous woodland. Litter based on plentiful leaf drop. Under natural conditions the soils would form under broadleaf forest which promotes rapid decomposition of plant residue and consequent recycling of plant nutrients.	Vegetation growth is limited due to the lack of warmth and waterlogging. Adaptive species such as mosses, lichens and marsh vegetation may occur.
Soil characteristics and processes	A heavy soil. Strong profile with clear horizons. A clearly defined iron pan. There is a build-up of iron and aluminium oxides and a 2–3 mm layer forms. Acidic soil from pines and needles. Humus formed is acidic (mor). Limited biota activity. Evidence of leaching. Litter based on coniferous vegetation. Presence of reddish-brown A horizon. Main process called podzolisation with strong influence from the climate, with lack of warmth and strong leaching of humus and oxides of iron and aluminium. Formation of an iron pan. Climate also discourages biota. Few animals, worms or bacteria to mix and aerate or fertilise the soil. Soil eluviates from the A horizon.	Horizons can be less distinct due to greater mixing. A milder, less acidic, slightly more alkaline soil. Litter from deciduous trees. Fertile soil with good root depth. Faster decomposition of litter and humus due to warmer temperatures and less water. Free draining. Lots of biota activity with action of worms, rodents and insects. A horizon is well aerated. Less leaching due to closer balance of precipitation and evaporation. Tree roots can penetrate to the C horizon encouraging mixing and aeration of the soil. Sufficient depth of soil parent material, which is neither extremely siliceous nor extremely calcareous, and which is **permeable** to permit free aeration.	Poorly drained, intrazonal soils. Waterlogged with shortage of oxygen in the pores. Bacteria action very slow. Blue grey in colour. A horizon is dark from organic matter. Slow decomposition so humus builds up. Poorly defined horizons. **Gleying** is the name given to the process when the pore spaces in the soil become saturated with water to the exclusion of air. The lack of soil movement and the impact of leaching means that a strong zonal soil occurs. Following waterlogging subsoil experiences lack of oxygen within pore spaces. Under such anaerobic conditions, insoluble iron oxides add a grey or bluish-grey colour to the subsoil. If this process is intermittent, **mottling** will occur when there is re-oxygenation of the subsoil.

▼ **Table 4.5** Summary and comparison of the three main soils *(continued)*

	Podzol soil	Brown earth soil	Gley soil
		A regime which promotes rapid decomposition of plant residues and recycling of plant nutrients. Where this happens the plant residues are broken down by fungi/bacteria to be incorporated into the soil by earthworms to create humus. High level of recycling of minerals. For example, the trees take in nutrients from the soil and return these nutrients following the autumn leaf fall.	
Human response	In the more remote areas this zone tends to be untouched by modern development. The iron pan restricts root penetration and waterlogging is a problem. Podzols are generally infertile and are physically limiting soils for productive use. They are extremely acid and lacking in nutrients. Where they are used for arable cropping, long-term fertilisation (lime) is required. They are also used for rough grazing (stock rearing) and for forestry or recreation (grouse moors).	Among the most fertile soils in Scotland. Due to the longer, warmer summers and the amount of biota activity, animal action and litter, this soil has far greater fertility than podzols. Given the deep nature of these soils, their free drainage and often high levels of natural fertility, brown soils are often cultivated. Occurs on gently undulating terrain, so is often in competition with settlement and industry.	Of limited agricultural potential. Main use is rough grazing (sheep) and forestry. People can influence gley soils by draining, ploughing and fertilising, but the yields and costs make it uneconomic to do so.

colder and wetter climate found in Scotland, our soils tend to be more organic, wetter and more leached, than soils elsewhere in the UK and Europe. It is possible to recognise some of the key soil types from the generalised soil map of Scotland shown in Figure 4.14 on page 135.

The James Hutton Institute has produced some very helpful summary sheets on podzol, brown earth and gley soils – go to www.hutton.ac.uk/learning/schools-colleges-and-universities/introduction-to-soils.

The study of the biosphere is often referred to as biogeography. As part of the background to the SQA Biosphere themes, it has been necessary to emphasise the importance of 'change' when studying soils and processes.

 Task

1   Write down three characteristics of a brown earth soil.
2   Draw a sketch profile of a brown earth and label the different horizons.
3   If you were looking for an example of a podzol, what key characteristics would you look for?
4   What type of vegetation is usually associated with podzols?
5   Draw a sketch profile of a podzol and label the different horizons.
6   Comment on the relief, climate and vegetation usually associated with the formation of gley soils.
7   Explain the formation processes connected with:
    a) podzols
    b) brown earth soils.

Summary

You have now completed this chapter on the biosphere and should be able to answer questions in the SQA Higher Geography examination Physical Environment topic, Biosphere. This chapter has provided you with additional background information on soils with regard to their location, features of relief, drainage, climate, natural vegetation and the human response. You should therefore have a breadth of knowledge as well as detailed information and understanding of the properties and formation processes of podzol, brown earth and gley soils.

SQA examination-style questions

Below are some examples of possible exam questions. These are by no means the only questions that could be asked but they give you an idea of what to expect. Some questions may be accompanied by diagrams or maps from which you can gather extra information to assist with your answer.

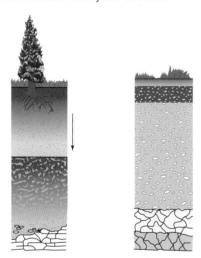

▲ **Figure 4.21** Selected soil profiles

1 Study Figure 4.21.
   a) Choose either the podzol or gley soil profile. Describe the characteristics of your chosen soil, including its horizons, colour, texture, soil biota and drainage.
   b) Explain how factors such as climate, natural vegetation, relief and drainage have contributed to the formation and characteristics of a brown earth soil.

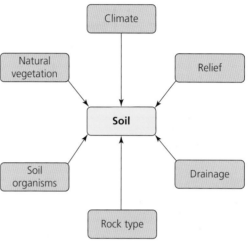

▲ **Figure 4.22** Physical factors affecting soil formation

2 Explain how the factors shown in Figure 4.22 affect the formation of:
   a) a gley soil *or*
   b) a podzol *or*
   c) a brown earth soil.

3 Figure 4.23 shows a cross section of soil types commonly found in Scotland.
   a) Explain the effects of climate, relief and drainage on the formation of the three soil types shown.
   b) Select one of the three key soil types and with the aid of an annotated diagram of a soil profile, show and explain the properties of the soil. (Your answer should mention horizons and movement of water.)

Did you notice that there is considerable overlap in terms of content in the three questions? What makes the Higher Geography examination a fair exam is that SQA describes very clearly what you need to know and then bases the question on that!

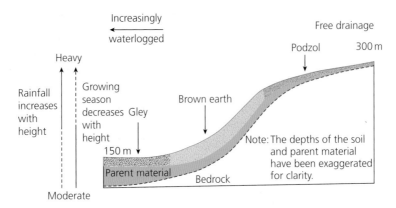

▲ **Figure 4.23** Cross section of soil types commonly found in Scotland

Chapter 5 Population

Introduction

What could be more important than a study of planet Earth and its people? Population is one of three Human Environment themes in the Higher Geography SQA course:

- Population
- Rural
- Urban

For the examination you may be given a question based on one or more of the following broad topics:

- methods and problems of data collection
- consequences of population structure
- causes and impacts relating to forced and voluntary migration.

SQA requires you to develop and apply geographical skills, knowledge and understanding of population issues within urban and rural environments in developed and developing countries.

As before, you will require additional background information to use your knowledge to best effect in the examination. Throughout the chapter there will be a variety of diagrams, tables, statistics and maps to enhance your application of geographical skills.

This chapter will consider the following:

- Global population, distribution and density
- Population indicators and definitions
- Global population change and growth
- Birth rates, death rates and natural increase
- Demographic transition model: population change, structure and impact
- Population pyramids
- Population structure
- Data collection
- Migration

5.1 Global population, distribution and density

Figure 5.1 is a population distribution map and Figure 5.2 is a population density map. Both show unevenness on a global scale.

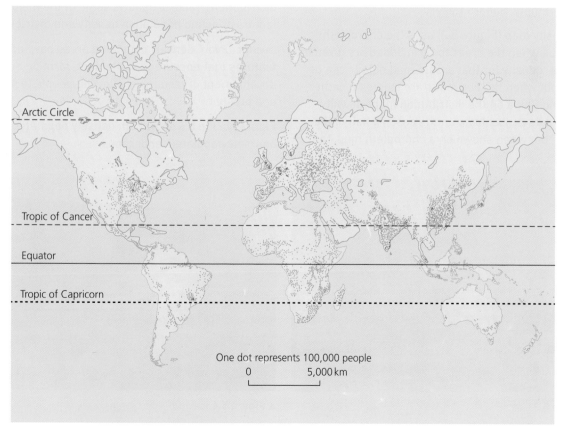

One dot represents 100,000 people

0   5,000 km

▲ **Figure 5.1** Population distribution map

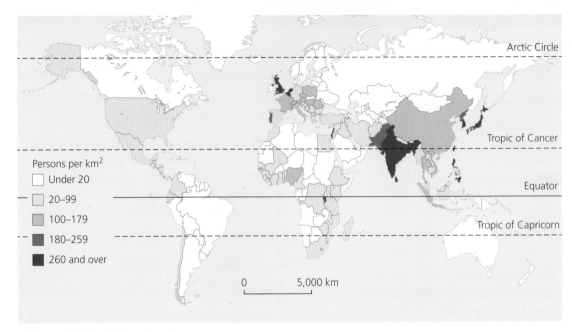

▲ **Figure 5.2** Population density map

Population distributions are often shown by a 'dot map', where every dot represents a certain number of people. In this case 1 dot represents 100,000 people. Such maps are visually strong. Study Figure 5.1 and you can pick out some very striking patterns, for example the densely populated Nile Valley in Egypt and the 'empty' Sahara Desert.

The density map (Figure 5.2) uses the choropleth technique when the areas to be included are given the 'average' density for that area. Small details can be picked out when the two maps are studied together. If you find China on the distribution map you will see the dots concentrate on the eastern half of the country, but when shown on a choropleth map, the whole country is shown as having a uniform density of over 100 persons per square kilometre (km²).

The two maps indicate that there are areas that are densely populated and areas that are sparsely populated.

Why is there such a variation in density and distribution? Table 5.1 shows some of the major factors affecting population density and distribution.

In conclusion: densely populated areas have positive features that encourage settlement, farming and development of resources, allowing people to survive and prosper.

Figures 5.3 to 5.6 show both densely populated and sparsely populated landscapes.

▲ **Figure 5.3** Cairo

▲ **Figure 5.4** Iceland

▼ **Table 5.1** Factors affecting population density and distribution

Factors	Sparsely populated areas	Densely populated areas
Physical terrain	High mountains. Steep slopes. Active volcanoes. High plateaux	Flat, lowland plains. River valleys
Climatic	Desert and semi-desert areas with low precipitation. Seasonal drought. Unreliability. Excessive rainfall. Very cold temperatures and short growing season. Excessively hot. High humidity	Areas that avoid extremes and are not too hot or cold, wet or arid. Rainfall should be reliable and a growing season long enough for at least one crop cycle to be completed
Soils	Thin unproductive mountain soils. Frozen and permafrost landscapes. Tropical leached soils. Seriously eroded soils	Ideally deep, humus-based soil, freely draining and sustainable. River alluvium-based deposits around rivers
Water	Lack of available water. Waterlogged land. Marshes	Populations need a reliable water base and supply. This can be from rivers, lakes, underground sources or canals
Vegetation	Dense tropical rainforest and cold barren northern coniferous forests	Temperate grasslands
Disease/insects	Areas that contain endemic diseases such as river blindness or insects associated with disease, e.g. malarial mosquitoes, tsetse flies	Areas where the climate does not encourage diseases or insects. Following industrial development, such issues can be eradicated
'Natural' resources	Areas lacking fertile soils or exploitable mineral resources such as oil or iron ore	Positive factors include energy or mineral deposits which can encourage industrial development
Communications/ accessibility/ remoteness	Usually as a result of other physical barriers such as mountains or dense vegetation. Cut off from the rest of the more 'developed' world	Where the construction of roads, canals, railways and airports is possible with little in the way of physical barriers
Economic opportunities	Areas that may lack the potential or opportunities to attract investment or development. May also include areas with subsistence economies	The key opportunities are in areas with farming, industry, resource development
Political/tensions/ war	Areas where development will not take place due to war or lack of control by the government	Countries with sound and stable political systems
Hazardous features	Earthquakes, volcanic activity, flooding, tropical storms	In Java for example, the volcanic lava flows quickly weather to become fertile

▲ **Figure 5.5** Himalaya Mountains

▲ **Figure 5.6** Shanghai

 Task

1   Look at Table 5.1 and choose five of the factors shown. Provide a named example for each of your chosen factors and a named location for both sparsely populated areas and densely populated areas. Then fill in a copy of the table below.

▼ **Table 5.2** Examples of factors associated with sparsely or densely populated areas

Factor	Sparsely populated areas	Densely populated areas

2   Explain the difference between population density and population distribution.
3   Discuss the relative strengths and weaknesses of a dot distribution map and a choropleth map.
4   Look again at Figures 5.3 to 5.6 and evaluate the reasons for either a low or high population density.

Let's do our sums. Our planet is made up of 70 per cent water, leaving 30 per cent land. Of this 30 per cent, only 11 per cent is 'perfect' for the cultivation of crops or has reasonable soils and is able to be productive for growing food. Of course, that does not mean that 89 per cent of our land surface is useless. As humans we are very good at making adaptations and getting the best we can from the available land.

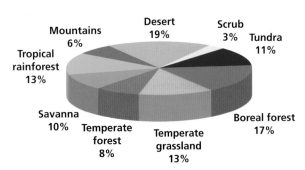

▲ **Figure 5.7** Pie chart showing percentage of land influenced by physical factors

5.2 Population indicators and definitions

Before we continue, we need to define a number of the most important words in our review of population Geography:

● **Demography:** Study of human populations
● **Birth rate (crude):** Number of live births per thousand people in a year
● **Death rate (crude):** Number of deaths per thousand people in a year
● **Life expectancy:** Number of years the average person born in a given year may expect to live
● **Infant mortality rate:** Number of infant deaths (under one year old) in a year for every 1,000 babies born
● **Natural increase:** Difference between birth rate and death rate
● **Fertility rate:** Average number of live births per woman in an area or country

Task

1 Distinguish between birth rate and fertility.
2 Why do you think infant mortality rate is a good example or indicator of a country's development?

5.3 Global population change and growth

The key idea is that populations are never static: they constantly change because of the influence of factors such as birth, deaths and migration. Population is therefore an example of an 'open system', with inputs, processes and outputs.

In this section on population change, considerable background information has been included because the factors influencing such change are the starting point for understanding and managing the consequences.

Here are some facts on global population:

- World population in 2018 was 7.6 billion.
- Of this 7.6 billion, 6.5 billion people live in less economically developed countries and 1.1 billion people live in more economically developed countries.
- The worldwide fertility rate is 2.5 but this ranges from 1.1 children in Taiwan to 7.5 children in Niger.

Task

▼ **Table 5.3** World population growth 1800 to 2014

Year	Population (billions)	Year*	Population (billions)
1800	1.1	1800	1
1850	1.4	1927	2
1900	1.7	1960	3
1950	2.6	1974	4
2000	6.1	1987	5
2014	7.2	1999	6
2050	9.3 (est.)	2011	7

*Year in which the population reached each billion total.

Look at Table 5.3. How would you describe this growth?

▲ **Figure 5.9** Newborn babies, China

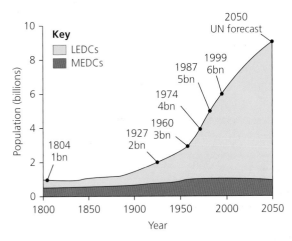

▲ **Figure 5.8** World population growth

▲ **Figure 5.10** Swimming pool in China

Since the 1950s the total population of our planet has grown at an exceptional rate (see Table 5.3). However, this growth has been uneven and some continents and countries have grown at faster rates than others. In general, Europe, North America and Australasia have experienced relatively low growth rates, while population growth in Asia, Africa and South America has been rapid. Of course, this is an oversimplification and fails to recognise individual countries, only continents.

Looking at Tables 5.3 and 5.4, we can see that:

- the population of the world has increased most rapidly in the last 50 years
- this will continue over the next 50 years, but at a lower rate of increase
- the less developed countries will continue to show the greatest increase in population
- the population of Europe is expected to reduce by 2050, while the population of Africa will increase
- fertility rates around the world will drop
- China and India will remain the two countries with the largest populations but it is expected that the population of India will overtake that of China within the next 20 years
- globally the rate of population growth is slowing down, although huge variations will continue.

Predictions of change will always be subject to debate. However, we also need to look to the future and make plans accordingly.

5.4 Birth rates, death rates and natural increase

Birth and fertility rates

When we study fertility and birth rates we consider the issues that influence both these key indicators. The crude birth rate is the number of live births per 1,000 people in a given year. This basic statistic does not take into consideration the sex and age of the population. We refine this definition through the **general fertility rate** – the number of live births per 1,000 women aged 15–44 for a given year. Fertility in demography is simply the average number of live births per woman in an area. **Age-specific fertility rate** refers to the number of births during a year to women in a particular age group, usually per 1,000 women in a five-year age group at mid-year. The **total fertility rate** refers to the average number of children that would be born per woman if all women lived to

▼ **Table 5.4** Selected population characteristics

	2017 population (million)	Births per 1,000 population	Deaths per 1,000 population	Rate of natural increase (%)	% of world's population 2017	Projected population 2030 (estimate)	% of world's population 2030	Density (people per /km²)
World	7,240	20	8	1.2	100	8,450	100	46
More developed	1,250	11	10	0.1	17	1,295	14	15
Less developed	5,990	22	7	1.4	83	7,155	86	56
Africa	1,136	36	10	2.5	16	1,637	20	37
North America	350	12	8	0.4	4	396	4.6	18
South America	618	18	6	1.2	8.5	710	8.4	30
Asia	4,351	18	7	1.1	61	4,907	59	98
Europe	741	11	11	0	10	746	8	20
Oceania	39	18	7	1.1	0.5	48	0.5	4.5

Source: Variety of sources

▼ **Table 5.5** Key fertility and mortality statistics for selected countries (2017)

	Crude birth rate/1,000 2017	Fertility: number of babies per mother	Crude death rate/1,000 2017	Infant mortality rate/1,000 2017	Life expectancy (years) 2017	Growth rate (death rate – birth rate/1,000)
UK	12	1.9	9	3.9	81	3
India	22	2.4	7	44	65	15
Mali	42	6.1	13	58	51	29
China	12	1.6	7	15	76	5
Niger	50	5.6	11	54	56	39

Source: Variety of sources

the end of their childbearing years and bore children according to a given set of age-specific fertility rates.

Overall fertility is the critical factor of population change and is more significant than mortality (death) and migration when considering population change. On a global setting the rates vary significant. We can also use these key population statistics to measure change over time, for example we can follow the rate of change in a country such as Scotland over any given time period.

Factors influencing fertility

A wide range of factors influence fertility rates, including religious, social, economic, family relationships and political, and many of these overlap.

Birth rates and fertility rates remain high when:

- children are viewed as economic assets because they work on a farm (e.g. Bangladesh) or in factories (e.g. Philippines)
- children can be used to care for parents as they get older (e.g. Mali) and as a form of 'family insurance'
- social pressures exist because children are viewed as an indicator of virility and as a status symbol (e.g. Mexico)
- it is important to continue the family name (e.g. South Korea)
- religious influences encourage fertility (e.g. Islam and Roman Catholicism)
- women have 'lower status' or opportunities for education (e.g. Afghanistan)
- early marriage is encouraged in less developed rural areas (e.g. Burkina Faso)

- there is poverty (e.g. Senegal)
- there are areas with high infant mortality (e.g. Ethiopia) or high death rates
- there is little programmed birth control (e.g. Niger)
- a country has a cultural tradition that demands high rates of reproduction. For example, in Vietnam 90 per cent of women who had two children did not want any more, while in Chad the figure was 5 per cent.

Birth rates and fertility rates drop when:

- infant mortality and death rates drop (e.g. Jordan)
- schooling becomes compulsory, especially for girls (e.g. Morocco)
- women achieve increasing equality and status (e.g. Tunisia)
- there is increasing affluence and economic growth (e.g. Malaysia)
- men and women marry later (e.g. Vietnam)
- the costs of raising children become an issue (e.g. USA)
- there is widespread use of and acceptance of birth control (e.g. Japan). In Brazil, too, contraception is practised by 75 per cent of women, up from 53 per cent in 2000
- improving health programmes are introduced (e.g. India)
- government policies strongly encourage smaller families (e.g. China).

Overall, it is difficult to name a country that has not experienced a drop in birth rates and fertility rates in the last 30 years.

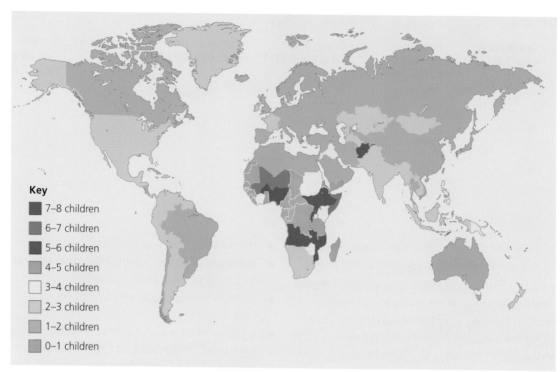

▲ **Figure 5.11** Global fertility rates

Key
- 7–8 children
- 6–7 children
- 5–6 children
- 4–5 children
- 3–4 children
- 2–3 children
- 1–2 children
- 0–1 children

Task

Compare, contrast and explain the fertility rate patterns shown for Africa and South America.

Mortality rates

The crude death rate is the number of deaths per 1,000 people in a given year, but this basic statistic does not take into consideration the age of the population. For example, in an **ageing** population country such as Japan, there will clearly be more deaths per 1,000 people since there are many older people. In a youthful population country such as Morocco, there are very few older people. There is no doubt that overall Japan is a richer and healthier country than Morocco. We refine this definition through the **age-specific death rate**. Here we work with the number of deaths per 1,000 people aged over a certain age, or between selected ages for a given year. The most effective of the age- specific measures is the infant mortality rate, but once again, globally the rates vary significantly. As with the birth and fertility rate, we can use mortality statistics to measure change over time or over a given time period.

The global trend in the last 20 years has been a marked decline in mortality as measured through increased life expectancy and life expectancy at birth, improved measures of falling infant mortality and falling death rates. It is difficult to find a country which has not experienced a decline in these indicators, which can be taken to mean that real social progress is at last being made.

Death rates and mortality rates remain high when:

- investment in areas such as health, education, welfare, wealth and pension provision is limited
- there is famine (e.g. Sudan), poverty (e.g. Bangladesh), war (e.g. Syria), drought (e.g. north-east Brazil) and disease such as AIDS (e.g. Zambia)
- internal civil war occurs (e.g. Afghanistan and Syria)
- there is overcrowding and insufficient infrastructure relating to water, sanitation, power and transport (e.g. shanty towns of India, South Africa, Brazil).

Death rates and mortality rates drop when:

- there is increased and sustained investment in health, education, welfare, wealth and pension provision (e.g. China)
- levels of infrastructure in water, sanitation, housing, power and transport continue to increase
- there is increased funding for medical care, hospitals, child vaccinations and the implementation of medical advances (e.g. Sri Lanka)
- there is improved diet and nutrition (e.g. Croatia)
- the output from agriculture improves (e.g. Taiwan)
- there are general medical and environmental improvements.

There has been an explosion in the global population over the last 30 years. Considering both mortality and fertility measures, all the indicators seem to point at lowering rates for both. However, a closer analysis of the data indicates that at a global level there has been a greater reduction in all mortality statistics than in fertility measures.

5.5 Demographic transition model: population change, structure and impact

'In the last 200 years the population of our planet has grown exponentially, at a rate of 1.9% per year. If it continued at this rate with the population doubling every 40 years, by 2600 we would all be standing literally shoulder to shoulder.'

Professor Stephen Hawking

In the 1930s, Warren Thomson developed the **demographic transition model (DTM)**, which not only attempted to explain but also predict population change in countries (Figure 5.12). The DTM has been brought up to date and is still a useful guide today. It is a valuable model to refer to when considering different population structures.

Originally the DTM showed four stages which attempted to show changing birth and death rates together with the subsequent change in population growth. It could be applied to an individual country over a period of time, as

Task

▼ **Table 5.6** Demographic data comparison of four countries

	Crude birth rate per 1,000 1980	Crude death rate per 1,000 1980	Natural increase (%) 1980	Crude birth rate per 1,000 2017	Crude death rate per 1,000 2017	Natural increase (%) 2017
Scotland	12	10	0.2	11	9	0.2
Nigeria	54	17	3.7	39	13	2.6
India	39	12	2.7	22	7	1.5
Japan	12	6	0.6	8	10	-0.2

▼ **Table 5.7** Demographic data for Morocco and Taiwan

	Crude birth rate per 1,000	Fertility rate 2017 – births per woman	Crude death rate per 1,000	Infant mortality rate	Life expectancy
Morocco	22	2.28	6	29	71
Taiwan	8	1.1	7	27	83

1 Using the information in Table 5.6, comment on the following changes:
   a) Nigeria 1980 and 2017
   b) Japan 1980 and 2017.

2 Comment on and explain the following changes:
   a) birth rate in India 1980 and 2017
   b) death rate in Nigeria 1980 and 2017.

3 Using the information in Table 5.7, describe and comment on the differences in the demographic data for Morocco and Taiwan.

well as used to plot all countries in the world at a fixed time. It also allowed comparisons between countries. The model is generally easy to understand since it is flexible over time and rates. However, more recently the model failed to predict what was happening in parts of Europe and so a fifth stage was added.

- Birth rates in several countries continued to drop with very low levels of fertility. Stage 5 predicted a drop in population numbers.
- A basic feature is that when birth rates are higher than death rates then there will be population growth and when death rates are above the birth rates then there will be a drop in the population.
- The model was devised in Europe (we call this Eurocentric since it has a bias towards the way we look at issues from a European perspective) and accounted for European-style changes. Recent evidence suggests that not all countries will change in this manner. For example, the pace of change will be faster in Singapore and Malaysia following very rapid industrialisation.

- The model does not include the impact of migration, which was significant, for example in Australia during the 1980s and 1990s and in the UK in the 2010s.
- The DTM also failed to predict the impact of centralised government policies such as the 'one child' programme in China.
- The DTM is essentially an optimistic review of population change. It anticipates and explains how population will grow, but in time, the population 'explosion' will become controlled and a sustainable pattern will emerge.
- More recently it has been noted that some countries may go backwards. For example, in Zimbabwe death rates have shown an increase, partially due to the impact of AIDS/HIV, famine and political strife.

A note of caution: in this section of the book there are many sets of statistics, for many countries, covering many years. It is important to remember that there are numerous contrasting viewpoints and sets of data available. The data is important, but focus on *general trends* rather than rigorously adhering to one set of statistics.

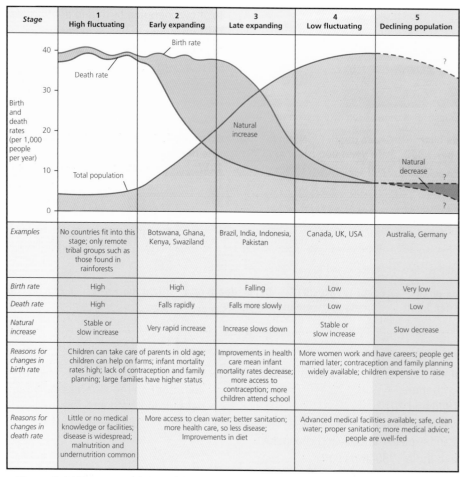

▲ **Figure 5.12** Demographic transition model

▼ **Table 5.8** Key features of the five stages of the demographic transition model

Stage 1 High fluctuating	Birth and death rates fluctuate at a high level, resulting in a small variable population growth. Causes of high birth rate: ● minimal birth control or family planning ● having many children in order to replace those that die in infancy in the hope that at least some will survive to adulthood ● many children are needed to work on the land ● religious beliefs. Causes of high death rate (especially among children): ● disease, war and plague (e.g. bubonic cholera, kwashiorkor) ● famine, unreliable food supplies and poor diet ● poor hygiene and impure water ● limited access to doctors, drugs and hospitals. Examples: Remote native groups, e.g. in the Amazon rainforest now/Scotland pre-1750 Example: Birth rate around 35/1,000; death rate 35/1,000; growth rate 0/1,000
Stage 2 Early expanding	Birth rates remain high but death rates fall rapidly, leading to a rapid population growth. Causes of high birth rate as above. Causes of falling death rates: ● improved medical care with vaccinations, new drugs, hospitals and more professional medical staff ● improved sanitation, hygiene and water supply ● improvements in food production, both in quality and quantity ● improved transport ● a decrease in **child mortality**. Examples: Zambia and Uganda now, Scotland 1750–1875 Example: Birth rate around 35/1,000; death rate 15/1,000; growth rate 20/1,000 or +2%
Stage 3 Late expanding	Birth rates are now dropping rapidly while death rates continue to fall slightly, resulting in slowly increasing population growth. Causes of falling birth rates: ● family planning with more acceptability and availability of contraceptives, sterilisation, abortion and government incentives and policies ● a lower child and infant mortality rate, leading to less pressure to have so many children ● increased industrialisation and mechanisation, so fewer labourers needed, as in India ● increased desire for material possessions (e.g. cars, holidays) and so children regarded more as an economic cost than a benefit ● an increased desire for smaller families ● emancipation of women, enabling them to follow their own career rather than simply perceived as child bearers ● government policies ● increasing personal wealth ● more compulsory schooling, making the rearing of children more expensive. Death rates remain low as above, but with continuing improvements in health, diet and sanitation. Examples: Cuba, India now, Scotland 1875–1945 Example: Birth rate around 13/1,000; death rate 10/1,000; growth rate 3/1,000 or +0.3%
Stage 4 Low fluctuating	Birth and death rates remain low and fluctuating, leading to a limited population change. Generally birth rates remain higher than death rates. Birth rates remain low, often due to increased access and demand for luxury goods, e.g. holidays, cars and electronic items. More women choose to work. Examples: Canada now, Scotland 1945–2000 Example: Birth rate around 10/1,000; death rate 10/1,000; growth rate 0/1,000

▼ **Table 5.8** Key features of the five stages of the demographic transition model (*continued*)

Stage 5 Declining population	Both birth and death rates remain low. However, death rates, with an ageing population, tend to be slightly higher, resulting in a declining population.
	Choice has been an important factor in births. A trend noted in several European countries is that with growing wealth, improved levels of education and equality for women, couples are making an informed decision to have far fewer (if any) babies increasingly later in life. Other factors include: social acceptance now favours small families rather than the norms of the previous periods; greater financial independence for women; an increase in non-traditional lifestyles, such as same-sex marriages and a rise in acceptance of the concept of being fulfilled yet childless.
	Medicine has perhaps also broadly reached the limits of how far we can go in terms of saving and prolonging life, and in the more developed world death rates are about as low as they can go. We are living longer and longer.
	Examples: Germany, Italy, Spain and Scotland (excluding migration 2000 to present)
	Example: Birth rate around 9/1,000; death rate 10/1,000; growth rate -1/1,000 or -0.1%

When answering exam questions based on the demographic transition model, try to remember the following:

- Note that there are two 'rate' lines drawn on the graph with five sector names. These lines show the birth and death rates over the years. The gap between the birth and death rate lines show the growth rate of the population. Also the five stages are usually marked and named as 'high fluctuating', 'early expanding', 'late expanding', 'low fluctuating' and 'declining'.
- The data can be overwhelming, so try to 'chunk down' the information into more easily digestible pieces of data.

Dependency ratio

The **dependency ratio** is calculated by using the formula below:

$$\text{Dependency ratio} = \frac{(\% \text{ children } 0\text{–}14) + (\% \text{ the 'aged' } 65+)}{\% \text{ economically active adults } 15\text{–}64} \times 100$$

'Economically active' refers to those aged 15–64, while 'dependents' refers to those aged 0–14 (children) and those aged over 65 ('aged'). Figure 5.14 shows global variations in dependency ratio.

A high dependency ratio can cause serious problems for a country because a large proportion of its government's expenditure will be on health, social security and education. These services are most used by the youngest and the oldest in a population.

It is the active population that generally provides the money for pensions, education and hospitals, which tend to be most heavily used by the young and the old.

Nevertheless, the dependency ratio ignores the fact that the 65+ are not necessarily dependent (an increasing proportion of this group is in active work) and that many of those of 'working age' are actually not working. Remember, too, that in some of the less developed areas of the world, children below 15 will be actively employed, so always regard dependency ratios with a degree of caution.

▲ **Figure 5.13** Egyptian children: 40 per cent of the population of Egypt is aged 15 or under

5.6 Population pyramids

We are now going to look at **population pyramids**. The standard pyramid carries information on age, gender and population structure in an area or country. A population pyramid can be used to compare countries, to show change in one country over time and even make a visual prediction for the future.

Population pyramids are helpful as they provide us with a visual method of showing the relative proportion of the population who are economically active and those who are dependents.

The diagram is drawn to show the shape and structure of the population in terms of percentage or numbers, with separate columns for men and women, **age structure** in five-year bands/cohorts (0–4, 5–9 and so on). The structure of a pyramid depends on birth and death rate and 'in and out' migration.

Task

1 Look at Figure 5.14 which shows the dependency ratio by country.
   a) Compare and contrast the information shown for Africa and Europe.
   b) Comment and suggest reasons for the differences.

2 Study Table 5.9. Copy and complete the figures for dependency ratios, then comment on your findings.

▼ **Table 5.9** Population comparison of countries

	% population aged 0–14	% population aged 15–64	% population aged 65+	Dependency ratio	Comment
Country A	15	66	19		
Country B	44	51	5		

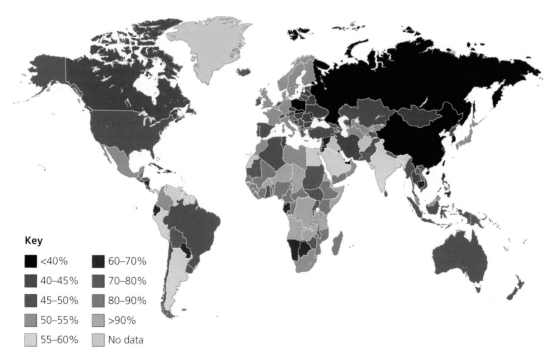

Key
- <40%
- 40–45%
- 45–50%
- 50–55%
- 55–60%
- 60–70%
- 70–80%
- 80–90%
- >90%
- No data

▲ **Figure 5.14** Global map, showing dependency ratio by country

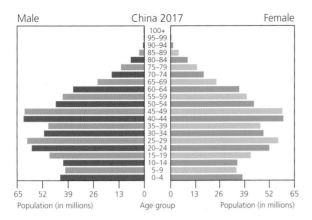

Male   China 2017   Female

65 52 39 26 13   0   0 13 26 39 52 65
Population (in millions) Age group Population (in millions)

▲ **Figure 5.15** Population pyramid, China 2017

Source: Adapted from US Bureau of the Census International Database

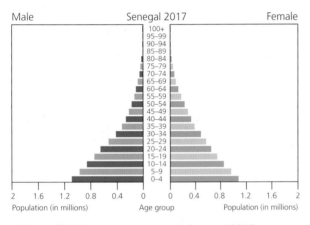

Male   Senegal 2017   Female

2 1.6 1.2 0.8 0.4 0   0 0.4 0.8 1.2 1.6 2
Population (in millions) Age group Population (in millions)

▲ **Figure 5.16** Population pyramid, Senegal 2017

Source: Adapted from US Bureau of the Census International Database

The seven key points when describing and explaining a population pyramid:

1 Note the country and the date.
2 Note horizontal axis: males usually to the left and females to the right.
3 Note the horizontal scale: percentages or raw numbers in millions
4 Note the age cohorts (usually in five-year bands).
5 Note the general shape.
6 Identify percentage in age cohorts. We suggest the young aged 0–14, the aged (usually 65+), the percentage of 85+. Then calculate the dependency ratio.
7 Look for gender differences, e.g. with the elderly, are there more women than men? Also are there more baby boys than girls?

Task

Using this seven-point scale, complete your analysis of the population pyramids for China and Senegal (Figures 5.15 and 5.16).

In summary, Figure 5.17 shows the five classic pyramid structures for the five stages of the demographic transition model (described in Table 5.10).

Population pyramids can show in detail the impact of significant social events, for example outward and inward migration, war, ageing, famine, population control programmes, the impact of a vaccination programme and even gender imbalance.

5.7 Population structure

Some countries, especially more developed countries such as the UK and Japan, are now experiencing an ageing population. Newly developing countries, however, often have a youthful population structure. We now look at the consequences of both an ageing and youthful population structure.

Consequences and issues of an ageing population structure

- In the UK today, when a person retires at 65 he/she would expect to live at least another 20 years.
- In a country such as Scotland, an ageing population implies a high dependency ratio.
- With so many older people, it is recognised that eventually there will be a need for greater provision of geriatric care, all of which will lead to extra costs for individuals, local authorities and the government.
- One way of dealing with this problem is to raise the retirement age and possibly raise tax contributions from the active working population. This is happening now! For example, a young teacher today may now have to work until they are at least 70 before accessing their pension.
- With more aged dependants in the population, there is more of a challenge on the working population to provide the money required to support them, for example state pensions are paid for by the working population through taxes.

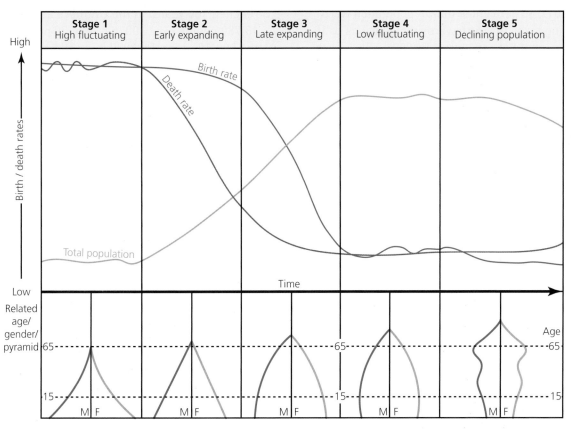

▲ **Figure 5.17** Demographic transition model and related population pyramids

▼ **Table 5.10** Five stages of the demographic transition model and related population pyramids (Figure 5.17)

Stage 1 High fluctuating	Stage 2 Early expanding	Stage 3 Late expanding	Stage 4 Low fluctuating	Stage 5 Declining population
Key features:	Key features:	Key features:	Key features:	Key features:
• Broad-based pyramid • High birth and high death rates • Short life expectancy • Very few old people • Youthful population • Very high child mortality	• Still a broad-based pyramid with high birth rates and falling death rates; mortality still high; slightly longer life expectancy • More people living into middle age	• Declining birth rates indicated by narrower base and continuing lower death rates and longer life expectancy showing with the increased percentage of older people	• Low birth rate • Low death rate • In balance with few fluctuations • Higher dependency ratio • 'Bullet-shaped' • Narrow base • Fewer young • Low child mortality • Increasing and high percentage of elderly • More older women than men • Long life expectancy	• A very narrow-based pyramid, showing very low fertility rates • Middle and top of pyramid shows an ageing population with high percentage of older people • Long life expectancy

- In 2017, 60 per cent of the UK population were paying taxes that go towards the pensions of 19 per cent of the population. By 2030, only 56 per cent of the population will be of working age, but the taxes they pay will have to pay for the pensions of 27 per cent of the population.
- There is concern over the inability of countries such as Britain to have enough people of working age, as there could be a shortage of workers.
- Young people need to plan for their retirement early in their working life.
- There will be less demand for other services such as maternity health care and nursery/primary education.
- A positive solution is to encourage migration into the country, attracting younger workers and their families.
- Another positive solution would be to encourage women to have more children. Various benefits and credits can support families if they take this step.
- Many elderly people in the UK at the moment live in poverty, relying on a state pension. It seems unlikely that this will change. At the same time there are many within this ageing population with savings, work and state pensions and investments. Many continue to work well into their 70s and contribute to the economy through taxes.
- Older people increasingly provide substantial child support for their own children and grandchildren.
- In 2017, more than 7,500 people received a congratulations card from the Queen for having reached 100 years. In the UK there are now 13,780 people over 100, a rise of 70 per cent over the last 10 years. By 2037 it is estimated that there will be 111,000 centenarians. The writer of this chapter will have to wait until 2055 before he gets his card!

 Task

With reference to at least one named country, what are the consequences of an increasingly aged population?

Consequences and issues of a youthful population structure

- In a country such as Senegal, a youthful population implies a high dependency ratio.
- A high proportion of national income will need to be spent on education and child health care.
- The youthful population will soon move into the active cohort requiring jobs, health care, houses, power and many other services. It may be that in the poorer areas of the world, there are insufficient economic resources to support this.
- A young population will eventually form the active working population, vital for the development of that country.

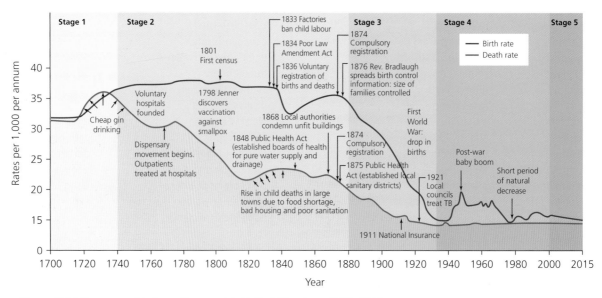

▲ **Figure 5.18** Demographic transition model: United Kingdom, 1700–2015

Task

With reference to at least one named country, what are the consequences of an increasingly youthful population?

Case study: UK and Scotland

As Figure 5.18 indicates, the UK has experience of all five stages of the DTM. Broadly speaking, the DTM for Scotland is very similar.

- Before 1750, Scotland had high birth and death rates. We know that during the sixteenth and seventeenth centuries there were plagues and famines that severely checked population growth.
- From 1750 to 1875 Scotland saw a marked drop in death rates as a result of improvements in diet, nutrition and water supplies, as well as an improvement in food supplies. However, urban areas remained unhealthy and birth rates remained high. There were some breakthrough medical advances, for example Edward Jenner invented the first vaccine in 1789 for smallpox and within three months 100,000 people had been vaccinated.
- From 1875 to 1940, Scotland continued to experience a decline in the death rate; there was acceptance of family planning and the country benefited from improvements in health care and medical advances. The 1920s was a time of medical advances, including the development of insulin to treat diabetes, vaccines for diphtheria, whooping cough, TB and tetanus and the discovery of penicillin. However, by now there were signs of a marked decline in the birth rate. At the beginning of this period, on average women were having 6 babies and by 1945 the average was 2.5. The impact of two world wars and high unemployment were also factors that led to fewer babies being born.
- From 1940 to 2000, Scotland benefited from medical advances that continued to keep death rates low. However, increasingly throughout this period birth rates dropped as a result of economic advances, the increasing status and aspirations of women, social changes which led to people having children later in life and the growing impact of consumerism (e.g. cars, holidays) on quality of life and having children. The causes of death moved away from childhood illnesses and disease towards the diseases of affluence, such as cancer, stroke and heart disease.
- Since 2000, Scotland has begun to experience many of the elements of the new, fifth stage of the DTM, with a decline in the population. The average number of births to each woman in Scotland is now 1.8, a figure below that of sustainability.

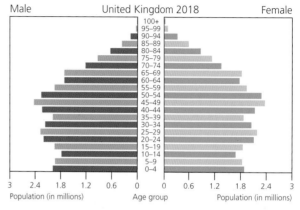

▲ **Figure 5.19** Population pyramid of the UK 2018 (n=66 million)

Task

Study Figure 5.18, the demographic transition model as applied to the UK, and Figure 5.19.

1 Describe and explain how birth rates and death rates have changed since 1800.
2 Select any three of the five stages and draw a sketch pyramid of the population structure at those times.
3 As the UK is now within Stage 5 of the DTM, what is the impact of an ageing population?

Case study: Population problems in the USA and Japan

Read the following articles about population and then answer the question below.

'About that population problem' by Jeff Wise

'The world's seemingly relentless march toward overpopulation achieved a notable milestone in 2011: Somewhere on the planet, according to US Census

Bureau estimates, the 7 billionth living person came into existence.

[However, birth rates are falling.] One of the most contentious issues is the question of whether birth rates in developed countries will remain low. The United Nation's most recent forecast, released in 2010, assumes that low-fertility countries will eventually revert to a birth rate of around 2.0. In that scenario, the world population tops out at about 10 billion and stays there. But there's no reason to believe that birth rates will behave in that way – no one has ever observed an inherent human tendency to have a nice, arithmetically stable 2.1 children per couple. On the contrary, people either tend to have an enormous number of kids (as they did throughout most of human history and still do in the most impoverished, war-torn parts of Africa) or far too few. We know how to dampen excessive population growth – just educate girls. The other problem has proved much more intractable: No one's figured out how to boost fertility in countries where it has imploded. Singapore has been encouraging parenthood for nearly 30 years, with cash incentives of up to $18,000 per child. Its birth rate? A gasping-for-air 1.2. When Sweden started offering parents generous support, the birth rate soared but then fell back again, and after years of fluctuating, it now stands at 1.9 – very high for Europe but still below replacement level.'

Source: Adapted from an article on www.slate.com – 9 January 2013

'Number of elderly in Japan hits record high'

'A record-high 31.86 million people, or about a quarter of Japan, were over 65 years old as of Sunday, up 1.12 million from a year earlier. The record high of 25.0 percent, was calculated based on

births and deaths registered since the 2010 census, the Internal Affairs and Communications Ministry said ahead of Respect for the Aged Day, a national holiday that falls on the third Monday of September. It attributed the growing number of senior citizens to the post-World War II baby boom. The National Institute of Population and Social Security Research said it expects 1 in 3 people in Japan to be over 65 in 2035. The number of men over 65 stood at 13.69 million, accounting for 22.1 percent of the male population, while women over 65 stood at 18.18 million, or 27.8 percent of the female population.'

Source: Adapted from an article in *The Japan Times*, 16 September 2013 (www.japantimes.co.jp)

Yes, you read it correctly, there is a national holiday in Japan called 'Respect for the Aged Day'. It was established in 1966 to pay respect to the elderly for their lifelong contributions to society. On Respect for the Aged Day, family members give gifts to their grandmothers and grandfathers to show their gratitude and appreciation. So, if you want to almost live forever, you should move to the island group of Okinawa and live on a diet of fish, seaweed, soya, vegetables, in a very pleasant climate within a close-knit family and community and adopt a healthy lifestyle.

Reflection

From each passage, pick out what you consider to be three or four key points expressed and note your own thoughts.

5.8 Data collection

In this section we look at demography and statistics.

'There are three kinds of lies: lies, damned lies, and statistics.'

This quote, attributed to Mark Twain, is often used to strengthen an argument through the selective and possibly biased use of statistics.

By the end of this section you should be able to answer the following questions:

- How do we collect information?
- Why do we collect so much information?
- What type of data do we collect?
- What do we do with all this information?
- What are the problems associated with a census?
- What data do we collect in the UK?

Collecting information

In the UK we have, since 1801, collected information every ten years about the people who live here and aspects of their lives and deaths in the form of a census. We have an almost unbroken record (the break occurred in 1941 due to war) charting social and economic change in the UK. A census is a snapshot of UK households at a fixed time (usually the third Sunday in April) and recorded every 10 years.

Every household in the UK receives a form, with what seems to be an increasing number of questions for completion. In Scotland the General Register Office (GROS) has the responsibility of completing the census. In England and Wales it is the Office for National Statistics (ONS). The ONS also collates the information from Northern Ireland, Scotland and England and Wales to provide a UK set of statistics.

A population census is a key system for assessing the needs of local communities. The questionnaires, including people's personal information, are kept confidential for 100 years before being released to the public and provide an important source of information for historical demography and genealogical research.

There were 56 questions on the 2011 census questionnaire. Of these, 14 related to the household and its accommodation and 42 were for each member of the household. Questions covered the themes of work, health, national identity, passports held, ethnic background, education, second homes, language, religion and marital status.

Concerns

In the UK, the main political parties all expressed some concern over the increasing costs and value for money of the national census (estimated to be over £400 million) and it was suggested that this may be the last of the decennial censuses to take place. It took almost three years for all the data to be processed and released, although the bulk of the key population data was released within a year.

There was concern by some groups in 2011 over the question, 'What is your religion?' Others regarded the census as snooping and an infringement of the right of individuals to keep personal matters private. A maximum fine of £1,000 was imposed for failure to complete and return the census form. The Office for National Statistics in England and Wales (ONS) believes it achieved a response rate of more than its target of 94 per cent. The remaining 6 per cent includes empty properties but the ONS believes that tens of thousands of households failed to respond. Following a freedom of information request by the 'World at One' on BBC Radio 4, the ONS said 22.9 million forms were returned out of the 25.4 million sent out. The Scottish Government said that around 2.3 million of the 2.5 million questionnaires they distributed had been returned.

We all use public services at various times, including schools, health services, roads and libraries. These services need to be planned and in such a way as to keep pace with the fast changing patterns of modern life. In order to do this, the government needs accurate information on numbers of people, where they live and what their needs are. While this is true for an MEDC such as the UK, it is also true for the LEDCs.

Civil registration in Scotland and the UK

We all recognise key life events, namely births, marriages and deaths, and in Scotland all three must be registered by the GROS. But who uses this information? The answer is, all levels of government (national and local) to recognise and plan changes for the future. For example, if a decline in the number of babies being born and an increase in the number of older people is noticed, then government will need to allocate resources from care and education of the young to more resources in housing and care for the elderly.

Many businesses are interested in demography changes and changing needs with regard to transport, holidays and migration. The argument is that census and data on key life events promotes efficiency and ensures that such businesses can actively plan and manage our requirements.

A census can also enable companies to target their marketing. For example, supermarkets may decide to stock more prepared foods in areas where there are greater numbers of young, single adults in employment!

Task

1 What are the main features of the UK census? How is statistical information on demography collected?
2 Why is so much information collected?
3 What type of data do we collect?
4 How is it used?

A global perspective on population data collection

The United Nations strongly supports all nations to collect data on a regular basis. While aware of the costs involved there is a belief that for every $1 spent on a census, savings of $8 in terms of efficiency can be made. Enumerators are those whose job it is to go out and collect the information from people.

However, LEDCs face many challenges. Table 5.11 describes some of these challenges using examples from different countries.

Task

1 What are the advantages of taking a national census in a country such as China or Brazil?
2 Why is it so difficult to get data which is accurate? Give reasons, using named examples from countries in Africa and Asia.

▼ **Table 5.11** Challenges of conducting a census

High cost of conducting a census	In China the last census cost $500 million.
	The 1996 census in Nigeria was cancelled since the country at that time could not afford the investment.
Low levels of adult literacy	In Sierra Leone, for example, adult literacy is only 35%, while in Nigeria, it is 72% for men and 50% for women. Literacy is important since most census forms are printed.
Consideration of the large number of languages and dialects within a country	In India there are 16 official languages and approaching 1,700 dialects! It becomes very difficult and expensive for a poor country to cover all languages and dialects.
Number of people, towns and villages in the country. Also sometimes the opposite with scattered settlements	In China there are over 1.3 billion people, 1 million villages and over 2 million enumerators! The organisation of such a massive task is expensive.
War, ethnic and religious tension and political rivalries	There are many examples of this in the modern world, e.g. war in Afghanistan and the Syrian civil war (over 300,000 deaths).
	Mexican drug disputes have been responsible for over 150,000 deaths in the last 10 years.
	Ethnic violence in South Sudan.
	Fundamental religious groups such as Boko Haram in Nigeria.
	It is not safe for 'government' administrators to enter areas of war and tension.
Suspicion from local people directed towards the government or enumerators	Those living in shanty towns; rural people may be suspicious of those from urban areas and fail to complete the census forms.

▼ **Table 5.11** Challenges of conducting a census *(continued)*

Costs of training and organising enumerators	Often huge numbers are required; there may be a need for enumerators to be multilingual.
Poor communications, difficult and hostile terrain and remoteness within a country	Inhospitable and remote mountainous areas of Borneo and Papua New Guinea. The size and remoteness of much of Brazil. This means that the accuracy and cover will be greatly reduced.
Migration within countries (rural to urban migration)	Over 2,000 people are estimated to move into Mumbai every day. In Shanghai (2013) there may have been as many as 9 million **migrant** workers.
Rapid demographic change	For example within a 10-year period the population in India grew by a massive 17%. The pace of change means that the census data will be very quickly dated and inaccurate.
Particular difficulties of rapid growth in urban/shanty towns	In cities such as Mexico and Rio de Janeiro, it is difficult to get enumerators into the shanty towns, because they are not only growing rapidly but local authority action is taking place to remove some of the settlements. It is a dynamic changing environment.
Deliberate manipulation of the data for political purpose	In Nigeria in the 1960s it was reported that numbers in certain regions were exaggerated for political representation reasons.
People choosing to 'go missing'	Following the 2011 census it was reported that one million people in the UK were not registered. In Scotland this may have been due to their objection to the poll tax (a local tax in force at that time) or homeless people or those who were in the country illegally. Since people have a choice whether to complete the census form or not, it can never be 100 per cent accurate.
Presence of illegal immigrants	In the last three censuses in the USA, a rough calculation has indicated that as many as 7 million illegal **immigrants** have chosen to be excluded from the count.
Mistakes in data collection and analysis	Simple human error as a result of the huge numbers of computations and numbers involved.
Nomadic populations	Always difficult to count. For example, the Fulani or Berbers of the Sahara/Sahel cross international boundaries. They could be counted twice or not at all.
Other concerns	In China there is a large imbalance in the percentage of baby boys being registered. Is this due to the 'one child' policy or female infanticide? Distrust of 'government snoopers'. Sensitivity towards personal questions.

▲ **Figure 5.20** Poster advertising the census in China – the 'Census benefits us all'

▲ **Figure 5.21** Completion of the census at an Indian home

Case study: Indian census

Since 1872 India has conducted a census, whose motto is 'Our Census, Our Future'. The last one was completed in 2011, when 2.7 million officials were involved in visiting houses in 600,000 villages. The information was classified under the four key headings of Gender, Religion, Education and Occupation. The cost was $360 million which worked out at approximately 50 cents per person. The census is completed every ten years. In the period 2001 to 2011, the population increased by 17 per cent and adult literacy rose by 9 per cent to 74 per cent. The census was collected in 16 languages.

 Task

In total there were 65 questions on the two census forms, some of which are shown in Figure 5.22. There is always a balance to be made between seeking information and being obtrusive. Looking at Figure 5.22, what are you views on this? Did the Indian Government get it right?

Building number	Ownership status of the house	Availability of kitchen
Census house number	Number of dwelling rooms	Fuel used for cooking
Predominant material of floor, wall and roof of the census house	Number of married couples in the household	Radio/transistor Television
Ascertain use of actual house	Main source of drinking water	Computer/laptop
Condition of the census house	Availability of drinking water source	Telephone/mobile phone
Household number	Main source of lighting	Bicycle
Total number of persons in the household	Latrine within the premises	Scooter/motor cycle/moped car/jeep/van
Name of the head of household	Type of latrine facility	Using banking services
Gender of the head of household	Waste water outlet connection	Seeking or available for work
Caste status (SC or ST or others)	Bathing facility within the premises	Travel to place of work
Name of the person	Other languages known	Birthplace
Relationship to head of household	Literacy status	Place of last residence
Gender	Status of attendance (education)	Reason for migration
Date of birth and age	Highest educational level attained	Duration of stay in the place of migration
Current marital status	Working any time during last year	Children surviving
Age at marriage	Category of economic activity	Children ever born
Religion	Occupation	Number of children born alive during last year
Scheduled caste/scheduled tribe	Nature of industry	
Disability	Trade or service	
Mother tongue	Class of worker	
	Non-economic activity	

▲ **Figure 5.22** Basis of questions from the Indian census of 2010–11

Source: Indian Government: A Census of India (2011)

Some key findings of the Indian census:

- The population on 1 March 2011 was 1,210,193,422.
- The increase since 2001 was 181.5 million.
- India has 2.4 per cent of the world's land surface and 17.5 per cent of the world's population.
- Adult literacy rates: men 82 per cent and women 74 per cent.
- Nearly half of India's 1.2 billion people have no lavatory at home, but more than 800 million own a mobile phone.
- Only 46.9 per cent of the 246.6 million households have lavatories while 49.8 per cent of people defecate in the open. The remaining 3.2 per cent use public toilets. More than half the population – 53.2 per cent – have a mobile phone.
- Census 2011 data on houses, household amenities and assets reveal that 63.2 per cent of homes have a telephone.
- Analysts say the data show the complex contradictions of the Indian system because the census reveals a country where millions have access to cutting-edge technology and consumer goods but a larger number of poor who lack access to even basic facilities.
- About 77 per cent of homes in the eastern state of Jharkhand have no lavatory, while the figure is 76.6 per cent for Orissa and 75.8 per cent in Bihar. All three are among India's poorest states with huge populations that live on less than a dollar a day.
- The data show that 47.2 per cent of households have a television while only 19.9 per cent have a radio.
- The number of people living in shanty towns/slum housing is 140 million.

The Indian Census Report states:

> 'The Population Enumeration provides essential Census data about land and its people in the present time. The survey reveals the current population trends, its varied characteristics that are valuable inputs for planning sound programs and policies aimed towards the welfare of India and her people and also for effective public administration.'

Developing nations like India are data intensive: they need socio-economic information about their population to design redistributive policies, especially in health, education, economic growth and development. In addition, given their obsession with global rankings, they also need information to compare themselves with other countries. However, India's official statistics are not free of errors.

Task

1 Can you identify instances where the data for India cannot be free from error?
2 Can you identify clear reasons for this lack of total accuracy?

Reflection

The Indian Census findings on this page reveal a complex pattern of inequality and disadvantage. From these findings, reflect on your thoughts and feelings about access to toilets. A web search will allow you to follow progress since 2011.

Research opportunity

A search of the internet will bring up masses of information regarding the 2011 UK census. You can look at the structure of the census form and the questions asked, study a timetable of 'online information release' and issues over how the census was organised. You can see how the data has been broken down into smaller districts and communities. From this you can see how information is available for planning in numerous areas such as health, education, housing, migration and transport provision. You can research changes in population in your local area and even research your own family history (or genealogy).

Here in the UK plans are currently underway for the 2021 census. At this stage it seems that online returns will replace the household visits.

Case study: China

For many years a study of Chinese demography has thrown up issues of the management and consequences of population structure. For example, China had to take steps to cope with the consequences of a rapidly youthful population. By 2015 there was concern about an ageing population.

Imagine a world with no aunts, uncles, brothers, sisters or cousins!

The population of China was increasing at a rate that could not be sustained: between 1962 and 1973 the population had increased by 39 per cent from 650 million to 950 million. Death rates were low and birth rates had fallen, but not by enough. Various family planning programmes had had mixed results, for example, the 'Later (marriage), Longer (space between births) and Fewer (children)' programme. In 1979 the government introduced the 'one child per family' programme, with inducements to participate that included:

- one child received free education and a whole mass of benefits
- parents were able to gain priority in housing and health
- parents qualified for a pension
- employment guarantees.

However, the Chinese Government has enforced the policy with considerable abuse of power and coercion, for example, women are regularly inspected to check if they are pregnant, even well into their 40s and 50s. Those who are found to be in breach of the one child policy can suffer forced abortions and even sterilisation. In millions of cases, families have been successful in hiding new children. The 1990 census recorded 23 million births but the 2000 census put the number of ten-year-olds at 26 million, suggesting at least 3 million babies had escaped the notice of family planning officials.

Those who are caught having more than one child can opt to pay a 'social upbringing fee', usually a multiple of the average income in the city where the child is born, which is designed to cover the cost of the child's education and health care.

Since 1979, there has been considerable relaxation and 'exceptions' introduced, but in the early years there were many instances of abuse of power and force applied to couples:

- Couples needed permission to marry and then needed permission to try and have a child.
- All inducements were withdrawn if a second child was born.
- There was massive community pressure to conform to the greater needs of the country.
- Considerable resources were concentrated on family planning, abortion, sterilisation and education.
- State employees lost their jobs if they failed to comply.
- There were many exceptions built into the programme, for example permission was granted to couples whose first child had physical or mental disabilities. In rural areas a second child was allowed if the first child was a girl!
- The policy has created issues over a huge number of 'little emperors/empresses' – only children stereotyped as being spoiled and pampered.
- There were reports of female infanticide. Ultrasound scanning allowed parents to establish the gender of their child and the sex ratio at birth appears to be skewed – in China for every 100 girls born there are 118 boys – a trend that is not seen in countries that do not place an emphasis on boys being the preferred sex.

By 2015 the relaxations allowed a couple to have a second child if both parents were only children. Wealthier Chinese may now opt to have more children, since they can afford to pay the 'fine'. In addition, the more affluent may choose to have their second and subsequent babies abroad. As you can see, the regulations have become very complex.

So what is the outcome of China's one child policy? It has largely been successful and, without it, the population would be some 400 million greater than it is today. However, a new problem is emerging for China – that of an ageing population!

Task

1   Study the table below which shows birth rates, death rates and growth rates for Thailand between 1960 and 2017.

Date	Birth rate/1,000	Death rate/1,000	Natural growth (%)
1960	46	18	2.8
1970	38	14	2.4
1980	30	10	2.0
1990	22	8	1.4
2000	18	8	1.0
2010	15	8	0.6
2017	14	8	0.6

2   What is the evidence that suggests that Thailand has moved from Stage 2 to Stage 4 of the DTM?

3   Draw a population pyramid that shows the structure of the population for Thailand in 1960 and 2017.

4   Match the three countries in Figure 5.24 with stages 1 to 5 of the demographic transition model.

5   For the Democratic Republic of Congo, or any other country you have studied with a similar population structure, describe and explain the conditions that resulted in such rapid population growth.

6   For Germany, or any other country you have studied with a similar population structure, describe and explain the conditions that resulted in a negative population growth.

5.9 SQA examination-style questions (focused on population)

Below are some examples of possible exam questions. These are by no means the only questions that could be asked but they give you an idea of what to expect. Some questions may be accompanied by maps or graphs from which you can gather extra information to assist with your answer.

'Both developed countries and developing countries need to have accurate population data.'

1   Explain why developing countries may find the collection of such data more difficult and why the quality of data obtained may be less reliable.

2   Study Figure 5.23. With reference to the Democratic Republic of Congo (or any similar country showing signs of a youthful population), explain the impact of such a population structure.

3   Study Figure 5.23. For Germany (or any other country showing features of an ageing population), explain the impact of such a population structure.

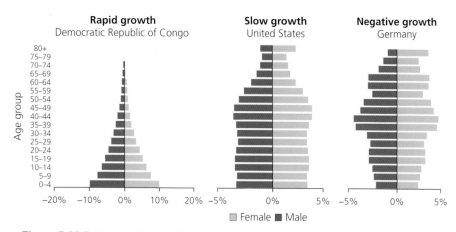

▲ **Figure 5.23** Patterns of population change

5.10 Migration

By the end of this section you should be able to:

- identify and define the various types of migration
- recognise the causes of migration
- assess the social, human, economic and political impact of migration
- apply your knowledge and understanding of migration within urban and rural environments in developed and developing countries through case study examples.

Types of migration

Human migration is the movement of people from one place to another with the intention of settling temporarily or permanently in the new location. This movement is often from one country to another (international migration) or within a country (internal migration). It may be from the countryside (rural) to the city (urban) or from one city to another. Migrations will involve individuals, family units or large groups. The cause of the migration can be voluntary (economic, social) or it may be forced (war, famine, persecution). People who move out of a country or area will be given the general name migrants, while people who migrate into a region or country are called immigrants.

Table 5.12 shows the different types of migration with examples of each. Note that it is possible for migrations to be classified under more than one heading, for example, a person fleeing Syria and going to Jordan (a refugee) is an example of a permanent, forced international movement.

▼ **Table 5.12** Types of migration

Type of migration	Examples
Temporary	Daily commuting, e.g. from Auchterarder to Glasgow for work. A student taking a year out to do voluntary work in Bolivia. A temporary job contract, as working for a British bank in Switzerland for a year.
Seasonal	Sometimes the word 'circulation' is used, since the person will return 'home' at some stage. A two-week holiday in Turkey or nomadic herders in the Sinai Desert in Egypt. University students staying at home during the holidays and in the university city during term time, for example, St Andrews.
Permanent	A retired couple leaving Scotland to live in Spain. A family moving to a bigger house at the edge of the city. Rural people moving from a village in the Indus Valley to Delhi.
Voluntary	Refers to people who are free and choose to move, usually for social or economic reasons, such as better living conditions, higher wages, access to good education, better employment prospects and better health care. A young couple from Edinburgh moving to Australia for a 'better life'. Young Polish workers coming to Scotland to work in the construction industry. West Indians moving to the UK in the 1960s.
Forced	Regretfully there are many examples of forced migration in the world today, as a consequence of war, famine or drought, ethnic cleansing, religious or political persecution. African slaves to America from the sixteenth century through to the nineteenth century. Jews in Germany in the 1930s and 1940s. Forced removal of shanty towns in Johannesburg during the 1970s and 1980s. Syria 2013 – present day.
International	Involves crossing national boundaries such as Mexicans into the USA. Workers from India coming to the UK. Turks into Germany or Poles into the UK.

▼ **Table 5.12** Types of migration *(continued)*

Internal/intra-national	Movement within a country or even within a city. A person moving from rural west China to Shanghai for work. A family in Scotland wishing to move to a small village for a better quality of life.
Economic	**Economic migrants** move to improve their quality of life and to earn more money for themselves and possibly their families. A young man moving from the countryside in Bangladesh to the city for employment. A young couple moving from Scotland to London to work in the City. A young person moving to earn a higher salary in the USA.
Refugee	A refugee is a stateless person who finds him/herself displaced and homeless. The United Nations' definition adds, 'a person who cannot return to his or her own country or region'. This may be because of war, famine, religious/ethnic persecution or 'cleansing'. A refugee is usually without documents, status or belongings. However, often the refugee, in time, may return to their country when the threat is removed, as happened in Kosovo.
Asylum seekers	**Asylum seekers** are people who claim to be refugees. They claim to feel threatened in their home country and on arrival at a new country declare themselves to be an asylum seeker. An asylum seeker is someone who has lodged an application for protection on the basis of the Refugee Convention or Article 3 of the ECHR (European Court of Human Rights).

In our study we will not include nomadic movements. This is because they are not regarded as migrations as there is no intention to settle in the new place and because the movement is generally seasonal. We will also exclude the movement of people for the purposes of travel, tourism, pilgrimages or commuting, since again, there is no intention to settle permanently in the new location.

Migration is not new. The initial populating of the planet was probably due to the hunter-gatherers spreading from Africa across the continents over a period of 50,000 years. From the sixteenth century through to the nineteenth century, slaves were shipped from Africa to the Americas and the Caribbean. During the nineteenth century almost 50 million people left Europe bound for North America and Australasia. In the twentieth century we had movement within the south of Asia involving Muslims and Hindus and Jews leaving war-ravaged Europe for many destinations including the new country of Israel. More recently we have had several waves of migrants leaving and entering the UK and Scotland. Migration reflects events of world history.

Migration patterns

In the 1880s Ravenstein (an English/German geographer) identified a number of 'laws' which explained the pattern of migration at that time. The key ones are described below:

- Most migrants travel short distances.
- Most migrants are adults.
- Migration occurs in waves and the 'vacuum' left as one group leaves is filled by a counter-movement of another group moving in.
- Migrants who move longer distances tend to choose big-city destinations.
- Urban residents are less likely to make international moves than people from rural areas.
- Families are less likely to make international moves than young adults.
- Large cities grow by migration rather than natural increase.
- Men tend to move longer distances than women.

By 2017 some new trends had been identified:

- Most migrants follow a series of small steps from the rural village to the city.
- People are leaving rural areas in vastly increased numbers.

- Migrants are getting younger (mainly in the 20–35 age range) and are increasingly male.
- There is an increasing number of migrants within the European Union.
- The majority of migrants move for economic reasons.
- There has been a significant increase in the number of asylum seekers and refugees.

▲ **Figure 5.24** Polish migrants leaving Warsaw to come to the UK

▲ **Figure 5.25** Rural poverty in China

▲ **Figure 5.26** Construction boom in Shanghai, China

▲ **Figure 5.27** London street scene

Migrations happen because people make decisions to do so. Sometimes it is a positive, deliberate choice, but sometimes it may be forced on them. Although most movements are positive, there will always be barriers that have to be considered and overcome. The most basic set of circumstances affecting and explaining migration is that of 'push–pull': 'push' at the place of origin and 'pull' at the place of destination. When combined, these factors can be grouped under the headings, Economic, Social, Political and Environmental. Note that sometimes a 'pull' factor is the exact opposite of the 'push' factor. For example, a 'push' factor could be a lack of educational opportunity and the 'pull' factor will be the presence of schools and opportunities. Table 5.13 describes some of the push–pull factors involved in migration.

Figure 5.28 shows Professor Everett Lee's migration model (push–pull model) which was developed in the 1940s and was an attempt to explain patterns of migration. He felt that migration was a decision made by an individual or a family (because of their needs and desires) and it was based on the positive and negative characteristics of the origin *and* the destination (push–pull factors) and the nature of the intervening obstacles.

Of course, there are positive and negatives associated with migration. For example, François Crepeau, Special Rapporteur on the Human Rights of Migrants (a United Nations body), stated that, in 2013, migrants sent about $404 billion (£251 billion) in remittances back home to family. He also pointed out that those moving from less developed to more developed countries achieved a fifteen-fold increase in income, a doubling in education enrolment rates and a sixteen-fold reduction in child mortality.

However, he added that many states were still failing to protect the most vulnerable in their societies,

Intervening obstacles may prevent migration from occurring or reduce the numbers migrating. These obstacles include distance and social and economic factors.

The +, − and 0 shown on the diagram represent positive, negative and neutral factors for the migrant viewing both their home settlement and the destination they wish to migrate to.

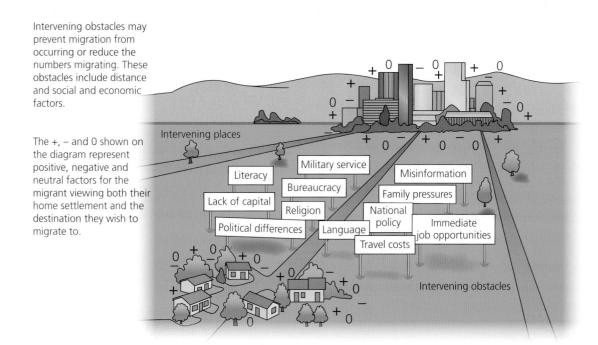

▲ **Figure 5.28** Lee's migration model

▼ **Table 5.13** Push–pull factors of migration

Push factors	Pull factors
Often negative, forcing or encouraging people to move away: • Not enough jobs and underemployment • Few opportunities • Lack of basic amenities such as sewerage, water or power • Desertification • Famine or drought • Political fear or persecution • Slavery or forced labour • Poor medical care • Poverty • Exposed to natural disasters • Death threats • Desire for more political or religious freedom • Pollution • Poor housing • Landlord/tenant issues • Discrimination • Poor chances of marrying • War • Ethnic cleansing • Low wages • Higher mortality rates and lower life expectancy • Population overcrowding • Very limited social and cultural amenities for young people (clubs/cinemas)	Positive and encouraging, drawing people to a new destination. The pull factors may be real, but often they are imaginary. It is the perception of a better life that is attractive. Some people use expressions such as 'attracted by the bright lights of the city', or 'the streets are paved with gold'. • More and a greater variety of job opportunities • Better living conditions • The belief that homes will have mains sewerage, power, water • The feeling of having more political and/or religious freedom • Enjoyment • Education beyond basic primary level • Better opportunities for girls • Better medical care • Less likely to be a victim to natural disasters such as drought or flooding • More security and freedom to follow personal religion • Improved salary and a higher standard of living • Better chances of marrying • A higher standard of living and freedom from poverty • Be able to send money back to family • An attractive climate • The pull of a bigger house, a better job, greater wealth, greater freedom and happiness and the chance of a new life

with some key industries – such as in construction, hospitality, extraction, fishing and agriculture – exploiting migrants as a source of cheap labour.

Such migrants experience multiple forms of discrimination, on the basis of nationality, legal status, sector of work, gender, age and ethnic, linguistic or religious identity.

The World Football Cup will be played in Qatar in 2022. This small but (very) rich country requires a massive construction programme to complete the stadia and the necessary infrastructure. From the Indian subcontinent and from across North Africa many workers have come to Qatar. The media (e.g. BBC News, February 2015) repeatedly report on the exploitation of the workers, virtual slavery (by impounding workers' passports), dangerous working conditions and poor accommodation. Despite this many new workers are still very keen to go to Qatar.

There are barriers to migration (Figure 5.29). It is evident that migration is a massive step and decision for individuals and groups to make.

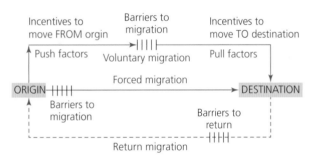

▲ **Figure 5.29** Migration model showing barriers

When migration is voluntary then planning and preparation is possible. Things to consider include the cost of transport and setting up home in another country. The distances involved can be a psychological barrier and there are often government restrictions in place in the new country (such as quotas and work permits). Other barriers include language difficulties, different food and culture, religious barriers and the trauma of leaving a family behind.

The model in Figure 5.29 also includes a route for return to the original country, but this is not always possible once the ties have been broken. For many migrants the move is successful and a new life is established. However, migration does not always work and the reality of the move may not lead to the

opportunities imagined. In other words, the 'pull' factors are not realised. Another factor may be that the reason for the migration has been removed, for example, in time, Syrians may be able to return home from Jordan or even Germany. It could also be that there were racial, cultural, language and religious tensions. However, some migrants return because they miss their family or simply because they have earned enough money to start a business in their home country.

Case study: Moroccan village to Marrakesh

Background to rural/urban migration in Morocco:

- Rural/urban migration has played a significant and important role in the economic and social development of Morocco.
- Most migration occurs among the 15–29 years age group.
- Most migrants are men from the poorest rural areas.
- The main motivation is the cash economy and job opportunities in urban areas such as Marrakesh.
- Strong links are maintained back to the village.
- Two-thirds of migrants return at least once a year to their village.
- Of those migrants questioned, 90 per cent say that they will return one day to stay in their village. It seems that in reality this will be closer to 10 per cent.
- At least 30 per cent of rural households receive money from relatives living in the towns and cities.
- This 'remittance money' is used to improve the quality of life in the village.

Zaouite Inkkal is a Berber village on the south side of the Atlas Mountains, some 100 km from Marrakesh. Here the Berbers are settled and farm the land. The village has been bypassed by the N5 road that links Marrakesh and the valleys of the Draa and the Drey. The road leads to Quarzazate and the desert. The village has fewer than 500 people from about 20 families. The village has electricity, an inadequate water supply and basic sewerage. There is a primary school in the village, a mosque, some artisan craft 'factories' and several small shops selling essential goods. Between the river and the steep mountain slopes, the land is farmed – grains, grass, roots, fruit, vegetables and some cattle and sheep/goats all provide a source of income. Most farming remains subsistence, but the big market in Marrakesh provides an income. Water comes from the streams flowing from the Atlas Mountains. In recent years there has been a problem, with not enough rain to fill water tanks nor irrigate the fields. Ironically the occasional flash flood not only fertilises the soil but can damage the fields and buildings. The environment is harsh because of the summer heat and aridity, the coldness of the winter, flash flooding and remoteness. There is no doctor or dentist in the village. Secondary education is available in a small town 10 km away, but a majority of children (especially girls) do not seem to complete their education. Those who wish to go to college or university must move to Marrakesh.

Marrakesh is expanding fast. It has become a tourist hotspot, popular with people from northern Europe seeking an exotic resort. It is also an industrial and commercial centre, growing at a rapid rate. A bus from Zaouite Inkkal to Marrakesh takes less than four hours. There are plenty of jobs available, either in the factories or working in the hotels and cafés in the city. With tips, it is possible to earn more in one day working as a guide in the souk (market), than can be made in two weeks of farming the land. In 2014, 14 men and 9 women migrated to Marrakesh from Zaouite Inkkal. Money from migrants has paid for improvements to the village mosque, school and water tank.

Task

1 Identify the push and pull factors when considering migrating from the village to the city.
2 Consider the life of a young girl who fails to complete secondary education and remains in her home village. What are her opportunities for marriage, employment and the future?
3 What would you consider to be some of the problems that migrants may face when they arrive in Marrakesh?

Case study: Rural to urban, Shanghai

Migration is not a new phenomenon in China and in the last 75 years there have been several waves of migrants.

● There has been mass movement from rural areas to the industrialising cities. Between 1950 and 1970, China's urban population grew from 11 per cent to 30 per cent, and by 2017 it was closer to 64 per cent.

● Migration to the cities is also linked to the political failure of Mao's 'Great Leap Forward' in the years 1958 to 1960, which resulted in very high levels of rural famine.
● Many Tibetans left their country as refugees, as a result of the policy of the Chinese Government to assist the Han Chinese and military to move into Tibet, thereby altering its ethnic balance.
● During the late 1960s, as part of another political upheaval (Cultural Revolution) many of the educated, middle classes were sent to live in remote rural areas.

In China, people have not always been able to move freely. Registration is required and permission can only be given to move if it is in the overall interests of the community. Foreign investment and rapid growth has resulted in factories booming, increased industrial demand and the creation of jobs and population movement to the cities. In addition, the construction of the Three Gorges Dam resulted in 1.3 million people being displaced from their homes. The Chinese National Highway, running 4,800 km from east to west, has become the national routeway for migrants to follow. The 2012 census revealed that 141 million Chinese were living in a different province from that in which they were born.

By 2017 many of these migration restrictions were being relaxed. In Shanghai, such is the demand for jobs in construction, manufacturing and the service industry (for example, maids and taxi drivers) that the city now has grown to over 23 million people.

▲ **Figure 5.30** Temporary accommodation for construction workers in China

▼ **Table 5.14** Impact of migrants from Sichuan to Shanghai

Sichuan costs	Sichuan benefits
Loss of young, dynamic and educated people creating a gender and age imbalance	Reduction of overcrowding and unemployment
Population decline	Remittance money being sent back greatly boosts local economy
Difficulty for women to find men for marriage	
Break-up of family	Returning migrants bring back many new skills
Shanghai costs	**Shanghai benefits**
Increased demand for housing, transport, power, education	City has grown to be a major centre for ships, industry, commerce and retail
Loss of political control, e.g. 'one child policy'	Increased wealth for whole country
Increased fear of crime	
Lack of integration	
Growth of shanty towns	
Growing clashes over different culture	

Case study: Poland to Scotland

In 2013, an estimated 353,000 (6.8 per cent) of the resident population of Scotland were born outside of the UK, a decrease of 22,000 on the previous year. Of those non-UK born residents, 182,000 were born outside the EU (51.6 per cent). An estimated 266,000 (5.1 per cent) of the resident population of Scotland held non-British nationality, a decrease of 19,000 on the previous year. Of those non-British nationals resident in Scotland, 101,000 held non-EU nationality (38.0 per cent).

The most common nationalities are from Poland (84,000), Republic of Ireland (15,000), India (12,000), United States of America (11,000) and Pakistan (10,000).

A key principle of European Union membership is freedom to live and work in any other EU country. Since 2004 the Polish population in Scotland has grown from 2,700 to over 80,000. At the time of writing this chapter, the UK and Scotland will be leaving the EU in 2019.

Table 5.15 shows the push–pull factors for those immigrating to Scotland (see also Table 5.13).

Many Poles have settled in Scotland but many have returned to Poland. This counter-migration followed the economic downturn of 2009–12 and some strong economic growth back in Poland.

▼ **Table 5.15** Push–pull factors for immigrants to Scotland

Push	Pull
In 2004 unemployment in Poland was around 20%.	The ease of migration to the UK, with unlimited migration.
Wages in Poland were about one third that of Scotland.	Positive currency exchange rate meant that sterling conversion into zloty was very favourable.
An acute shortage of housing in Poland meant that many young couples had to live with their parents.	In the UK it was common to earn more than enough to live on and have money to send as remittance back to Poland.
State benefits in Poland are very low compared to Scotland and the UK.	There were plenty of available jobs with decent wages in parts of the economy that appeared to have a shortage, such as in construction and trades such as plumbers and electricians.

Consequences and impact of Polish migration to Scotland

- **Human**: Scotland has an ageing population. Without an influx of younger people, Scotland will face difficult economic issues in the future, as it will be unable to generate sufficient wealth to look after non-productive and dependent groups of the population. Migrant Poles tend to be younger and have a higher birth rate than indigenous Scots. Young, dynamic Polish families bring new life to communities.

- **Political**: Some politicians and newspapers were concerned with the influx of Poles into Scotland. There were also fears that the country would be 'overrun' by Romanians and Bulgarians and other EU migrants coming to Scotland. Sometimes the 'facts' reported were exaggerated and problems and clashes were overemphasised. As geographers we have to take a balanced view. Migration is often mis-reported in the media, with a negative bias. The reality is that Scottish politicians and communities have welcomed such migrants.

- **Economic**: In Poland there are fewer young, educated and dynamic workers and so less tax would be collected. This has been partially overcome through the remittance money sent back to Poland. Generally most immigrants, and Poles in particular, have a positive work ethic, and have been a strong and positive influence on Scottish society. They work, pay taxes and contribute to the economy of Scotland.

- **Social and cultural**: Migrants in general bring enrichment to the culture of the destination country, whether it be music, dress, food or language. Unfortunately, some people remain challenged by new ideas and change. At the time of writing this chapter (early 2019) the UK is planning to leave the European Union. As a result there will be considerable changes to the status of EU migrants within the UK and the opportunities for new migrants wishing to come to the UK.

Case study: India to the UK, an example of voluntary, international permanent migration

Those migrating from India to the UK are an example of voluntary, international permanent migration. This is summarised in Table 5.16 below.

Case study: Refugees caught up in the Syrian civil war

This is an example of forced migration.

▲ **Figure 5.31** Syrian refugee camp in Jordan

▼ **Table 5.16** Migration from India to the UK: impact and consequences

Host/destination country: UK	Origin country: India
Pull factors:	**Push factors:**
• Commonwealth link. • Higher wages and high standard of living, good job prospects. • Good education and health services.	• Rural poverty and unemployment. • Lower quality of life, especially in health, education and support. • Poorer-quality housing and poverty. • Caste system and religious tensions.
Positive impact and consequences of migration to the UK:	**Positive impact and consequences of migration to India:**
• Enrichment of UK culture, especially music, fashion, cinema and food. • Migrant skills fit in well with UK needs in health, textiles and retail. • Proven to be creative and enterprising. • A more youthful population with a higher birth rate that will help to balance the UK's ageing population structure.	• Reduced pressures on unemployment. • Reduced overcrowding on the land and pressure on limited health, housing and educational resources. • Impact of remittances.
Negative impact and consequences in the UK:	**Negative impact and consequences in India:**
• Discrimination, often fuelled by the media, which works on the idea of blaming the migrants as the cause of all the problems in the country. • Migrants are often blamed for shortages in housing, pressures on education and health. • Differences in language, culture, religion, food and dress can create insecurity and unease in the indigenous population.	• A loss of mainly young, educated and dynamic people. • The population left behind will be imbalanced with a high proportion of young, old and women.

- By August 2018, 7.4 million people had been displaced in Syria while more than 3 million refugees had fled to Lebanon, Jordan and Turkey. The charity World Vision estimated that over 14 million people in Syria needed humanitarian assistance in 2018.
- The United Nations states that this is 'the largest humanitarian emergency of our era'.
- The cost to Lebanon of supporting the refugee camps has reached $1 billion.
- The most needed items are tents, water filters, rechargeable lights, stoves and blankets.
- The European Union has sent $2 billion in aid.
- Between 2010 and November 2018, Germany had accepted 80,000 refugees from war zones in the Middle East, and the UK had made a commitment to accept 20,000 Syrian refugees by 2020. Scotland, by 2018, had resettled over 2,000 Syrians. The USA's acceptance policy altered significantly in 2016 (with the election of President Trump) and, during the whole of 2018, the country accepted 51 Syrian refugees.

Syrian refugees may be housed in temporary camps for many years before a more permanent solution can be found. The countries surrounding Syria are poor and struggle to cope with the huge numbers of refugees. The civil war has claimed a quarter of a million lives and at the time of writing (June 2019) there is no end in sight.

What is the background to this dispute? The conflict started between forces loyal to President Bashar al-Assad and those opposed to his rule. The recent dispute dates to March 2011 following clashes in the south between the people and soldiers before escalating countrywide. The civil war is now sectarian with the country's Sunni Muslim majority against the President's Shia Alawite sect. Jihadist groups, including Islamic State (IS) have now entered the war fighting alongside the Sunnis.

All wars are horrific but this one has documented war crimes committed by both sides (including murder, torture, rape, dropping 'dirty' bombs (devices that combine conventional explosives such as dynamite with radioactive material) and the use of gas and chemical weapons. It is estimated that there are over 100,000 Islamist and Jihadists fighting for IS and that they have taken control of large parts of Syria and

Iraq. We also know that significant numbers of foreign fighters have entered Syria supporting the rebels. The UN, USA, UK, European Union and many other groups or countries are all actively trying to find a peaceful solution but with very limited success so far. In time, this remains the only hope to reduce tension and violence.

Iran and Russia and Shia groups support the President's troops, while Turkey, Saudi Arabia, Qatar, the USA, UK and France have given degrees of support to the Sunni opposition. However, the rise of Sunni Islamic militia within the rebel ranks has created real conflict and confusion for these countries.

Meanwhile, life in refugee camps such as Zaatari in Jordan remains appalling.

Reflection

Consider the material that has been made available to you in this case study. What are your thoughts? What can a country such as the UK do about it? Should we be involved? This may form the basis of a classroom discussion. Note: This information was correct as of June 2019 and so you may need to update these notes.

This Syrian case study has local, global and international issues.

Local impact and consequences:

- Massive population loss and upheaval, with 14 million refugees forced to move, almost half of whom have left Syria.
- The UN estimate that 333.000 Syrians have died over the last eight years.
- There has been destruction of the infrastructure, education, health and industry in many cities such as Damascus.
- Whole villages have been destroyed.
- Destruction of cultural sites such as at Palmyra and the Great Mosque at Aleppo.
- Amnesty International state that 3 million Syrian children have not attended school in the last two years.

- Collapse of the local economy. The value of Syrian trade in 2010 was $2.73 billion, the 2018 value was $0.7 billion.

Regional and global impact and consequences:

- There is a need to preserve key cultural sites. All six UNESCO **World Heritage Sites** have been damaged.
- The political impact has affected the West's relationship with the Arab world and Russia and China.
- Neighbouring countries, such as Turkey, Lebanon and Jordan, cannot deal with the pressures from the refugees (needing accommodation, health facilities, food and water). Such countries do not have the capacity to cope.
- Unstable governments may be more likely to fear the rise and growing confidence of terrorist organisations (for example, Tunisia).

At a global level any unrest can add to uncertainty about economic trade and markets (for example, oil markets and prices).

Why is migration important for us today?

Migration has become a contentious issue. While writing this chapter, I was very aware of alternative viewpoints. For example, when researching the case study on Poles to Scotland or Syrian refugees I drew on several sources including the BBC, newspapers, specialist agencies such as the United Nations and other websites. As young adults you will have to adopt a 'social science' approach and methodology of understanding about what is happening in the UK today. Be aware of bias, mischief, misinformation and overt racism. Countries and their politicians and people have widely contrasting views. Be very careful in your examination answers to show your understanding of the issues and use words carefully to express the wide range of views. This theme is one that the writers of this book feel that you should consider reading and researching further. Here are some issues to guide your research:

- Confusion over definitions of asylum seekers/ refugees/economic migrants.
- Newspapers, bias and confusion over actual numbers.

- Disputes about the value of migrants to the UK economy.
- Impact on the culture and enrichment of UK life.
- Growth of extremist groups in the UK and other countries such as the USA, Syria and Germany.
- The impact and consequences for Scotland and the UK following Brexit, as the UK still prepares (as at June 2019) to leave the European Union.

Summary

At the beginning of this chapter we posed the question, 'What could be more important than a study of planet Earth and its people?' Barely a day will pass without stories in the media relating to the concerns and issues of this chapter. Demography, the study of human population, involves change, both in terms of population numbers and population movement.

You will agree, we hope, that a study of population and migration is important. Through the inclusion of background information, theory and case studies it has been shown that demography affects us all. The greatest movement of people on our planet is from rural areas to the urban areas of the world. We live on a planet with finite resources but with increasing demands from increasing numbers of people, all of which creates tension. In the UK we have a changing population structure, an ageing population and in-migration. It is more important than ever to recognise that our dynamic population presents us with new opportunities as well as new challenges.

SQA examination-style questions

For the SQA Higher Geography examination, you will be given a question based on one or more of the following broad topics:

- Methods and problems of data collection
- Consequences of population structure
- Causes and impacts relating to forced and voluntary migration.

1   Outline the ways in which countries can obtain accurate population data.

2   With reference to a named LEDC (less economically developed country) such as Kenya, explain why the collection of such data may be difficult and less reliable.

3   Figure 5.32 shows a refugee family holding numbered placards as they pose for a photo during a census conducted by the Thai authorities at Mae La refugee camp, near the Thailand-Myanmar border in Mae Sot district, Tak province, north of Bangkok.
     Why is it difficult to conduct an accurate census in a camp such as this?

4   Look at Figure 5.33.
     a)   Discuss the consequences for the UK of the population structure shown.

▲ **Figure 5.32** Refugees holding placards during a census conducted in Thailand

b)   Discuss the consequences for a country such as Pakistan of the population structure shown.

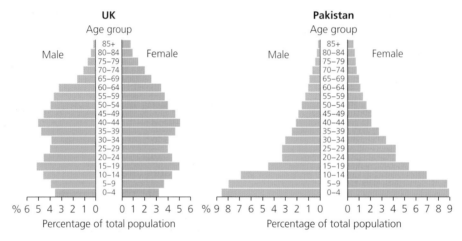

▲ **Figure 5.33** Population structure of UK and Pakistan

5   Look at Figure 5.34.
     a)   Explain the causes of voluntary migration from rural areas to urban areas in a country such as Morocco.
     b)   For any named voluntary migrations you have studied, explain the impact of such migrations on both the area/country losing people and the area/country receiving people.

▲ **Figure 5.34** Moroccan rural landscape

Introduction

Rural is one of three Human Environment topics in the SQA Higher Geography course.

For the examination, you may be given a question based on one or more of the following broad topics:

- impact and management of rural land degradation related to a rainforest or semi-arid area
- rural land use conflicts and their management related to either a glaciated or coastal landscape.

This chapter is concerned with causes, impact, management and conflict.

Degradation affects areas of the developed and developing world (the MEDCs as well as the LEDCs). The MEDCs can at least use their wealth to tackle the problem by managing large-scale regeneration schemes to compensate for the declining fertility of the land. Rich areas can also use their wealth to ensure that the human, economic and social impact is not life threatening. All this cannot be said for the LEDCs, where the impact can be very damaging. A crop failure in Texas does not result in famine and death, but such a failure in Ethiopia does.

- Land degradation is about the reduction in the productivity of the land, as a result of physical and human activity.
- Land degradation can occur naturally (e.g. storms, flooding, fire, volcanic eruption) but is more likely to be accentuated by human activity.

For the examination you may be given a question on a broad theme, for example 'the impact and management of rural land degradation related to a rainforest or semi-arid area'. The keywords are 'impact', 'management', 'rural', 'land degradation', 'rainforest' and 'semi-arid'.

As with previous chapters, you will require additional background information to use your knowledge to best effect in the examination. Some specific case study exemplars are also provided. SQA requires you to study examples from the rainforest and semi-arid areas.

You are required to have background knowledge and understanding of the following:

- The nature and processes of soil erosion and degradation, impact of vegetation removal, soil erosion by water (sheet, rill, gully) and soil erosion by wind.

- The problems posed by climatic variability such as those caused (for example) by variable movement of the intertropical convergence zone (ITCZ) across Africa (north of the equator) and by intensity of rainfall in the tropics (see section on the ITCZ in Chapter 1 of this book).
- The modification of ecosystems caused by human activity, deforestation, monoculture, over-cultivation, overgrazing, inappropriate cultivation and irrigation techniques.
- The consequences of soil erosion and degradation (desertification), including the physical impact on landscape and climate, social impact on people and economic impact on the traditional ways of life.
- An understanding of traditional patterns of life in semi-arid areas and the rainforest.
- Specific examples of soil conservation and land management strategies; case studies from the selected area contexts of semi-arid regions and rainforests.

The first part of this chapter will consider the following topics:

- An introduction to land degradation
- The impact and management of land degradation in the rainforest
- The impact and management of land degradation in semi-arid areas

6.1 Introduction to land degradation

▲ **Figure 6.1** Primary rainforest (Amazon)

▲ **Figure 6.2** Deforestation and degradation (Amazon)

▲ **Figure 6.3** Desertification of semi-arid land (Sahel)

Rural land resources are subject to degradation, which may be as a result of natural processes and/ or human activities. The decline in land productivity and other issues associated with land degradation has direct social and economic consequences and has led to the development of soil conservation and land management strategies.

The population of the world continues to grow, putting an increasing demand on available resources. Increased land is needed for food, crops, animals, fish, water, oil, space, wood and so on. This growth puts pressure on the environment and increasing damage to soils, forests and grasslands has been noted, which is beyond the natural rate of recovery (sustainability). The result is land degradation, soil erosion and desertification.

The Food and Agricultural Organisation (FAO) of the United Nations recognises land degradation as the reduction in the ability of the land to provide food, resources and services over a period of time for the benefit of the people. Land degradation affects large areas and many people in semi-arid and rainforest regions. Increased population pressures and increasing migration into semi-arid lands during wet periods leave a legacy in that when the drier period inevitably returns there will be more people, animals and farming pressures on the land. The FAO suggests that:

> '... the removal of the protective cover to reduce competition for water and nutrients, ploughing, heavy grazing and deforestation all leave the soil highly vulnerable to wind erosion particularly during severe droughts. Heavy grazing around water points or during long droughts prevents or delays the regrowth of vegetation or favours only unproductive shrubs.'

During research for this chapter we found many sources of information, but one that you may consider using is the 'Millennium Assessment', launched by the UN General Secretary Kofi Annan in 2001. Over 1,250 scientists from 100 countries (in collaboration with numerous other international organisations such as the World Bank) wrote a series of academic papers looking at **ecosystem** change, the impact on humans and the options for response to these changes.

According to the FAO (2018):

> 'Land degradation costs an estimated US$44 billion annually worldwide' ... without taking into account hidden costs of increased fertilizer use, loss of biodiversity and loss of unique landscapes.'

Further the FAO believes that the consequences of land degradation include reduced land productivity, uncertainty with food security, migration, limited development and damage to ecosystems. Degraded land is costly to reclaim and, if severely degraded, may not recover again.

Research opportunity

1   Define the following keywords: 'impact', 'management' and 'land degradation'.

2   For each, identify possible issues of concern in the world today.

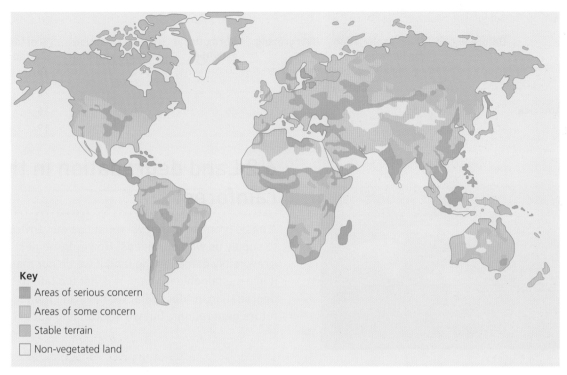

Key
- Areas of serious concern
- Areas of some concern
- Stable terrain
- Non-vegetated land

▲ **Figure 6.4** Global distribution of areas of degradation

Task

Using Figure 6.4 and focusing on South America, Africa and south-east Asia, describe the distribution of:

- areas of serious concern
- areas of some concern
- areas of stability.

Look at Figure 6.4 and note the following:

- Firstly the geographical extent of concern seems to cover all continents, with stability from degradation covering only around 40 per cent of the Earth's surface land area.
- Concern is noted in western South America, Central America, the Sahel and the Mediterranean coast of North Africa, the Kalahari area of south-west Africa, much of the Middle East into the Thar and Gobi Deserts, most of China and western India, the area in north-east Brazil and the island of Madagascar. Degradation is also found in North America and throughout Europe.
- You should also distinguish between varying degrees of risk. In general, land degradation is most common in tropical and sub-tropical areas, particularly in the semi-desert environment.
- In land such as the cold deserts of Greenland and the hot desert of the Sahara, there is little degradation due to the fact that there is little potential for change in areas that are of very limited potential.
- An initial study reveals the key causes of land degradation are deforestation, over-exploitation for fuelwood, overgrazing, agricultural activities, industrialisation and mining.

▲ **Figure 6.5** Burning of the rainforest, Brazil

▼ **Table 6.1** Causes of land degradation (%) 2018

	Deforestation	Over-exploitation for fuelwood	Overgrazing	Agricultural activities	Industrialisation including mining	% of land degraded
World	25	7	35	27	5	**18**
Africa	14	12	44	25	5	**22**
South America	41	5	23	26	5	**14**
Asia	40	6	23	26	5	**19**

▲ **Figure 6.6** Impact of gold mining, Peru

Interpreting data

It is important to be able to interpret information given in a table. The data shown in Table 6.1 was obtained from a variety of sources including the FAO and the World Resources Institute. The final column was obtained from Wikipedia (your teacher may tell you that this source should be checked for validity, but all sources may be subject to bias and misinformation). The most recent information I could find was for 2012. Is that a problem? It could be in a theme involving rapid change. The data relates to continents but in some ways that is inaccurate, because within a continent such as Asia for example there are massive variations: cold and hot deserts, high mountains and examples of all the major climatic types, from tropical to arctic.

The case studies that follow examine in more detail the information referred to in Table 6.1. Apart from variations between the continents, tables and data can also be used to show change over time. Are the figures in Table 6.1 changing or are they static? As a geographer, your enquiring mind wants to know more. You may wonder about the causes of overgrazing, or why deforestation is such a major cause of land degradation.

We will now consider the background to and then the impact and management of rural land degradation related to a rainforest.

6.2 Land degradation in the rainforest

A basic premise is that we must use our environment to supply us with our needs. However, neglect irreversibly damages the land if we do not manage it in a sustainable manner. It is not too late to stop the degradation, protect what we have and manage it for future generations, but we are running out of time.

'Forests ... are in fact the world's air-conditioning system, the very lungs of the planet and help to store the largest body of freshwater on the planet, essential to produce food for our planet's growing population. The rainforests of the world also provide the livelihoods of more than a billion of the poorest people on this Earth ... In simple terms, the rainforests, which encircle the world, are our very life-support system – and we are on the verge of switching it off.'

Source: HRH The Prince of Wales, Presidential Lecture, Jakarta, Indonesia, November 2008

'I used to worry that all the trees in the jungle would be cut down to make paper for their reports on how to save the rainforest!'

Source: Nick Birch, entomologist and ecologist

'The simple fact is that the world is not paying for the services the forests provide. At the moment, they are worth more dead than alive, for soya, for beef, for palm oil and for logging, feeding the demand from other countries. I think we need to be clear that the drivers of rainforest destruction do not originate in the rainforest nations, but in the more

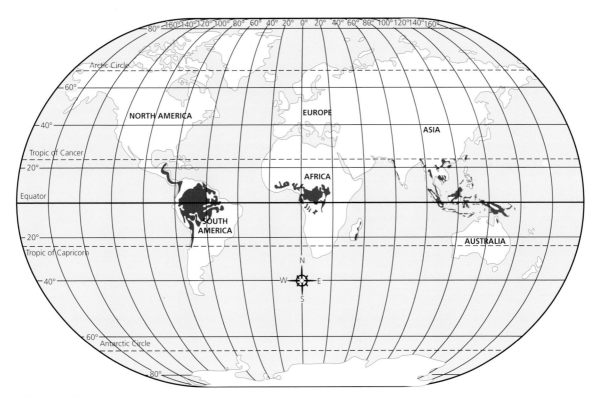

▲ **Figure 6.7** Global distribution of rainforests

developed countries which, unwittingly or not, have caused climate change.'

Source: HRH The Prince of Wales, Presidential Lecture, Jakarta, Indonesia, November 2008

 Reflection

What is your reaction to these quotations? Do you agree with what they say?

 Reflection

You will not be asked a question about the traditional way of life in the rainforest, but you do need background information to be able to answer a question on impact/consequences and management of change in the rainforest. If you feel that you have insufficient background knowledge you should undertake some additional research into these areas.

When we study the degradation of the rainforest we start by considering the drive towards deforestation, the cutting down of trees, which is recognised as the main threat to the sustainability of tropical rainforests.

However, we need to consider:

- the underlying causes of deforestation
- the act of deforestation or logging
- other threats to the rainforest
- the negative impact of deforestation on the environment and the forest people
- the positive impact of deforestation on the environment and the forest people
- management strategies to reduce the impact of land degradation
- the success of such management strategies.

More than half of the Earth's rainforests have already been lost forever to the unrelenting human demand for wood and arable land. Rainforests that once grew on 15 per cent of the Earth now cover only about 7 per cent. If current deforestation rates continue, this ecosystem could completely disappear from the planet by the year 2100.

The reasons for the attack on rainforests are mainly economic. Wealthy nations create the demand for tropical timber and weaker governments

▼ **Table 6.2** Background notes to the rainforest

Location	Tropical rainforest zones of South America, tropical Central Africa and south-east Asia.
	Example of people living in the rainforest are the Boro Indians of the Amazon.
Keywords	Subsistence, shifting, peasant/traditional, low technology, extensive, low output per worker.
Settlement	There are 340 million people worldwide living in rainforest areas with low population density (i.e. 1,000 hectares required to support one person).
	Low population density occurs as a result of isolation, climate, dense forest and limited land fertility that cannot support increased population density. Settlement is dispersed, with small clearings ('chagras') with community houses ('malocas' or longhouses).
Methods	Clearings are created using 'slash and burn' techniques.
	Machetes are used to cut down vegetation which is then burnt.
	Ash used as fertiliser.
	Crops such as manioc, maize, yams and cassava are planted using basic stick tools.
	Heavy rains cause soils to be leached, washing out fertility.
	Clearings abandoned (every four or so years) and left to regenerate (which takes a minimum of 40 years).
	Local people have a continual battle against encroaching secondary forestry and weeds.
Landscape	The largest trees and fruit trees were traditionally left in position.
	Highly labour intensive agriculture with little use of machinery.
	The native people can grow crops all year round, with usually two or three harvests per year.
	Little fertiliser is added, therefore **leaching** limits cultivation to every three or four years.
	Gathering, fishing and hunting still practised.
	Little or no surplus either for sale or storage.
	The patches of land cultivated tend to be irregular in shape and pattern.
	When left alone, this farming system is hard and harsh for the traditional people but is sustainable.
Concerns and impact	Deforestation because of ranching, mining, lumber, sedentary farming, damming (HEP) and roads.
	Rivers are vulnerable to being choked following clearance and deforestation.
	There is destruction of the native culture and the forced introduction of a 'westernised' lifestyle.
	There is soil erosion on the fragile land and concern over global environmental issues.
	The quality of the land is being degraded with concern over a lack of sustainability.

(especially in the last 30 years) encourage logging companies by selling concessions to exploit this resource, often at a fraction of the land's true value.

Causes of degradation and deforestation

Shock images such as that in Figure 6.9 show the destruction of the rainforest but reacting with anger is too simplistic. For many people who live in relative and absolute poverty in the developing rainforest regions of the world (e.g. Borneo or Suriname), development may mean progress in the form of jobs and a better quality of life and even improved health and education.

Cleared land formerly occupied by rainforest has an economic value. Regretfully, if a profit can be made, then the forest is vulnerable to clearance and development.

Small-scale farming

In some ways this is an expansion of the subsistence pattern of farming, although now it is no longer shifting and instead is likely to be permanent and settled. With increasing population numbers it is no longer possible to allow shifting cultivation

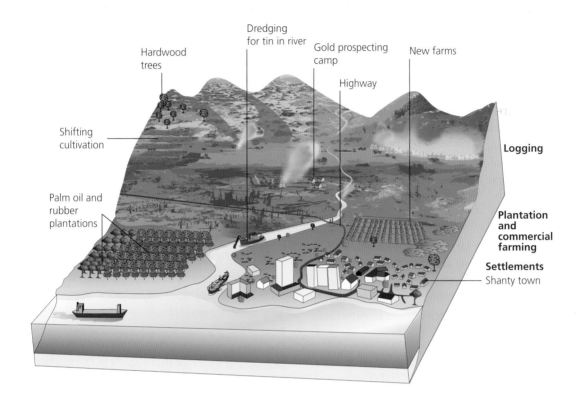

▲ **Figure 6.8** Development of the rainforest

▲ **Figure 6.9** Impact of deforestation in the Amazon

to continue. Small-scale farming is likely to be sustainable but may require some assistance to prevent the soil from being overused and washed away by heavy rain storms. Subsistence farmers slash and burn rainforest for firewood and to make room for crops and grazing lands.

Commercial logging

There is worldwide demand for timber products. Logging interests cut down rainforest trees for timber used in flooring, windows, doors and furniture. The paper industry turns huge tracts of rainforest trees into pulp. In the Congo, the government estimates that 80 per cent of logging is illegal.

The methods used for deforestation or logging can be destructive:

- Destruction by fire is considered to be the easiest and fastest way to clear the forest for an alternative use but it is clearly wasteful and environmentally destructive.
- Trees can be destroyed when valleys are flooded to create reservoirs for new HEP projects.
- Not all tropical rainforest trees have a high economic value and so there is less demand for them, but those that do have value, such as teak or mahogany, are targeted for clearance.

Commercial agriculture

Agricultural interests, particularly for the soya, palm oil and cacao markets cause the forests to be cleared. The cattle industry uses slash-and-burn techniques to plant pastures for vast cattle ranches. There are now extensive rubber and palm oil plantations. In Mexico, in response to increasing debt, the government has increased agricultural exports and reduced imports. This has meant an increase in cattle ranching for export and plantations of cash crops such as tobacco, pineapples and sugar cane.

Industry

Mining operations clear forests to build roads and dig mines. Bauxite, gold, silver and iron ore are mineral resources found in rainforest areas. Hydroelectric projects flood huge areas of rainforest. Power plants and other industries cut and burn trees to generate electricity.

Improvements to infrastructure

Governments and industry clear rainforests to make way for services and transit roads.

Political concerns

Many governments consider it important for there to be routes into all parts of the country in order to produce a cohesive nation that the state can influence and control.

New settlements

New settlements may be required to cope with an increase in population.

Impact of deforestation

Deforestation and degradation within the rainforest can have environmental, social and economic impacts, as shown in Table 6.3.

Other issues associated with deforestation

Overhunting and poaching

Traditional hunting was sustainable, but with increasing population numbers there is now a higher demand for meat from wild animals. Hunting has become more commercialised and therefore beyond the levels of sustainability. Poaching involves both plants and animals that have a value (such as skins, tusks and other animal parts for decoration and medicines) being illegally taken or killed. Examples include killing elephants in Cameroon and Borneo, and the clouded leopard and tapir in Malaysia.

Climate change

It appears from research in Brazil and Sabah, Borneo that climate change is having an impact on the rainforest. Research continues but early indications

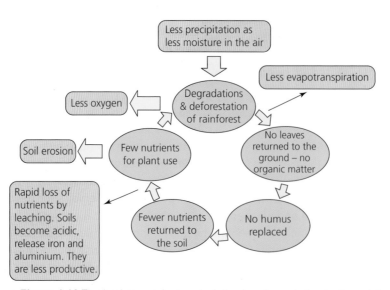

▲ **Figure 6.10** The broken nutrient cycle following degradation in the rainforest

▼ **Table 6.3** Impact of degradation and change in the rainforest

Negative impact	Positive impact
Social: • Native people will lose their homes, land and culture. • Loss of traditional livelihoods in farming. • Increased risk to local people from 'western' diseases. For example due to lack of immunity to influenza the numbers of Nukak people (Amazon) have been reduced by 50 % since 1995. • Migration: Sometimes people are 'forced' to make way for development. For example the Guarani people in Brazil were evicted to make way for cattle ranches and sugar plantations. • Conflict between the competing groups of people. For example the native people, mining, HEP and logging companies and landowners. • New roads can divide communities, traditional native groups and encourage migration to the shanty towns and favelas. • Local languages and traditions may be lost.	**Social:** • Quality of life for some local people will improve as there may be more jobs. • Profits from selling resources can be used to improve a country's infrastructure. For example profits from the sale of rainforest resources can be used to build schools and hospitals. • New roads allow people to move freely and seek out a better future in the cities. • Large-scale farming brings money into the country and provides food and jobs for the country's growing population. Small-scale farming provides food for rainforest communities and the landless poor of Brazil and Sabah, Borneo.
Environmental: • Habitat loss and an increase in endangered species and plant loss. • There will be a break in the nutrient cycle (see Figure 6.10). • Reduction in **biodiversity**. • Logging leaves vulnerable soil open to leaching. The heavy rains can now wash away the rich nutrients from the soil, increasing surface run-off and increasing the risk of flooding. • Deforestation is a likely factor in climate change. Trees remove CO_2 from the **atmosphere**. Fewer trees mean more CO_2 in the atmosphere, increasing the greenhouse effect. • Deforestation reduces rates of evapotranspiration. This results in less atmospheric water vapour, fewer clouds and a reduction in precipitation. As a result there will be an increased risk of unreliability and drought. • The threat of increased drought may also lead to forest fires which destroy large areas of forest.	**Environmental:** I have thought hard about this section on environmental positives and tried not to leave this box blank! • It is not too late to stop the destruction. While it seems as if we are on course for complete degradation of the rainforest ecosystem, this will not happen. We will have a reduced rainforest which will continue to have a positive influence. • We have an increased awareness of the pressures for change. The richer parts of the world now realise that there are steps that can be taken (see the section below on management). • New trees can be planted, e.g. eucalyptus trees, which will create a new ecosystem. • We can continue to make the world aware of this valuable ecosystem and manage **ecotourism** to generate income yet retain the rainforests.
Economic: • It is important that there is sustainability in the opportunities that arise from logging, mining and farming. Cash crops, logging and mineral exploitation can bring money into the country. • Such opportunities need to be balanced with tree replanting and careful management of the new farmland. • In the long term deforestation and mineral extraction can deplete resources, leaving the country with little to show for the loss of the forest because the profits from timber and minerals often go back to MEDCs or the large overseas based companies rather than benefiting the rainforest communities.	**Economic:** • Jobs are created in the new logging, mining, power and farming industries. In Borneo over 350,000 people are employed in these industries. Over 60,000 people are now employed in gold mining in Peru. • Money can be created from selling the timber, minerals and farm products. For example Brazil made $15 billion in exports from cattle products in 2014. Mineral deposits in the Amazon include bauxite (the main constituent of aluminium), iron ore, manganese, gold, silver and diamonds. Minerals can be sold for large profits. • New roads and airports can open up the forest allowing products to be exported.

appear to show that in some areas rainfall is decreasing and temperatures are slowly increasing, resulting in periods of unexpected drought (e.g. the severe droughts in the Amazon, Brazil, in 2003, 2010 and 2015).

The American Meteorological Society found that when the Amazonian tropical forests were replaced by degraded grass (pasture) there was a significant increase in the mean surface temperature (about 2.5°C) and a decrease in annual evapotranspiration (30 per cent reduction), precipitation (25 per cent reduction) and run-off (20 per cent reduction) in the region.

Source: Adapted from The American Meteorological Society

What will this mean? It is likely we can expect the following:

- degradation of freshwater systems (rivers and lakes)
- loss of ecologically and agriculturally valuable soils
- increased erosion
- decreased agricultural yields
- increased insect infestation
- increased spread of infectious diseases.

Over time, global climate change and more deforestation is likely to lead to increased temperatures and changing rain patterns in the Amazon, which will undoubtedly affect the region's forests, water availability, biodiversity, agriculture and human health.

Between 25 per cent and 50 per cent of the Amazon rainforest could become a dry savanna. A rise of 4°C could kill off 85 per cent of the Amazon rainforest.

Of course, there is a massive amount of research being carried out around the world at the current time and as a geographer you need to place all of this in context. We are not short of information. Be aware of findings that range from a prediction of the 'end of civilisation as we know it' to those in denial who claim 'there's nothing to worry about'.

Cattle ranching

According to Greenpeace:

> *'Cattle ranching is now the biggest cause of deforestation in the Amazon, and nearly 80 per cent of deforested areas in Brazil are now used for pasture.'*

Brazil has the largest commercial cattle herd in the world; since 2003, the country has also topped the world's beef export charts and the government plans to double its share of the market by 2018. Greenpeace is a respected pressure group that works with governments and raises awareness of issues of conflict. However, as a geographer you should always be aware of a bias that can creep into the press statements of such groups.

▲ **Figure 6.11** Impact of cattle ranching, Brazil

Land ownership

One of the major problems of deforestation has been over the ownership of the land. Native people do not have bits of paper stating that they own the land. Unscrupulous people can come along with land ownership papers and claim the land as their own. However, land can be bought by conservation groups and returned to the native people.

 Task

1. What are the key features of the traditional cultural way of life in the rainforest?
2. What are the causes of deforestation?
3. What negative impact does degradation of the rainforest have on the native people?
4. What negative impact does degradation of the rainforest have at a global level?
5. Is it all bad news? What positives can we take from economic and social levels?
6. Do you think we can ban logging? Explain your answer.

Let's remind ourselves of the broad theme of this topic, 'The impact and management of rural land degradation related to a rainforest or semi-arid area.' So far we have covered 'impact related to a rainforest'. We will now move on to look at the aspects relating to 'management'.

Management strategies to reduce the impact of land degradation

Many rainforest countries are relatively poor and are currently going through a process of development, so leaving the rainforest untouched is not an option for them. It is therefore necessary to manage development and take steps to reduce the negative impact of land degradation, yet allow and support the development of such countries. Poverty does not help us to solve this global issue.

Uncontrolled and unchecked exploitation can cause irreversible damage such as loss of biodiversity, soil erosion, flooding and climate change. It is therefore necessary to find a balance by undertaking sustainable development of the forest as this will meet the present day needs of rainforest people without compromising the needs of future generations. The keyword here is 'management'. So who manages? Below is an impressive list of good ideas and strategies but the problem remains to convince landowners, governments and commercial logging, mining and farming interests.

Encouraging agro-forestry

This is the practice of growing trees and crops at the same time. Agro-forestry encourages farmers to take advantage of shelter from the canopy of trees, helping to prevent soil erosion and enabling crops to benefit from the nutrients in the dead organic matter. People could be encouraged to harvest the forest's bounty (nuts, fruits, medicines) rather than clear-cutting it for farmland. For example in the Eden Foundation programme in Nigeria, farmers grow perennial plants to protect the soil against heavy rain. This prevents **rainsplash** from dislodging fine sand and soil particles, makes sure that the soil is not exposed and that the roots bind the loose soil.

Sustainable logging

Can we ban logging? No, but we could control it. Degradation is a problem when an area is cleared, leaving the soil exposed to heavy rain. By being more selective and felling trees only when they reach a particular height, young trees could be given a guaranteed life span. Rainforest trees reach maturity between 40 and 60 years. This means that the canopy and structure of the forest remains and the forest is able to regenerate and become sustainable. The problem is that often the trees that are in highest demand do not grow in stands (meaning they do not grow together). Clearance is wasteful with heavy machines damaging the fragile forest floor and the trees that are not of value to loggers are often burnt. Trees such as teak can be grown under plantation conditions in many parts of south-east Asia and South America.

Replanting and afforestation

Governments in Vietnam and Peru have plans to replant extensive areas of rainforest. Peru alone intends to replant over 150,000 hectares of forest by the year 2020. To allow for biodiversity a variety of hardwood trees should be planted, to encourage sustainability of fauna and flora. Who pays for all this? As the producing developing countries achieve higher levels of development, such projects will become self-funding. Until then the developed world may consider this to be a worthy act in the face of climate change and resource sustainability.

Ecotourism

This can be defined as:

> '... responsible travel to natural areas which conserves the environment and sustains the livelihood of local people'.

Source: National Geographic

Good ecotourism benefits the local economy, does not harm the environment and can be combined with research and educational benefits. There are some excellent examples: for example, in the Danum Valley (Sabah, Borneo) and in Costa Rica, ecotourism brings in money and jobs and this funds protection of the environment from development. However, there are lots of examples of bad ecotourism and the term is used by unscrupulous travel companies to fool people that there is genuine care and concern for sustainability.

Education

To ensure that those involved in the exploitation and management of the forest understand the consequences behind their actions, more campaigns are needed to educate people about the destruction caused by logging in the rainforest.

Reducing global demand

In the West we continue to buy hardwood furniture from natural rainforests. Some people regard this as an act of great selfishness and no more than a fashion trend that encourages high prices and therefore demand for the furniture. If there was no demand for teak, ebony or mahogany then there would be no need to cut down these beautiful trees. We can take action on this by banning the import of such timber or charging high tax rates on these imported hardwoods. Brazil has banned mahogany logging since 2001. The problem is that the rewards from illegal logging are still sufficiently high that companies are willing to take a chance.

Regulation and protection

It would be wrong to assume that rainforest countries do not have a concern about the degradation of the forest. Many of them have environmental laws. For example in Brazil, landowners are required as part of the Brazilian Forest Code to keep 50–75 per cent of their land as forest. However, this is often difficult to enforce when taking into consideration the vast areas and the scattered and sparse population. We can create forest reserves – areas protected from exploitation.

Brazil has set up a vast national park and nature reserve to protect its rainforest (see case study on pages 192–193). The Central Amazon Conservation Complex is a UNESCO World Heritage Site and is the largest forest reserve in South America, with restricted entry. Where there is such high level protection (government and United Nations support) then damaging activities such as poaching, logging

and mineral exploitation can be monitored and prevented. Local people can also be employed. Governments could place a temporary restriction (moratorium) on road building and large infrastructure projects in the rainforest, as has occurred in the Danum Valley area of Sabah, Borneo.

Burma (Myanmar) placed a self-imposed ban on the export of teak logs. Good? Well yes and no. The keyword here is 'logs'. They intend to continue to sell teak but now will concentrate on exporting the higher value cut and shaped planks and products. This shows why it's always important to read beyond the headlines.

Illegal logging

This involves cutting trees without permits or removing trees from protected areas. While illegal logging occurs in many parts of the world, much of it is concentrated in the tropics, where prized hardwoods are taken to make furniture. In 2008 the US Congress passed amendments to the Lacey Act, a century-old law that combats trafficking in illegal plants and wildlife, and closed the entire US market to illegally sourced wood. Illegal logging occurs outside of government regulation and oversight. As a result, it can cause excessive forest damage and ecosystem impoverishment, loss of biodiversity, changes in soil nutrients and increased susceptibility to clearing for agriculture, pastureland and other uses. Illegal logging depresses world timber prices and reduces the competitive advantage of legal loggers and producers. Globally, illegal logging and the associated trade in illegal wood costs governments and businesses an estimated $10 to $15 billion in losses per year.

Monitoring

It is possible to create numerous management strategies to tackle the problem of deforestation, but to do so requires knowledge about what is happening and the ability to step in and take action. Satellite technology and photography can be used to check that any activities taking place are legal and following guidelines for sustainability. Not all countries have the technology or the money to do this so assistance from wealthier countries is needed. In the most remote rainforests of South America, Amazon Indians (Amerindians) are using Google Earth, global positioning system (GPS) mapping and other technologies to protect their fast-dwindling homes. They are combining their traditional knowledge of the rainforest with western technology to conserve forests and maintain ties to their history and cultural traditions.

Certification and sponsorship schemes

Certification involves the introduction of a form of 'barcoding' all timber to make sure that it can be validated as 'eco-friendly' or from a 'sustainable' forest. Charities and pressure groups are involved in sponsorship schemes (see case study on page 191).

Reduction of debt and poverty

Another way to manage the degradation of the rainforest is to reduce debt and poverty. Many tropical rainforests are in less economically developed countries, such as Nigeria, Belize and Vietnam. Countries borrow money to help pay for improvements to the quality of life of their people, especially in health, education and infrastructure. A large number of these countries are in debt to richer countries and organisations such as the World Bank. Logging, mineral exploitation and commercial farming is a source of income that can help to reduce this debt, but reducing or cancelling debt would mean countries no longer need to do this. The problem is getting wealthier countries or organisations to reduce the debt owed to them, but even then there is no guarantee the money saved would be spent on conservation. In 2008, the USA reduced Peru's debt by $28 million in exchange for rainforest conservation. It should be noted that many of the rainforest countries are also rife with corruption.

Success of management strategies

Problems are often dependent on who has power: governments, mining, cattle ranching and logging companies have power and the drive for economic growth and profits may be stronger than conservation and management measures. For example, just because the Brazilian Government sitting in Brasilia passes legislation does not automatically mean that it is enforced in the rainforest 2,500 km away. Laws exist to limit the amount of land that can be used for activities such as logging and mining, but they are difficult to enforce. However, as stated above, the use of satellite technology may make it possible to detect what is happening in even the most remote areas.

Environmental groups such as Greenpeace and Friends of the Earth have more power than ever before. They often have an influence on western governments and are large enough to object to developments and organise protests as well as having resources to encourage sustainable development. By encouraging and promoting 'Fair Trade' products, such as tropical fruits, products have a good chance of being sustainable.

In conclusion:

- Many rainforests continue to suffer from deforestation and degradation.
- World awareness is at its highest level and the rate of destruction is slowing down.
- Countries are realising that rainforest development can be sustainable.
- It is important to conserve rainforests to protect local and global environments to enable native people, their language and cultures to survive.
- Local people rely on and need the forest to provide them with food and shelter.
- LEDCs depend on the natural resources obtained from the rainforest (logging, mining and commercial agriculture) to provide them with income and fund development.
- All agree that management is important in order to balance competing social, environmental and economic needs.
- Successful management strategies must be sustainable.

Task

1 For each of these eight concluding comments write a short summary outlining the background to the comment.

2 Referring to management strategies described in this chapter, create a summary table, using the headings: *Management strategy*, *Brief summary*, *Evaluation*.

We will now consider the use, misuse and protection of the rainforests by looking at a wide range of case studies. You should read these carefully as you may be required to draw on aspects of this information in the examination.

Case study: Ethical forestry

'Timber is a valuable commodity and like all commodities (such as oil and gas) it is constantly in demand. According to the United Nations, the global demand for timber is projected to double by the mid part of this century, driven by the requirements of the rising global population expected to peak at 9 billion by 2050. The two largest economies in the world, the USA and China continue to dominate the timber import industry. In the USA, the majority of homes are framed using timber. Moreover, China's demand for imported wood increased by 415% between 1997–2012, according to a report by the RISI. The 2013 China Timber Outlook also revealed that "China's import demand is already equal to 10% of the world's total timber harvest even a relatively slower growth rate will still mean a substantial increase in demand."'

Source: www.ethicalforestry.com

'China provided the biggest source of wooden furniture imports into the UK in 2009, valued at £137 million. This was a whopping 224% increase in value since 2004. During the same period Vietnamese wooden furniture imports increased by 230%, Malaysian by 204% and Indonesian by 95%. Chinese companies are heavily implicated in deforestation across the world, from Burma to Madagascar to the Democratic Republic of Congo. More illegal timber is imported into the UK than any other European country. Approximately half of the wood imports into Vietnam from neighbouring countries between 1987 and 2006 were illegal. The demand for cheap furniture in the West has also driven rapid deforestation in Laos, Thailand and Cambodia.'

Source: www.ethicalconsumer.org

'Illegal timber includes timber harvested in national parks, outside of logging concessions, or from illegal plantation expansion. It is then laundered into the global timber market where it is packaged up into consumer goods that find their way to a store or the pages of catalogues.

EIA's timber trade investigations have demonstrated how numerous powerful and well-connected international criminal syndicates conspire with corrupt officials and international companies to steal huge volumes of high value timber from the world's last remaining tropical forests, usually in developing countries. Many of these networks, operating in countries including Indonesia, Malaysia, Vietnam and China, have also directly supplied western furniture markets.

At its peak, illegal logging is estimated to have cost its developing country victims up to £7.5 billion a year through the theft of public assets and non-payment of taxes. From 2000-2005 Indonesia suffered losses of US $20 billion from the illegal timber trade. The costs for forests, local livelihoods and ecosystem services are incalculable.

No laws were being broken by companies or consumers in the UK. This was even where it could be shown that timber on sale was from an illegal source in another country. In such "no-questions-asked" markets, governed by laws that could not discriminate between legal and illegal timber, legal timber finds it hard to compete with illegal supplies, particularly from south-east Asia, Africa, and South America.'

Source: www.ethicalconsumer.org

Task

Using these two sources (www.ethicalforestry.com and www.ethicalconsumer.org) summarise the problems they identify and consider any issues that need to be overcome.

Case study: The work of the Rainforest Foundation

There are several UK-based and many global charities concerned about the degradation and potential destruction of the rainforest. Table 6.4 describes the work of the Rainforest Foundation.

Case study: Ecotourism

Ecotourism is concerned with conservation, communities and sustainable travel. This means that those who participate in ecotourism activities should follow the following ecotourism principles to minimise their impact and to build environmental and cultural awareness and respect.

Ecotourism:

- minimises impact and does not harm the environment
- provides a source of income for local people by providing accommodation and transport and guiding services
- provides positive experiences for both the visitor and the host
- should be small-scale, helping to minimise the environmental impact and increase sustainability
- helps the sustainable development of an area because quality of life is improved yet preserves those resources for future generations
- should reduce the need for mining, logging and farming to generate income so fewer trees are cut down
- should support international human rights and sustainable principles
- should support education and research.

However, all of this needs to be policed, managed and enforced. There is considerable mis-selling and confusion over exactly what is ecotourism. For example, building a nature path through a rainforest is not really ecotourism. Is it possible to avoid cultural and environmental negative impact? Ecotourism needs to be supported and it consumes resources, such as travel, shelter, water and food. There can be tensions due to the unequal relationship and wealth of the visitors and their hosts, and through cultural differences in customs, behaviour and clothes.

▼ **Table 6.4** Work of the Rainforest Foundation

The situation we are facing	What we set out to do	Successful results
The rainforests of the world are under increasing pressure from agro-industrial expansion, extractive activities, infrastructure development and industrial logging. They are also home to millions of people. Indigenous and forest populations living in and around the rainforests depend on the forests for shelter, food, medicine and livelihoods. In many cases, the basic rights of these people are threatened or undermined by forest destruction, land theft and resource exploitation.	The Rainforest Foundation is working to ensure the long-term protection of rainforests by securing the rights of indigenous and forest peoples to land, life and livelihood. They are working in 21 countries and across four continents, supporting hundreds of communities.	The approach is working. Research has shown that indigenous peoples' areas in the Amazonian rainforest are now better conserved than even in some protected areas. Significant evidence from the Amazon Basin now shows that, where forest communities have gained legal title to land, levels of deforestation and forest destruction are far lower even than in strictly protected areas such as national parks. To date, they have protected over 11,700,000 hectares of rainforest following this approach.

Source: Adapted from www.rainforestfoundationuk.org

Case studies: Sarawak and Sabah, Borneo

▲ **Figure 6.12** Baku National Park, Sarawak, an example of a successful ecotourism project

Background: Sarawak and Sabah are two Malaysian states located on the island of Borneo. The area is situated near the equator with a tropical climate. The natural vegetation is rainforest, which has been considerably depleted over the last 50 years. The two states have a population of 5.5 million and 35 ethnic groups with a wide variety of cultures and customs. Over half of the land is now covered by national parks.

Case study 1

The Baku National Park is home to a rich variety of fauna and flora, such as the orang-utan, proboscis monkey, crocodiles, pitcher plants and wild orchids. The park has beaches, caves and coral reefs and attracts adventurers from all over the world. The entrance fee is approximately £2. Activities include mountain biking, sailing, snorkelling, jungle trekking and rafting. You can even enjoy the 'longhouse experience', living in a real native house! Is this ecotourism? Possibly not! Just because you stay with locals in their homes and see the exotic animals and plants you may feel that you have experienced something authentic. You have also contributed to the local economy, assisted with employment opportunities, discovered and experienced traditional life and had a good time!

Case study 2

The Iban Longhouse community in the Mulu National Park have a long cultural heritage and proud tradition. Tourists arrive by boat and stay in a 'longhouse'.

Local women cook for visitors using local produce (fish, eggs and vegetables).The income from tourists has paid for improved infrastructure such as septic tanks and a generator. An ecotourism company has sponsored young Iban students to train as teachers to provide education for children in the areas. The Iban culture is preserved and life is sustainable, with the addition of extra income from the tourists.

Case study 3

The Danum Valley in Sabah, Borneo, is a primary, undeveloped, lowland rainforest area with outstanding flora and fauna. It has escaped logging, commercial farming and plantation development and is one of the last remaining natural rainforests in Sabah. It is managed by a charitable trust devoted to education and research. A visitor will see evidence of this in the form of laboratories, monitoring stations and sensitively placed platforms, canopy towers and walkways. It is an area of rich biodiversity with 120 species of mammals and primates (including the clouded leopard, Borneo hippopotamus and the orang-utan) together with over 300 species of birds. There are links to universities in many countries and the trust hosts ecology and environment courses. There are lodges for people to stay and night walks and jungle treks are available.

Task

1 For case studies 1–3 above, decide which (if any) are examples of ecotourism.
2 What do you think is meant by ecotourism?
3 Compare and contrast the case studies of the Danum Valley with that of the Baku National Park in terms of examples of ecotourism management strategies to reduce the impact of land degradation.

Case study: Central Amazon Conservation Complex (CACC)

The CACC was established in 2003 and has acquired World Heritage Site status and incorporated four reserves, including the Jaú National Park. It covers a total of 6 million hectare (49,000 km²), is a massively important biodiversity area with the aim of:

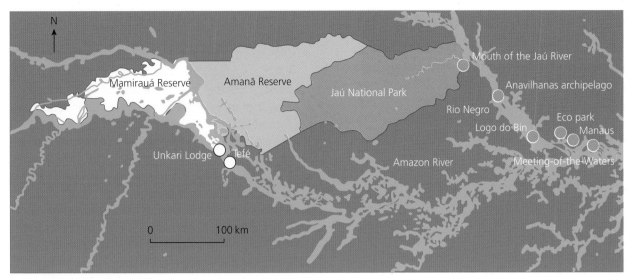

▲ **Figure 6.13** The Central Amazon Conservation Complex

'... protecting endangered species whilst allowing locals to live and use the land in a sustainable way'.

The Complex includes rainforest, rivers, lakes and flooded wetlands. An additional focus has been on allowing local people to continue to use the forest for their livelihood in a sustainable way.

Management of the CACC involves the Brazilian Government, local government, the Brazilian Institute of the Environment and Natural Resources, research institutes and representatives from the mining and tourism industries. Local people are represented.

So how does it work? There are different levels of management and control:

- Total protection: very restricted access and no development.
- Sustainable use: areas where the local natives can hunt, fish and farm at a subsistence level (with limits).
- Rehabilitation: areas of the reintroduction of native people back to their traditional pattern of sustainable life.
- Experimental use: areas where researchers and scientists can try out new seeds, crops and afforestation.

Entry from the outside is limited and there are controls on development. There are no dams or plans for power development, mineral exploitation, pipelines or commercial logging.

Economic Alternatives Programmes (EAP) have been established where local communities run fisheries, handicraft, ecotourism and sustainable agriculture programmes, all providing a direct income.

Impact of the management strategies:

- The number of animals in the key endangered species in the park has increased since 2003.
- There are reduced levels of poverty (household income up by 66 per cent) following the EAP initiatives.
- Local farmers now sell their crops through an association guaranteeing increased income.
- Ecotourism has brought jobs and money with low impact on the environment.
- Locals have been trained in health and education related activities.
- There has been a drop of 55 per cent in infant mortality and more children now attend school.

However, there are limitations:

- The Complex is very large and difficult to monitor.
- There are not enough guards and rangers.
- Locals still migrate to the cities and favelas.
- Poverty levels remain high when compared with the rest of Brazil.
- Corrupt officials and the power of the illegal loggers and poachers still present major challenges.

Case study: Demand for rubber tyres

'Global demand for tyres is ravaging forests'

'Demand for rubber fuelled by the tyre industry will destroy vast areas of natural forest inhabited by endangered gibbons, clouded leopards and elephants in south-east Asia, a study has warned.

Up to 21 million acres of additional rubber plantations will be required to meet global demand for tyres by 2024, according to research by the University of East Anglia.

Expansion on this scale will have a 'catastrophic' effect on wildlife comparable to the damage done by the expansion of the palm oil industry. The demand is such that rubber plantations are expanding in Sundaland (Malay Peninsula, Borneo, Sumatra, Java and Bali) and in Indo-Burma (Laos, Cambodia, Vietnam and Burma) and south-west China. With concern it is noted that even 'protected' forests have been cleared. Mention is made that 70 per cent of the Snoul sanctuary in Cambodia has already been cleared for rubber plantations. Loss of animal, fish and plant life has resulted in loss of biodiversity.'

Source: *The Times*, 17 April 2015

Conclusion

Here are some final facts to consider with regard to rainforests.

- Eighty per cent of our food originally came from rainforests. Some of the more popular examples include coffee, chocolate, rice, tomatoes, potatoes, bananas, black pepper, pineapples and maize.
- Rainforests only cover about 7 per cent of the Earth's surface, but they are home to more than half the world's total plant and animal species.
- In a primary rainforest, the forest floor is almost completely dark – with less than 5 per cent of the available sunlight making it through the tree canopy above.
- Today, the rainforests are being destroyed at a rate of one hectare every second.
- With deforestation continuing at such a fast rate, we've created the most rapid extinction rate in the history of the world. Almost 150 rainforest species are exterminated completely every single day.
- Of the medicines we use today, 25 per cent have their origins in the rainforests. So far only about 1 per cent of rainforest plants have been examined for their medicinal properties.
- We often think that the soil in the rainforest is really fertile to support such a huge range of plant and animal life, but in fact it is not very good for farming. Once cleared, and after a few years of farming, the land is totally deficient in nutrients.
- If deforestation continues, we'll completely lose the rainforests within the next 80 years.
- Over 3,000 species of fish live in the Amazon River – more than all the known species of fish in the Atlantic Ocean.

 Task

In the case studies there have been numerous references to the problems of degradation, the management strategies and the impact of some of these management decisions. We have referred to Brazil as a case study on several occasions. From these notes plus any additional research you may wish to conduct, compile your own report on: 'The impact and management of rural land degradation related to the Brazilian rainforest.'

▲ **Figure 6.14** Model of management strategies

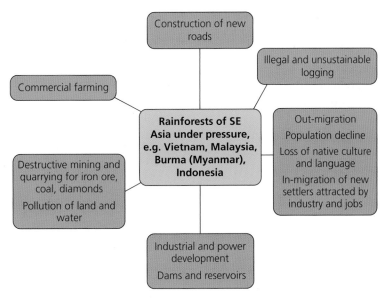

▲ **Figure 6.15** Rainforests of south-east Asia under pressure

6.3 SQA examination-style questions

1 Look at Figure 6.14 and select four of the strategies shown.
   a) Explain the ideas behind each of your chosen management strategies.
   b) Comment on the effectiveness of each strategy.

2 Look at Figure 6.15.
   a) Explain and comment on the impact of these pressures.
   b) Select three of the pressures and comment on how they can be managed.

6.4 Land degradation related to a semi-arid area

It is time to remind you again about the question you may be given in the exam: 'The impact and management of rural land degradation related to a rainforest or semi-arid area.' We now move to consider semi-arid areas.

The definition of a 'semi-arid' landscape is important. In this textbook we have used the Koppen Climate Classification which recognises both hot and cold semi-arid areas. There is agreement in textbooks about the key features of a semi-arid area:

- Precipitation range will be approximately 250–600 mm.
- The region supports short or scrubby vegetation with grasses and shrubs.
- Rainfall patterns are inherently erratic and variable.
- Rains fall (infrequently) as heavy showers and are lost to run-off.
- A high rate of evapotranspiration.
- A majority of the population of semi-arid lands depend on agriculture and pastoralism for subsistence.

Semi-arid areas are not deserts (which by definition are too dry, with precipitation at below 250 mm).

Semi-arid areas are not savannas (which by definition receive rain in a wet and dry seasonal pattern).

A cautionary note: It is not really possible to draw with any precision any of these climatic regimes on a map. Deserts, semi-arid lands, savanna grasslands and rainforests merge over 2,000 km as you head north from the equator in Africa. Added to this is change. At the moment the desert areas appear to be expanding in area as the semi-arid lands are increasingly becoming deserts and the savanna lands are becoming semi-arid. Confusing? Try the task related to Figure 6.16.

Task

Study Figure 6.16 and, using an atlas, identify the countries that appear to be hot semi-arid and cold semi-arid.

Hot semi-arid areas tend to be found in sub-tropical areas across Africa (the Sahel), parts of west India, parts of Mexico, bordering areas in Texas, USA and in Australia circling the desert.

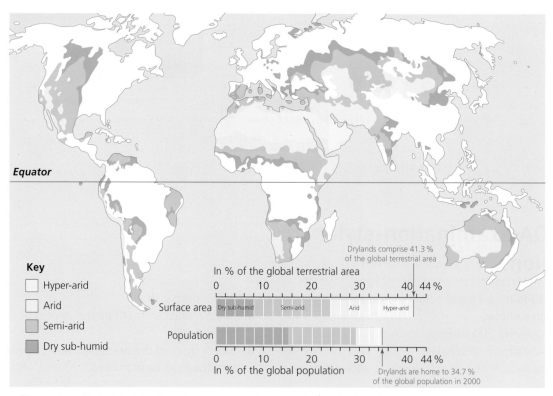

Key
- Hyper-arid
- Arid
- Semi-arid
- Dry sub-humid

Equator

Drylands comprise 41.3 % of the global terrestrial area

In % of the global terrestrial area

| 0 | 10 | 20 | 30 | 40 | 44 % |

Surface area — Dry sub-humid | Semi-arid | Arid | Hyper-arid

Population

| 0 | 10 | 20 | 30 | 40 | 44 % |
In % of the global population

Drylands are home to 34.7 % of the global population in 2000

▲ **Figure 6.16** Global distribution of arid and semi-arid lands (dryland systems)

Cold semi-arid areas are found in continental interiors cut off from the influence of oceans. The summers can be hot with cold winters. The map shows extensive areas in the west of the USA (the 'Dust Bowl') and across China into Russia.

Wind and water processes linked to degradation of the land and soil

Degradation involves the removal of vegetation cover. Vegetation protects the soil by binding it together, intercepting the falling rain and protecting the soil from the effects of the wind. Following practises such as mono-cultivation and over-cultivation nutrients are lost from the soil. Although chemicals, fertilisers and pesticides can strengthen the soil, they can also weaken it through inappropriate use. Acid rain can degrade soil, as can over-irrigation that can cause deposition of salts on the surface. The dumping of hazardous waste can also cause contamination through water seepage. Soil can be compacted and damaged through the tramping of animal feet or the overuse of heavy machinery, so that water cannot drain through the soil properly and root growth is held back. Surface vegetation and soil is also removed to create quarries and opencast mines. Steep bare land left exposed to the 'elements' will quickly degrade.

This section is brief and selective, but will give you an idea of some of the processes involved. The Rural question in the examination paper will not ask you about processes, only about 'impact and management of land degradation'.

Water degradation processes

There are four main processes of water action that can have an influence on the land:

- **Rainsplash**: The impact of raindrops on the soil can dislodge and move soil either outwards (flat land) or downhill (on a slope).
- **Sheet erosion**: The removal of the surface topsoil by heavy rain gently flowing down a slope.
- **Rill erosion**: The creation, by heavy rain, of small (usually temporary) water channels, which over time can lead to larger gullies.

- **Leaching**: When heavy rain washes out minerals from the topsoil.

Such processes can be 'natural', for example following heavy rainfall or flash flooding on an exposed soil, but human activity can speed up the erosion process.

Wind degradation processes

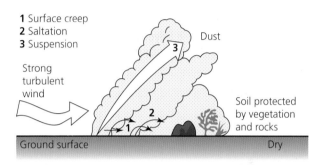

▲ **Figure 6.17** Selected processes of wind erosion

There are three main processes of wind action:

1 **Suspension**: The dust storm is a dramatic feature, when fine soil is blown away, suspended by strong winds.
2 **Saltation**: The most common movement occurs when soil particles close to the ground move in a series of jumps, bounces and rolls.
3 **Surface creep**: A very slow movement over the ground, usually larger particles of soil or stones, rolling and sliding.

Once again wind erosion may be a natural process but the areas that will be studied in this chapter have experienced human influence as part of the process. Ideal conditions include a dry, bare soil and a flat, exposed, windswept surface.

Research opportunity

If you feel that you would like to know more about these water and wind degradation processes try doing an internet search.

Relationship between degradation, soil erosion and desertification in semi-arid lands

Rural lands can be subject to degradation, which may be as a result of natural processes and/or human activities. Increasing damage to soils, forests and grasslands has been noted. This decline has environmental, social and economic consequences and has led to the development of soil conservation and land management strategies.

The decline is happening beyond the natural rate of recovery (sustainability) and the result of this degradation is shown as desertification and soil erosion. Desertification is defined as land degradation in semi-arid areas.

When you compare Figure 6.4 (page 179) and Figure 6.16 (page 196) it is possible to identify a pattern. Those areas of the world identified as being semi-arid seem to coincide with areas of 'serious' and 'some' concern.

 Task

Look at Figure 6.4 (page 179) and Figure 6.16 (page 196) and write your own short report on the desertification of semi-arid lands.

Desertification

A simple statement of desertification is the process by which land deteriorates in quality, where sustainability is not possible, resulting eventually in the land dying. In other words a 'desert' is created.

The best (or worst!) example of the process is found within the Sahel belt that runs across Africa from the Atlantic to the Indian Oceans. Its key geographical features include:

- low, unreliable and variable rainfall resulting in frequent drought
- heavy, intense tropical downpours
- tree, shrub and grass vegetation
- a desperately poor landscape
- low life expectancy, high population growth and local people following 'traditional' styles of life.

There is some debate about the true extent of the Sahel. It is defined as:

> 'A semi-arid region of north-central Africa south of the Sahara Desert.'

Source: The Free Dictionary

Since the 1960s the Sahel has been afflicted by prolonged periods of extensive drought. Agriculture can be sustained as long as the pressures placed on the land can be controlled and measured. Traditionally, arable farming (barley, millet) and pastoral farming (cattle, goats, sheep) are found. However, the land cannot support or sustain intense demands.

About one third of the world's land surface is arid or semi-arid and the prediction is that this will increase by 20 per cent by 2100.

Physical and human causes of rural degradation in semi-arid areas (desertification)

It has been calculated that the Sahel is migrating southwards at a rate of between 5 and 10 km each year.

Desertification is regarded as a natural process intensified by human activities. A United Nations Commission in 2009 stated that it is a combination of increasing animal and human population numbers with elements of climate change that caused the effects of a drought to become more severe. When fragile land is placed under increased pressure, then rapid change and degradation is an outcome.

 Task

1 Explain the link between overgrazing and desertification.
2 Look at Table 6.5 which shows the causes of desertification. Create a table with two columns labelled 'Physical causes' and 'Human causes'. Complete your table using the information from Figure 6.18.
3 In your judgement, which factor appears to be the most significant when identifying cause? Explain your answer.

Table 6.5 Four main causes of desertification

Climatic variability and change:	Deforestation and the search for fuelwood and shelter:
• A problem occurs when a number of 'wet' years give false hope to the local people about the land's capability. Ploughing, planting and settlement take place and when the climate switches back to a dry pattern the vegetation dies, the soil becomes degraded, crops fail and grazing is destroyed. • Variability may mean high seasonality or total failure. • Climate change has been discussed in detail in the accompanying textbook, *Global Issues*.	• In the West, we may talk about the energy crisis and the high cost of power. In the semi-arid lands the crisis is about wood and roots for cooking, keeping warm and shelter. Loss of protective cover from grass, shrubs, trees, leaves and branches allows the rain to erode the soil and the sun to parch the soil. Loss of vegetable matter breaks up the nutrient cycle. Once again there is degradation of the soil as the root system cannot bind the soil, **evaporation** increases and run-off and wind can pick up the dry light soil. • The problem is that this activity for fuel is not sustainable.
Overgrazing:	**Over-cultivation and poor farming practices:**
• This is the increase in animals above the 'carrying capacity'. In Mali, the number of cattle, sheep and goats increased by 40% between 2005 and 2015. There is a tendency to equate wealth and security with the number of cattle a farmer may have. The issue should really be about quality of meat rather than the quantity. Land can only be sustainable if there is a balance between the inputs and the demands on it. Too many animals will compact the soil and, put simply, they will eat too much! When compacted, the soil cannot absorb the rain, leading to greater run-off, while the trampling increases the impact of wind erosion. The vegetation will be eaten, the roots exposed, the soil exposed and degraded and the vegetation cannot re-establish itself. Where boreholes and wells have been dug, this increases localised overgrazing and degradation. • Early nomad pastoralists living in semi-arid areas moved their small groups of animals in relation to grazing and water availability. With increasing population numbers and density and increased government control, nomadism as a way of life is diminishing.	• If too much is taken from the soil without replacing the nutrients, it is inevitable that deterioration will take place. Growing single crops year after year (monoculture), failing to rest the land (fallow) or being over-ambitious during 'wet' times, can all result in too much pressure on the soil. • Populations have increased in all of the semi-arid lands. Many of these rural people wish to continue to farm. More people means more demand for food and increased strain on the land. This can result in more crops being grown, fewer fallow periods and an increasing tendency to grow 'cash crops' intensively. • Traditional farmers may lack the experience or knowledge to farm this 'marginal' land.

Impact of degradation in semi-arid areas

The impact (or consequences) of degradation following desertification are serious and can be categorised as:

● environmental
● economic
● social/cultural.

The impact is overwhelmingly negative and it is difficult to consider any positives in the degradation of the semi-arid environment.

Management strategies to combat degradation and desertification in semi-arid lands

One of the strengths of Geography is our skill in being able to identify problems and find ways to combat them. As with the issue of deforestation, there are no simple answers.

▲ **Figure 6.18** Summary of the main causes of desertification

▼ **Table 6.6** Impact of desertification and subsequent degradation

Environmental	Economic	Social and cultural
A reduction in the land available for cropping and pasture.	Reduced income from pastoralism and the cultivation of food crops.	Forced migration due to food scarcity to the towns and cities. Migrants tend to be young males, creating additional problems in the shanty towns.
Expansion of the desert into the semi-arid land.	Increased rural poverty.	Governments and charity organisations may have to set up refugee camps. Conditions are likely to be appalling, with overcrowding and insufficient health and education facilities.
Increased environmental damage as a result of wind and water erosion.	A decrease in available fuel-wood, resulting in people buying alternative fuels (e.g. oil and kerosene).	Increase in social tensions.
A change and loss of fauna and flora and a reduction in the biodiversity of the landscape.		A loss of traditional knowledge and skills.
The semi-desert will become a desert.		Psychological impact as many people will have an increased dependency on international aid.
Loss of sustainability.		People will die, communities broken up and a way of life lost.

The case studies that follow provide more detail on the issues of impact, management strategies and solutions. We will consider:

- the Dust Bowl of the Great Plains, USA
- north-west and west China
- the Sahel.

Case study: The Dust Bowl of the Great Plains, USA

'Houses were shut tight, and cloth wedged around doors and windows, but the dust came in so thinly that it could not be seen in the air, and it settled like pollen on the chairs and tables, on the dishes.'

John Steinbeck, *The Grapes of Wrath* (1939)

▲ **Figure 6.19** Dust storm, Texas, 1935

▲ **Figure 6.20** Dust Storm, Oklahoma, 2012

Dust storm damage, 1930–40

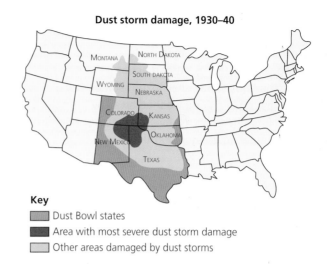

Key

- Dust Bowl states
- Area with most severe dust storm damage
- Other areas damaged by dust storms

▲ **Figure 6.21** Dust Bowl states and the extent of the dust storms

Why is a case study on the 1930s Dust Bowl included here? It is a classic study of what happens when we fail to care. The soil conservation strategies used then still have relevance today.

The Great Plains cover an area which stretches from the southern parts of the Canadian prairie provinces (Alberto, Saskatchewan and Manitoba) down the eastern side of the Rocky Mountains to the Dust Bowl states of Colorado, Kansas, Oklahoma, New Mexico and Texas. Rural land degradation is a combination of physical, climatic and human influences. For centuries the Native Indian people hunted and gathered in a sustainable manner across the Plains. As the 'West' was colonised, cattle ranchers and arable farmers moved in, and not only destroyed the traditional way of life, but imposed a new, alien structure and system on this balanced landscape, with damaging effect.

Physical causes of land degradation in the Dust Bowl

The area is in the rain shadow of the Rocky Mountains and far from the sea, with variable low to moderate precipitation, sometimes resulting in drought as in the 1930s, early 1980s 2012 and again in 2018. However, during the 1990s there was above average precipitation with flash flooding and water erosion of the landscape. The rural landscape has suffered from degradation with the grassland progressively destroyed over the years (both naturally because of lightning strikes and by human action). If left bare and dry, the light sandy chernozem soil can by picked up easily by the wind and washed away by the rain and from flash flooding. Native grasses have been removed following 'deep ploughing'.

Human causes of land degradation in the Dust Bowl

The worst years occurred in the 1930s when farmers over-cultivated the land by ploughing the marginal farmland and overgrazing. This was worst on the western, drier parts of the Plains. The farmers often were guilty of monoculture (especially wheat) without crop rotation or fallowing and as a consequence the soil structure was weakened and yields fell. Such farming practices were more suited to the wetter parts of eastern USA. The 1930s was a time when new machines (such as tractors with heavy, deep ploughs) ripped apart the land and there was a total lack of environmental understanding.

Environmental impact

The topsoil was eroded and blown away in massive dust storms that were described as 'black blizzards'. The soil became barren and infertile, smothering vegetation, choking wildlife and blocking sunlight. The fragile soil that took centuries to fully develop was destroyed in just a few years.

Social and economic impact

Farms were abandoned, settlements were depopulated and there were growing levels of poverty. Many farmers and their families migrated to cities such as Los Angeles and states such as California in search of employment. Communities were split and the area was left with a general feeling of helplessness, depression and despair.

Solutions and strategies to prevent further land degradation

The federal government was involved as early as 1933, when FD Roosevelt created government programmes for better 'stewardship of the land'. The Civilian Conservation Corps (CCC) restored balance by planting trees and many projects attempted to educate farmers and encourage alternative forms of employment (e.g. the construction industry). The US Soil Conservation Service was formed to oversee and advise, to manage and to regenerate the area. Strategies included shelter belts, the introduction of fallowing and crop rotation, diversification of crops, contour ploughing, soil banks, strip cultivation, trash farming and stubble mulching, reducing the intensity of farming, encouraging alternative sources of employment in the area, returning marginal land to native grassland, and so on (see Table 6.7). From the 1950s to the 1990s new sources of underground water were exploited with large-scale irrigation available on the carefully managed farms.

▼ **Table 6.7** Examples of soil conservation strategies

Shelter belts	Planting of trees at right angles to the direction of the prevailing wind. This acts as a barrier for the land behind. A 10 m high tree can break the force of the wind between 80 and 100 m downwind. Shelter belts are effective, but can be costly and they require maintenance, take up farmland space and require many years (25–50) before their impact can be really felt. Used extensively in the Dust Bowl and across the semi-arid areas of China.
Contour ploughing	Ploughing around a hill rather than up and down the slope. The rainfall and water movement will be checked and 50% is more likely to infiltrate the soil, rather than form rills and gullies. Contour ploughing is effective in that soil moisture level is increased resulting in more vegetation growth. Ploughing this way does take longer and, to be really accurate, it is necessary to mark the contours with posts. Once again, used extensively in the Dust Bowl semi-arid lands.
Terracing	Especially used in areas with steep slopes. A series of steps can be created in the side of the hill, forming a number of flat (sometimes flooded) fields. Again, the negative effect of rainwater and surface run-off can be checked, as well as reducing the chance of rills, gullies or even a landslip developing. Terraces are very effective long-term solutions but they take time to construct and require regular maintenance. Found within the hillsides of the Tennessee Valley and in the Sahel zone in Africa.

Evaluation of the solutions and strategies used in the Dust Bowl

Let's consider the storms of 2012. During this exceptional year there was drought, combined with exceptionally high temperatures, strong winds and an economic depression, in fact the same conditions as 1935. So what happened? The area did not return to the 'black blizzards'. However, there are real problems waiting to surface again. The water table is dropping, irrigation water is declining, there is clear evidence of climate change giving higher temperatures and less rain in the area and there is increased population pressure and increased demand for food, forcing farmers to push for more output from less productive land.

The Dust Bowls of the 1930s have not returned, the area is now more diversified in terms of employment structure and there has been no return to the poverty and despair of those years. The wind is now used for power generation but settlements such as Boise City continue to shrink (an 18 per cent reduction in population since 2000). Wells are drying up and cattle are being sold at the market for very low prices as the pasture diminishes in quantity and quality.

Case study: China

China has serious land degradation because of desertification. Forty per cent or 3.5 million km^2 of the country is desert or semi-arid. Just 8 per cent of the land feeds the Chinese population of 1.4 billion people. China has made incredible economic and social progress in recent years, but at serious environmental cost. According to the China State Forestry Administration, the desert areas are still expanding by between 2,500 and 10,000 km^2 per year. Up to 450 million people live in areas that are at risk of desertification – 37 per cent of the total land area. Some of this is happening around the expanding desert but much of it is at the edge of the settled area. This suggests that both physical and human activities are to blame.

Physical and human causes of land degradation in China

The degraded area for this case study is found in north-west and north China, covering land which is arid or semi-arid. Rainfall is low (200–600 mm) and unreliable, often falling as intensive thunderstorms.

There has been an acceleration of soil erosion (caused by both wind and water), drought, livestock overgrazing, poor agricultural practices (over-cropping, mono-cropping, no fallow period, cultivating steep slopes), excessive logging on the more humid mountain slopes and excessive cutting and gathering of fuelwood. Land is also lost to urbanisation and industrialisation.

Coal mining and oil extraction is also causing not only a loss of agricultural land but also river, land and air pollution. Beijing has massive issues with the quality of its air. Some of this has an industrial origin, but dust storms are now more than an occasional problem, causing health issues more than once a year. The value of the loss of pasture, fewer livestock and a reduction in commercial farming has been put at over $18 billion a year – about 4 per cent of GDP.

Reuters, the news agency, reported that 40 per cent of China's arable land is degraded and unless action is taken now, by 2030 agricultural productivity will have dropped by 10 per cent.

Regional impact is greatest in the Loess Plateau area and in the extensive regions of the north-west and west. Poverty and land degradation are closely correlated. The direct causes include ongoing deforestation of steep slopes, over-intensive use of grasslands for livestock production, neglect of community conservation practices under the new rural system and use of biomass for energy in rural areas.

Other concerns include:

● grain production in dryland areas without soil conservation
● poor management of groundwater resources
● improper management of soil and water on irrigated lands
● loss of agricultural land through urban and industrial expansion.

Solutions and strategies to prevent further land degradation

There are generic strategies that are applied to land degradation in semi-arid areas: these are standard responses that are used in areas throughout the world. The Chinese response to land degradation is to manage the issues. In China, there is a pattern of strong government involvement in all aspects of economic and social life; while this is less than in the past, local area committees still have an influence over management. Regretfully there have also been many publicised examples of government corruption in large public programmes. Some examples of the strategies employed in China are described below.

Deforestation and fuelwood collection

Strategies include encouraging agroforestry (combining agriculture with woodland planting), protecting existing areas, restricting collection of 'live' wood for fuel (enforced by fines) and encouraging the use of cheap alternative fuels such as kerosene or oil. These strategies have been reasonably effective. However, it may take a minimum of 40 years before the benefits of tree planting are felt and there are always problems enforcing restrictions.

Alternative fuels are not always available or cheap; ovens may not be adaptable to the new fuels and expensive to replace.

The strategies used to manage overgrazing, poor farming practices and attempts to stop desertification are similar to those outlined earlier in this chapter, but the Chinese have come up with a few extra strategies.

The China National Research and Development Centre on Combating Desertification was established as the core group to manage the problem and work with outside organisations such as the United Nations and other countries to combat desertification by developing profitable techniques and environmentally sound practices. This includes fixing sand through planting native grasses, covering the sand with oil based chemicals, water saving techniques through modern irrigation systems such as drip irrigation and eliminating water seepage and loss through evaporation. A massive forest shelterbelt programme was launched in 1978 which brought 10 per cent of the desertified semi-arid land back under control again. Groundwater projects in Shaanxi Province have meant that cropping on irrigated land is possible and shifting dunes have been stabilised. Here, forest coverage has increased from 2 per cent to 38 per cent. In Jiangxi Province,

bamboo contour trenches were dug to prevent soil erosion, community methane tanks installed and shrubs planted primarily for fuelwood.

China is developing rapidly but there remains considerable variation between the wealth of rural and urban people. It is accepted that the Chinese Government is committed to managing their environmental problems.

Evaluation of the solutions and strategies used in China

A recent UN report on the causes and consequences of degradation stated that China suffers from degradation as a result of both physical and human factors. Economic growth and population pressures are placing a great strain on China's environment. There have been impressive results, but the rate of desertification appears to be exceeding the rate of environmental restoration (Table 6.8). Population and economic pressures continue to place a strain on China's environment.

Task

Identify some of the environmental, economic and social consequences of the impact of land degradation/desertification in north-west and west China.

Case study: Burkina Faso in the Sahel

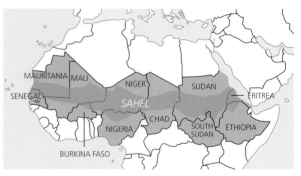

▲ **Figure 6.22** Map showing the Sahel countries

▼ **Table 6.8** Summary of impact, management and evaluation of China case study

Impact	Management	Evaluation
• Very high pressures on land resources • Concerns over serious environmental costs • 450 million people live in areas at risk of desertification • Accelerated soil erosion, drought and overgrazing • Rural poverty • Drop in agricultural output • Loss of forest • Out-migration to cities	• Willingness of the government to support short- and long-term programmes • Taking steps to tackle corruption • Breaking down the problems into individual parts • Continuing with an afforestation programme • Support use of alternative fuels • Continue to educate farmers to implement positive agricultural practices • Stabilisation of the shifting dunes	• Government supporting regional governments • Very severe penalties being imposed • Completion of 5, 10 and 20 year plans • Since 1977 a massive area has been afforested. Successful but regretfully the spreading of the semi-desert continues • Only successful when the alternatives such as kerosene are subsidised and government gives subsidies • Successful when it works but Chinese farmers are very conservative in their traditions • Usually very successful, since many people available to work on such projects

▲ **Figure 6.23** Drought and decreasing water reserves in Burkina Faso have resulted in failed crops and a lack of pasture

'The Sahel covers parts of (from west to east) Senegal, southern Mauritania, central Mali, northern Burkina Faso, extreme south of Algeria, Niger, extreme north of Nigeria, central Chad, central and southern Sudan, northern South Sudan and northern Eritrea.'

Source: Wikipedia

Other sources describe six Sahel countries, but whether it is six or eleven countries is mainly irrelevant since the focus is on a growing and changing problem that has a global impact. It is estimated that 30 million people are affected by land degradation across the Sahel.

The key locational features of the Sahel include:

- low, unreliable and variable rainfall resulting in frequent drought
- occasional heavy, intense downpours
- native tree, shrub and grass vegetation
- social challenges, poverty, low life expectancy, high population growth and a 'traditional' culture and lifestyle.

Agriculture can be sustained as long as the pressures placed on the land can be controlled and measured. Traditionally arable farming (barley, millet, peanuts, sorghum and rice) and pastoral farming (cattle, goats, sheep) are found but the land cannot support or sustain intense demand.

Physical and human causes of desertification with land degradation in the Sahel

Burkina Faso is a landlocked country, located between 9 and 15 degrees north. It is a desperately poor country with a life expectancy of 56, chronic malnutrition affecting 36 per cent of the population and 50 per cent of the population surviving on less than $1 per day.

To the north, the landscape is part of the wider belt known as the Sahel and this has a semi-arid climate.

It has been calculated that the Sahel is migrating southwards at a rate of between 5 and 10 km each year. In Burkina Faso the following features have been noted:

- Recurring drought (possibly linked to the unreliability of the ITCZ and climate change), with the most recent droughts being in 2012 and 2017.
- Overgrazing (cattle are regarded as a measure of wealth and status).
- Overcropping because of the pressure to feed people.
- Urbanisation and pressures put on the land.
- Poor irrigation and drainage practices, leading to saltation and leaching.
- Over-intensive farming and too many small farms, especially in 'marginal areas'.
- Rapid population increase (over 2.5 per cent per year) and increasing demand for food.
- Wet productive years in the 1960s and 1970s encouraged agriculture that subsequent drought conditions have been unable to support and sustain.
- Shortage of alternative fuels encourages over-exploitation of wood and deforestation.
- The best land is used for cash cropping (e.g. cotton, rice), putting more pressure on marginal areas.
- Flash floods are experienced.
- Poor farming techniques and practices.
- Extreme poverty and reliance on international aid.
- Increasing market prices for foods.
- Civil unrest and the recent overthrow of the President (2014).

 Task

Organise the notes above into a list of physical and human factors.

Social and economic impact

The resulting drought and degradation has resulted in migration from affected rural communities into new areas as well as into the cities such as the capital, Ouagadougou. This has created strain in the shanty towns and pressure on the land elsewhere. The people of Burkina Faso experience malnutrition, famine, crop failure, increasing mortality levels, ill health and death. The traditional way of life is under threat and there is growing conflict between nomadic pastoralists and the fixed farming communities. There is a shortage of wood for cooking and building. Incomes are low and there is a growing reliance on overseas aid from countries, international organisations and charities. Debts are building up. Following civil unrest in Mali, there are now Malinese refugee camps within the border of Burkina Faso, adding to the stress on resources.

Environmental impact

The soil is exposed, breaks up and is eroded by the wind, meaning that fragile soil is permanently lost. The soil dries up, the water table drops and so the land is increasingly becoming arid with little economic value. The World Resources Institute claim that Burkina Faso loses 35 tonnes of soil per hectare per year.

Solutions and strategies to prevent further land degradation

For over 40 years the MEDCs have been active within the Sahel zone. The best approach to the problem of degradation is to consider each specific issue and then find the best way to resolve that issue.

In addition to the various strategies mentioned in the Dust Bowl and China case studies, the following have been introduced in the area north of Ouahigouya in northern Burkina Faso.

Gullies have been filled in and stone walls (diguettes) built to reduce the impact of run-off. In an attempt to reduce the power of the wind and stop the physical movement of the sand, drought-resistant shrubs and trees have been planted and sand dunes stabilised. Land has been fenced off to give protection from uncontrolled goat and sheep grazing. Farmers are being educated to use more appropriate techniques such as terracing, fallowing, strip cropping and irrigation. Through both local schemes with community involvement and co-operation and large-scale projects there are numerous attempts to improve the water supply and increase irrigation, for example three dams and reservoirs have been constructed. Local people are encouraged to use appropriate and intermediate technology, such as the use of basic but effective fuel-saving stoves.

Outside of Burkina Faso, the Eden Foundation programme in Nigeria encourages farmers to grow perennial plants to protect the soil against the heavy rain. This prevents rainsplash from dislodging fine sand and soil particles and ensures that the soil is not exposed and that the roots bind the loose soil.

Stone lines slow down run-off, increase water infiltration and form the basis for improved production in semi-arid areas. At the same time, sediment is captured behind these semi-permeable barriers. Stone lines were originally a traditional technique in the Sahel (for example in Mali and Burkina Faso), but have been improved by careful construction and through aligning the lines along the land contours. Stone lines are suited to low slopes, high run-off and hand labour. It is a simple remedy that really works.

Evaluation of the solutions and strategies used in Burkina Faso

So what is the outcome of all this activity? There is no doubt that without such initiatives and programmes the area would be even more desperately poor than it already is. When linked to small-scale local projects and using local people, there is a far greater chance of success, especially with regard to irrigation, drainage and reforestation. Although there are successes the desert continues to track south and desertification continues to degrade the land, making life uncertain for the people of northern Burkina Faso. Many people believe that the underlying problem in such areas is poverty. This area has the combined disadvantages of climate change, population pressure, overgrazing, Aids/HIV, poverty and debt.

 ## Reflection

Now that you have completed this section on rural land degradation, look back at the quote from HRH Prince of Wales in which he comments that 'forests ... are in fact the world's air-conditioning system ...' (page 180). What are your views on his comments?

 ## Task

'Land degradation involves two interlocking, complex systems: the natural ecosystem and the human social system.'

'Nomadic peoples lived in harmony with drylands for thousands of years. Land degradation begins when populations increase to the point that the land can no longer sustain the people.'

1 Explain the background to these quotations using examples from the case studies on the Dust Bowl or the Sahel.

'People use wood for cooking and heating. When the population is too large, forests are destroyed to obtain wood. Forests are also cut or burned to make way for crops (slash-and-burn agriculture), or to obtain wood for export.'

2 A cause of land degradation in both the rainforest and the semi-arid lands has been deforestation or the removal of vegetation for fuelwood. Using examples from any affected area:
a) explain why this has happened
b) examine and comment on the impact of these practices
c) give examples and evidence to support the management strategies that have been attempted to resolve the issue
d) comment on the successes or limits of these strategies.

6.5 Rural land use conflicts and their management

In Chapter 3, Lithosphere, we studied in some depth the formation of erosional and depositional features of coastal and glaciated landscapes. In this section we are going to consider *rural land conflicts and their management related to these two landscapes.*

Conflict Geography has become a very important subject in recent years and can be looked at on a variety of levels – international, national, regional and local.

For the purposes of the Higher Geography course and exam paper we will be studying land use conflicts at the smallest scale (i.e. locally focused on a small part of a region or country).

A conflict is defined as:

> *'A state of opposition, disagreement, argument between those with opposing ideas, interests, or beliefs.'*

Adapted from the Collins Dictionary

Conflicts can be caused by a number of issues but here we will focus on land disputes and in particular about land usage. Different people or groups of people will have different relationships with the landscape and equally varied opinions on how it should be managed and developed or whether it should be developed at all. Anyone who has active interest in a specific area, or is affected by activities in that area, is known as a stakeholder. Stakeholders could include the inhabitants of the local area, regular visitors or tourists, people with a passion for a particular way of life or appearance of an area, local businesses, industrialists and conservationists. The list of stakeholders can be extensive, as can the variety of beliefs, ideas and responses they have.

Of course it is impossible to include every possible conflict within the areas we are studying or to give every point of view. Instead, we will give a general outline of the possibilities and some examples of conflict and management. It is therefore important that you become aware of the landscape, how people use a particular area and what it is they want to either preserve or change. Geography is a living topic and it is up to you to look for additional examples and research for the most up-to-date information.

Glaciated landscape conflict

While recognising that there are many areas open for conflict in lowland glaciated landscapes, we have chosen to highlight those in previously glaciated areas in upland areas. These are areas of particularly delicate environments which have become major areas of conflict.

Glaciated upland landscapes are very recent in geological terms; much of the development of soils, for example, has only been in the last 10,000 years, on steep slopes in difficult climatic conditions. Here, due to altitude, there is increased precipitation, often snow during winter, and lower temperatures in general. Some of the higher areas experience strong winds and this creates difficult conditions for soil development, agriculture and human occupation in general.

The steep slopes and mountains helped to create the isolation that these areas experienced and this, along with the natural conditions described, resulted in those who lived here developing their own traditional agriculture and human landscapes to meet their needs.

Striking scenery, potential for active and passive tourism, traditional landscapes and a feeling of solitude make glaciated upland areas extremely attractive to visitors. Modern transport networks and cars, together with increased affluence and leisure time, have increased the attraction of these areas as well as the potential for conflict.

Other natural features make suitable conditions for exploitation:

- Large areas of igneous and metamorphic rocks are targeted by companies to quarry for financial gain.
- Rugged, varied and difficult terrain is ideal for military training.

It should be realised that although they are famed for their isolation, upland glacial areas are used for many activities, both economic and recreational (Table 6.9).

Reflection

You are planning a week's holiday in an upland former glaciated area. The purpose of your holiday is to relax and enjoy the scenery. How could the activities of exploitation shown in Table 6.9 affect your holiday?

▼ **Table 6.9** Examples of ways that upland glacial areas are used

Agriculture	Traditionally the land on the valley floor is used for grazing cattle or arable farming, usually to provide feed/fodder for farm animals. Near the farm buildings some crops are grown, including root vegetables, but mostly for personal rather than commercial use.
	Further up the sides of the valley beef cattle continue to graze but as climatic conditions and steepness of slope increase this decreases.
	Although sheep may not prefer these conditions, they are able to withstand them and provide farmers with purposeful economic use of this land.
	In winter conditions animals are traditionally brought from the higher ground to lower areas near the farm.
Forestry	The bases of glacial troughs and the well-drained deposited materials at their sides, together with the availability of a good water supply due to high rainfall, provide ideal conditions for commercial forestry.
Reservoirs and hydroelectric power	Deep glacial troughs with their **impermeable** igneous and metamorphic bedrock in an area of high rainfall provide perfect conditions for damming and the creation of reservoirs. The water supply can then be used in the creation of hydroelectric power (HEP). The igneous and metamorphic rocks also provide solid bases for dams.
	Hydroelectric power may also necessitate the building of pylons and cables.
Wind farms	Wind turbines can be located on mountainsides to take advantage of the stronger winds.
Rock climbing, hill walking, mountaineering	The natural features of this area create great potential for these kinds of sports and recreational activities. Steep valley sides and corrie headwalls provide challenging climbs while arêtes offer often difficult and/or exciting routes for the hillwalker. For mountaineers pyramidal peaks give access to a number of different and varying climbing experiences.
Cycling	Various forms of cycling are becoming increasingly popular in these areas. The steep slopes provide difficult challenges for those on roads or paths but off-road cycling is becoming increasingly popular even in some of the more extreme locations.
Winter sports	The higher precipitation and low winter temperatures result in greater levels of snowfall in the mountains. Corries are particularly suitable for winter sports as they collect and maintain snowfall for longer periods of time. Their shape allows a variety of slopes to be experienced from very steep, through steep to gentle. Increased popularity of skiing and snowboarding leads to a demand for additional and improved winter sports facilities.
Sightseeing	The spectacular scenery of steep mountains, impressive valleys, waterfalls and lakes makes them popular for sightseeing visitors, resulting in an increase in the number of cars and even coaches using the roads.
Hunting	Moorland has been exploited for use in hunting. Acidic soils and a lack of other appropriate economic use has enabled this activity to develop. In Scotland this may include grouse, pheasant and deer shooting.
Fishing	Some fjords (sea lochs in Scotland) allow sheltered areas for fishing boats to be able to fish. Ribbon lakes tend to attract more rod or small net fishing.
Harbours	The deep water in fjords can provide sheltered harbours, enabling large ships such as ore carriers or oil tankers to come close in to shore. However, problems include: • the bar at the fjord mouth may make the entrance too shallow • there may only be limited land available at the fjord head, making port development difficult • the mountainous **hinterland** may make it impossible or very difficult to transport goods into or out from the port.
Military	As noted above, plus the steep and deep valleys provide challenging low-level flying environments.

▼ **Table 6.9** Examples of ways that upland glacial areas are used *(continued)*

Settlement	In general this is likely to be dispersed and isolated. Larger settlements tend to be limited in their location and are more likely to be: • at the heads of fjords (sea lochs) • on land raised above potential flooding on the valley floor • on the sides of the valley facing the south so as to receive sunlight and warmth.
Communications	The difficulty of developing communications into and within glaciated upland areas has until recently helped to maintain their isolation. The creation of roads or railways through mountains is difficult, dangerous and very expensive and may require tunnelling, large spans of bridges or complex hairpin roads. This has resulted in few methods of transport into an area and roads which are difficult and narrow.

Reflection

Reflect again on your holiday to an upland glaciated area. What kind of facilities would you need or want to be provided so that you gain maximum enjoyment from your stay?

Sources of conflict in upland glacial areas

Conflicts over land use are often complex and may involve many groups. However, to simplify things, we will look now at the likely players and some of the main issues. We have attempted to identify whether these are environmental conflicts or socio-economic conflicts, as exam questions may specify a response about one or the other.

Local residents/conservationists and visitors (day trippers, tourists, active recreation)

- Increased traffic on local roads resulting in:
  - *Environmental* – additional noise, increased air pollution, more dangerous road conditions including crossing roads (especially for children)
  - *Socio-economic* – increased journey time because of traffic congestion, hold-ups for those on business, increased danger for livestock.
- *Socio-economic*: Farm gates left open can lead to the loss of valuable livestock.
- Litter:
  - *Environmental* – makes the area look dirty and untidy.
  - *Socio-economic* – paper bags, bottles, cans and plastic can cause livestock to choke and die.

- *Environmental* – wildlife can also be harmed and the smallest of creatures may become trapped or drowned in bottles or cans.
- *Environmental*: Walkers and cyclists can wear away the top levels of soils in this fragile environment. Damage may be permanent or it may take a long time for the land to recover. A worn path can often act as a channel for water causing even greater erosion of soil. It is not only the soil that disappears but the vegetation too, including protected species of plants that only exist in these tundra-like conditions. Wildlife habitats can be trampled on, run over and destroyed.
- *Socio-economic and environmental*: Dogs being let off their leads may chase, attack and even kill farm animals and wildlife. Simply being chased may cause animals to miscarry and for a farmer this results in a loss of revenue, increased vet bills or payment for the disposal of animal carcasses.
- *Socio-economic*: Increasing numbers of tourists often encourages a change in use for local shops to those that cater almost exclusively for the tourist. Shops catering for the everyday life of local people become fewer in number and prices increase.
- *Environmental*: Additional noise by tourists in the form of partying and late-night drinking can disrupt the normal working life cycle in the area, both within settlements and in the countryside. Those who have moved to experience solitude and quiet find their idyll being destroyed. Noise may have similar effects on wildlife and farm animals as those noted from being chased by dogs.
- *Environmental*: Skiing facilities with their buildings, chairlifts, funicular railways, access roads and car parks damage the view, and the flora and fauna. Skiing or snowboarding on only a light snow cover can damage the soil and/or vegetation beneath, leading to soil erosion and scarring of the landscape.

Long-term residents and holidaymakers/inward-moving house buyers

- *Socio-economic*: Popular areas find themselves under pressure from those who either wish to have a regular holiday home to visit, or people who wish to move into the area because of its attractive qualities. This demand causes an increase in house prices, often to a level that is unaffordable to those who may have lived in the area for generations. Wages in the local area, especially those associated with agriculture, are often low, meaning that local people cannot compete with those who have moved from areas with greater employment opportunities and higher wages. The result is that younger members of the local community are often forced to leave the area. A further source of conflict is that many holiday homes lie empty for long periods of the year.

Local residents/conservationists/tourists and power generation

- *Environmental and socio-economic*: The creation of hydroelectric power schemes has caused great conflict and controversy as they entail the building of vast dams, visible pipelines, turbine buildings and electricity pylons. Whole valleys are often flooded, resulting in the loss of the most viable farmland on the base of the valley floor and even the eviction of the communities who lived there. These projects are seen to be for the national good, providing clean, renewable energy, but local people may lose their homes and farmland, and the natural scenery can be severely damaged.
- *Environmental*: Controversy over power generation has increased in recent years with the introduction of single wind turbines or even wind farms consisting of many turbines. Concern has also been raised over this renewable source, not only for being a perceived blot on the landscape but for the damage it can do to the fragile environment. Construction of wind turbines requires vehicular access to upland areas, electricity cables being dug into the ground and a great deal of activity on the surrounding land. Thus the natural environments of local flora and fauna can be severely disrupted and soil erosion may occur. In addition, many conservationists highlight the killing of protected species of birds as they fly into the turbine blades.

Construction of both hydroelectric plants and wind turbines increases construction traffic, adding to the noise, air pollution and traffic problems experienced by local people and tourists.

Local residents and other local residents/tourists/conservationists

- *Socio-economic*: For some local residents the opportunities provided by quarrying, construction work and tourism greatly outweigh the changes to the landscape and the community. In areas of low employment such developments provide employment opportunities that are often better paid than jobs in the agricultural sector.

 Task

Note: We have described just some of the possible conflicts that occur in upland glacial areas, as they are too numerous to describe in full.

1 Think about the conflicts that could occur due to the following land (and in one case, water) uses:
- large-scale plantation of a single type of conifer tree
- military training exercises
- building a modern housing estate at the edge of a traditional local village
- building a visitor centre at a place of scenic value (i.e. a beauty spot)
- using jet-skis or powerboats on ribbon lakes.

2 For each example above, describe the types of conflict likely to occur and the groups of people involved on each side.

3 For the people on both sides explain the reasons for their point of view and what they would wish the outcome to be.

4 Try to identify some solutions to the problems but also highlight any potential problems with the solutions you come up with.

Resolving conflicts

While we may have some understanding of the methods used to make people aware of a point of view within a conflict, or even what the conflict is based on, conflict resolution can be multi-layered and very difficult.

Awareness campaigns may take the form of:

- leafleting
- public meetings
- social media campaigns
- publicity stunts
- appearing on television or radio
- creating information media (e.g. a conflict newspaper, or a video/DVD)
- letters to MSPs, MPs, interested parties.

The above are only limited methods of creating awareness.

Conflict resolution can be much more complex and the same methods do not work for every issue. Figure 6.24 shows a *simplified* model of conflict resolution for important and/or contentious land-use issues. Examples of solutions:

- Limiting access to areas where damage may be caused.
- Channel tourists and visitors to areas of attraction where they can be controlled and educated, for example by the provision of parking, toilet facilities, rubbish bins, picnic areas/cafés, an education centre, maps and routeways signposted

to reduce the possibility of people wandering and causing damage. In some areas specially created walkways have been built to limit damage to flora and fauna and reduce footpath erosion.

- Restricting access to areas at particular times of the day.
- In areas with narrow roads, creating one-way systems and banning parking, both in settlements and the countryside.
- Limiting the times when explosives may be used for quarrying.
- Limiting when vehicles that transport rock from quarries are allowed on the roads to prevent small roads being blocked during peak traffic times and to reduce noise at night.
- Strict licensing agreements to prevent clubs or pubs creating unnecessary noise late at night and similar restrictions for camp and caravan sites.
- Speed restrictions for both road vehicles and those on waterways and lakes.
- Providing clear signposting to direct walkers and cyclists to those area where they are allowed to be. Signposting can also include expected behaviour information and reasons for limitations.

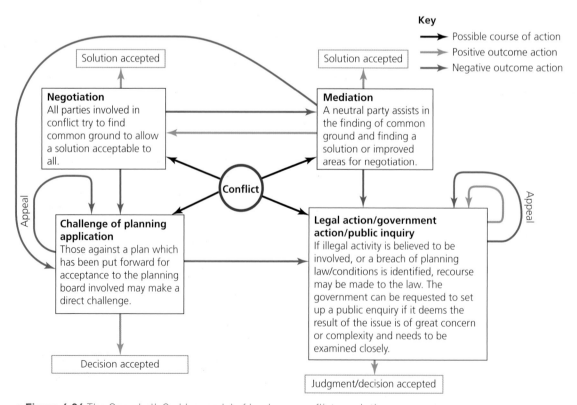

▲ **Figure 6.24** The Campbell-Geddes model of land-use conflict resolution

- Building tourist buildings in a manner that merges with the traditional styles of the area and/or locating them where they are not easily visible to passers-by (in hollows in the landscape; planting trees or bushes to camouflage them).

Local authorities have the ability to create bylaws to enforce the above through fines.

Areas of scenic, ecological, environmental, historic or cultural value that are under threat can be specially protected by law. There are different ways that this is done, with probably the best-known approach being through the creation of **national parks** and **National Scenic Areas** (Scotland). A variety of other options are available throughout the United Kingdom to protect areas of scenic, **biodiversity** and **geodiversity** value. However, these areas can cause their own conflicts as they try to uphold their statutory obligations. National parks in England and Wales (at the time of writing this book there are none in Northern Ireland, although one is proposed for the Mountains of Mourne) have two statutory obligations:

- To conserve and enhance the natural beauty, wildlife and cultural heritage.
- To promote opportunities for the understanding and enjoyment of the special qualities of national parks by the public.

The statutory obligations of Scotland's national parks (the Cairngorms, Loch Lomond and the Trossachs) (Figure 6.25) are as follows:

- To conserve and enhance the natural and cultural heritage of the area.
- To promote sustainable use of the natural resources of the area.
- To promote understanding and enjoyment (including enjoyment in the form of recreation) of the special qualities of the area by the public.
- To promote sustainable economic and social development of the area's communities.

While not a statutory obligation, the national parks in England and Wales are also expected to 'foster the economic and social well-being of local communities' in a manner similar to the fourth obligation of those in Scotland.

The obligations and responsibilities of these parks are difficult to balance. Here are a few possible conflicts:

- House prices rise when a developer is forced to use traditional stones, heights, sizes and, at times, methods to match the look of the area. Local people struggle to afford these or feel this is unfair.

- Restriction of economic development such as quarrying, forestry and industry means that local people find it difficult to obtain employment and may have to leave the area.
- If economic development is allowed in order to create jobs and improved lifestyles for local people, tourists and conservationists may object to what they see as spoiling of the land.

Research opportunity

Try to find out more ways that the landscape is protected. To begin an internet search you could try the following keywords and phrases: protection of UK landscapes; protected landscapes UK; protection of Scottish landscapes; conservation in the United Kingdom; conservation in Scotland.

Task

1 In your own words explain what is meant by a conflict.
2 Evaluate the conditions within glaciated upland areas and explain why this makes them suitable for exploitation.
3 Look at Table 6.9 (pages 209–210) which gives examples of how upland glacial areas are used. Select five of these uses and then for each of them:
   a) assess the suitability of a glacial upland for the activity's use
   b) explain any difficulties that may be experienced when undertaking the activity selected (both physical and human).
4 For each of the facilities that you identified:
   - Assess their likely effect on the landscape.
   - Assess whether the facility could stimulate conflict and, if so, between which groups.
   - If there is potential for a conflict state the basis for each conflicting group's argument.
   - Critically examine the conflict and decide what solutions could be put in place.
5 Explain the methods used to reduce the impact of quarrying.
6 Explain in your own words why national parks were set up.
7 What are the statutory obligations of national parks in Scotland, and also in England and Wales?

▲ **Figure 6.25** National parks and the location of the Lake District

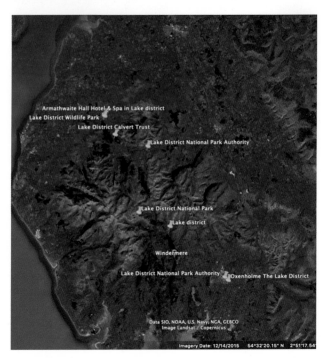

▲ **Figure 6.26** The Lake District

Case study: Lake District

It is possible to look at case studies in almost any region of glaciated uplands and scenery in the British Isles, with good examples found in Loch Lomond and the Trossachs, Arran and the Cairngorms. The reason for choosing the Lake District is the length of time this area has been dealing with the conflicts and pressure put on it by the demand for resources and high visitor numbers (see Figure 6.26). When you have finished this case study, try to look at other examples, maybe in your own local area.

Until the nineteenth century areas such as the Lake District were seen as isolated, untamed and even dangerous places. However, interest was stimulated by the Romantic poets, especially William

Wordsworth, who were inspired by the spectacular glaciated scenery and ribbon lakes (Figure 6.27) and this led to their growing popularity as a place to visit.

It was not until the early twentieth century that the Lake District became a target for any serious levels of tourism. There was a growing appreciation of outdoor exercise and fresh air with many people wishing to escape from the cities and industrial towns. Many travelled to the Lakes via the railway network.

By the 1930s outdoor leisure enthusiasts (ramblers, hillwalkers and cyclists) and conservationists were visiting in increasing numbers. As the century went on and workers became better paid and gained extra free time the number of visitors rose. Eventually concerns were raised about preserving the Lake District and in May 1951 it was designated a national park.

Since then increased car ownership, the development of a national network of motorways, greater affluence and increased holiday periods have led to greater access to the national park and visitor numbers have increased dramatically. It is now possible to drive to the Lake District from London or Aberdeen in around five hours, or travel by train in around three to four hours.

▲ **Figure 6.27** Typical Lake District scenery

Key facts

- The park is managed by the Lake District National Parks Authority (LDNPA).
- It is England's largest national park, covering an area of 2,992 km².
- Only one of the bodies of water within the Lake District is called a lake: Bassenthwaite Lake near Keswick.
- There are 16 bodies of water that are considered to be the main 'lakes':

Bassenthwaite Lake	Grasmere
Buttermere	Haweswater Reservoir
Coniston Water	Loweswater
Crummock Water	Rydal Water
Derwentwater	Thirlmere
Elterwater	Ullswater
Ennerdale Water	Wast Water
Esthwaite Water	Windermere

- The glaciated mountains in this area are usually referred to as 'fells'.
- Depending on which definition you choose there are between 210 and 214 fells.
- The main glacial troughs and ribbon lakes radiate out from the centre of the Lake District.
- There are 14,650 archaeological sites and historical monuments recorded.
- There are 1,760 listed buildings within the Lake District.
- There are 23 conservation areas covering historic towns and villages.
- Nearly 41,000 people live within the park and population density is 18.4 per km².
- There are 22,930 homes (dwellings), of which owner occupied housing is 67.7 per cent and rented housing is 32.3 per cent; 15 per cent of all homes in the Lake District are holiday or second homes.
- Each year the Lake District receives 15.8 million visitors and there are 23.1 million tourist visiting days (i.e. the number of days spent in the Lake District that the 15.8 million visitors accumulated).
- Each year over £1,050 million is spent in the national park by tourists.

Examples of issues and their management

There is no doubt that the majority of conflicts are as a result of the large numbers of tourists and day trippers who visit this area. The Lake District National Park Authority has put in place a number of solutions to what are seen as the key issues (Table 6.10).

▲ **Figure 6.28** Water run-off gully on a footpath in the Lake District

There are numerous areas where there is severe path erosion and repair and maintenance must be carried out. Local stones are often brought in to stabilise banks and assist with the infill of pathways as they blend in with the landscape. Re-seeding assists with the binding of slopes and the reintegration of the path into its natural surroundings (see Figure 6.29).

▼ **Table 6.10** Solutions to key issues in the Lake District National Park

Type of conflict/issue	Groups involved	Detail	Solutions
Environmental: access to and usage of land areas and pathways	Sightseers/ conservationists/ locals/tourists *versus* walkers/ hilltwalkers/ mountain bikers	**Footpath and hillside erosion** Walkers/hilltwalkers/mountain bikers wish access to areas of beauty and challenge (slopes and ridges) while sightseers/ conservationists/locals/and other tourists view overuse and misuse by these activities as causing damage to the environment. Walkers and cyclists wear away the top levels of soils in this fragile environment. Damage may be permanent or it may take a long time for the land to recover. A worn path can often act as a channel for water causing even greater erosion of soil. Not only does soil disappear but vegetation too. Wildlife habitats can be trampled on, run over and destroyed. Scarring can be seen on the landscape, destroying its natural appearance and attractiveness.	• Refill eroded pathways using a variety of methods to suit the local area through camouflaging with the natural surroundings and make the paths more resistant (Figure 6.28). • Signposts to encourage use of reinforced pathways or to divert from areas of overuse/misuse. • Zigzag pathways built up hillsides. The zigzag ensures that erosion does not create top-to-bottom gullying and rapid run-off on slopes. • Limitations on areas that allow off-road cycling. Designated areas such as Whinlatter Forest and Grizedale Forest are criss-crossed with routes with varying degrees of difficulty from beginner to challenging.
Socio-economic: access to agricultural areas	Tourists/walkers/ cyclists *versus* farmers	**Farm gate opening, climbing field walls and fences, trampling across fields** Tourists/walkers/cyclists wish access to areas which they perceive to suit their activities, from picnicking, walking, cycling, to having access to the best place to take a photograph. Many appear unaware that much of this land is used for farming and their actions can have a financial impact on the farmers. By using farm or field gates and leaving them open, valuable livestock may escape risking their injury or death (e.g. being run down by motor vehicles on roads). Climbing on drystone walls (drystane dikes) or fences can damage these and again allow animals to escape. Walking across fields causing erosion of topsoil, removal of rough pasture, or damage to planted crops. Damage to livestock, fences and walls, land and crops, all result in an economic loss due to the need for vet bills, replacement and repair, or the loss of resources which reduces profit or viability of the farm.	• A programme is in place to install self-closing and kissing gates to remove the need to open farm gates or to climb over walls. Many existing styles are also being replaced by the more easily accessed self-closing or kissing gates. • To give greater access many kissing gates are made wide enough for pushchairs and wheelchairs. • Signposting of footpaths to avoid trespassing and prevent damage to agricultural land or environmentally sensitive areas. • Information posters showing the location of path and gates and educating visitors about how to behave in rural areas and the problems which could occur due to their actions.

▼ **Table 6.10** Solutions to key issues in the Lake District National Park *(continued)*

Type of conflict/issue	Groups involved	Detail	Solutions
Environmental: access to and use of places and areas of specific attraction	Tourists *versus* locals/conservationists	**Overcrowding at popular places (countryside, historical sites and settlements)** Places of extreme beauty or interest attract the most people and these are known as **honeypots**. This is a reference to bees being attracted to the sweetest honey. This results in a high volume of visitors to these places and can create numerous problems: ● footpath erosion ● noise ● increased litter ● traffic congestion (especially on narrow roads due to volume of traffic and limited parking) ● off-road or verge parking causing damage and erosion ● damage to environmentally sensitive landscape, flora and fauna ● the need to create tourist facilities such as toilets and car parks ● all of the above reducing the natural beauty of the area.	● Limiting access to particular sites or areas. ● Encouraging visits to other areas through education, free maps and signposting. ● Creating alternative honeypots where visitors can be controlled more easily. An example of this is Brockhole (The Lake District Visitor Centre) overlooking Windermere. Here the visitor is provided not only with somewhere to look at the scenery, but car parking, a picnic area, toilets, a shop, free entrance to Brockhole House and its Arts and Crafts gardens, adventure playgrounds, events and a café.
Environmental: refuse disposal	Tourists/campers/others *versus* locals/conservationist/tourists	**Littering/dumping refuse** Many tourists and others are concerned at the lack of places to dispose of rubbish. Some indiscriminately leave their refuse where they have picnicked, camped or parked. Recent years have seen an increase in the amount of litter being dumped around the Lake District. Much of this is in designated parking areas and picnic spots where people think that rubbish is regularly collected. This is not the case and much of it has to be picked up by park rangers and volunteers. Locals/conservationist/tourists object to the dumping of refuse and littering as it destroys the natural beauty of the area and can be scattered by the wind or by animals opening rubbish bags. It also creates smell from decomposing food and attracts vermin. This makes the environment poorer, creates eyesores and reduces the pleasantness of picnic areas or places for parking. Where dumped off road within the countryside (e.g. on mountains) it is difficult to ensure that it will be cleared. Knock-on effects may be injury to farm animals and wildlife, or to individuals who come into contact with the refuse (e.g. broken glass).	It has been judged impractical and unattractive to place rubbish bins on hillsides or in areas of natural beauty due to the difficulty in emptying and removing refuse from such a large, mostly remote area where access can be very difficult. Bins in such locations would simply overflow and become another eyesore and replicate the problems already being experienced. Methods to deal with general problem include: ● increased education, signs and posters around the park explaining the need to take home litter/refuse for recycling ● encouraging the use of litter bins where available, especially at the alternative honeypots where collection is made ● encouraging local sale of foods and other produce without wrappers or with limited disposable wrappers ● employing more national park wardens during the tourist season to actively enforce environmentally sensitive practices ● imposing fines for fly-tipping and littering.

▼ **Table 6.10** Solutions to key issues in the Lake District National Park *(continued)*

Type of conflict/issue	Groups involved	Detail	Solutions
Environmental and socio-economic: building and industry within national park boundaries	Conservationists/tourists *versus* locals/farmers/businesses/second-home purchasers	**New housing/agricultural/buildings/industry** Many people view the traditional housing and buildings of the Lake District as being as important as the scenery and want these traditions to be maintained. Locals may need affordable new housing and without new housing stock they may be forced to leave the area. Forcing locals to build with traditional materials and to traditional styles increases the cost of such houses and again may make them unaffordable. To improve the viability of their farms or bring them to acceptable modern standards farmers need to build new buildings. Not being able to do this can cause extreme financial hardship, unwanted and forced changes in farming type, or the farm owner being unable to continue farming. Extractive industries, for example quarrying, see the underlying rock types as valuable resources for both their own businesses and the nation's economy. Locals may also see employment in these extractive and other industries as vital in tackling unemployment and improving wages.	• There are guidelines for the kinds of materials and building types that are allowed, including the need for quality design and use of materials sympathetic to the national park to fit in with the surrounding environment. • Planning conditions and consent must be obtained before any building can take place. • Building in hollows, camouflaging with bushes or trees may also be utilised to hide new buildings. • Some flexibility is allowed to ensure that the economic and social well-being of local communities is protected while ensuring that measures are taken to limit the environmental impact. • Great limitations are put on those extractive activities that are permitted to be carried out, including noise restrictions, limits on operational times and vehicle use and screening by natural methods such as trees.
Socio-economic: house purchasing	Locals *versus* holiday home owners/outsiders buying homes/Lake District National Park	**Lack of affordable housing for locals** As mentioned earlier, locals were often priced out of the housing market in the Lake District and were forced to leave the area. This was due to the low availability of housing and the popularity of the Lake District for holiday, second, retirement or relocation homes. This pushed prices up to levels that the lower-paid locals could not afford.	• Since the early 1990s virtually all new housing that has been given the go-ahead in the national park is restricted to local needs (i.e. may only be bought by those who live or are employed in the area). • Houses built must be at a price that is affordable to local people. • Sell-on clauses mean that those who buy these houses can only sell them on under the same restrictions, to stop the houses becoming holiday, second, retirement or relocation homes.

▼ **Table 6.10** Solutions to key issues in the Lake District National Park *(continued)*

Type of conflict/ issue	Groups involved	Detail	Solutions
Environmental and socio-economic: road traffic volume	Tourist car drivers *versus* locals/tourists	**Traffic congestion and traffic hazards** Access to the Lake District National Park by road has become relatively straightforward with large conurbations within easy reach. The average journey time from London and the south-east is about five hours. It takes about one and half hours from Manchester and two hours from York. Even Glasgow and Edinburgh are only around two and a half hours away. The M6 running to the east of the Lake District makes access relatively simple. However, the road network in the national park is not suitable for high-volume traffic with single-track roads, steep slopes and even A roads can be quite twisting. These slow down traffic and make passing difficult. Over 70% of all visitors to the national park arrive in private cars and this causes a variety of problems, including noise, air pollution, traffic congestion and additional traffic dangers. The traffic congestion also hinders the day-to-day activities of businessmen, farmers, suppliers and locals.	Various solutions have been employed: • Seasonal one-way traffic on narrow or dangerous roads and in popular sightseeing areas to reduce the potential for traffic jams, congestion and road accidents. Various roads within the park have warning signs stating that both the one-way system and road layout sometimes change. A good example can be found on the popular scenic route along the banks of Derwentwater. • Selected road widening and improvement schemes. • 'Park and ride' schemes where visitors are encouraged to park their cars during the busiest areas and then make use of the shuttle buses which run to a variety of key places. These can greatly relieve congestion and parking issues in honeypot areas. • Specialist buses such as the 'Mountain Goats' that take, for example, hillwalkers, climbers, cyclists and canoeists to locations where they can take part in their activities. Many buses are fitted with cycle racks, roof racks and even canoe holders. These buses run regularly and pick up those who have been dropped off earlier. The Borrowdale Rambler, for example, operates all year round from Keswick as far as Seatoller at the head of the Borrowdale Valley. Or seasonal services such as the Honister Rambler takes in Borrowdale, the Honister Pass, Buttermere, the Lorton Valley and Whinlatter. All these measures reduce the number of vehicles that need to go into these areas and therefore congestion and verge-side parking on narrow roads. • Designated cycle lanes and routes such as the A591 cycle route between Winster and Crosthwaite (near Windermere). There is now a network of these routes across the Lake District. These encourage people to use their bikes while separating them from the dangers of motor vehicle traffic.

Table 6.10 Solutions to key issues in the Lake District National Park *(continued)*

Type of conflict/ issue	Groups involved	Detail	Solutions
Environmental and socio-economic: use of off-road vehicles for recreational activity	Locals/tourist/ off-road vehicle users *versus* locals/tourists/ farmers/ conservationists	**Off-road vehicles** (e.g. 4 wheel drives (4WDs) or motorbikes) This is becoming an increasingly more popular sport with the rugged landscape of the Lake District providing challenging and entertaining surfaces and inclines. Many tourists wish access to this to take part in the sport. Some locals also see this as a way to earn income from the tourists (this may include diversification by farmers to subsidise and increase their income). Others see these vehicles as disrupting and damaging the environment. Recreational vehicles such as these create conflicts around noise, pollution, soil erosion, frightening horses, farm animals and wildlife and interfering with other activities.	• Restricted parking zones to prevent narrow roads becoming blocked. Elterwater at the entrance to Langdale Valley is a small village that came under severe visitor and traffic pressure. Parking made it impossible for buses to travel through the village. This measure was also supported by the provision of extra parking spaces in peripheral car parks along with speed restrictions (20 mph zones) through Elterwater. Resident-only parking areas were also created. • Roads being changed to access only for residents. • A co-ordinated and unified approach to transport encouraging the use of rail, Lakeland boat services and buses with a single ticket system allowing for hop-on/hop-off use. • Tight restrictions have been put in place with only specific areas and types of roads being allocated for use. Pathways and tracks have been banned for use by these vehicles with notifications posted. • In 2015, 36 unclassified roads and a footpath/bridleway were added to those where 'propelled vehicles' were banned, although 75 routes which allow such activities still remained. • Maps showing permitted areas for off-road use and routeways and codes of conduct have been made easily available as leaflets which can be downloaded or picked up at tourist information centres, honeypots, hotels and local shops.

▼ **Table 6.10** Solutions to key issues in the Lake District National Park *(continued)*

Type of conflict/ issue	Groups involved	Detail	Solutions

Environmental: caravanning and camping in areas of isolation and scenic beauty	Campers/ caravanners *versus* locals/ tourists	**Setting up camp or parking caravans and areas of solitude and scenic beauty**
		
		Many tourists choose to stay in tents or caravans when in the Lake District. Many do so as it is a cheaper alternative to hotels or bed and breakfast facilities. For some campers it is to be closer to nature.
		
		Much of the conflict against this is that tents and caravans can disrupt the look and natural beauty of isolated spots. Concerns are also raised over refuse dumping and littering.
			• The Lake District National Park Authority has no legal right to stop camping on its land. It is however illegal to camp without the permission of a landowner.
			• Caravans, mobile homes (overnight stays) and tents are banned from car parks.
			• People choosing to camp or caravan illegally can be removed and maybe fined.
			• Official touring caravan and campsites have been created which offer various facilities, for example:
			  ▪ Throstle Hall, Caldbeck – a small touring caravan or motorhome site on a working farm
			  ▪ Church Stile Farm Holiday Park, Wasdale, with space for 70 tents or motorhomes
			  ▪ Parkcliffe, Windermere, with 20 specified tent pitches and a smaller area for self-pitching, plus 70 caravans or mobile homes.
			
			These allow camping and caravanning but also provide places for litter and refuse with controlled collection.
			
			For those who wish to experience 'wild camping' in isolated places the national park has the following guidelines:
			• Camp above the highest fell wall, well away from towns and villages.
			• Leave no litter – this includes *not* burying any litter and removing other people's.
			• Do *not* light any fires, even if there is evidence that fires might have been lit previously.
			• Stay for only one night, keep groups very small – only one or two tents.

▼ **Table 6.10** Solutions to key issues in the Lake District National Park *(continued)*

Type of conflict/issue	Groups involved	Detail	Solutions
			• Camp as unobtrusively as possible with inconspicuous tents that blend in. • Leave the campsite as you would want to find it. • Carry out everything you carried in. • Do not bury tampons and sanitary towels as animals dig them up again. • Choose a dry pitch rather than digging drainage ditches around a tent or moving boulders. • Perform toilet duties at least 30 m (100 ft) from water and bury the results using a trowel. • At all times, help protect the environment.
Environmental: use of the lakes	Tourist/speedboat and jet-ski users *versus* locals/tourists	**Unlimited use of the lakes** The lakes provide opportunities for utilisation by a variety of water-related activities. Some people wish to use these for fast-moving watercraft due to the length and the opportunity to build up great speed. This has been prompted for many by historical world water speed record attempts on Windermere. Concerns mostly focus on the noise and dangers from fast-moving boats (including speedboats) and jet-skis on lakes used for a variety of other activities such as fishing, swimming and canoeing. Fast-moving craft could collide with the other users. The wash created by these boats and jet-skis can also topple or swamp small boats, canoes and swimmers or disrupt fishing.	To limit the dangers created by fast-moving water vehicles and large numbers of such vehicles, the national park has developed restrictions on their usage: • Bylaws have been put in place banning motorised craft from 20 small lakes and tarns. • Speed restrictions of 10 mph have been placed on Coniston, Derwentwater, Ullswater and Windermere. • Compulsory registration of powered water vehicles on Windermere to discourage these from being brought by tourists and to limit craft on the waters.

▲ **Figure 6.29** Footpath restoration in the Lake District: a) the western slopes of Helvellyn; b) the ridge of Yoke, Kentmere Horseshoe walk

🌐 Task

1 Look back at the Lake District 'Key facts' (page 215).
   a) Create a bar graph or pie chart showing the different percentages of home occupancy: owner occupied, rented, and holiday homes or second homes.
   b) Calculate how many actual homes there are in each category.
   c) Determine the average number of visitors per day.
   d) Calculate the average amount of money spent per day by tourists.

2 Look back at Table 6.10 and choose six from the ten examples shown and for each one:
   a) Explain the issues that create the conflict.
   b) Identify the groups involved, explain each one's point of view and suggest reasons why they are involved.
   c) Evaluate the solutions put into place, highlighting the positive value of them and any negatives which you have identified.
   d) State whether any of the groups involved in the conflict would be disappointed with the solutions and why.
   e) From your evaluation do you foresee any future conflict due to the solutions put in place? If yes, who would be involved and why?

3 SQA suggests that role playing is a good activity to assist with your learning. You could try a number of different approaches to this:
   a) Organise, prepare for and take part in a debate about a geographical issue.
   b) Look at an existing issue and decide which side of the conflict you support, then prepare for and deliver a speech in the role of a character for whom the issue would be important.
   c) Create a campaign to support one side of a conflict and research facts, figures and viewpoints.

Some possible issues are described below:

● A proposed introduction of downhill-mountain biking on the slopes of Cairngorm Mountain, in the Cairngorm National Park. This is intended to provide an alternative use to the slopes during the summer season when the skiing facilities are underused and to provide year-round employment.
● Increased numbers of visitors walking up to the summit of Ben Nevis has raised concerns at the increasing amount of footpath erosion. What should be done to tackle this?
● A proposal to reintroduce wolves to Scotland in areas such as the Alladale Estate in Sutherland. Should these plans be given the go-ahead and what are the possible effects on land users, biodiversity and tourism?

6.6 Coastal landscape conflict

Much of what has been said about upland glacial areas and the need for preservation/protection as well as the causes of conflict also applies to coastal areas: footpaths are eroded and delicate ecosystems such as those found on sand dunes can be badly damaged or destroyed by those walking through them. Although there are other problems linked to the specific circumstances of coastlines, tourists and day trippers are also a major cause of conflict because of their desire to travel to see spectacular coastal scenery and enjoy beach activities.

Coastal stakeholders include:

- local residents
- employers/businesses/industries
- land developers
- transport companies (land- and water-based)
- recreational sailors/watersport enthusiasts
- farmers
- fishermen
- port authorities
- tourists
- conservationists/environmentalists.

In the case study that looks at the **Jurassic Coast** (below), geologists are also an important stakeholder. Each of the stakeholders listed above have their own needs, expectations and viewpoints, many of which will not be accepted by the other stakeholders and therefore will lead to conflict.

Case study: Jurassic Coast

The Jurassic Coast is a 155 km long stretch of coastline consisting of headlands, cliffs and bays that runs from near Exmouth in East Devon to Studland in Dorset, southern England (Figure 6.30). It gets its name due to the geological evidence (rock types and fossils) found there from the Jurassic Period although the site includes rocks from the Triassic and Cretaceous Periods as well. The Jurassic Coast is recognised as the only place on Earth 'where 185 million years of the Earth's history are sequentially exposed'. When walking eastward there is a movement through geological history from 250 million to 65 million years ago (Triassic through Jurassic and into the Cretaceous Period).

The importance of this coastline was confirmed in December 2001 when it was awarded **World Heritage Site (WHS)** status by **UNESCO (United Nations Educational, Scientific and Cultural Organisation)**. The status is only awarded to places of 'outstanding universal value' and is the world's highest level of designation for areas of natural significance.

In addition to WHS status the Jurassic Coast is also protected by 13 **Sites of Special Scientific Interest (SSSIs)** protecting wildlife covering 149.5 km of the complete 155 km coastline. Seventy-five per cent of the area is also designated a **Special Area of Conservation** covering both flora and fauna. Most of the site is also covered by **Area of Outstanding Natural Beauty (AONB)** status.

The management of the Dorset and East Devon Coast World Heritage Site is carried out by a committee known as the Steering Group (most often referred to as the Jurassic Coast Steering Group). This is made up of numerous stakeholders (including scientific/geological/ecological experts) and is led by the Dorset and Devon County Councils who originally applied for WHS status. Through discussion and negotiation the steering group creates a management plan (The Shoreline Management Plan) to ensure that the WHS is protected.

For the purpose of this case study we will look at two examples of conflict:

- tourists/day trippers
- offshore wind farm development.

▲ **Figure 6.30** Location of the Jurassic Coast, Lulworth Cove and Durdle Door

▲ **Figure 6.31** Jurassic Coast

While noticing the possibilities in Table 6.11 for conflict it is important to note that in 2015:

- only 10 people actually lived within the boundary of the designated WHS
- 326,000 people live within 10 miles of the Jurassic Coast
- the main man-made frontages of Exmouth, Sidmouth, Seaton, Lyme Regis, West Bay, Weymouth, Portland and Swanage are excluded from the site
- there were over 80 separate landowners, the largest of which is the National Trust.

▼ **Table 6.11** Jurassic Coast and conflicts between stakeholders

Stakeholder groups	Reasons for conflict
Coastal settlements and their inhabitants	Storm danger, possible flooding, loss of homes and businesses
Businesses/industry	Loss of buildings, loss of trade, difficulty in being insured
Home owners	Flooding, loss of buildings, difficulty in being insured, loss of house value
Farmers and landowners	Flooding, loss of buildings, difficulty in being insured, stock killed or injured, loss of land
Tourists	Loss of famous landscapes, possible loss of facilities/hotels, etc., holiday disruption and cancellation
Local councils	High cost of maintenance or replacement of roads/pathways and other council facilities.

Task

1 What is the formal name for the Jurassic Coast?
2 Explain why the Jurassic Coast has been designated a World Heritage Site.
3 How are the flora and fauna of the area protected?

Tourists/day trippers at Lulworth Cove

▲ **Figure 6.32** West Lulworth and Lulworth Cove

Lulworth Cove (Figures 6.30 and 6.32) is a small bay which attracts an estimated 500,000 to 750,000 visitors each year. Lulworth Cove is certainly a honeypot attraction. Of the visitors/day trippers:

● 35 per cent arrive in the six weeks between July and August, creating a very crowded period
● 10 per cent visit between November and February
● 95 per cent of all visitors are day trippers
● over 90 per cent arrive by car.

The village of West Lulworth is located beside Lulworth Cove and has a population of 714. It is at the end of a small B class road. The area benefits enormously from the influx of tourists, with millions of pounds reaching the local economy, opportunities for employment (although mostly seasonal) and an improvement in local infrastructure such as roads.

People are drawn to Lulworth Cove because of the cove and the spectacular surrounding coastal scenery

as well as its position on the Jurassic Coast near the sea arch known as Durdle Door (Figure 6.33). A large variety of water-based sports are available and beaches are rated at a high standard for water cleanliness. However, Lulworth Cove is the focus point for a number of conflict issues, as shown in Table 6.12.

▲ **Figure 6.33** Durdle Door

Task

1 What are the features or activities that attract tourists and day trippers to Lulworth Cove?
2 Of the possible annual 750,000 visitors, how many would be expected to visit in July and August (give your answer as a figure, rather than a percentage).
3 Using your answer to the question above, on average how many people visit Lulworth Cove per day during that period?
4 If 90 per cent of the total 750,000 visitors arrive by car, we can estimate the number of cars by assuming the number of people in each car is four. How many cars will visit each year?
5 Take some time to consider the conflicts in Table 6.11 and then organise them into a list in descending order of importance (i.e. the most important at the top of the list). Justify your decision for organising the conflicts in this way.
6 Would you have made different choices if you were a member of one of the conflicting groups and, if so, why?

▼ **Table 6.12** Solutions to key issues in the Lulworth Cove area

Type of conflict/issue	Groups involved	Detail	Solutions put in place
Environmental and *socio-economic*: land use and access to and use of places and areas of attraction	Military *versus* tourists/locals/ conservationists	**Noise from military activity, restriction on access, possible damage to the landscape, flora and fauna** The military identified a large area in this locality as being suited to military training 'in the national interest'. The activity includes the use of large military vehicles, including tanks, and live firing exercises. This creates a great deal of noise and necessitates the closure of the land area, roads and footpaths for safety reasons. Some tourist-related businesses are concerned that the noise and lack of access may reduce tourist activities on which they depend. Closure of areas of land, roads and footpaths restricts access to some of the most interesting scenic points and beaches for tourists. Conservationists voice concerns that the military activity (vehicles and explosions) causes damage to the landscape, destroys flora and fauna and encourages erosion.	The Ministry of Defence negotiated the following solutions: • Access is allowed to the land during weekends and busy holiday periods. • Access roads (especially to beaches) are kept open during the busiest holiday periods. • Reduced live firing exercises to lower noise levels during weekends and busy holiday periods. • Signage to inform visitors when the coastline is closed and which particular areas or paths cannot be used. While the military maintain the right to continue training 'in the national interest', it is impossible to fully protect the landscape, flora and fauna. The Ministry of Defence has stated that it is aware of concerns and takes action to limit any damage and to allow areas to recover.
Environmental: tourism, refuse and vehicular traffic	Tourists *versus* locals in West Lulworth/ environmentalists	**Increased noise and litter/increased traffic/noise and air pollution/congestion/difficult access to cove/ inconsiderate parking** Lulworth Cove acts as a honeypot site within the Jurassic Coast, with the Cove itself, beaches and other natural features such as Durdle Door sea arch in the vicinity. Tourist numbers are very high both for day visits and longer stays and this results in increased noise pollution, littering and traffic congestion (especially as the roads are narrow, steep and lead to a dead end). Parking on the narrow streets, verges and steep slopes further increases congestion. Congestion in West Lulworth could become severe.	Trying to find solutions to additional noise is difficult if it refers to individuals and can only be dealt with through the normal legal channels. Some solutions have been attempted to reduce the problems from cars and other motor vehicles: • Lulworth Estate has provided a large car park (for over 500 vehicles) outside the village (money collected from parking is reinvested in the local area to fund facilities for tourists, conservation schemes and employment for local people). This car park may become another point of conflict as the Council of Europe has identified it as needing to be moved or to be significantly screened to reduce its visual impact. • A mini roundabout has been constructed at the entrance to the car park to allow for easy access and exit to encourage swift traffic flow, reducing congestion.

▼ Table 6.12 Solutions to key issues in the Lulworth Cove area (continued)

Type of conflict/issue	Groups involved	Detail	Solutions put in place
			• Lulworth Estate subsidises a bus service from the local railway station to encourage visitors to leave their cars at home. • Restricted entry for vehicles to West Lulworth (residents only). As a response to litter, Lulworth has no litter bins and instead encourages visitors to take their rubbish home.
Environmental: land use and its effect on the visual environment	Lulworth Estate's local holiday park (static and touring caravans, tents) *versus* locals/ tourists/ conservationists	**Large area of mostly white caravans that are unsightly and out of context with the landscape** To provide a camping and caravanning site with facilities for tourists who wished to visit Lulworth Cove, Lulworth Estate provided a facility on its land. This large site has come in for criticism as it does not blend with the landscape and is viewed as an eyesore by locals and visitors who wish to see the natural scenery and conservationists.	• Lulworth Estate plans to invest in natural screening (trees and plants) sympathetic to the local environment to reduce the visual impact (camouflage).
Environmental: footpath erosion	Tourists/day trippers/walkers *versus* locals/ environmentalists/ WHS	**Coastal footpath erosion** The South West Coastal Path (a 1014 km path around the coastline of south-west England): the section between Lulworth Cove and Durdle Door is one of the most heavily used sections and experiences considerable erosion. This has damaged the footpath and the fragile grasslands, causing soil erosion.	Solutions employed so far have included the following: • Re-routing pathways. • Where the conditions allow, direct reseeding. • Building steps into steeper sections to discourage straying from the path. In some areas the steps are ignored because walkers view them as unnatural and they prefer to walk on the grass, causing additional erosion. • Resurfacing paths with stone (such as the one from Lulworth Cove to Durdle Door, paid for by Weld Estate, the Countryside Commission and Purbeck District Council), although these have been criticised for encouraging more walkers and scarring the landscape with white lines.
Socio-economic: house purchasing	Locals *versus* second home/ holiday home owners	**Housing** The popularity of this area has meant that many people wish to move here or to purchase a second home or holiday home. Because of competition for housing and strict planning rules against the building of new homes, house values are very high, ruling out many local people who wish to purchase them. This can result in locals being forced to move outside the area.	At present, no major solution to this problem appears to have been found.

Offshore wind farm development

When the first edition of this book was being written, the Jurassic Coast Steering Group was nearing the end of a conflict with the company wishing to create an offshore wind farm (the Navitus Bay wind farm proposal), which would have been visible from the coastline. The Planning Inspectorate submitted recommendations to the Secretary of State for a final decision. The Navitus Bay project highlights the limitations of case studies in textbooks such as this as they can quickly go out of date, but it also shows the importance of up-to-date research for Geography students. Take time to research the most current information on the project.

The details of the proposal were as follows.

Navitus Bay wind farm proposal

- In a joint venture Eneco Wind UK Ltd (Eneco) and EDF Energy Renewables propose to locate an offshore wind farm (Figure 6.34) off the Dorset and Hampshire coasts, to the west of the Isle of Wight, approximately 17.3 km off Scratchell's Bay (south of the Needles on the Isle of Wight) and 14.4 km from Durlston Head (on the Isle of Purbeck).
- There will be up to 194 wind turbine generators occupying an area of 153 km².
- It is intended that as a renewable energy project the wind farm will provide a clean and sustainable source.
- The energy created will be transmitted by undersea cables to the coastline to be used within the National Grid (the UK's electricity network).
- It is estimated the wind farm will generate enough energy to power up to 700,000 homes per year.

- The company suggests that if this scheme was to replace a carbon-dioxide-emitting generation source it would reduce CO_2 emissions by approximately 1,290,000 tonnes per year.
- A minimum of 1,700 local jobs will be created during a four-year period of construction and 140 local permanent jobs for the full 25 years' operational life of the project.
- The project offers opportunities for local businesses to become part of the project supply chain by providing services and products.

The Jurassic Coast Steering Committee objected because of the perceived impacts on the WHS and believes that the wind farm goes against the principles accepted when the WHS was set up:

- At only 22 km distant the wind farm will be a dominant feature, clearly visible to visitors to the World Heritage Site, particularly between Studland and St Aldhelm's Head in Dorset.
- Within the World Heritage Convention, Article 4 states that the WHS Steering Committee is charged with ensuring the site's 'protection, conservation, presentation and transmission to future generations'. The proposal would substantially modify the views from the WHS and reduce the cultural and sensory experience of the site and therefore be against Article 4.
- With the proposal in place the WHS would be transmitted in a form significantly different from that when WHS status was granted through changing the seascape characteristics.
- At particular locations the wind farm would visually overlap with natural scenery and impact on the setting in its natural context and the cultural and sensory experience.

The decision

The Government turned down the application to build the £3.5 billion wind farm off the Jurassic Coastline. Lord Bourne (the Energy Minister at the time) rejected the plan as it would 'undermine the local tourist industry, which benefits from the nearby Jurassic Coast, a UNESCO World Heritage site'. As you would expect, this decision both delighted and dismayed the various interest groups.

So, what now?

▲ **Figure 6.34** Offshore wind farm

Task

You have been presented with:

- background information about this area
- the proposal
- the arguments both for and against the proposed wind farm
- the outcome and the reasoning behind the decision.

What are your reflections on this case study? Do you agree with the outcome?

This decision, in the context of the politics of 2016, was not unexpected. However, there is a fundamental issue. As a society, we need to make a commitment to expand non-carbon sources of renewable and sustainable forms of power.

If you are interested in energy, the environment and conflict, you may wish to research further examples of such proposals. For example, in 2018, an offshore wind farm opened off the Cumbrian coastline in north-west England. At this site, the largest offshore wind farm in the world, with 87 turbines and covering an area of 145 km by 145 km (the size of 20,000 football pitches!), was created. Local objections were considered of less importance than the energy requirements of the UK, the environment and the economic impact on the local area.

Summary

There were several key themes in this chapter on Rural environment:

- The impact and management of rural land degradation related to a rainforest or semi-arid area
- Rural land use conflicts and their management related to either a glaciated or coastal landscape.

In this chapter you have considered the nature and processes of soil erosion and degradation, and the impact of vegetation removal, soil erosion by water (sheet, rill and gully) and soil erosion by wind. In addition, you have investigated the effects of climate change. Human activity has led to deforestation, monoculture, over-cultivation, overgrazing, inappropriate cultivation and irrigation techniques, and these actions have modified the environments of both rainforests and semi-arid lands. The consequences of land degradation are now of considerable worldwide concern. Through case studies you have considered the traditional patterns of life in semi-arid areas and the rainforest, with specific examples of management strategies, and comments on the successes and failures of such strategies.

Conflict is an important part of Geography. In this chapter the focus has been on the causes, impact and management strategies in selected glaciated and coastal landscapes.

Task

1. Looking at the evidence above (and any further research you undertake) critically examine the wind farm proposals and the WHS's objections. Write out your own decision, describing the reasons for your choice.
2. As we saw in the glacial landscape conflict section (page 208), the SQA suggests that role playing is a good activity to assist with your learning. Look at the example below and suggest who would be in conflict in this issue.
   A request to build a wind farm in Ayrshire at Knoweside Hill on the coastline, close to and in view of the National Trust for Scotland's Culzean Castle and its Country Park. The wind farm would initially have 15 wind turbines measuring up to 76 m in height.
3. In detail, explain the arguments both for and against the proposed wind farm.
4. Decide which side you would be on in the conflict and discuss the reasons for your support.

SQA examination-style questions

It is likely that a question will ask you to explain conflicts 'within an area you have studied'. These will only be about glaciated or coastal landscapes. If you are asked to discuss or explain these 'within an area you have studied', you will be expected to give an actual named example of the location you are talking about and examples of real rather than potential events. You may also be asked to either explain solutions that have been put in place or evaluate their effectiveness.

Possible example questions:

1 Referring to named examples from any rainforest that you have studied, explain the soil conservation strategies that have reduced rural land degradation.
2 For any semi-arid or rainforest area you have studied, comment on the effectiveness of the strategies used to manage land degradation.
3 Referring to either a named rainforest or a named semi-arid area, explain the techniques used to combat rural land degradation.
4 In a glaciated/coastal landscape you have studied, explain conflicts that arise due to tourism.

5 In a glaciated/coastal landscape you have studied, explain the conflicts which arise.
6 For either a glaciated or coastal landscape you have studied, evaluate the solutions put in place to counter high numbers of tourists.
7 Many coastal and glaciated areas have competing land uses and users that create conflict.
Referring to a coastal or upland glaciated area you have studied:
a) identify three issues of conflict
b) explain the strategies used to manage these conflicts
c) comment on the effectiveness of these strategies.

Introduction

Urban is one of three Human Environment topics in the SQA Higher Geography course.

Throughout this chapter there will be a variety of diagrams, tables, statistics and maps to enhance your application of geographical skills.

▲ **Figure 7.1** Edinburgh from Calton Hill

For the examination you may be given a question based on one or more of the following broad topics:

- the need for management of an aspect of recent urban change (housing and transport) in a developed world city and in a developing world city
- the management of strategies employed
- the impact of the management strategies.

The keywords are 'change', 'strategies', 'management' and 'impact'. A variety of case study exemplars will be considered, looking at cities and urban areas from both the developed and developing world. As with previous chapters, before you study change, management and impact, some additional background information is helpful.

- What is meant by site and situation and the relevancy of this in the growth and development of urban areas.
- Functions of settlements.
- Hierarchy and sphere of influence.
- What is urbanisation?
- Global growth of cities.
- Models of land use within urban areas.

Having considered the above background information, this chapter will then consider the following:

- Background to urban development.

- Aspects of urban change and management.

Most of us in the UK live in urban areas. The most significant movement of people in the world today is from rural areas into cities and towns within the developing world. As shown in Chapter 5 Population, this movement takes place mainly as a result of 'push and pull' factors (this may be a good time to check your notes on this). This chapter includes some additional material that will provide some ideas for your assignment.

Urban areas can be seen as exciting places to live and work. Cities and towns attract people for employment and better opportunities for education, health and leisure. They can also be seen as places of conflict. For some people in the developing world the streets are 'paved with gold' and opportunities open up. For others the movement to the city merely exchanges one form of poverty and disadvantage for another. Traffic congestion, urban pollution, crime, exploitation and poor housing are all part of the urban problem.

7.1 Background to urban development

Site and situation

- Site refers to the exact location of a settlement, the actual land on which it is built. To explain site, it is necessary to look at both physical and economic/human reasons, although physical factors were probably more important from a historical perspective than they are today. Factors include the following:
  - Relief: High enough to be safe from flooding, yet low enough to be sheltered from the cold and wind.
  - Defence: Sites such as a hill top, above a steep slope, or on the inside of a meander were desirable.
  - Transport: At a crossroads, a bridging point over a river or at the head of a valley.
  - Soil: A deep fertile soil, on gently sloping land, made farming and subsistence possible.
  - Water: For drinking, irrigation, cooking and cleaning.
  - Resources: Such as stone, coal or timber (for building, fuel for cooking and warmth).

▲ **Figure 7.2** Durham: an example of a defensive site

Situation is the position or location of a settlement in relation to the surrounding area, for example fertile soil, valleys, hills, the coast, river and routes. The site and situation factors can encourage the original growth of a settlement and will have an influence on whether the settlement continues to grow.

Case study: Glasgow

Glasgow was once just another small village positioned beside the River Clyde. However, it grew at a rate that soon left all the other villages behind. A combination of physical factors and chance made Glasgow grow from the early thirteenth century:

- The River Clyde was shallow enough to be crossed by people with their horses and carts.
- An early bridge encouraged routes to converge at the lowest bridging point, thereby encouraging people to gather at the site. There is extensive research about the first bridge, which was possibly a timber bridge built around 1340. A stone bridge was constructed in 1345.
- A ridge of higher ground provided a good position for a fort, which gave protection to early inhabitants.
- The raised site provided a dry point site above the level of any flooding.
- Fertile soil allowed a food surplus to be produced and a thriving market was established for trading.
- The secure site encouraged the growth of a church (later a cathedral) and a university.
- The river was able to be deepened, allowing the largest ships of the day to reach into the heart of the settlement.
- The west coast location placed Glasgow in a perfect position for trade across the Atlantic to America.

- The Atlantic trade opened up opportunities for tobacco, sugar and cotton manufacturing in the city.
- Crucial raw materials and resources such as coal, iron ore and limestone encouraged manufacturing industries.
- Railways and roads converged on Glasgow and reinforced the city as a communication centre.
- As the population grew the city became a service centre with a strong 'pull' across central Scotland.

 Task

1 Explain the difference between site and situation.
2 Looking at the factors that led to Glasgow's growth, which are still relevant today?

Functions of settlements

The **function of a settlement** is what is does. All settlements have shared functions, such as residential (e.g. housing) or a service centre (e.g. shops); they will all have businesses and/or factories, transport hubs and even some local government administration. However, a settlement may become notable for a particular function:

- Blackpool: Tourism, recreation and conferences
- Edinburgh: Political centre and administration, shopping, tourism
- Oxford: University, publishing
- Canterbury: Cathedral and religion
- Dover: Ferry port and terminal
- Newcastle: Industry, port, shopping
- Aberdeen: Port, oil
- Kilmarnock: Education, the arts, retail.

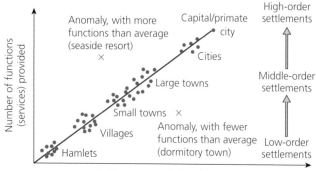

▲ **Figure 7.3** Settlement hierarchy: relationship between size and function

Hierarchy and sphere of influence

Settlements can be arranged in a 'rank order' using various criteria, such as population or by the number and range of services found (Figure 7.3).

A rank order of settlement could be:

1 Isolated farm
2 Hamlet
3 Village
4 Town
5 City
6 Conurbation
7 Capital or primate city.

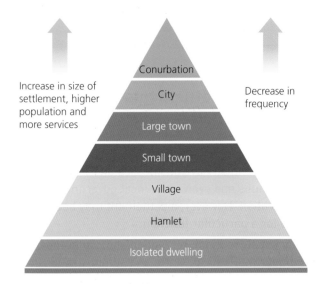

Increase in size of settlement, higher population and more services

Decrease in frequency

▲ **Figure 7.4** Settlement hierarchy

The **sphere of influence** is the area served by a settlement or the area over which the settlement has an impact. The key relationship tends to be between the population size and the number and range of services found. The larger the settlement the greater the number and range of services and the greater the 'sphere of influence'. Sphere of influence is linked to the range – the distance people are normally prepared to travel to use a service and the threshold – the minimum number of people needed to support that service.

Case study: Dundonald, Ayrshire

In a village such as Dundonald, Ayrshire, with a population of 3,000+, there are half a dozen shops/

▼ **Table 7.1** Settlement hierarchy and sphere of influence

Service order	Range	Threshold	Example
Low order	Small and limited area; local.	Can be as low as a few hundred people.	Convenience shops selling newspapers, milk or bread, e.g. the local 'Spar'.
Middle order	Within a town and surrounding villages.	A few thousand people.	Shops found in a town, but not in a village, e.g. a shoe shop.
High order	Large range where people will travel to; services that go beyond daily needs.	Large numbers of people will be needed to support the services.	City centre services and specialised shops. Comparison shops, furniture shops.

services, including a chemist, newsagent, butcher, takeaway and general convenience store. Locals buy their day-to-day basics in the village. However, for the weekly food shop or for clothes and services such as a travel agent, Dundonald folk travel to Kilmarnock or Ayr. For that special clothes outfit or more specialised services or for 'comparison shopping' they will travel to Glasgow, possibly the modern south side shopping site at Silverburn, or into the city centre.

Task

Look at Figure 7.3 and describe what it shows.

Research opportunity

You may decide to choose a settlement study for your assignment as there are many possible topics. Here are a few ideas; we will provide some further suggestions later in this chapter:

- An investigation into site and situation factors.
- Sphere of influence study of a village.
- A mapping study of the growth of a settlement.

7.2 Urbanisation and global growth of cities

Three main phases in the growth of urban areas have been recognised:

1   Some five or six thousand years ago, in areas such as Mesopotamia (mainly modern Iraq) and Egypt, India and China, agricultural surpluses allowed merchants, traders, craftsmen and government officials to concentrate in central areas.
2   In the eighteenth and nineteenth centuries within a number of European countries, such as the UK and Germany, industry based on resources, trade and economic and political expansion resulted in the spectacular growth of cities such as London, Liverpool, Glasgow and Hamburg.
3   More recently, certainly over the last 25 years, in the less economically developed countries (LEDCs) of the world there has been a mass movement of people from the countryside into the 'magnet' cities, such as Mexico City and Mumbai, India.

In 1801 there was only one city in the world with over 1 million people – London – but by 2014 there were 350 and by 2025 there could be as many as 500!

▼ **Table 7.2** Urban change (1950–2025)

Population in urban areas (%)	1950	2000	2015	2025
World	30	51	60	71
Less economically developed countries (LEDC)	17	40	55	70
More economically developed countries (MEDC)	53	74	78	79

Rise of the megacities

In 1950, New York and Tokyo were the world's only megacities – urban agglomerations with over 10 million residents. Now there are 35 and by 2025 the UN predicts nine new megacities in Asia will help bring the total to 44. All but eight will be in the developing world – and the quality of life for millions will be determined by the quality of their cities. Tokyo is forecast to remain the world's most populous urban agglomeration in 2025, with 37.2 million people, but Tokyo's growth has slowed down and fast-growing rivals such as Delhi, Shanghai and Mumbai are closing in. There are now 13 cities with over 20 million people.

There are a lot of statistics but how accurate are they? Of course it is difficult to be exact and urban areas showing rapid growth are notoriously difficult in which to collect accurate census information. But what are we measuring? For example as Shanghai grows it will swallow up surrounding settlements, so do we now count all these people as part of Shanghai?

There are five phases of urbanisation (see Figure 7.5) and these processes may happen one after the other as a country develops, or they may be happening at the same time, but possibly in different areas of the city.

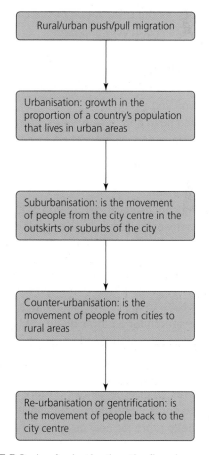

▲ **Figure 7.5** Cycle of urbanisation: the five phases of urbanisation

Reasons for urban growth in developing countries

- Cities attract large numbers of migrants due to perceptions of better health, employment opportunities and education ('pull' factors).
- Rural populations are more affected by famine, war, drought, poverty ('push' factors).
- Migrants are usually younger with higher fertility and birth rates.
- Improved diet, clean water, vaccination programmes and overall improved health provision reduces infant mortality rates and death rates.

Reasons for urban stagnation in developed countries

Cities such as Tokyo, Berlin and even London have very low growth rates, while for others in developed countries such as the USA, Japan or the UK in general, city life is still very appealing.

- Increasing prosperity and car ownership (with improved public transport) mean that more people are prepared to commute long distances from rural towns and villages.
- Decreasing birth and fertility rates, combined with later marriage and concentration on careers, have had an impact on population growth in cities.
- Planning legislation often places a barrier on outward growth.
- Increasing concern over perception of crime and other urban social issues such as poverty.

Counter-urbanisation

Counter-urbanisation is the recent movement from urban areas back to the countryside and is often linked to the search for a better quality of life. The desire for a less stressful life, cheaper housing and fear of inner-city crime, terrorism and drugs are some of the factors that have encouraged the more affluent to seek an alternative life in more rural areas. In addition, in some cities older areas have been cleared to make room for new development and this has given many people the chance to move out of the city and into the surrounding areas, for example from Glasgow to East Kilbride. However, there is concern

that the more affluent are choosing to abandon the city for a new life; an option that is not always available to those who are less wealthy. A further trend has been identified, that of **gentrification**, where the older inner-city and city centre houses and flats are renovated and new luxury apartments are being built. This has been noted in London, for example, with very prestigious apartments being developed at addresses such as in Belgravia, where five-bedroom houses sell for between £15 to £35 million (May 2019)!

▲ **Figure 7.6** Belgravia, London

7.3 Models of land use

The SQA examination paper may include a question on change, strategies and impact, with a focus on housing and transport. However, a wider focus is required so that you can put these changes in context.

Geographers look for order and pattern in urban areas in the developed world and the developing world.

We begin by looking at the distinct districts/zones found in the urban areas of the developed world. For most of you this is not new as you will have studied this at National 5 level. Descriptions of the districts/zones can be as simple or as complex as you wish, but most geographers recognise the following:

- Central business district (CBD)
- The inner-city – an area of older nineteenth century housing and industry
- New housing and industrial zone (suburbs)
- Rural-urban fringe.

▼ **Table 7.3** Key features of districts found in urban areas

Central business district	Inner-city housing – old (often nineteenth century)
Located near the geographical centre.	Surrounding the CBD.
Concentration of roads, often in a grid-iron road pattern.	Grew rapidly during industrialisation over 100 years ago and has seen very considerable change and **redevelopment**.
Bus and train stations.	Mixture of high-density tenements or terraced housing, often in a rectangular, grid-iron pattern. Houses often constructed quickly and cheaply which became slum housing; some housing of higher quality.
High density of buildings.	
Concentration of shops, financial and legal services, entertainment (cinemas, clubs, theatres), public buildings (town hall, government offices, university, concert hall, museums) and churches.	Busy roads passing through the area into CBD.
	Often lacking open space.
Very little in the way of open space, industry or housing.	Very congested streets with little parking.
High density of vehicles, traffic congestion.	Linked closely to older industry.
Comparison and specialist shops, often in pedestrianised areas; modern shopping malls.	Often areas of **urban deprivation**.
	Associated with crime/vandalism and social and economic issues.
Land expensive (high land values).	High density of housing with many one-person households.
	Significant ethnic minority and migrant population.
	Low order shopping.
Inner-city industry – old (often nineteenth century)	**Suburbs – new (twentieth century housing)**
Surrounding the CBD.	Known as the suburbs, suburbia or the outskirts.
Grew rapidly during the industrial revolution.	Local authority and private housing in separate estates.
Close to housing (source of labour) and linked historically to railways, canals, rivers and roads.	Variety of styles and layout of houses including high-rise, flats, semi-detached and detached; densities lower nearer the edge of the city.
Industry mixture of small workshops and large factories.	
Scene of dereliction, decay and abandonment.	Gardens, more space and parks.
Environment traditionally dark and environmentally negative.	Environmentally more attractive.
Area of considerable redevelopment and change, with a range of new functions (exhibition, concert and conference arenas, hotels, new housing, marinas, retail parks, museums).	Street patterns smooth and curved (crescents) with culs-de-sac.
	Busy roads separate from housing.
	Slower traffic.
Limited open space.	Commuting.
Industrial areas – new (twentieth century)	**Rural-urban fringe (suburbs)**
Usually separate from housing, located on industrial estates or industrial parks – planned landscape.	This zone includes twentieth century housing and industry, but also includes the 'fringe' at the edge of the town.
Room for expansion and low buildings within landscaped grounds.	Located on the outskirts of the town/city, houses are a mixture of modern attractive designs, located in an area of higher environmental attractiveness, within commuting distance of the city, e.g. detached houses with gardens in an area with woodland, parks and local shops.
Good links to roads and motorways.	
Less polluted.	
	Suburbs have separate retail parks, science parks, golf courses, modern roads and country parks.

▲ **Figure 7.7** George Square and City Chambers, Glasgow

▲ **Figure 7.8** Riverside Development, Glasgow

▲ **Figure 7.9** Newton Mearns suburb, Glasgow

▲ **Figure 7.10** Silverburn, south Glasgow

▲ **Figure 7.11** River Clyde, Glasgow

▲ **Figure 7.12** River Clyde shipyards and tenements

Task

Look at Figures 7.7–7.12 and decide which image relates to which zone and explain the land uses associated with each image.

It is clear that there are differences in land use moving from the city centre, through the inner-city and the suburbs before reaching the fringe or edge of the urban area.

Land use transects

Three factors explain the sequence of zones, moving from the city centre to the edge of the city: accessibility, age of development and land values.

Accessibility

The CBD is the focus of roads and rail routes and is the most accessible part of a city, which is why most shops and offices are located in the centre.

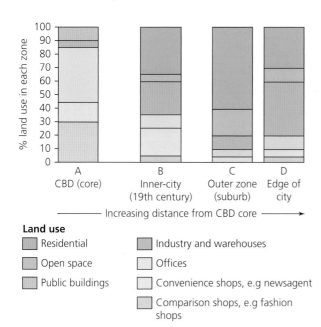

▲ **Figure 7.13** Land use transect from the CBD to the edge of the city. This diagram shows how land use changes as you move from the CBD to the suburbs

Age of development

Generally, moving from the centre outwards the buildings become more recent in construction. However, in the older parts of the city, modernisation and redevelopment have been necessary to replace old, worn-out buildings that are no long fit for purpose in the modern world. In the nineteenth century the main growth and demand was for housing and industry – this explains the position of the inner-city zone. During the twentieth and twenty-first century modern buildings have been located in the suburbs where there is space.

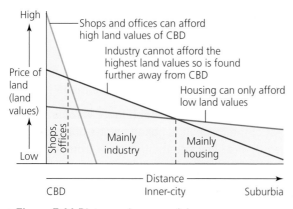

▲ **Figure 7.14** Distance decay model

Land values

There is competition for land in the most accessible part of the city. Space is limited and so land prices are high. As competition decreases, land values fall as distance from the CBD increases. This is called 'distance decay' (Figure 7.14).

Relationship between the distance decay model and land use

Shops and offices need to locate in the CBD to be accessible. This central area has high land values, so shops need to attract large numbers of customers. Many buildings, particularly those housing offices, are constructed with many levels in order to make maximum use of limited ground space. Think of the commercial premises found in the CBD: only those making large profits can afford the high rents associated with the high value of the land.

Early industrial development tagged around the CBD at what was then the edge of the settlement. Railways and canals linked into this area and since people walked to their work, houses developed alongside industry. In time this mixed housing/industry zone was engulfed by more housing developments and the site became congested and unsuitable for modern housing and industries, which needed more space and better access to road networks. Newer industries and housing were therefore attracted to the suburbs because of the space and lower land values.

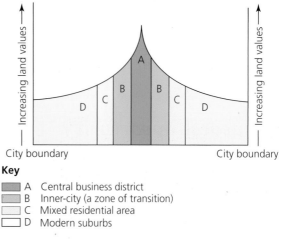

▲ **Figure 7.15** Land use values and land use zones across a city

Generally, land values become lower as you move out from the CBD and this explains the lower densities of housing and open space with parks and golf courses that can be found, as well as relocated offices, retail parks and industrial estates.

Newer residential developments near the outer part of the city/town are more desirable. Houses have space for gardens and expansion, and the pleasant environment can lead to a better quality of life.

Research opportunity

Choose a town or city that you know well and take a walk from the CBD through the inner-city to the suburbs. You will find a large-scale map of the route, a note book and a camera useful. Keep a record of changing land use and how the quality of the environment changes.

Urban zones and models of city development in the developed world

It is clear that there are different zones within any town or city and this is true within the developed and the developing world. Geographers over the years have attempted to show these patterns in diagram form using models. These models allow us to simplify urban structures and help us understand how cities grow. In order to be able to understand the issues, change, strategies and impact we need to briefly outline the three key models shown in Figures 7.16, 7.17 and 7.18. They show that cities grow in circles from the centre or grow sector by sector, or a combination of both.

Research opportunity

Select any one of the urban models shown here and on page 241 (Figure 7.16, Figure 7.17 or Figure 7.18) and describe its key features.

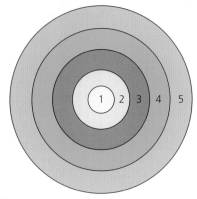

Key

- ☐ 1 Central business district (CBD)
- ☐ 2 Wholesale light manufacturing (transitional)
- ◼ 3 Low-class residential (inner-city)
- ◼ 4 Medium-class residential (inter-war)
- ◻ 5 High-class residential (suburbia)

▲ **Figure 7.16** Burgess concentric model

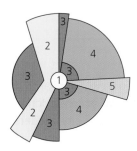

Key

- ☐ 1 Central business district (CBD)
- ☐ 2 Wholesale light manufacturing (transitional)
- ◼ 3 Low-class residential (inner-city)
- ◼ 4 Medium-class residential (inter-war)
- ◻ 5 High-class residential (suburbia)

▲ **Figure 7.17** Hoyt's sector model

There are many models showing urban zones. Indeed, if you are really inventive you could research fully into this theme and create your own unique model!

The Burgess concentric model (Figure 7.16) is the simplest of the three. It is based on age of building and wealth and shows that cities grow from a central source (the CBD). The city is older at its core and newer at the fringes, and the model assumes that growth is even in all directions. It ignores physical

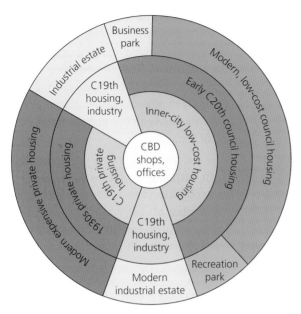

▲ **Figure 7.18** The UK industrial city model (Mann)

features (rivers, hills and coastline) and the influence of transport routes (railways, canal, roads, rivers). It does not really consider the variety of fringe land uses in the modern city, such as industrial estates, green belts and out-of-town shopping centres.

Hoyt's sector model (Figure 7.17) introduces the idea that cities grow from the centre outwards but not in uniform rings. Hoyt noted that American cities also grow along route ways (rivers, roads, railways) and that industry follows these sectors, attracting low-cost housing. The spaces between the sectors become filled with housing.

Both these models have been criticised as being too simple. Zones rarely have distinct boundaries and in reality merge into each other.

The third model (Figure 7.18) works well with UK industrial cities. Once again, it combines the idea of outward growth, sector growth linked to industry, large-scale redevelopment and **urban sprawl**.

Land use changes over time. Older buildings can be replaced and areas may lose their key features. For example in Glasgow, the old industrial/shipbuilding zone along the side of the River Clyde has changed greatly in appearance and function over the last 30 years. New uses and buildings include concert and conference halls, leisure and sporting venues, restaurants, the BBC and Scottish Television buildings, hotels and housing.

Urban zones and models of city development in the developing world

There are many similarities between some of the biggest cites in both the developed and developing world: a CBD, traffic congestion, areas of high and low quality housing and areas devoted to industry and shopping. There are also areas of change and conflict, but most people are simply going about their business, trying to do the best for themselves and their family. The CBD in Lagos, Nigeria, is like other CBDs in Berlin, Shanghai or London, with the same characteristic features described above. However, there are differences, with some real challenges brought about by rapid growth from rural to urban migration and natural population increase.

Key characteristics of developing world cities

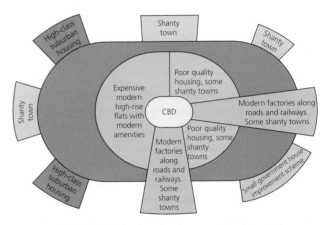

▲ **Figure 7.19** Model of urban land use and residential areas in a developing country

▲ **Figure 7.20** Rich/poor side by side

▲ **Figure 7.21** Rio de Janeiro

Figure 7.19 shows a model that is a combination of concentric rings, showing that the city has grown outwards in sequential stages based on age of development, as well as wedges or sectors, usually along a main road. The structure is different from the so-called developed world city models described above, in that growth has only been rapid over the last 30 years. The CBD does exist, with international banks, offices and the main shops and shopping malls.

Many cities in Africa and Asia have a colonial link to the past. For example, the streets in the French sector in Shanghai have been laid out with a very strong French influence. It is notable that just outside the CBD there exists a zone of houses for the wealthy landowners, merchants, administrators and business people. These old colonial villas and luxury apartments are often gated communities with high security. They are found near the centre and extend outwards along major communication lines. Beside these expensive houses there is lower and middle quality housing and industry. Shanty towns have grown wherever there is space, often close to the centre, but also on any unwanted or undesirable land. Factories tend to locate along the roads and railways. It is clear that the pattern of housing is very mixed. Generally housing deteriorates as distance from the centre of the city increases; wealth or the lack of it determines where you live in such a city.

Features of life in a developing world city

- People are attracted by the perception of a better quality of life. While many will achieve this, others will drift towards the shanty towns and continue to live in poverty.
- While there are many opportunities for jobs in the booming industries, there are still not enough for the number of migrants.

- There is a very strong informal or 'black' economy (e.g. car repairs, shoe shining, touting tourists to buy fake watches) which provides limited financial opportunity.
- Long commuting journeys from the housing areas to the industrial areas have to be made on roads that are increasingly congested and polluted.
- The visible disparity between the poor and the rich can lead to social tensions.

It is important, however, to avoid viewing such cities as only being a problem. Although problems exist, such cities still offer many opportunities. Later in this chapter you will consider a number of case studies drawn from cities of the developing world. In particular, there is a case study on shanty towns: their growth, issues and solutions.

Task

Select *one* of the images shown in Figures 7.7–7.12 (page 238) and Figures 7.20–7.21 and identify what it shows.

7.4 Aspects of urban change and management

In the SQA Higher Geography examination, questions will consider management strategies and the impact of change in housing and transport. It is important to understand the reasons for the changes.

7.5 Urban transport and traffic congestion

A simple definition of traffic congestion is when a road is overused and vehicles using it are unable to move freely. A survey concluded that in the year 1900, a horse and cart could move across London at an average speed of 14 mph. In 2018 approximately the same route was followed and the average speed was 13 mph. So much for 118 years of progress! It is obvious that most of our cities pre-date cars and buses. City centres often have narrow roads, narrow pavements and a tight network of roads. By definition, city centres are places where people and routes concentrate. The CBD is often the oldest part of the city and as such, the streets were not designed for cars. Since people now demand greater mobility, flexibility and accessibility, the number of cars has increased.

Statistics relating to traffic congestion

In this section, case studies are drawn from the developed world (e.g. London, York, Edinburgh, Glasgow) and from the developing world (e.g. Mumbai and Marrakech). Shanghai is also considered. This city is part of both the developed and developing world. The western core of the city shows all the features of a developed city, whilst the surrounding areas still clearly exhibit features of a developing city. The following is some background information.

Traffic congestion is a worldwide problem. Look at these statistics from the USA and the UK.

- A Harvard study (USA) indicated that in 2014 traffic congestion in the country's top 75 cities resulted in the premature death of 2,500 citizens and a cost of $20 billion to public health.
- A citizen of Los Angeles commuting into the city 250 times a year will, on average, sit in traffic jams for 185 hours! The total cost has been calculated (for the top ten cities in the USA) to be close to $200 billion in time and fuel!
- Research shows that building a new road seems to encourage more people to use it. The more roads created, the more cars they attracted. In California, for example, a 2000 study found that a new highway will reach 90 per cent of capacity within just five years.
- At certain times of the day, up to a third of cars on roads in Glasgow city centre are drivers looking for a place to park. In San Francisco and Moscow there are 'smart' systems and even apps to assist drivers to find the nearest parking space.
- According to the Department of Transport, in 1994 there were 21.2 million vehicles licensed in the UK. By 2018 this figure had risen 79 per cent to 37.9 vehicles, of which 31.3 million were cars.
- In 2018, trips by car accounted for 64 per cent of all trips made and 78 per cent of distance travelled.
- On average, females made more trips than males, but males travelled much further each year.
- People in the highest household income group made 28 per cent more trips than those in the lowest income group and travelled nearly three times further.
- Estimated average annual car mileage was 8,200 miles.
- There are over 38 million driving licences in the UK.

Reasons for congestion and its impact

- City centre streets were not designed for cars, since they are often in the oldest part of the city, with narrow roads and, in the case of some cities, old city walls. Figure 7.22 identifies a number of the issues linked to the impact of congestion and traffic.
- Generally there is a shortage of off-street parking, so many drivers are forced to park on the roads, reducing throughflow even further.
- People are often reluctant to use public transport, since it may be less convenient, expensive, inflexible and sometimes not available.

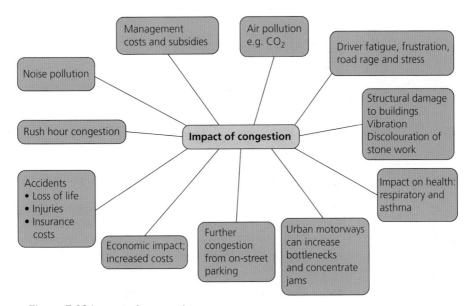

▲ **Figure 7.22** Impact of congestion

▲ **Figure 7.23** Congestion in Xiang, China

- Since people choose to own cars they generally want to use them.
- Traffic congestion at rush hour times not only clogs the city streets but also causes motorways to funnel the traffic to bottlenecks, such as a city bridge or tunnel.

Traffic management strategies in London, York and Edinburgh

London, York and Edinburgh all suffer from traffic congestion and a number of strategies have been introduced to try to manage and reduce this.

London: congestion charge zone

The congestion charge was introduced in 2003 and involves a system of cameras that register car licence plate numbers as vehicles enter and leave the city centre zones. The set-up costs were high (over £200 million), but congestion has fallen by 25 per cent and traffic is down by 18 per cent, with 70,000 fewer vehicles per day. Businesses are divided over whether it has improved trade or discouraged it. The charges are hefty (see Transport for London's website for details of current prices – www.tfl.gov.uk) and fines are significant (over £100).This system may be effective but it is not popular and few urban areas have followed suit.

London: Oyster cards

The Oyster card is a pre-paid electronic smartcard and now 80 per cent of tube journeys and 90 per cent of bus journeys are made using it. This has resulted in reduced queueing and faster transfer of people at tube stations. Overall it has reduced public transport costs. Drawbacks are that some people find the card system confusing and it is prone to system failure.

York: park and ride

York's medieval core within the old city wall is not capable of accommodating heavy traffic loads. The streets are narrow and haphazard with no space for parking. Six sites with good access from the surrounding areas were selected at the edge of the city and now visitors park their car at a site and travel into York by bus. The system appears to be successful, fast and efficient and has reduced both pollution levels and congestion. Combined with York's cycle and bus lanes and its encouragement of car sharing and walking, the 7 million visitors to the city appear to be well managed.

Case study: Edinburgh management strategies and impact

Edinburgh is a capital city and tourism hotspot, with major road, rail, air and sea links within Scotland, the UK and beyond.

Traffic congestion in Edinburgh arose from a number of changes:

- growing car ownership linked to increasing wealth
- growth in commuting from towns and villages in Fife, Lothian and the Borders
- growth in new shopping centres such as The Gyle, which attracts close to 400,000 vehicles per month
- tourism, which brings in several million visitors a year – city routes can be choked with the countless tourist buses
- new retail parks, e.g. IKEA
- growth of Edinburgh Airport.

Edinburgh is a city with a reputation for being 'car unfriendly' but this is perhaps unfair. Edinburgh has tried many strategies, from creating car parks in gap sites, multistorey parking, metres and wardens, congestion relief roads, a southern bypass and 'Greenways' bus lanes.

At rush hour, it took three times as long for buses to travel from the outskirts of the city to the city centre as it did at quieter times. The introduction of dedicated lanes for buses/taxis greatly reduced commuting time by bus and the city now has 65 km of these bus lanes, known as 'Greenways'. However, bus lanes were often simply created by restricting movement on the existing road layout, but this meant that the road capacity for all other transport was reduced. Motorists tend to be confused with bus lanes, often not entering the lane even when restrictions are lifted outside the rush hours.

In 2014 a new tramway system was completed. This electrified system has reduced air and noise pollution and cut travel time from the airport and Leith to the city centre. The costs rose considerably to over £600 million and the project was years behind schedule. Some locals felt that the upheaval was unnecessary in a city that had an excellent bus system, but an early evaluation indicates that locals and tourists are impressed with the simplicity of the system.

The Edinburgh city bypass was completed over 20 years ago and is one of the key roads in Scotland. The idea was simple: construct a 21 km dual carriageway to the south of the city, eliminating the need to enter the city. It has been effective in reducing the number of vehicles entering the city but, due to its design and the need for roundabouts linking the numerous arterial roads, combined with the rise in vehicles on the road, the A720 is very congested at peak travel times.

The River Forth flows to the north of the city, with traffic crossing over the heavily congested Forth Road Bridge. The construction of the Queensferry Bridge, opened in 2016, was part of a programme to relieve congestion of traffic entering and leaving Edinburgh across the River Forth, and to revitalise the economies of the surrounding areas. Opinions are divided over the impact of this crossing, which is still being assessed, but it is hoped that there will be a positive effect on traffic flow. The park and ride sites are located off the main roads and buses take passengers into the city centre. The Ingliston site to the west, for example, has space for 550 cars. An evaluation indicates that together the park and ride schemes save some 50,000 car journeys into and out of the city every business day.

In 2005 Edinburgh people were asked whether they supported a London-style 'congestion charge'. This was rejected by 75 per cent of residents.

Other strategies to improve transport links and flow into the city include:

- railway station improvements (e.g. £25 million upgrade at Haymarket)
- improvement of key roads, pavements and footpaths

- easy and clear ticketing on the buses
- new bus shelters and pedestrian crossings
- additional 20 mph restrictions
- easier access to buses and real time bus tracking
- alternative ways to pay for on-street car parking (via mobile telephone).

There remains much to do. In 2011, Edinburgh was the second most congested city in the UK (after London), with 31 per cent of roads classified as 'regularly congested'. However, the city has been aware of the problem of transport and congestion for many years and has shown initiative by introducing a whole raft of ideas. How effective have they been? The park and ride schemes have been very effective and, on average, local people use their local buses 190 times each every year – twice the national average. The trams are running, the railway stations and airport are modern. The main concerns are congestion around the city to the north, the lack of capacity on the city bypass to the south and the large number of motorists who still want to drive into the city.

Case study: Cairo

Cairo is one of the largest urban areas in the world. It has been ranked by the World Bank as the fourth worst city in terms of congestion. In this book, we have added this case study as an example of traffic congestion in a developing country. Clearly, it is a desirable place for many millions of Egyptians to live and work. The city now has over 20 million inhabitants and the city has expanded across both banks of the Nile. There are extreme contrasts of wealth and poverty with expensive new settlements often close to the city's shanty towns.

There is a need to manage transport provision in the city. The roads are chaotic, congested, polluted and it's almost impossible to find a place to park. The World Bank has concluded that it is faster to cross the city by walking than using a vehicle! Also, the Bank has calculated that the cost of congestion to the economy is close to £5 billion, or 4 per cent of GDP. There are 4 million vehicles in the city and suburbs. The bridges over the Nile, including the 6th October and the Qasr El Nile bridges, are choked. The writer has recently visited Cairo. He was informed that traffic lights were introduced in 1967 but people have not really got into the habit of looking at them. Fuel is highly subsidised. Egyptian motorists tend not to follow a code, with vehicles just as likely to drive along either side of the road in any direction. Vendors frequently set up stalls in the middle of roads and donkey carts are prominent, competing for space with cars.

Figure 7.24 Traffic congestion in Cairo

Transport has to be managed better than it is at the moment. New roads and flyovers are being constructed, bringing in even more vehicles from the suburbs. There is a good metro system crossing the city and carrying several million passengers daily. So what else should be done to manage congestion?

There are several standard approaches that can be applied and improved, such as:

- continuing to expand the metro system with designated bus lanes and subsidised pricing structures
- regulating the police and city officials to enforce existing laws and regulations
- educating drivers to work towards a 'common good' with a 'care and concern' for other road users
- expanding traffic control measures such as traffic lights, parking restrictions, widening roads, new roads, flyovers and investment in new bridges.

Other suggestions that relate to the Cairo problem are to:

- cut fuel subsidies for cars, making driving in the city more expensive
- implement stricter controls over the registration of new cars
- reduce public transport prices
- ban carts from certain roads at peak times
- ban vendors from selling products in the middle of the road and at junctions

- introduce more flexible working hours to spread the congestion
- assist businesses to relocate away from the congested centre and suburbs
- invest in new bridges across the Nile
- use new technology to manage traffic flow. For example, some universities are working with car manufacturers to develop mathematical programs (algorithms) to prevent traffic jams from forming, rather than trying to find solutions for when they have occurred. Smart signage can reroute cars away from traffic 'hot spots'.

Will these measures be successful? There are obstacles to overcome, for example financing the changes, persuading Egyptian drivers to uphold traffic laws and securing the commitment of city authorities to enforce those laws.

Case study: Shanghai

Shanghai is an example of a global megacity with elements of both a developed and developing city. Shanghai is a massive city with 23 million inhabitants and a core road network built around an old city. Today the city is booming with massive construction and economic growth and new areas such as the Pudong financial centre. This means that an increasing number of commuters travel in from the suburbs. Shanghai is one of the largest urban concentrations on the planet and consequently the city has a very extensive public transport system. Shanghai is a polluted city as a result of this growth. Oil and coal power stations, industrial waste and vehicle exhaust fumes produce toxic smog that can hang over the city. The December 2013 smog was the worst in recent memory.

▲ **Figure 7.25** Air pollution in Shanghai

▲ **Figure 7.26** Shanghai Expressway network at night

In Shanghai there are:

- 7 million cycles
- 35,000 taxis
- 200,000 scooters/motor bikes
- 3 million vans, lorries, buses, mini buses, government and company cars
- a growing number of private cars.

The metro now connects (by subway or light railway) to every urban district. There are 14 networks and 329 railway stations with 538 km of track, making it the largest and longest network in the world. On a single day in October 2018, 8.1 million people passed along this network. There are over 1,000 bus lanes, with a massive modernisation programme in progress and taxis in Shanghai are both plentiful and cheap. Shanghai has four main railway stations and a new high speed train, the Meglev, connects the new airport at Pudong with the city in a journey time of just 8 minutes. The Meglev is the fastest commercial train in the world, capable of reaching speeds of 430 km/hour.

Shanghai is a major hub of national expressways, such as the G2 which runs from Shanghai to Beijing, and municipal expressways. Rush hour traffic moves at a very slow pace. There are several elevated expressways to lessen traffic pressure on surface streets, but traffic in and around Shanghai is often heavy and traffic jams are commonplace during rush hour. There are bicycle lanes separate from car traffic on many surface streets, but bicycles and motorcycles are banned from most main roads including the elevated expressways.

In the 1990s when the first elevated ring roads and motorways were being constructed, these multi-lane highways were constructed across existing houses and businesses. People were given the option of being moved to a new flat or compensated with money before the bulldozers moved in. When the new airport at Pudong was being constructed, the first some farmers knew about it was when construction began!

In 1985 the only way to cross the Huangpuy River was by ferry. By 2018 there were 36 major bridges, two underground metro tunnels and one road tunnel, the most recent being the Shanghai Yangtze River Tunnel and Bridge.

Private car ownership in Shanghai has been rapidly increasing in recent years, but a new private car cannot be driven until the owner buys a licence in the monthly private car licence plate auction. Around 8,000 licence plates are auctioned each month and the average price is about £4,500. The purpose of this policy is to limit the growth of automobile traffic and to alleviate congestion.

There is strict parking enforcement in Shanghai, with many wardens/traffic police imposing fines and towing away cars. Street parking is relatively expensive but in the city centre and in affluent areas such as the French Concession, all major new buildings must have underground car parking facilities. Traffic lights, one-way streets, traffic calming, wardens and police all attempt to manage vehicle movement. How successful has all of this been? The issue is balancing the economic and industrial success of the city with the damaging cost to the environment, health and the economic costs due to congestion. While Chinese society is very ordered, in a big city such as Shanghai not everyone follows the rules and the local authorities have even narrowed the pavements, cycle lanes and bus lanes to try and cope with the increasing demands of traffic. Many claim that the urban expressways don't deserve their name. During peak hours, commuters face congested traffic over 15–25 per cent of their route. The average vehicle speed on main roads in rush hours in Shanghai is only 15–16 km per hour (8 mph) and, according to the local newspaper, the *Oriental Morning Post*, it's even slower for buses.

While Shanghai's population has grown by 43 per cent in the last 10 years, the traffic has seen a 53 per cent increase, registered vehicles have doubled and cars have tripled. However, the traffic capacity has been increased only by 10 per cent, which is insufficient for the increased demand.

Shanghai is used as an example of a developing world city. Some geographers may see it as a part of the developed world, but it is considered an acceptable developing world example.

You can use the information in Table 7.4 and apply it to an urban area that you know well. As you are aware, you may be asked a question about impact, strategies and effectiveness of those strategies in the question paper. It is important that when you use the information in this table, you select your own case study city and use detailed and informed local examples, names and issues.

In this section we have seen that there are many ways of dealing with urban traffic congestion, but do they work? A successful management plan tackles congestion and pollution at several levels, as demonstrated by the model shown in in Figure 7.27, which recognises:

- flow management
- improvements in public transport
- changes in the design of roads
- parking management
- innovation.

Task

Study Figure 7.27. Identify an urban area in the developing or developed world that you are familiar with.

1   Comment on the features of congestion in that area.
2   Identify strategies in place that control or manage traffic flow.
3   Comment on the effectiveness and impact of these management strategies.

Most of you reading this book will be approaching age 16, 17 or 18. For most young people, getting a driving licence is one of life's big targets and it is unlikely that demand for travel, mobility and car ownership will reduce in the foreseeable future. Without the strategies mentioned above, the problems of congestion and pollution would be far worse; it is clear that we can manage and control but not eliminate this problem of development and urbanisation.

▼ **Table 7.4** Traffic congestion impact and management strategies

Impact of traffic congestion	Strategies to manage traffic congestion
Vehicular emissions can damage and discolour stonework in buildings.	Making catalytic converters compulsory.
Exhaust emissions cause acid rainwater.	Running cars on unleaded petrol.
Nitrous oxides can form smog and damage lung tissue causing emphysema and bronchitis.	Promoting the use of electric and hybrid cars.
Traffic is noisy and unsightly.	Promoting the use of newer cars through the recent car scrappage scheme, where owners of a car aged 10 years or more were given £2,000 towards the cost of a new car if they scrapped their older one.
Emissions affect respiratory conditions such as asthma. Research indicates that organic compounds are produced which can create ground level ozone, which irritates the respiratory system, causing coughing, choking and reduced lung capacity.	Ensuring that cars pass an annual emissions test as part of the MOT.
	Modifications to the road network by increasing the size of roads and the number of lanes.
Carbon monoxide is produced which is an odourless poison for humans.	Congestion zone charging in London.
Traffic congestion slows down essential emergency service vehicles.	Introducing variable speed limits because when cars all move together at a similar speed there is a reduction in flow break-down and therefore traffic jams. Reducing a speed limit from 70 mph to 50 mph in peak periods can keep all traffic moving.
Congestion can affect people's mental health, who may react by demonstrating 'road rage' – a relatively recent phenomenon.	Charging for road use via toll roads.
	Promoting other forms of transport, such as the the 'Bike to Work' scheme that allows people to buy their bike cheaply by paying for it from their salary before tax is deducted.
Congestion has an economic impact as goods sit in traffic queues, costing companies in lost time and sales.	Metro/subway services (e.g. the Glasgow, and Tyne and Wear metro) receive subsidies and grants, and the rail and bus networks are also financially supported by the government to provide a cheaper service.
Traffic congestion is highly wasteful of oil, a finite resource.	

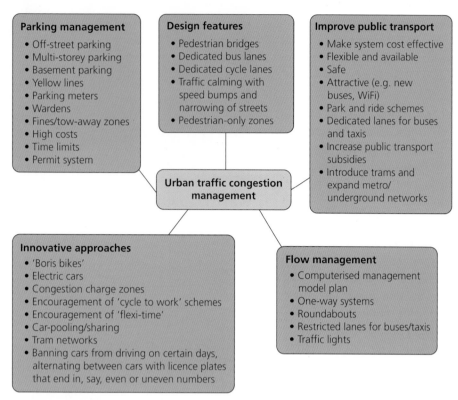

Parking management
- Off-street parking
- Multi-storey parking
- Basement parking
- Yellow lines
- Parking meters
- Wardens
- Fines/tow-away zones
- High costs
- Time limits
- Permit system

Design features
- Pedestrian bridges
- Dedicated bus lanes
- Dedicated cycle lanes
- Traffic calming with speed bumps and narrowing of streets
- Pedestrian-only zones

Improve public transport
- Make system cost effective
- Flexible and available
- Safe
- Attractive (e.g. new buses, WiFi)
- Park and ride schemes
- Dedicated lanes for buses and taxis
- Increase public transport subsidies
- Introduce trams and expand metro/ underground networks

Urban traffic congestion management

Innovative approaches
- 'Boris bikes'
- Electric cars
- Congestion charge zones
- Encouragement of 'cycle to work' schemes
- Encouragement of 'flexi-time'
- Car-pooling/sharing
- Tram networks
- Banning cars from driving on certain days, alternating between cars with licence plates that end in, say, even or uneven numbers

Flow management
- Computerised management model plan
- One-way systems
- Roundabouts
- Restricted lanes for buses/taxis
- Traffic lights

▲ **Figure 7.27** Model of urban traffic congestion management

7.6 Housing: management, strategies and impact in the developing and developed world

SQA asks you to consider change and aspects of management, strategies and impact (evaluation) of housing. The case studies in this section look at:

- shanty towns (Mumbai) and redevelopment (Marrakesh)
- Glasgow (redevelopment and renewal).

Shanty towns and housing in the developing world

In this section we will consider the:

- background to the growth of shanty towns
- social, economic and environmental challenges that have been created by the growth of shanty towns

- methods used to manage and improve the quality of these areas
- effectiveness or impact of these strategies.

We begin by considering the general issues and solutions before applying this knowledge to the examples of Mumbai and Marrakesh.

Shanty towns

A shanty town, also known as a spontaneous settlement or squatter town, is a settlement usually built using materials such as plywood, plastic and corrugated iron. These settlements are often located in environmentally deficient sites, such as city rubbish dumps, marsh land, river flood-plains, steep slopes, remote sites or beside railway tracks. They are also deficient in infrastructure, sanitation and sewerage, electricity, clean water and communications. Shanty towns are a feature of developing countries but can also be found in many developed countries/cities. They tend also to be associated with social problems such as crime, drugs, suicide and disease. Shanty towns are given different names around the world, such as:

- bidonvilles (former French colonial areas)
- townships (South Africa)
- bustees (India)
- favelas (Brazil).

These slums are also found in cities such as Madrid, Marseilles, Paris, Lisbon (Baracas) and, according to the *Daily Mail*, in south London, where dwellers may be part of the itinerant immigrant population. Shanty towns can grow very quickly within the centre of a city on land awaiting development.

It is very easy to over-generalise the problems within shanty towns – in an exam you should never say there is *no* electricity, *no* jobs, *no* sewerage, *no* clean water or *no* paved roads – every shanty town is different. Shanty towns serve a purpose as they provide houses and shelter for many people and conditions vary from place to place. People do their best to live a clean and dignified life, attempting to feed and look after themselves and their children, but life within the shanty towns is hard.

Growth of shanty towns

Shanty towns grow as a result of 'push' and 'pull' factors. They are a reaction to high population growth and movement and for many they provide a stepping stone to a better way of life. Since the countries with shanty towns are poor, these settlements are the inevitable response to that growth and the inability of the local authorities to cope. Globally, as many as 50 million people may live in these temporary/spontaneous settlements.

Social, economic and environmental challenges

There are 2.5 million slum dwellers in about 200 settlements in Nairobi, Kenya, representing 60 per cent of the Nairobi population. One of these slums, Kibera, houses 900,000 people. It is the biggest slum in Africa and one of the biggest in the world.

▲ **Figure 7.28** Children playing beside an open sewer, Kibera, Nairobi

▲ **Figure 7.29** Rio de Janeiro, Brazil

Shanty towns are overcrowded to an unimaginable degree – for example, over 10,000 people per km^2 in parts of Mexico City. They develop rapidly without structure or planning and the authorities cannot cope with the numbers of people. The population is very youthful (in Nairobi over 55 per cent of the shanty town population is under 15 years of age). Living conditions can be dreadful, with lack of space and privacy. There are higher levels of infant mortality and lower life expectancy for slum dwellers and although schooling and basic health care may be available, it is often inadequate. Such townships may become centres for crime, disorder and vice (Soweto in South Africa has been reported as a 'no-go' zone for police) because people are poor and living on the edge of society.

There are jobs in the shanty towns, but not enough. Many people, including children, will travel by bus to the city centre some distance away for employment. Transport systems are inadequate, relatively expensive and very overcrowded. The infrastructure within a shanty town is weak and often there is a lack of clean water and sewage disposal and an unreliable electricity supply. The streets are often unpaved, but crowded and congested.

From an environmental viewpoint the townships are unsightly (building materials are often scrap stone and brick, corrugated tin and wood), with poor quality air and water. If built near the town rubbish dump they will be smelly and unhygienic, or dangerous if built close to railway tracks, especially for children. Since shanty towns are built on the cheapest land rejected by other developers, the sites may be open to landslides, flooding or be beside rubbish dumps or even railway yards.

However, shanty towns can be constructed cheaply and quickly and with their network of workshops and small industries they provide work, and the closeness of the people sharing adversity allows a community spirit to exist. For many of the people they are a temporary home, before they move on. While not in any way ideal, shanty towns are better than sleeping rough on the streets.

Strategies to improve the quality of shanty towns

The shanty town people often organise themselves into self-help groups (especially in India and Brazil). This empowerment of the local people, combined with support from the urban authorities, churches or charities (e.g. Médecins Sans Frontières or Christian Aid), can lead to improvements, such as installing sewerage systems, paving roads or supporting a health clinic. What is often needed to improve life in the shanty towns is some money, a level of organisation, people with the skills and time to make the changes and a limit on the number of people moving in. For example, in Dharavi, Mumbai, the authorities provided a sound foundation for a house and a link to sewerage and electricity. Bricks can now be delivered to a central source and a paved road can be provided. Families can then build their own house using the materials provided. Some of these townships become established and are recognised by the local authority who then will

install sewerage, power and even undertake refuse collection. This type of improvement works well since it is cheap and there is a level of involvement from local people. In Rio de Janeiro, there are schemes where banks lend government money at low interest rates to communities and individual families. However, in Marrakesh the shanty towns are being removed as the bulldozers move in, but this only works if there is somewhere else for the people to move to. Sometimes these relocation schemes involve forcing people to another site.

As we have said earlier, it easy to regard shanty towns as 'bad', but they fulfil a need and, in time, people will generally move on and out of the town. Solar power does not require an elaborate support system, so many houses are now generating their own electricity and it even seems that tourism is growing in some of the 'safer' favelas in Rio de Janeiro.

One final strategy in preventing the rise of shanty towns is to improve the quality of life in rural areas. By creating more opportunities it may prevent people from moving to the cities – investment in rural areas can have a positive impact on urban areas.

Impact of strategies to improve the quality of shanty towns

A fundamental problem of shanty towns is that improvements in their living conditions increases their pull so that more people come to live in the shanty town. Projects involving improvements to the quality of life, health and education have positive outcomes, but the more money that is put in, the more money is needed! Many people are reluctant to move away from the city centre shanties because location is important and so many of the pressures remain.

Relocation projects have a limited history of success, because many people do not wish to move again. Self-help schemes tend to be successful, since they are dependent on both local need and community spirit. Other ways of improving people's lives include:

- enabling local people to get a loan to improve their lives
- the authorities leaving a pile of breeze-blocks and ceramic roof tiles for local people to collect and use to make their houses stronger and waterproof
- building schools and hospitals to improve the education and health of the local population

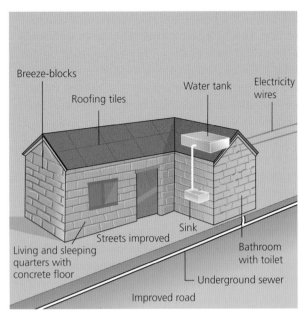

▲ **Figure 7.30** Model of a self-help house

- installing water pipes to provide fresh water and plumbing in toilets, so all waste is taken away, preventing the spread of disease
- tarring dirt roads so when it rains they do not turn to mud, making travel easier.

In the long term the best strategies remove the need for migration and result in a general improvement in the overall wealth of the country.

Case study: Dharavi, Mumbai, India

▲ **Figure 7.31** Dharavi slums close to the railway line

'The people of Dharavi may be poorer in material wealth but are richer socially.'

Source: HRH The Prince of Wales (2011)

▲ **Figure 7.32** Slums of Mumbai, showing high densities

Background

Dharavi is one of several shanty towns in Mumbai, the Indian city which was founded in 1882 during British colonial rule. The city centre is crowded with people and polluting industries, and there was a forced movement to an adjacent island site. The population of Dharavi (estimated to be between 500,000 and 1 million) live in a very densely populated area. Despite the amazing growth of its national economy, India still has over 65 million people living in conditions that the United Nations recently described as 'slum accommodation'. While it is easy to focus on the problems, Dharavi gives hope, shelter and employment to many people. Mumbai's history dates back over 125 years, but it is a city of change and many people who live there today choose to stay, even though they could afford to move out.

Challenges

Typing Dharavi into a search engine will reveal scenes of real poverty and challenge: overcrowding, poor sanitation and drainage, shortages of electricity, unpaved roads, limited rubbish collection, open sewers, diseases such as diphtheria and polluting industries such as tanneries. For many there is a lack of dignity, with few enclosed toilets and a real lack of privacy. Housing varies but there are many poor quality houses, plus unemployment and underemployment.

Dharavi has a history of flooding (2005, 2013 and 2017) and fires (occurring almost yearly, often with serious damage and loss of life). A majority of residents do not have any legal right to the land they live on and there is a feeling of lack of power or political representation.

Water is often rationed to just two hours a day and the city tanneries remain. Recently, a massive recycling industry has developed, often employing very young children who should be at school. You may also be aware of reports of the clothing sweatshop factories that are found in areas such as this. The infant mortality rate within the shanty town remains high at 40/1,000. The Mumbai road network cannot cope and there is congestion, leading to high levels of pollution and long journey times.

Hope for the future

However, Dharavi is a city within a city. Because it is so huge, there are wide variations between areas that are in dire poverty and some areas that could almost be described as wealthy. The shanty town has a central location, close to the financial centre of the city, and communications are good immediately surrounding Dharavi, with two railway lines, lots of buses and roads. Rents are low, with over 5,000 established businesses and 15,000 single-room factories. People are generally enterprising and hard-working and this area exports to the world. Of those people in Dharavi who do work, 85 per cent work within the area. Accommodation does vary with many people choosing to remain in their 'city'. Often, if you explore and go behind the street scene, you will find houses that are clean with curtains, balconies and flowers. There is pride and immense dignity, with a very high level of family and community support.

So is life getting better for the inhabitants of this shanty town? In some ways it is, but the scale of the problem is so large, it can be very difficult to gauge progress.

Development

There are plans to develop the area of Dharavi, backed by the Mumbai authorities and foreign investors from the USA, UK, Dubai and Singapore. Since 2004, the Indian Government has backed projects to clear Dharavi's slums and create a new independent legal township. This has resulted in new apartments, a water and sewerage system, hospitals and schools. Some residents were concerned that such redevelopment would destroy their existing livelihoods and the community spirit of the areas. The Slum Sanitation Programme (started in 1996) built almost 350 new communal toilet blocks. Parts of Dharavi lie very close to the financial centre which is looking to expand. The money generated by the financial centre can be used for schools, infrastructure and hospitals and clinics and the cost is put at £1.1 billion, which seems to be a modest amount.

There are issues over compensation (amounts awarded are low and very selective) and legal issues over how a person can be compensated for being moved from land over which they have no legal right. There is also pressure from many developed countries to improve the working conditions for the people who work in the factories, rubbish dumps and recycling sites. The public transport system in Mumbai is being developed, with a new metro system being constructed. The first line is already open.

Charities and other organisations such as the Society for the Promotion of Area Resource Centres are involved in smaller projects that tackle child poverty or supply materials (e.g. pipes and breeze-blocks) or focus on the education and opportunities for girls.

So what is changing? If you were to join the tourist trail through Dharavi (genuine!), your senses would be challenged. You would see the extremes of human existence, smell the infrastructural inadequacies and may have a feeling of despair but you would also experience hope.

Impact of management strategies in Dharavi

Dharavi offers the extremes of human hope and despair. As you read through the previous section, it is clear that there are many positive things happening. Money is being used for better schooling, health clinics and infrastructure. Mains water connections are increasing and there are more communal toilet blocks. Legal rights of land and home ownership are being established, and global pressure appears to be ensuring that working conditions in the factories are (possibly) improving. Of greater significance is the impact of the huge number of creative and proud people living in Dharavi. However, so much has yet to be done.

Task

1 Urbanisation within the developing world can help to solve poverty issues in the countryside. However, it also causes new problems in the urban areas. To what extent do you agree with this view?

2 Consider Dharavi or another shanty town that you have studied or plan to research (e.g. Kibera in Nairobi). Write some summary notes using the following headings: Challenge, Hope and Development.

Case study: Housing in Marrakesh, Morocco

Background

Marrakesh is located in central Morocco, some 560 km south of Gibraltar. Founded in 1062, it grew as a centre of culture, education, religion and trade. The city initially grew within the old red clay walls, but quickly expanded across the flat plains. Marrakesh now brings in over 2 million visitors a year, attracted by the culture, climate, the souks (markets) and the wonderful landscape to the south. Today, Marrakesh has a thriving industrial quarter but it was a magnet for hippies in the 1960s and 1970s. The city attracts many migrants from the rural areas around and by 1990, the city was struggling, as the old core of the city could not cope with in-migration. There was intense poverty and high unemployment.

Some features of Marrakesh:

- Old city core, containing mosques and the palace, located within the walls.
- Medina quarter located within the walls and the souks.
- Gardens and palmeries (areas of oasis) surrounding the city; once farmed they are now a fashionable area of hotels and expensive houses.
- Former French colonial sector to the west of the city, with wide tree-lined streets, modern hotels, shops and high-rise housing.
- Shanty town ghettos.
- Suburbs, each with its own shopping centre and containing a mix of older and new medium rise flats.
- New towns and industrial zones.

Government intervention

The existing housing stock was dated and deteriorating and the continued in-migration from the rural areas resulted in several large shanty towns (known as bidonvilles). In 2003 the government began a programme called 'Towns without slums', that aimed to deliver a six-pronged attack on housing poverty by providing:

- a clean water supply
- proper drainage systems
- proper sewerage systems
- organised regular waste/litter removal
- electricity
- street lighting.

In Marrakesh the plan was to upgrade the bidonvilles rather than remove them. This was decided so that poor families could retain their strong community links, gain improved access to the above and build up savings to perhaps find better housing in the future.

The authorities were determined not to allow new shanty towns to be constructed. Since it is inevitable that new migrants would continue to arrive in Marrakesh, the solution was to knock down any new shanty town construction and to build new towns around Marrakesh. An example of such a 'satellite settlement' was Tamansourt, some 7 km outside Marrakesh and it is intended that Tamansourt will eventually be home to 300,000 people. This planned community will be a mix of housing, industry, shopping, entertainment, education and health care. It is intended to be an independent settlement so that people will not need to commute to Marrakesh. Housing will be range from good quality social housing to high end expensive villas. The plan shows Tamansourt as a pleasant place to live. The national motorway, the N7, will pass through the new town and there will be a network of fast local roads within the city, which will have parks and water features because Moroccans love to walk in their parks in the evening. The plan is that industries will be attracted to the area following government incentives and that all of this will relieve the stresses from Marrakesh. In addition the government has backed low-cost loans for people moving to the area.

Rehabilitation of the Medina

Marrakesh has a large Medina (Old Town) which is the centre of much commercial activity today. The area positively bustles day and night as people buy, sell and barter and it is also a great attraction to visitors. The Medina is surrounded by the old city wall and, despite it covering an area of just 6 km², over 150,000 people live within it. The population density is therefore very high. Within the Medina, you will find souks (the markets where there are shops and trades), small craft industries (textiles, metal work, shoes), **riads** (large houses with interior gardens), **dars** (houses without a garden) and hotels and guest houses. The richness of the architecture has been recognised as a UNESCO World Heritage Site.

However, many of the traditional family homes are ageing and their owners are of limited means and cannot afford to renovate their homes, so often they sell up and move out. Since the 1990s the Medina has seen a big boom with property developers and European second home owners moving in, financially squeezing locals out.

The Medina now has many hotels and restaurants occupying the old homes. The authorities cannot afford to renovate the houses as homes for local people and so the Medina will continue to change. Commercial businesses wish to buy out the locals and develop their own enterprises. However, the government, through a scheme called 'RehabiMed', recognises the importance of the heritage characteristics of the area and is supporting low-income families to remain inside the Medina.

Impact of changes in Marrakesh

Morocco attracts foreign investment since it is viewed as a stable North African country and the King is progressive in wishing to improve the overall situation of the people.

The city still attracts migrants from the surrounding plains and mountains. The Medina and riads are being renovated and the development plans appear to be having a positive impact on the remaining shanty dwellings, with the new towns continuing to show growth. Poverty and unemployment still exist, but through 2015 to 2019 the city was continuing to recover from a recession, with new housing, an expansion of the airport, new industries, shopping malls, golf courses and conference facilities picking up again.

The King has made it a priority to eliminate the bidonvilles and they are now almost all cleared. New settlements have been built, although many Moroccans seem reluctant to move away from the city.

 Task

For Marrakesh or another shanty town that you have researched, carry out the following tasks:

1 Explain the background to the growth of your selected shanty town.
2 Describe what the problems were and explain why they needed to be managed.
3 Outline the strategies that were introduced to reduce the impact of the shanty town.
4 Evaluate the success of the strategies.

 Task

Consider these aspects of tourism in Marrakesh and reflect on the impact that each development has had on local people:

1 New hotels, holiday homes and golf courses that are transforming Marrakesh into a mass tourism destination.
2 Seventeen golf courses have been built (a further ten are at the planning permission stage).
3 Foreigners have bought and restored more than 1,000 riads in the Medina, creating much needed work for local craftsmen.
4 The restored riads have pushed up house prices by 500 per cent in the last ten years.
5 Moroccans who have become rich through tourism provide jobs and money to many local people.

Housing: rural-urban fringe and suburbs in the developed world

Cities are dynamic – they grow and develop with time, with changes taking place both within the city as well as at the periphery. Urban sprawl is taking place in virtually all cities as they expand, both in the less developed world and the more economically developed world. The rural-urban fringe is the interface between the countryside and the town and it is where there can be a clash for competing uses. In the face of change we need to manage and control but it is not possible to please everyone and compromise is necessary.

A **greenbelt** is an area around a city mainly left as farmland and woodland in which development is not permitted. Most people would agree that the idea of a greenbelt is good, allowing some of the environment to remain green, quiet and peaceful. If only! Despite regulations that forbid development, sometimes the pressure is too great and planning permission is given, particularly if the development is considered to be in the interests of the wider community. For example, In Glasgow, the route of the M77 is across greenbelt land and permission was also granted for many new homes to be built in Newton Mearns and Darnley Mains, both formerly within the greenbelt. The area immediately outside the greenbelt can also be placed under immense pressure. For example, around Glasgow such has been the demand for

housing that prices have soared in settlements such as Fenwick and Eaglesham to the south, Bishopton and Kilbarchan to the west, and Strathblane and Torrance to the north.

Task

Choose a city rural-urban fringe that you have studied.

1. Explain the background to the growth of your chosen example.
2. Account for some of the conflicts that occur between users.
3. What strategies were introduced to reduce the impact of the growth?
4. How successful have these strategies been?

Sustainable cities

Planners and geographers are now trying to make cities sustainable. 'Sustainable' means doing something in a way that minimises damage to the environment and avoids using up natural resources, for example by using **renewable resources**.

A sustainable city balances quality of life for all residents today, with no damage to the environment, while creating a city for the future, where resources and services are available for all.

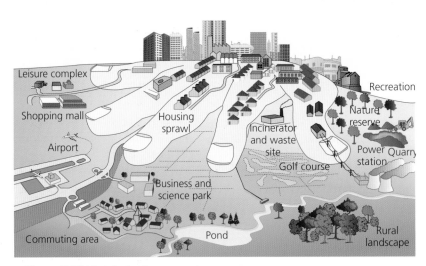

▲ **Figure 7.33** Model of urban sprawl

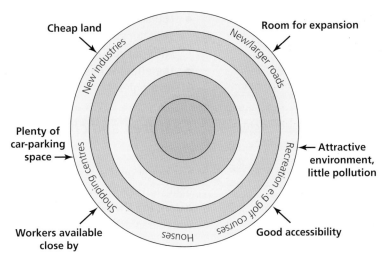

▲ **Figure 7.34** Benefits of the rural–urban fringe for economic development

▼ **Table 7.5** Urban sprawl: causes, problems, solutions and effectiveness

Causes	Problems and conflicts
Pressure for retail and commercial expansion.	Loss of farmland (often high quality).
Rehousing development from the inner-city.	Loss of existing woodlands, school playing fields.
New housing estates with schools, shops and health clinics.	Conflicting demand from infill sites and refuse sites.
Pressure to find space for urban waste.	Conflicting demands from other uses such as recreation, transport, retail, industry, transport, airports.
Recreational demands for land, e.g. golf courses. Pressures to improve transport links, e.g. ring roads.	Loss of community spirit in existing villages as they merge with the city.
Growth of villages in the commuter belt.	As the fringe areas grow the CBD 'dies a little'.
Other developments such as:	Blight of the rural-urban fringe with increase in vandalism and a loss of quality of life.
<ul><li>business and science parks</li><li>country parks and woodland walks</li><li>airport expansion</li><li>industrial expansion due to cheaper land, better transport links and less congestion</li><li>demand for new hotels and conference centres.</li></ul>	Possible increase in pollution (transport, industry, quarrying, infill). Encroachment bit by bit on the greenbelt.
Strategies	**Effectiveness**
Planning controls, restrictions and zoning regulations to protect the countryside.	There is a demand for new developments and this is difficult to stop.
A 'master plan' so that development can be controlled.	People generally want to improve their quality of life to live, play and shop in planned, environmentally positive sites.
Encouraging development in other areas through the use of grants and loans (e.g. 'Enterprise Zones') and encouraging growth in new towns.	Local authorities are aware of the impact that out-of-town shopping centres will have on the CBD and use their powers to veto some developments.
Encouraging redevelopment of **brownfield sites** (older derelict industrial sites).	The creation of restrictive zoning and the inclusion of greenbelts in planning has had an impact, but when land for development becomes restricted land prices increase markedly.
Encouraging and allowing redevelopment within the CBD and inner-city.	Often plans ignore the social and human needs of people.
Counter-urbanisation strategies to encourage developments within existing city boundaries.	Greenbelts may have some success but not all cities have them and development often 'leap frogs' over the protected area.
Making the core of the city more attractive so there is less need for people and services to move to the fringes.	Whatever developments take place, it is impossible to satisfy everyone and compromises can mean no one is entirely happy.

Research opportunity

Typing 'sustainability' into a search engine will produce many results, but some of the common themes are as follows:

- All new buildings should be energy efficient.
- Community links should be strong and people should work together to tackle social issues such as crime and poverty.
- All resources used should be renewable and recycling should become the norm.
- Social amenities, housing and open space should be accessible to all.
- Walking and cycling should be safe.
- Public transport should be cheap, safe and available to all.

Task

1 Compare your home town/city with this list of sustainability themes. How does it score for sustainability?
2 Five cities have a strong reputation for sustainability:
   - Vancouver, Canada
   - San Francisco, USA
   - Oslo, Norway
   - Curitiba, Brazil
   - Copenhagen, Denmark.
   Select one of these cities and give an account to justify its claim to be 'sustainable'.

Housing: management, strategies and impact in the developed world

SQA asks you to consider change and aspects of management, strategies and impact (evaluation) of housing. The case studies in this section look at the city of Glasgow – not just at housing, but taking a somewhat broader approach.

Urban decay and regeneration/renewal

In this section we will consider:

- the background to the issue of urban decay in the UK and look at the economic, social and environmental issues

- the solutions and management of urban regeneration/renewal (management strategies), with particular reference to Glasgow and housing
- the effectiveness and outcome of regeneration strategies.

Features and characteristics of urban decay

For many people a study of urban decay is mainly associated with the decline of the inner-city and to an extent the CBD. Refer back to Table 7.3 on page 237 which describes the key features of each zone.

Figure 7.35 shows the key features of urban decay and images in Figures 7.36 and 7.37 clearly show the problems. There are four strands recognised in the model. Over time there is decay in the basic housing and industrial stock of the area, which then results in further damage to the environment and social structure of the area.

There was incredible growth and expansion during the nineteenth and early twentieth centuries in many of the key cities in the UK. This was often linked to the industrial revolution, when migrants from rural areas poured into the urban areas in search of work. Technological advances combined with the expansion of the market in the UK and overseas meant that there was high demand for industrial products. Cities grew at a rapid pace and within the city factories and houses for workers were built quickly and cheaply. For some cities the pace of development meant that the environment was of lesser importance than the push for economic growth, but by the 1950s and 1960s cities such as Manchester, Bristol and Glasgow were showing the results of this drive for growth at all costs. The tenements and terraced houses were no longer fit for purpose. Too many of the old housing stock had poor facilities, such as outside toilets and no hot water or central heating. They were overcrowded with a legacy of poor maintenance, leaky roofs and windows, crumbling stone work and shabby 'closes'.

The key Victorian industries were in decline with insufficient new growth industries to take their place. The iron works, railway works, shipyards and countless small workshops were poorly placed to compete in a changing modern world. Industrial decline led to unemployment and poverty. The city

A model of urban decay

Housing	Industry	Social	Environment

• Ageing housing stock
 	
• Poorly maintained
 	
• Empty properties
 	
• Large/small site clearances
 	
• The gap between abandonment and renewal
	• Decline of old industrial core, e.g. shipbuilding, iron/steel
	
	• Industrial relocation
	
	• Sites abandoned
	
	• Loss of industrial location factors
	
	• Loss of jobs
	
	• Factories derelict
	
	• Some key industries located overseas
		• Unemployment
		
		• Increasing levels of poverty
		
		• Less money to spend
		
		• Social decay –
		    crime
		    vandalism
		    drugs
		    graffiti
		
		• Loss of community spirit
		
		• Deterioration in health, education, aspiration, equality
		
		• Out-migration, especially of the skilled and young
		
		• Closure of shops and services
			• Old industrial landscape
			
			• Abandonment
			
			• Waste land
			
			• Unattractive gap sites
			
			• Visual pollution
			
			• Housing abandonment
			
			• Empty houses
			
			• Graffiti, vandalism, fly-tipping

▲ **Figure 7.35** Model of urban decay

▲ **Figure 7.36** Old tenement building awaiting demolition in Glasgow

▲ **Figure 7.37** Glasgow slum

authorities were well aware of this decline, and strategies and plans (see below) were put into place. In some ways this story is far too neat. For most people who lived in these troubled areas, life carried on in a dignified way, but in time there was a feeling of blight. There was an increase in vandalism and crime and as properties became empty there was graffiti and further vandalism. Those who could, moved out. Those left behind felt abandoned. Some buildings were knocked down, gap sites appeared and rubbish dumps gathered. There seemed to be an increase in social disharmony with more split families, poor health, low life expectancy and low levels of aspiration.

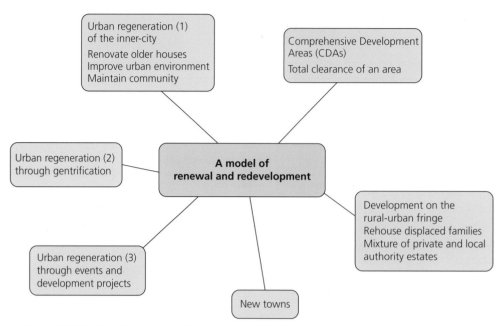

▲ **Figure 7.38** Model of renewal and redevelopment

Summary of the causes of decay

- A decline in the quality of the housing stock. The Victorian and pre-1914 housing deteriorated fast. Quality was often poor to start with, but low maintenance, age, overcrowding and lack of facilities fuelled the pace of decline.
- Out-migration – those who could afford to do so moved out, along with the more skilled and younger dynamic population. Many people migrated to Canada, Australia or the USA. Others moved to the suburbs or the new towns being created throughout the UK.
- Industrial decline – there are several reasons for this change, including changing market conditions and the rise of overseas competition, and the development of new greenfield sites that were more attractive and desirable for the new industries.
- The inner-city had a high concentration of low income groups. Possibly attracted by low rents, the poorest groups (including recent **immigrants**, the old and disadvantaged) seemed to find it difficult to break out of the cycle of poverty, poor health and low educational achievement.

- There was clear neglect by governments and local authorities during the previous 50 years. Government grants and incentives often favoured the areas that were growing without a troublesome legacy from the past.
- Age – many of the houses, factories and communities were over 100 years old.

Management strategies for urban regeneration

Cities cannot be allowed to die. In some respects the causes of **urban decline** can be classified under 'push and pull' factors. Parts of the CBD and especially the inner-city had lost any advantage that they once had, while at the same time there were developments pulling people, services and jobs away from the core of the city towards the suburbs and beyond. The lure was a new job, a new house and the chance for a better quality of life. As will become clear below, since the 1950s many strategies have been introduced, some of which worked and others that had more limited success. A number of terms were used to describe these changes: urban renewal, urban redevelopment and urban regeneration. All UK cities have their own development programmes, but they tend to share some common features, as outlined in Table 7.6.

▼ **Table 7.6** Urban renewal and redevelopment in Glasgow

Initiative	Effectiveness and impact
Comprehensive Development Areas (CDAs) and renewal If an area is beyond fixing then the solution may be to send in the bulldozers and clear the site. Once cleared it is then possible to start from a fresh plan which will include the number, size and design of the houses to be built, the environment and service provision. In Glasgow the construction of the inner ring road, the M8 and M77 cut through the suburbs, inner-city and CBD. Glasgow embraced high-rise flats with over 300 blocks constructed. Emerging from the ruins came a new feature in the city landscape. Rebuilding featured many high-rise flats, a cheap and quick solution to the housing problem.	In a city such as Glasgow, 29 CDAs were identified. It became clear that it is relatively easy and fast to clear a site, but rebuilding takes years. Many of the sites remained undeveloped for years and indeed there are still gaps in 2015. When building did take place the planners did not always get it right. In the 1960s and 1970s the trend was high-rise flats. Families were split up during clearance and only 25% of former residents could come back to the new houses. The impact was massive. In retrospect, 50 years later, what may have seemed to be a real positive step to rehouse people, was clearly a mistake. The CDA programme was never completed, problems quickly arose over families being split and they were unhappy with the new high-rise housing. Total clearance was also expensive and unnecessary. See case studies below on Gorbals and Hutchesontown and the Red Road Flats.
Urban regeneration of the inner-city (1) It became clear that total clearance of a site was unnecessary and very expensive. Regeneration became preferred and involved knocking down only what was necessary. Many of the houses could be renovated and improvements made to the environment and upgrading of education, health and other services.	In general regeneration has been successful. If the basic core of the tenement was sound, it was possible to reroof, replace windows, rewire, double glaze, install a secure entry system, clean the building by sandblasting, combine two small flats into one decent flat, improve the landscape by landscaping, build new social facilities and encourage new business and industry with grants and loans. This was popular since families could remain close and people could stay in their own area.
Development on the rural-urban fringes From the 1950s there was massive expansion of housing on the outskirts of Glasgow in local authority schemes such as Drumchapel, Castlemilk, Pollok and Easterhouse. Over 200,000 people were relocated to these four areas.	These housing areas promised new decent housing, often with gardens and a new start for the family. An evaluation of the rural-urban fringe development is that many of the areas were successful and popular, but there have been some issues. Often a family was broken apart and ended up in different schemes, often miles apart. Most people had little say in where they were moved to. The schemes were often rather remote and although there were buses, the journey into the centre of the city was long and often expensive for many people. The planners forgot that a new community requires shops, services, youth clubs and jobs and sometimes these social and economic services were not a priority. For some people, the schemes were isolated, for example Drumchapel had only one post office, one telephone box and a half-hourly bus service to the city centre. The worst areas of Pollok and Easterhouse have already been demolished less than 40 years after they were built (see below for the case study on Easterhouse).

▼ **Table 7.6** Urban renewal and redevelopment in Glasgow *(continued)*

Initiative	Effectiveness and impact
New towns A new town is a planned settlement, outside the city, on a greenfield site. New towns offered a new start and in Scotland five were built (Irvine, East Kilbride, Cumbernauld, Livingstone and Glenrothes). These towns were built to a plan with some key features – a purpose built modern town centre, separate housing and industrial estates and a modern road network, all surrounded by open space and green fields. Cities may also have 'overspill' agreements with other towns to take some of the displaced families.	Many families were attracted to the new towns. Amazingly, by the 1950s it became clear that Glasgow needed to rehouse 500,000 people. Within the city boundaries the CDAs could only rehouse 200,000, estates on the edge of the city could take another 100,000, leaving 200,000 to move outside the city to new houses and other settlements. New towns offered a new start, the chance to bring up children in a safe environment away from the stresses of poverty, poor housing and limited job opportunities. Although they have been caught up in recent economic downturns and their growth has been cut, on balance most people would agree that the new towns have been a successful strategy.
Urban regeneration through gentrification (2) This refers to the renovation of older inner-city and city centre houses and flats together with new luxury apartments being built. Since 2000 we seem to be rediscovering the attractiveness of the city centre.	In Glasgow the Merchant City is now a fashionable and stylish area. Once this was the main city trading area where tobacco and cotton merchants met and conducted their business. Then the CBD moved to the west and this area declined. It became an area of warehouses, older properties and low quality shops. Gentrification has been centred round Ingram Square and the Italian Centre, with stylish housing, cafés, bars and boutiques. Properties in Merchant City are expensive and exclusive. Once an area has been gentrified it moves out of the price category of the people who once lived there. On balance, however, the impact of this strategy has been successful and popular.
Urban regeneration (3) within the CBD and inner-city, based on events and development projects Glasgow's wealth was once centred on the River Clyde, with trading, shipbuilding and docks. At its peak there were over 55 separate docks and yards, but by 2015 there were two shipyards and one dock. Urban regeneration goes beyond the redevelopment of the physical area of a location to tackle the social and economic problems in the area, such as poverty, poor health and unemployment. Urban regeneration projects are major interventions, requiring considerable financial contributions from both the public and private sectors.	Since the 1980s Glasgow has become a desirable city for events, including the Garden Festival (1988), the European City of Culture (1990), the City of Architecture and Design (1999) and most recently City of the Commonwealth Games (2014). All of these events had a very positive impact at the time. We talk of a legacy nowadays and need to consider the lasting impact of such developments on local people, the city and people in Scotland. An example of regeneration is given in the case study on the Clyde waterfront regeneration.

Case study: The Gorbals and Hutchesontown

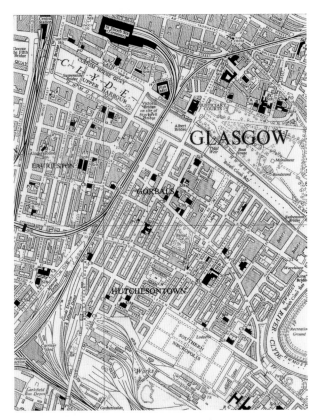

▲ **Figure 7.39** 1950s Gorbals and Hutchesontown

From the early nineteenth century the Gorbals was both home and workplace for many thousands of migrants. These migrants came from the rural areas of Scotland, where they had been displaced by sheep, land confiscation and poverty, as well as Irish people fleeing famine and Jews leaving behind persecution in Europe. Houses, mostly tenements and many quite stylish in design, were built to house both working-class and middle-class families. These communities had shops and cinemas, churches, schools and many small and larger factories and workshops. By the 1930s its 90,000 population was served by 1,000 shops and 130 pubs.

However, by the 1920s the middle classes started to move out and, combined with the decline of many of the jobs, rising unemployment and the deterioration in the quality of the ageing houses, the area began to deteriorate. By the 1950s the Gorbals was identified as one of Europe's worst slums and the census of 1951 found that 50,000 people lived in overcrowded high-density housing.

During the 1960s and 1970s Hutchesontown was identified for redevelopment, becoming the first of Glasgow's CDAs. Virtually all the old historic buildings were demolished along with the tenements. The author of this chapter visited the area in 1970 as part of a university field trip to see the demolition of one of the tenement blocks. The solution was thought to be high-rise blocks of flats. The Hutchie E maze of precast concrete wind tunnels lasted less than 20 years before they were demolished in 1987 and the award-winning Queen Elizabeth Court tower block followed in 1993. However, it is worth mentioning that not everyone hated the high-rise blocks and the remaining blocks are being softened to blend more into the community.

By 1991 the population of Hutchesontown was close to 10,000, but what is the area like today? For many it is uplifting. Hutchesontown is undergoing intensive redevelopment of mixed housing association and private housing. Modern, well-constructed four-storey tenements have been built. The area has a buzz to it and it is just a ten-minute walk across the suspension bridge to the city centre and Glasgow Green. The Gorbals Initiative, a local enterprise company, provides access for local people to nearby job opportunities and stimulates the local economy. In some parts gentrification is taking place, giving life and wealth back to the area. However, for some people there is a problem: the huge rise in property prices has forced the traditional working-class families out of the area as they cannot afford to rent or buy in this area. As a result, resentment from the remaining locals may be directed against those they consider to be 'outsiders'.

 Task

Summarise the impact and evaluate the changes in housing within the Gorbals and Hutchesontown.

Case study: Red Road Flats

▲ **Figure 7.40** View of the Red Road flats

▲ **Figure 7.41** Demolition of Red Road block

The Red Road flats (located to the north-east of the city of Glasgow), consisted of eight multi-storey blocks (of between 28 and 31 floors) and were designed to accommodate 4,700 people. Opened in 1966, they quickly gained a reputation for anti-social crime. The residents disliked these 'cities in the sky' and, combined with the dangers of asbestos in their construction and poor maintenance, proved to be unpopular. By 1980, two of the blocks were declared unfit for families and converted into student and YMCA accommodation. The other blocks did see some renovation (such as security access and concierge facilities). By 1990 the flats had become home to refugees and asylum seekers from Kosovo, Somalia and elsewhere. Their unpopularity and the high cost of maintenance meant that the blocks were now targeted for demolition (Figure 7.41). Two were demolished in 2012 and 2013, and the remaining six blocks were knocked down in 2015.

Case study: Easterhouse

▲ **Figure 7.42** Easterhouse: 1960s style flats

The scheme at Easterhouse, six miles to the east of Glasgow's CBD, was built in the mid-1950s to provide better housing for 50,000 people from areas such as the Gorbals and Hutchesontown. Initially the houses were three- or four-storey tenement-style flats with two or three bedrooms and separate kitchens and bathrooms. However, the planners did not get it entirely right because a community needs more than houses. The area lacked amenities such as shops, sport and youth clubs, cinemas, pubs, transport links and employment opportunities. Today, Easterhouse remains an area of lower life expectancy, higher levels of smoking, crime, poverty and unemployment than the rest of the city. However, since the 1990s a programme of demolition and renovation has seen a more attractive and varied urban landscape, with detached and semi-detached houses, better transport links, improved amenities and public and private investment. In time the planners may be seen to be getting it right!

Research opportunity

An internet search will reveal some excellent memories from older residents of areas such as the Gorbals and Easterhouse and what it was like to live and grow up in such areas of the city.

Case study: Clyde waterfront regeneration

The Clyde waterfront regeneration is one of the UK's largest renewal projects, with over 200 individual developments and an investment so far in excess of £6 billion. This money has come from local authorities, the Scottish Government, Scottish Enterprise and

European funding. An internet search will reveal details about the projects and current developments.

Case study: Impact and evaluation

Selected sites and projects at the Clyde waterfront:

- Grade 'A' offices in the city centre (creating over 15,000 jobs).
- River walkways and environmental landscaping.
- Improvements to the local roads and bridges (e.g. the 'squinty bridge').
- Braehead retail and leisure centre. This complex has 115 shops in the main covered section, with a further 10 large retail premises in a separate retail park (e.g. IKEA). Adjacent is the Braehead Arena, the Xscape ski slope, an IMAX Cinema and the Braehead Business Park.
- Glasgow Harbour has a significant and very popular housing development. This old dockland area, with its abandoned granaries and shipyards, has been turned into upmarket apartments, flats, offices and restaurants. 2,500 new flats have been constructed and 250,000 m² of office space. Forty per cent of the area has been left as public space, cycle paths, parks and walkways.
- Leisure and conference facilities, including the SECC, the Clydeside Auditorium (Armadillo), the Hydro, hotels, restaurants and parking.
- Pacific Quay with its modern business and office complexes, such as the BBC Scotland headquarters and the Scottish Television Studios, Glasgow Science Centre and a marina in part of the old Princes Dock.
- The Riverside (Transport) Museum.

In conclusion, the key benefits of regeneration are firstly to the local communities, who have seen improvements in leisure, retailing, business opportunities and jobs and transport. Generally these developments on brownfield sites have been welcomed. Not only have the old derelict docks, warehouses and slum housing been cleared, but the modern and environmentally attractive urban landscape is appealing to locals and tourists. A downside is that former docklands families have often been forced to move away from the area since the new housing and facilities tend to be expensive and many of the new jobs require high skill levels, for example jobs at the BBC are mainly media and digital jobs.

Research opportunity

Assignment opportunities and further research

We have considered some changes within cities in the developed world. In particular we have considered in detail the Glasgow story. One area you may choose to study for your assignment is the legacy from the 2014 Commonwealth Games, Glasgow. For example, you could investigate:

- the impact of the Athletes' Village which was built to accommodate the games competitors (1,440 houses)
- the impact of improved services (shops, infrastructure, school and sporting facilities) in the Dalmarnock area of the city.

Research opportunity

Changes in retail/shopping: ideas for assignment

Since the 1960s, the number of people living in UK city centres (both in the CBD and the inner-city) has markedly decreased.

Retail change and impact

In recent years the city centre as a retail centre has had to overcome new patterns and trends in shopping in the form of out-of-town shopping parks, for example Silverburn and Braehead in Glasgow and The Gyle in Edinburgh.

The £275 million Silverburn Shopping Centre, next to the M77 motorway on the south side of Glasgow, has the largest Tesco in Scotland, while the mall has a Debenhams as its premier store. However, it appears that Silverburn is likely to be one of the last out-of-town retail centres in Glasgow, since future large projects may not get planning permission because of real concern over the further decline of the CBD.

Retail revolution

So what has caused this retail 'revolution'?

- Cities and town centres may have struggled to cope with changes in mobility (the rise in car ownership).
- Over the last 30 years local authorities have granted planning permission for superstores, regional shopping centres and retail parks at the edge of towns.
- Since 2000, over 80 per cent of new retail floor space has been built on out-of-town sites.
- The 1980s saw the development of non-food retail parks, with furniture, DIY, carpet stores, food retail parks, garden centres, cinema complexes, restaurants, electronic warehouses and so on.

- There has been a vast increase in personal mobility in the form of car ownership, encouraging people to travel further for their shopping and entertainment. This, combined with new road networks, has increased the accessibility of these new retail areas.
- There have been changes to our patterns of shopping. We are more likely to shop in bulk and shop in the evening and at weekends, often as a family unit. Shopping is perceived (by some) to be an activity that can be combined with leisure activities (cinemas, skating) and eating.
- There has been an increased desire to shop in warm, covered, traffic-free, safe areas.

▼ **Table 7.7** Advantages and disadvantages of the high street versus out-of-town shopping

High street – advantages and positive impact	High street – disadvantages and negative impact
Traditional place to shop.	High business costs (rent and rates).
Allows comparison shopping to take place.	Can be busy and overcrowded.
Accessible by bus/train and car.	Expensive and difficult to park.
Routes converge.	Sometimes a lack of food shops.
Has a variety of other functions, e.g. banking, offices, local authority buildings.	Can be dangerous for pedestrians because of cars/buses.
Easy for staff to reach their work because of public transport, central location.	Can feel an unsafe place to be at night.
	Affected by poor weather.
Often location of most of the 'big names' in retail, e.g. Marks and Spencer.	Lack of space for expansion.
	Difficult to bring in delivery lorries.
Local specialist shops.	Too many charity shops.
	Too many discount shops.
Out-of-town – advantages and positive impact	**Out-of-town – disadvantages and negative impact**
Parking is usually free.	Often inaccessible for those without a car.
Accessible by cars.	Shops often very similar.
Buses now run between local housing areas and the shops.	Very few independent specialist shops.
Covered shopping, safe and dry.	In direct competition with high street, which may suffer as fewer people use the high street, leading to shop and restaurant closures and job losses.
Offers a range of modern comparison shops.	
Bright, attractive environment.	
Usually room for expansion.	Objections from local people who may live in the area.
Desirable place for the whole family to shop together.	Planning permission required.
May be part of a complex of bars/restaurants/cinemas.	Congestion and pollution may increase in surrounding areas.
Attracts high status shops (e.g. IKEA).	
Creation of jobs and generation of money.	

The high street fights back

Many councils are now trying to find ways to entice shoppers back to the CBD and high street retail areas, for example:

- pedestrianisation (e.g. Sauchiehall Street in Glasgow)
- creation of centrally located attractive shopping malls, e.g. Buchanan Galleries and St Enoch Centre in Glasgow, offering a range of shops and restaurants
- street landscaping, such as benches and sculptures
- street entertainment
- specialist food shops such as Tesco Express
- high status shops, for example Harvey Nichols in Edinburgh
- government and local authorities now prepared to block further planning permission for out-of-town developments
- planning permission for out-of-town shopping centres now requires the permission of Scotland's First Minister; very often this is refused.

Research opportunity

Using some of the ideas from Table 7.7, apply this knowledge to a shopping area that you know, then try one of the following:

- Research an out-of-town retail centre close to you or one of the big centres in Scotland (e.g. Braehead or Silverburn in Glasgow or The Gyle in Edinburgh) and measure the impact it has on the locality.
- Research a well-known, established retail park such as the Metro Centre in Gateshead.
- Conduct your own research by comparing your local high street with your nearest out-of-town retail park. You may find it helpful to interview an older person about their shopping experience in the past compared with today. You can also read internet articles on 'the death of the high street'.

Summary

You have now completed the final chapter of the Physical and Human Environment section of Higher Geography.

This chapter began with some additional background about urban life, site and situation, hierarchy and sphere of influence. As you saw in Chapter 5 Population, cities are always changing and in this chapter we have looked at the growth of the megacity, in-migration, urban decay and regeneration. Cities are exciting places to live in but they are also places of social challenges and problems. Cities need to be understood and managed and this chapter has considered urban models of development as well as breaking down the city into smaller 'urban zones'.

For the SQA examination you need to consider 'change, strategies, management and impact' and we have done this in this chapter using case studies from both the developed and the developing world.

SQA examination-style questions

The SQA examination question on Urban Geography will cover one or more of the following broad topics:

- The need for management of recent urban change (housing and transport) in a developed world city and a developing world city.
- The management of strategies employed.
- The impact of the management strategies.

1 Cities are being threatened by traffic congestion. In London, a congestion charge has to be paid by all drivers wishing to enter the centre of the city. For London or any other city you have studied, explain the management strategies attempted to reduce the impact of traffic congestion and evaluate the impact of these strategies.

2 Around 1.2 million people live in the shanty towns of Rio de Janeiro. For any named shanty settlement, explain the need to manage this feature of urban change in a developing city.

3 In the UK, the government and local authorities have realised that cities cannot be left to die. For a named city in the developed world, evaluate some strategies that have been used to improve the quality of housing.

4 Rapid urbanisation in developing world cities has resulted in many housing problems. With reference to Figure 7.31 on page 252, evaluate the impact of strategies employed to manage housing problems in a developing world city you have studied.

Exam preparation

You have now reached the end of this book and should have completed all the tasks and spent time trying to learn the processes and interactions at work within the topics covered. However, do not just rely on the information staying in mind – keep returning to it to refresh your brain. It may also help to spend some extra time researching other books and the internet as you may find methods, questions or graphics that help you with anything you find difficult. Your research could also turn up something that gives you that little extra for your exam. Remember: no book or teacher can teach you everything and only you can do the learning.

Glossary of key terms

Ablation: removal of material from the surface of an object by vaporisation, chipping or other erosive processes. In glaciation this refers to the removal of snow and ice from a snowpack, glacier or iceberg by melting or evaporation

Ablation till: an unstratified/unsorted glacial deposit consisting of rock fragments of various sizes (e.g. sand, clay and boulders) which initially accumulated in a supraglacial position (on the glacier's surface) and was later lowered to the ground surface by under-melting during glacial retreat

Abrasion: in general, this is the mechanical scraping and wearing away of a rock surface by friction between rocks and other particles being moved by the agents of erosion (wind, glaciers, waves, gravity and running water). Surfaces become smoothed and polished over time. Angular debris may leave scratch marks (striations) on the rock

Acid rain: rain and any other form of precipitation that has increased levels of acidity, which can harm living creatures and plants and erode rocks and buildings. The level of acidity within the precipitation is caused by the amount of gases, especially sulphur dioxide and nitrogen dioxide within the atmosphere. Human activities such as industry, use of motor vehicles and use of fossil fuels for power generation have added large amounts of acid rain-creating chemicals to the atmosphere

Ageing: an increase in the proportion of the population in the older age groups. May also be measured as an increase in the median age of the population

Age-specific death rate: the number of deaths per 1,000 people in a specific age band

Age-specific fertility rate: the number of births during a year to women in a particular age group, usually per 1,000 women in a five-year age group at mid-year

Age structure: distribution of a population according to age, usually by five-year age groups

Albedo: the intensity of light (e.g. solar energy) reflected from an object, such as a planet or a surface

Alluvial fan: a fan- or cone-shaped river/stream deposit caused by an abrupt decrease in velocity, reducing the river's ability to continue to carry material it is transporting. Often found at the base of a steep slope or cliff (e.g. at the foot of a waterfall)

Alluvium: loose soil or sediment which has been eroded, reshaped by water (streams, rivers, lakes) and re-deposited in a non-marine setting

Antarctic Circumpolar Current (ACC): ocean current and the dominant circulation feature of the Southern Ocean moving around 125,000,000 m³ of water per second. This current keeps warm ocean waters away from Antarctica allowing the continent to maintain its ice sheets (also known as the West Wind Drift)

Anticyclone: a weather system with high atmospheric pressure at its centre (where the air is sinking) which decreases as one moves outwards from there. Air slowly circulates in a clockwise (northern hemisphere) or anticlockwise (southern hemisphere) direction around the centre. Anticyclones are associated with calm, fine weather

Arch: an opening through one side of a headland to another formed by wave erosion. This is as the result of enlargement of the sea cave through a headland or the meeting of two caves from opposite sides, leaving a bridge of rock (the keystone) over the water

Area of Outstanding Natural Beauty (AONB): an area of land designated for conservation due to the attractiveness or value of the landscape in England, Wales or Northern Ireland

Arête: a narrow, saw-toothed edged mountain ridge developed by glacial erosion from parallel glacial troughs or adjacent corries

Asthenosphere: part of the upper mantle just below the lithosphere. It is a thin, semi-fluid, highly viscous layer approximately 100–200 km below the surface. In some regions it can extend as deep as 700 km. Although generally solid some of its regions are believed to be in liquid form such as those below mid-ocean ridges, where it is the source of basalt. It is believed to be able to flow both vertically and horizontally enabling the overlying lithosphere to subside, rise and move laterally

Asylum seekers: people who are refugees and who claim to feel threatened in their home country, so on arrival at a new country declare themselves to be an asylum seeker. An asylum seeker is someone who has lodged an application for protection on the basis of the Refugee Convention or Article 3 of the European Convention on Human Rights

Atlantic-type coastline: see discordant coastline

Atmosphere: a layer of gases surrounding a planet or other material body of sufficient mass. Earth's atmosphere is composed of layers of gases surrounding the planet that are held in place by Earth's gravity and is a mixture of (approximately) nitrogen (78 per cent), oxygen (21 per cent), and other gases (1per cent)

Atmospheric circulation: the large-scale movement of air and the means (together with the smaller ocean circulation) by which thermal energy is distributed across the surface of the Earth and within the atmosphere

Atmospheric pressure: the pressure exerted by the weight of the atmosphere at any given point (which at sea level has a mean value of 101,325 Pascals or one atmosphere). Pressure reduces with altitude. Also known as barometric pressure

Attrition: a form of coastal or river erosion, where the bedload is eroded by itself and the bed. Due to the movement created by waves or a river, pieces of rock debris (the load) impact against each other causing them to be broken up into smaller fragments. The load is also smoothed and rounded

Autumnal equinox: the point in the year when the Sun passes across the plane of the equator making day and night of equal length. This happens around 23 September in the northern hemisphere (the Sun tracking southwards) and 21 March in the southern hemisphere (the Sun tracking northwards)

Avalanche: a mass of snow or ice (though may also refer to rock, sand or other materials) that suddenly slides or falls downhill

Axial obliquity: see axial tilt

Axial tilt: the Earth's axis is not perpendicular but lies at an oblique angle. This tilt is what gives the planet its seasons. The northern half of the Earth (the northern hemisphere) has its summer when the North Pole is tilted towards the Sun. At the same time the South Pole is tilted away from the Sun bringing winter to the southern half of the planet (the southern hemisphere). Six months later, the Earth has reversed this positioning giving the north its winter and the south its summer

Axis: a fixed, straight line around which a body rotates. The Earth rotates around its axis once every 24 hours

Azonal soils: immature soils that lack the development of a B horizon. They tend to be associated with recent glacial deposits, volcanic (tectonic) soils, scree slopes, sand dunes, salt marshes and even fresh river alluvium

Backwash: the movement of water back down into the ocean/sea/lake having previously been moved up onto a beach by the swash of a wave

Bankfull discharge: maximum discharge that a particular river channel is capable of carrying without flooding

Bar: there are numerous types of bar but in general these are elevated regions of sediment deposited by water

Basal sliding: a glacier sliding over the bed due to meltwater under the ice acting as a lubricant (also known as basal slippage)

Basal slippage: see basal sliding

Basal till: an unstratified/unsorted glacial deposit consisting of rock fragments of various sizes (e.g. sand, clay and boulders) laid down or smeared subglacially when debris was released directly from the sole (underside) of the ice. Also known as lodgement till

Basalt: a common volcanic (igneous) rock formed from the rapid cooling of basaltic lava exposed at or very near the surface. It is a dark coloured, fine grained rock, the grains being smaller due to relatively swift crystallisation at the surface

Baseflow: represents the normal day-to-day discharge of a river

Basket of eggs topography: a term used to describe a landscape comprising a large grouping (swarm) of drumlins tightly packed and aligned. This is said to be reminiscent of the mounds of eggs placed together in a basket

Bay: an inlet of water connected to an ocean, sea or lake, where the coastline curves in so that the body of water is surrounded by land on three sides

Bay bar: deposited beach materials which have accumulated to form an above sea level ridge that lies across a bay and connects headland to headland. A feature which results due to the processes of longshore drift

Bayhead beach: coastal beach formed from sediment deposited in a bay between headlands. These beaches are typically crescent shaped

Bed deformation: a process of glacier movement found at the ice/rock interface beneath the glacier. Movement is accomplished due to the deformation of the rock material that underlies the base of the glacier, which tends to happen when the underlying rock is a weak rock or soft sediment

Bed load: materials being transported by a river along its bed by traction and saltation

Bedrock: solid unweathered rock that lies underneath the loose surface deposits (e.g. soil)

Bergschrund: a crevasse often found near the head of a mountain glacier where moving glacial ice is separated from stagnant ice or the firn above. In a corrie this may be seen where the bergschrund separates the ice attached to the headwall from the moving ice

Berm: a flat strip of land, a raised bank; a beach berm is a raised area at the rear of a beach (backshore) formed by deposition through constructive waves

Biodiversity: short for 'biological diversity', it is the term used to describe the variety of life found on Earth and all of the natural processes. This includes ecosystem, genetic and cultural diversity and the connections between these and all species

Biogenesis: life created from living matter

Biomass: the total sum of all living organisms (see biota)

Biopoesis: life created naturally from non-living matter such as simple organic compounds

Biosphere: the part of the Earth and its atmosphere in which living organisms exist or where life could be supported. Sometimes referred to as the zone of life

Biota (soil): consists of micro-organisms (bacteria, fungi and algae), soil animals (protozoa, nematodes, mites, springtails, spiders, insects and earthworms), plants living all or part of their lives in or on the soil and decayed organic matter (from leaves, roots, leaves, pine needles and dead vegetation)

Birth rate (crude): number of live births per 1,000 people in a year

Boulder clay: now mostly obsolete term for glacial till

Brown earth: a major soil type, found in temperate deciduous forest areas

Brownfield site: a derelict inner-city site which can be cleared and reused for new housing or development

Calving: see ice calving

Cap stone: a resistant rock that forms the top of a waterfall

Capillary action: process whereby water and minerals in solution can be drawn upwards when the rate of evapotranspiration is greater than precipitation

Catena: a sequence of soil types down the slope, where the soils are related to the topography of the slope

Cavitation: air bubbles collapse, usually where a fast river flow is constricted (e.g. in a crack in the rock of a river bank). This collapse of the bubbles creates a small shock wave that weakens the rock. Although the shock waves are relatively weak, the process repeats over time and so weakens the rock. Eventually, pieces of rock break off

Central business district (CBD): the commercial and business centre of a town

Channel flow: water flowing in a river; also known as the river discharge

Chemical weathering: a process of weathering causing the breakdown of rock as a result of chemical reactions (also known as decomposition)

Child mortality: Sometimes known as 'under-5 mortality', it is the term used to include the death of infants and children under the age of five

Cirque: the internationally accepted term for a glacially enlarged hollow found near the tops of mountains. See corrie

Clay: a type of soil where the soil particle size is less than 0.002 mm

Climate: the average pattern of the elements of weather prevailing in an area over a long period of time (usually around 30 years or more to create meaningful averages)

Climate change: statistical (evidence based) alteration of the climate system over an extended period of time, regardless of what has caused its modification. In addition to this it may also include a redistribution of the frequency or intensities of weather events around the average conditions

Climatologist: a person who studies or practises climatology, the study of climate

Coastal platforms: flat areas of land formed on coastlines by wave action. An alternative term for a wave-cut platform

Cold-based glacier: ice that is below the pressure melting point throughout the glacier and is frozen to the underlying rock. The glacier can only move through internal flow

Concordant coastline: where beds or layers of differing rock types run parallel to the coast. The outer hard rock provides a protective barrier to erosion of the softer rocks further inland. Results in few bays or headlands (also known as Pacific-type coastline)

Condensation: the change in the atmosphere when droplets of water vapour cool and change back into liquid water. This liquid takes the form of water droplets or clouds

Congestion: overcrowding on roads, leading to traffic jams and pollution

Constructive waves: waves that result in the build-up of a beach. More likely to be found in calmer weather and less powerful than destructive waves. The wave's swash is more powerful than its downwash and so projects material upwards and onto the beach

Continental crust: the layer of igneous, sedimentary and metamorphic rocks which forms the planet's large landmasses and the shallow seabed (continental shelf) around their shores. Continental crust is, on average, around 35 km thick and is less dense than the oceanic crust. Continental crust is more complex in its structure and less dense than oceanic crust. Like the oceanic crust, continental crust floats on the denser layers below

Continental glacier: see ice sheet

Convection: the transfer of heat in fluids such as liquids or gases, where heat energy is transferred from hot places to cooler places by convection (particles with a lot of heat energy move and take the place of particles with less heat energy)

Convection cell: a self-contained area in a fluid in which upward motion of warmer fluid in the centre is balanced by downward motion of cooler fluid at the periphery. In the atmosphere wind circulates in each hemisphere in three distinct cells which help transport energy and heat from the equator to the poles. The winds are driven by the energy from the Sun at the surface as warm air rises and colder air sinks (see also Hadley, Ferrel and Polar cells). The process of convection also assists in the forming of thunderstorms. Convection cells are also formed in the Earth's mantle powered by the heat at the Earth's core

Convection currents: the pattern of movement caused by convection, which forms a cyclical pattern. (The heat energy in the fluid rises to the top then increases in density because it is farther away from the heat source at the bottom. The fluid then sinks to the bottom and the heat source, heats up and becomes less dense causing it to rise. This repeats, forming a cycle.) Can be seen within the atmosphere, oceans and within the mantle material. In the mantle, this assists in the movement of the lithospheric plates and plays a key role in plate tectonics

Coriolis effect: a deflection of moving objects when the motion is described relative to a rotating reference frame. In a reference frame with clockwise rotation, the deflection is to the left of the motion of the object; in one with counter-clockwise rotation, the deflection is to the right. On Earth the movement of air undergoes a deflection from its path due to this. Air moving from high to low pressure in the northern hemisphere is deflected to the right. In the southern hemisphere, air moving from high to low pressure is deflected to the left

Coriolis force: causes the deflection of moving objects when the motion is described relative to a rotating reference frame. See Coriolis effect

Corrasion: mechanical erosion caused when materials are transported across the Earth's surface by running water, waves, glaciers, wind or gravitational movement downslope. At coastlines rock debris is thrown by waves against rock faces which in turn becomes eroded

Corrie: a steep-backed bowl-shaped hollow, at the upper end of a mountain valley, formed by glacial erosion (also known as a cirque or cwm)

Corrie lochan: a small, deep lake occupying a corrie (also known as a tarn)

Corrosion: where rocks dissolve in water due to the addition of chemicals which cause a chemical reaction e.g. limestone reacting to dilute acids in rainfall or seawater (also known as solution)

Counter-urbanisation: the movement of people from the cities back to the countryside to live

The tail may also have some deposited material

Creep: the slow downslope movement of particles that occurs on every slope covered with loose material (e.g. sand dunes). Even soil covered with close-knit sod creeps downslope, as indicated by slow but persistent tilting of trees, poles, gravestones and other objects set into the ground on hillsides. For creep movement within glacial ice see internal deformation

Crevasse: a deep crack or fissure in a glacier or other body of ice. Usually caused by differential movement of parts of the ice over an uneven landscape causing fracturing due to the limited flexibility of the ice

Cumecs: measurement used to describe river discharge. Cumecs represents 'cubic metres per second'

Cut-off: also known as a meander cut-off; happens when a pronounced meander in a river is breached by a flow that connects the two outer bends closest to the entry and exits of the meander. The river takes a new straighter course and water is cut off from the old meander

Cwm: see corrie

Cyclone: atmospheric system characterised by the rapid inward circulation of air about a low atmospheric pressure centre, usually accompanied by stormy, often destructive weather. Cyclones circulate counter-clockwise in the northern hemisphere and clockwise in the southern hemisphere (also known as hurricane, typhoon, or tropical storm)

Dar: In Morroco, a dar is a house without a garden

Death rate (crude): number of deaths per 1,000 people in a year

Debris: loose natural material consisting especially of broken pieces of rock

Decomposition: breakdown of plant-derived material into simpler organic constituents

Deforestation: process whereby natural forests are cleared through logging and/or burning, either to use the timber or to replace the area for alternative uses

Degradation: reduction or loss in arid, semi-arid and dry sub-humid areas of the biological or economic productivity and complexity of rain-fed cropland, irrigated cropland or range, pasture, forest and woodlands. Degradation can result from land uses or processes arising from human activities and habitation patterns

Delta: a landform that forms from deposition of sediment carried by a river as it leaves its mouth and enters slower-moving or stagnant water (ocean, sea, estuary, lake, reservoir, or another river). The sediment builds up, creating new land and the river separates into multiple channels passing through the build-up of sediment

Demographic transition model (DTM): a population model, first developed in the 1930s, it describes the stages in the relationship between birth and death rates and overall population change. It predicts that in time, all countries will reduce birth, death and growth rates and that populations will have lower levels of mortality and longer life expectancy. The classic DTM had four stages, with a fifth one added in the last 10 years, to cover those countries now experiencing a decline in population

Demography: the study of human populations

Denudation: the long-term sum of processes that cause the wearing away of the Earth's surface (e.g. wind, rain, ice, running water and the sea/oceans) leading to a reduction in elevation and relief of landforms and landscapes. Denudation can involve the removal of both solid particles and dissolved material

Dependency ratios: also known as the age dependency ratio and the total dependency ratio, this is the combined child population (people below age 15) and elderly population (people aged 65 and above) per 100 people in the labour force age group (those aged 15–64)

Deposition: the laying down (dumping) of the materials that have been transported following weathering and erosion. This adds to the landmass or landforms

Depression: also referred to as a 'low', these are areas of low atmospheric pressure at the surface. The pressure gradually rises as one moves away from the centre. Air is rising and as it rises and cools, water vapour condenses to form clouds and perhaps precipitation. As a result, the weather in a depression is often cloudy, wet and windy

Desertification: land degradation in which a relatively dry land region becomes increasingly arid, typically losing its bodies of water as well as vegetation and wildlife. It is caused by a variety of factors such as climate change and human activities

Destructive waves: waves that assist in the erosion of coastal material. These are high energy waves where the backwash is more powerful than the swash, resulting in materials being removed

Differential erosion: erosion that occurs at varying rates, caused by the differences in resistance and hardness. Less resistant rocks (softer and weaker) are worn away more quickly than resistant (harder) rocks

Discharge: rate of flow passing a specific location in a river or other channel. River discharge is the volume of water flowing through a river channel. This is the total volume of water flowing through a channel at any given point and is measured in cubic metres per second (cumecs). The discharge from a drainage basin depends on precipitation, evapotranspiration and storage factors

Discordant coastline: where bands of different rock types run perpendicular (at right angles) to the coast. The differing resistance to erosion leads to the formation of headlands and bays (also known as Atlantic-type coastline)

Diurnal temperature variation: the difference between the daily maximum and minimum temperatures experienced at a location (also known as diurnal temperature range)

Doldrums: a term used to describe those parts of the Atlantic Ocean and the Pacific Ocean affected by the intertropical convergence zone, a low-pressure area around the equator where the prevailing winds are calm. It is characterised by calms, light winds, or squalls

Drainage basin: area of land drained by a river

Drainage density (DD): total length of all the streams and rivers in a drainage basin divided by the total area of the drainage basin. It is a measure of how well or how poorly a watershed is drained by stream channels.

Drainage density = sum of length of all the rivers ÷ area of drainage basin (measured in km per km^2)

Drift: see glacial drift

Drift-aligned coast: a coastline oriented at an angle to the prevailing waves

Drumlin: an oval-shaped hill, largely composed of glacial drift (basal till), formed beneath a glacier or ice sheet and aligned in the direction of ice flow. The shape is reminiscent of an egg sliced along its longest axis. Its steep slope marks the direction from which the ice was moving when it was deposited

Drumlin swarm: a group of drumlins (glacially deposited, elongated hills composed primarily of basal till). Drumlins within a swarm display a similar long-axis orientation to their neighbours and are closely packed

Dust Bowl: The Dust Bowl was an area in the Midwest of the USA that was severely affected by drought between 1930 and 1939. The drought killed crops that had previously kept the rich black soil in place. When winds blew, they raised enormous clouds of dust that deposited mounds of soil over the landscape. The drought and dust storms destroyed a large part of the fragile agricultural system

Economic migrants: people who move to improve their quality of life and to earn more money for themselves and possibly their families

Ecosystem: a community of living plants and animals within an environment

Ecotourism: responsible travel to natural areas which conserves the environment and sustains the livelihood of local people

Eddies: currents of water or air moving in a direction that is different from the main current. These usually move in a circular motion and so are a form of turbulence

El Niño: a warm phase in the circulation pattern of waters within the Pacific Ocean. It is associated with a band of warm ocean water that develops in the central and east-central equatorial Pacific (between approximately the International Date Line and 120°W), including off the Pacific coast of South America

Eluvial: the soil horizon where leaching takes place by a process known as eluviation

Emergent coastlines: these appear from the sea (either due to the land rising through isostatic recovery or through the sea level dropping), e.g. raised beaches

End moraine: all the debris scooped up and pushed by the front (snout) of glacial ice and deposited as a large mound of rocks, soil and sediments

Englacial moraine: material that is found trapped within the body of glacial ice and includes material which has fallen into the glacier via crevasses

Enhanced basal creep: a process of glacier movement found at the ice/rock interface beneath the glacier. The lowest layer of ice is pushed against obstacles larger than 1 m wide and the pressure causes the ice to plastically deform/bend around the obstacle

Environmental conflict: a disagreement over values, usage and claims to a natural resource. This often overlaps with quality of life or socio-economic needs, ambitions or wants

Equinox: refers to the time, occurring twice a year, around 20 March and 22 September, where the duration of daytime and night time are equal (or approximately so)

Erosion: the wearing away and removal of material (soil, sediment, regolith and rock fragments) by water (in liquid form: rivers, seas/oceans), wind and ice (glaciers)

Esker: an elongated curving, narrow fluvioglacial deposit that forms along a meltwater stream channel, developing in a tunnel within usually near the terminus of a glacier. The ice-contact margins of the esker are often slumped and mixed with till

Eustatic change: the global rise or fall of sea levels due to an alteration in the volume of water in the oceans or, alternatively, a change in the shape of an ocean basin resulting in a change in the amount of water in the ocean/sea. Can be caused by climate change

Evaporation: the process where a liquid is changed into a gas. An example is the oceans being warmed by heat from the Sun and this energy causing water to be turned into vapour, which rises into the atmosphere

Evapotranspiration: total amount of moisture removed by evaporation and transpiration from the land surface

Exfoliation: the process by which concentric scales, plates, or shells of rock are stripped or spall from the bare surface of a rock mass

Exosphere: the outermost layer of the Earth's atmosphere. It lies above the thermosphere and merges into interplanetary space. Molecules with sufficient velocity can escape the Earth's gravitational pull and move into interplanetary space from this layer

Fauna: the animals of a particular region, area, habitat, environment, time or period

Ferrel cell: part of the Earth's atmospheric global circulation that assists in the transfer of thermal energy. In the three cell model of atmospheric circulation it is the middle cell of three in each hemisphere (Hadley, Ferrel and Polar). Air converges at low latitudes to rise along the boundaries (meeting points) of cool polar air and warm subtropical air. This happens at around 60° North and South of the equator and with sinking air at around 30° North and South. This cell moves in the opposite direction to the other two

Fertility rate: average number of live births per woman in an area or country

Fetch: the distance travelled by wind or waves across open water

Firn: a type of snow left over from the previous year's snowpack. It has developed from névé, but has re-crystallised into a slightly denser substance. It is an intermediate stage in the formation of glacial ice, is relatively hard and has the granular appearance of wet sugar

Fjord (fiord): a long narrow inlet of the sea in mountainous areas. Noted for their steep, high cliffs these are flooded glacially eroded valleys

Flood: when the capacity of a river to transport water is exceeded and water flows over the river bank

Floodplain: an area of low-lying ground beside a river, mainly formed by the deposition of river sediments (alluvium) when the river floods

Flora: the plants of a particular region, area, habitat, environment, time, or period

Fluvial processes: processes that are associated with rivers and streams (erosion, transportation and deposition) and the ability of a river or stream to alter the landscape

Fluvioglacial: relating to the action of meltwater from glaciers or ice sheets

Freeze–thaw: a type of physical/mechanical weathering (disintegration) in which jointed rock is forced apart by the expansion of water as it freezes in fractures. It occurs in cold climates where temperatures are often around freezing point and fluctuate from above to below 0°C. This allows the freezing and melting that creates increased pressure on the rock (also known as frost shattering, ice crystal growth or ice wedging)

Function of a settlement: all settlements have shared functions, such as residential or as a service centre (e.g. shops); all will have factories, transport hubs and even some administration

General fertility rate: number of live births per 1,000 women (aged 15–44) in a year

Gentrification: when rundown houses, usually in the inner-city, are improved, allowing people to return to the cities to live. Older properties are modernised, bringing growth and money back into the area

Geodiversity: variety of different earth materials (minerals, rocks and the like)

Geological period: one of the geological sub-units of time. It lies between eras (longer) and epochs (shorter) in the geological time scale hierarchy

Geological time scale: a method of dividing the geologic history of planet Earth (since its formation) into units and sub-units of time. In descending order of duration the units are: eons, eras, periods, epochs and ages

Geothermal: relating to heat from the interior of the Earth

Glacial abrasion: the mechanical scraping of a rock surface by friction between rocks and moving particles being transported by the base and sides of a glacier

Glacial budget: the balance between the rate of accumulation and the rate of ablation within a glacial system

Glacial drift: all material deposited by glacial ice

Glacial horn: another term for a pyramidal peak although more regularly used for one where the attached arêtes have been eroded leaving only the horn shape with steep rock faces

Glacial quarrying: see plucking

Glacial till: also referred to as till, this is an un-stratified/unsorted glacial deposit consisting of rock fragments of various sizes (e.g. sand, clay and boulders). Originally eroded and transported by a glacier and left behind after ablation and retreat. May be deposited over a larger area. Formerly known as boulder clay

Glacial trough: a valley shaped through erosion by ice, in particular valley glaciers. Often referred to as a U-shaped valley although may have an inverted parabolic shape

Glacier terminus: see snout or terminus

Gley: a major soil type, associated with poorly drained environments

Gleying: processes at work associated with poorly drained environments

Global energy budget: see global heat budget

Global heat budget: the usable energy maintained by the Earth as a balance between energy received by the planet (input) through insolation and that which is radiated back out into space (output) (also known as the global energy budget)

Global Ocean Conveyor: see thermohaline circulation

Global temperature gradient: refers to the change in temperature that exists in the atmosphere from the equator to the poles

Global warming: although seen by some as being synonymous with climate change it is more accurately described as the more recent worldwide increase in temperatures believed to be created by human activity that releases greenhouse gases into the atmosphere. In particular this refers to the period of global industrialisation

Gorge: a narrow steep-sided valley, typically with rocky walls and a stream running through it

Gorge of recession: a narrow, steep-sided valley, typically with rocky walls and a stream running through it, created by the backward erosion of a waterfall cutting a slice through the surrounding landscape

Granite: a common type of igneous rock, rich in quartz and feldspar. It is generally a light coloured rock with large grains, which are attributed to the slow cooling process of magma beneath the Earth's surface

Gravel: a loose aggregation of small water-worn or pounded stones (such as through glacial action)

Gravitational potential energy: the energy held by an object because of its position in a gravitational field. On Earth, where we always have gravity acting on us, the potential energy of an object is greater with increasing height

Greenbelt: an area left around a city in which development is not permitted. Established by legislation, it is meant to prevent urban sprawl, to stop towns from merging as a city grows and to preserve the special characteristics of towns. Not all cities have green belts

Greenhouse effect: the manner by which certain gases warm the atmosphere of a planet by capturing or trapping heat that would otherwise have escaped into space. This acts to warm the planet's atmosphere

Greenhouse gases: gases that absorb infrared radiation, trap heat in the atmosphere and contribute to the greenhouse effect. Carbon dioxide and chlorofluorocarbons are examples of greenhouse gases

Ground moraine: material (e.g. rock debris) carried at the base of a glacier or ice sheet. Following ablation and retreat this may be left *in situ* or washed out by meltwater streams. When left *in situ* these tend to form a rolling landscape which varies in thickness and topographical features

Groundwater: water that is stored within rocks, rock pores and joints

Groundwater flow: water flowing below the water table through permeable rock

Gulf Stream: a warm ocean current in the Atlantic originating at the tip of Florida and flowing along the eastern coastline of the United States before crossing the Atlantic Ocean towards western Europe

Gyre: a circular or spiral motion or form, especially referring to the large-scale circulating oceanic surface current

Hadley cell: part of the Earth's atmospheric global circulation that assists in the transfer of thermal energy. In the three cell model of atmospheric circulation it is the cell closest to the equator of three in each hemisphere (Hadley, Ferrel and Polar). Hadley cells extend from the equator to between 30° and 40° North and South. The air rises near to the equator, flows towards higher latitudes and then sinks to create dry, high-pressure regions. Air then returns at this lower level towards the equator

Halophytic: an adjective used to describe plants adapted to living in saline (salty) conditions, such as in a salt marsh or sand dune

Hard engineering strategies: projects that involve the construction of artificial structures that prevent a river from flooding, e.g. dams

Harmattan: a very dry, dusty easterly or north-easterly wind affecting West Africa and usually occurring from December to February. Linked with the movement of the intertropical convergence zone (ITCZ)

Headland: a point of land, usually high and with cliff edges, extending out into a body of water (ocean, sea, lake). Formed in coastlines with alternating bands of resistant and less resistant rocks. The less resistant rock erodes more quickly leaving the more resistant rock to jut out into the sea (also known as a promontory)

Headwall: is the highest cliff of a corrie, usually its backwall

Heat equator: see thermal equator

High water mark: a point that represents the maximum rise of a body of water over land (e.g. highest sea level)

Hinterland: a term used to refer to the backcountry (land to the rear of) of a port or coastal settlement. This is the outlying region which would be intended to support a settlement or port

Horizon (soil): horizontal layers found within a vertical cross section of soil (soil profile)

Horse latitudes: these are two belts of latitude at around 30° and 35° North and South of the equator which experience subtropical high pressure. There is very little precipitation and the winds are variable and often calm. In the three cell model of atmospheric circulation this is where air descends from both the Hadley and Ferrel cells creating this high-pressure zone

Humification: breakdown or decomposition of plant remains leading to the formation of different types of humus (mor and mull)

Humus: partially decayed remains of plants and animals; forms the organic portion of soil

Hurricane: see cyclone

Hydraulic action: erosion that occurs when the motion of water against a rock surface produces mechanical weathering. This includes air becoming trapped in joints and cracks on a cliff face. When a wave breaks, the trapped air is compressed which puts stresses on the rock and weakens the cliff. Following the retreat of the wave the explosive release of air can break off pieces of rock

Hydraulic pressure: the force exerted by liquid under pressure

Hydroelectric power (HEP): the production of electrical power through the use of the gravitational force of falling or flowing water

Hydrograph: a graph that shows river discharge and rainfall over time. The hydrograph shows the monthly river discharge over one year. Measurement will be taken daily, averaged out for the month and then plotted on the graph. If measurements are taken for many years, it is possible to see the long-term pattern. Variations from year to year can also be recorded

Hydrological cycle: describes and explains the movement and circulation of water (as a liquid, solid or vapour) between the oceans, atmosphere, vegetation and land

Hydrosphere: the liquid water component of the Earth. It includes the oceans, seas, lakes, ponds, rivers and streams. The hydrosphere covers about 70 per cent of the surface of the Earth and is home for many plants and animals. Hydrology is the study of water and anything linked to water is part of the hydrosphere

Ice age: a period of geologic time in which the Earth's climate sees a dramatic drop in surface and atmosphere temperatures resulting in episodes of extensive glaciation. These episodes of glaciation ('glacials' or 'glacial periods') alternate with periods of relative warmth known as 'interglacials'

Iceberg: a large piece of freshwater ice that has broken off from a glacier or an ice shelf and is floating freely in open water (usually an ocean or sea)

Ice calving: the breaking off of a large mass of ice at the end of a glacier (also known as iceberg calving or calving)

Ice cap: a thick mass of glacial ice covering an area of land, such as a small region or the peak of a mountain for a long period of time (smaller than an ice sheet)

Ice sheet: a thick layer of glacial ice covering an extensive region over a long period of time, e.g. Antarctica and Greenland (also known as a continental glacier)

Ice shelf: a thick floating platform of ice that forms where a land-based glacier or ice sheet reaches a coastline. The glacier/ice sheet extends onto the water and floats on the ocean surface

Ice stagnation: a mass of ice which is no longer moving and melts *in situ*. This may happen due to it becoming detached from the accumulation zone or through a change in climatic circumstances resulting in glacial retreat

Igneous: one of the three main rock types along with sedimentary and metamorphic. Igneous rocks derive their name from the Latin word *ignis* meaning fire. Igneous rocks are formed by the cooling and solidification of magma or lava

Illuvial: the lower soil horizon where the accumulation of washed-down materials occurs

Immigrants: people who migrate into a region or country

Impermeable: a rock that will not allow water to pass through it, e.g. clay

Infant mortality rate: number of infant deaths (under one year old) in a year for every 1,000 babies born

Infiltration: process of water soaking into and moving through the soil. Influenced by the permeability and porosity of the soil. Once the soil is saturated, then further infiltration is blocked

Infra-red (long-wave) radiation: invisible radiant energy, electromagnetic radiation with longer wavelengths than those of visible light

Inner-city: the part of the city surrounding the CBD which in the past contained older houses and industry; these areas have experienced extensive urban renewal

Inorganic: parts of the soil which do not come from living organisms; the rock and mineral portion of the soil

Inputs: any item or object joining a system. In the drainage basin, this is precipitation in the form of rain or snow

Insolation: the amount of solar radiation energy received on a surface during a given time. It is also known as solar irradiation. Although taken from the Latin *insolare,* meaning exposure to the Sun, it is often shown as meaning **IN**coming **SOL**ar radi**ATION** which, although inaccurate, is a good method of understanding its general connotation

Interception: process by which raindrops are prevented from directly reaching the soil surface. Vegetation (e.g. leaves) is capable of breaking up the fall of precipitation

Interglacial: a geological interval of warmer average temperatures lasting thousands of years that separates consecutive glacial periods within an ice age

Interlocking spurs: narrow necks of high land extending into a river valley as the river moves down course. These 'overlap' as the river winds from one side to the other around them. They appear to interlock like the teeth of a zip

Internal deformation: when the weight of the ice (in a glacier) causes ice crystals to distort and realign in the direction of the movement of the ice, allowing ice crystals to slide past one another. This allows the glacier to move downhill even as the lower portions of the glacier stick to the underlying rock due to friction. The layers above slip forward in a manner similar to a deck of cards on an angled table. As the glacier's weight becomes too heavy to maintain the shape of the glacier it starts to move, ice layers slipping within the glacier. This type of movement is the only type that occurs in polar glaciers, but it also occurs in temperate glaciers

Internal flow: see internal deformation

Internal migration: Movement within a country

International migration: movement from one country to another

Intertropical convergence zone (ITCZ): an area of low atmospheric pressure where warm, humid air converges (the north east and south east trade winds), rises and cools, forming clouds and frequent heavy showers. The ITCZ appears as a band of clouds, usually thunderstorms that circle the globe near the equator. The ITCZ is formed by the rising leg of the Hadley cell

Intrazonal soils: soils that do not reflect climatic or vegetation standard influence. Associated soils may be very heavily influenced by one particular factor, such as chalk or peat

Isostasy: where the Earth's lithosphere behaves as if it is floating on the underlying mantle and creates/maintains a state of equilibrium between the lithosphere and the asthenosphere. This is a vertical movement. When a load is put on the plates they sink downwards to compensate for the change. In the same way, if a load is removed the plates will rise. These alterations to regain equilibrium are known as isostatic adjustment

Isostatic adjustment: alterations in the levels of the lithospheric plates to regain equilibrium with the asthenosphere

Isostatic rebound: the upward movement of the lithospheric plates to regain isostatic equilibrium following the removal of load/material from the plate

Isostatic recovery: the process whereby the lithosphere returns to a state of equilibrium with the asthenosphere. It is often inaccurately used to describe only the upward movement as the lithosphere compensates for the removal of load/material

Isostatic uplift: see isostatic rebound

Jet stream: narrow bands of fast-moving air (normally 160–320 km/h but can reach speeds as high as 480 km/h which assist with the rapid transfer of energy around the world. Jet streams meander around the globe in a west to east direction and are caused by temperature differences between tropical and polar air masses

Jurassic Coast: a 155 km long stretch of coastline of headlands, cliffs and bays running from near Exmouth in East Devon to Studland in Dorset, southern England. It is a designated World Heritage Site (also known as a the Dorset and East Devon Coast World Heritage Site)

Kinetic energy: the energy that an object possesses due to its motion. It gains this energy during acceleration and maintains this unless its speed changes

Knickpoint: a sharp break (change in height) of slope in the smooth, concave, river long profile. It is usually marked by a waterfall (or a series of rapids). At this point vertical erosion associated with rejuvenation is at its greatest. The knickpoint retreats upstream over time

Lagoon: stretch of salt water separated from the sea by a low sandbank, bay bar or reef

Lag time: time interval from the centre of mass of rainfall excess to the peak of the resulting hydrograph. Lag time is the period of time between the peak rainfall and peak discharge

Land management: process of managing the use and development (in both urban and rural settings) of land resources. Land resources are used for a variety of purposes which may include agriculture, reforestation, water resource management and eco-tourism projects

Landslide: a collapse of a mass of earth and/or rock from a mountain, steep slope or cliff

La Niña: refers to a period of extensive cooling within the central and eastern tropical Pacific Ocean. La Niña happens for at least five months and sea surface temperatures across the equatorial Eastern Central Pacific Ocean will be reduced from normal conditions by approximately 3–5 °C

Lateral beach: a beach formed along a straight coastline where sediments can be moved along their length by longshore drift

Lateral moraine: this is a ridge of glacial load found at the sides of a glacier or deposited as till along the sides of the valley which was formerly occupied by a glacier

Latitudinal temperature gradient: the change in temperature over latitude (North or South). This is caused by the unequal heating of the Earth's surface

Lava: molten rock (magma) once it has reached the Earth's surface through a volcano or fissure, vent or crack

Leaching: removal of soluble minerals, salts and humus, which are washed downwards through the soil and may accumulate in what is called the subsoil; occurs when precipitation is greater than evapotranspiration, causing a downward movement of water in the soil

Lee: shortened version of leeward. See leeward

Leeward: on or towards the side sheltered from the wind; downwind. Alternatively, to the side away from where an object or element (e.g. glacial ice) moves towards a feature

Levee: a natural embankment or ridge on the banks of a river formed by sediment deposited as the river overflows its banks (the river slows and loses energy as it flows onto the shallower land at the river's bank and so deposits sediment)

Life expectancy: number of years the average person born in a given year may expect to live

Life expectancy at birth: average number of years a group of people born in the same year can expect to live if mortality at each age remains constant in the future

Lip: the ridge of rock at the exiting (downslope) edge of a corrie. Formed due to the reduced erosional power of glacial ice as it moved upwards as part of its rotational movement within the mountain hollow

Lithology: the physical character of a rock or rock formation

Lithosphere: the crust and the uppermost mantle, which constitute the hard and rigid outer layer of the Earth. It varies in thickness being on average around 55 km thick underneath the oceans and can reach up to about 200 km on continents

Lithospheric plates: see tectonic plates

Littoral cave: see sea cave

Littoral zone: a term referring to the foreshore of a coastal beach

Local isostasy: a theoretical view on how the lithosphere reacts during isostasy, which suggests that the lithosphere acts as if it is made out of numerous relatively small blocks. These react individually (in isolation) to the addition, or removal, of weight/mass in isolation to maintain equilibrium (a state of balance) between gravity and buoyancy obtained from the asthenosphere

Loch Lomond readvance: see Loch Lomond stadial

Loch Lomond stadial: the final period of extreme cold and glacial conditions affecting the British Isles, around 10 to 11,000 years BP. This reinvigorated glacial advance in Scotland created small ice caps and glaciers in the Scottish Highlands. The largest ice mass developed in the western Grampians and the North-West Highlands and extended from the north-west to Loch Lomond in the south and Loch Tay in the east. During this period, relatively small valley glaciers and cirques developed in most mountain areas in the British Isles such as the Lake District and as far south as the Brecon Beacons. Permafrost and tundra conditions returned to the lowlands. (Also known as the Loch Lomond re-advance)

Lodgement till: see basal till

Longshore drift: the process through which material is moved along a coast by waves which approach at an angle to the shore but whose backwash recedes directly away from it

Lower beach: the part of a beach that extends from the average high tide mark out to and including the nearshore

Lower course: the final section of a river as it flows toward its mouth. The volume of water in the river is greatest here, its channel deep, the main fluvial process is deposition, and the land around the river is an almost flat floodplain. The river's course is sinuous (winding)

Low water mark: the level reached by seawater at low tide or by other stretches of water at their lowest level

Mass movement: bulk movements of weathered material (rock debris) and soil down slopes. Often assisted by the presence of water

Meander: a winding bend in a river

Mechanical weathering (disintegration): see physical weathering

Medial moraine: when two glaciers merge this is formed from the two joining lateral moraines and results in a linear moraine feature running down the centre of the new larger glacier. Following ablation and the retreat of the glacier this will result in a linear ridge of till along the centre of the valley

Megacity: a large city with a population in excess of 10 million

Meltwater: water formed by the melting of snow and ice, especially from a glacier

Mesosphere: a layer of the atmosphere positioned above the stratopause and below the mesopause. It is located between the altitudes of around 50 km and 85 km

Metamorphic rock: one of the three main rock types along with igneous and sedimentary, formed by the transformation of existing rock types. The transformation is caused by physical or chemical alteration by heat and pressure acting on the original rock type usually while buried within the Earth's crust

Mid-latitude westerlies: winds that blow poleward from approximately 30° to 60° North and South

Middle course: the second section of a river as it flows towards its mouth. Its surrounding landscape is gentler than the upper course that it has left. The valley has widened, the valley sides are gentler. The channel has deepened and widened. Lateral erosion has started the widening of the channel and the valley bottom, allowing the river to wind

Migrants: people who move out of a country or area

Migration: movement of people from one place to another with the intention of settling temporarily or permanently in the new location

Mono-cultivation: the agricultural practice of producing or growing a single crop or plant species over a wide area, for a large number of consecutive years. Widely used in modern industrial agriculture, its implementation has allowed for large harvests from minimal resources, but it requires large input from chemical fertilisers and is not a practice that works in areas of degradation with a fragile and changeable climatic pattern

Moraine: an accumulation of unconsolidated debris (soil and rock) carried and finally deposited by a glacier

Mor humus: found under coniferous woodland or heather moorland under cool, wet conditions; plant matter breakdown is slow due to the limited activity of soil biota

Mottling: rusty 'mottles' occur in soils such as gleys where zones may be enriched with ferric compounds within well-aerated pathways (such as old root channels)

Moulin: a roughly circular, vertical well-like shaft within a glacier through which water enters from the surface

Mountain glacier: see valley glacier

Mudflats: coastal wetlands formed when mud is deposited by waves, tides or rivers (also known as a tidal flats)

Mudflow: very fast, surging flow of debris (soil and fine grained rock debris) that has become partially or fully liquefied by the addition of significant amounts of water to the source material

Mull humus: found under deciduous woodland (brown earth) where the plentiful plant matter is actively broken down by prolific soil biota

National parks: in the United Kingdom these are areas of protection set up with two statutory purposes: conservation and enhancement of the natural and cultural heritage of the area, and to promote understanding and enjoyment of the special qualities of the area by the public. Scottish national parks have two additional purposes: the promotion of sustainable use of the natural resources of the area, and to promote sustainable economic and social development of the area's communities

National Scenic Areas (NSA): designated in Scotland, these are areas of outstanding scenic interest or unsurpassed attractiveness which are given protection to conserve and enhance the landscape. This is similar to the AONB (Areas of Outstanding Natural Beauty) designated in the rest of the United Kingdom

Natural increase: the difference between birth rate and death rate

Neap tide: occurs when the sun and the moon are at right angles to each other in relation to the planet Earth. The gravitational forces counteract each other and create weaker tidal forces. This results in the least difference between high tide and low tide and occurs just after the first and third quarters of the Moon

Needle: a feature formed off the tip of a headland from a sea stack. A stack is worn into a pointed shape principally by sub-aerial processes

Negative regime: in a glacial system when the level of ablation is greater than that of accumulation and results in a negative mass balance. This results in glacier retreat

Névé: snow that has accumulated during a snow season and has become partly melted, refrozen and moderately compacted. It has granular appearance and is an early stage in the development of glacial ice

North Atlantic Drift: an extension of the Gulf Stream (the most important ocean current system in the northern hemisphere), it brings warm waters from the Caribbean north-eastwards and is responsible for moderating the climate of western Europe (also known as the North Atlantic Current or North Atlantic Sea Movement)

Oceanic circulation: the large-scale/global movement of waters in the ocean basins. Winds drive surface circulation, and the cooling and sinking of waters in the polar regions drive deep circulation. Oceanic circulation works with atmospheric circulation to transfer and redistribute heat more evenly around the planet

Oceanic crust: part of the Earth's lithosphere, it is younger, thinner (usually less than 10 km) and denser than continental crust. It is formed at mid-ocean ridges where plates are diverging. As the plates part, this allows magma to rise into the upper mantle and crust where it eventually solidifies to form new crust. The newest crust is found closest to the faults (plate boundaries) from where the mantle rises

Oceanic plates: see tectonic plates

Offshore wind farm: wind turbines placed in bodies of water to generate electricity from wind

Orbit: the movement (usually a curved path) of a celestial body (such as a planet, moon or comet) or an artificial satellite as it moves around another body due to mutual gravitation. In simple terms it may be described as a regular, repeating path that one object in space takes around another one

Organic: generally considered to mean components of the soil which come from living organisms

Output: any item or object leaving a system. In nature an example would be all the moisture which leaves a river system, e.g. by evaporation or entering the sea. In manufacturing outputs could be the product, waste, or even profit

Outwash plain: an area of relatively flat land formed of fluvioglacial sediments deposited by meltwater at the terminus of a glacier. Also known as a sandur

Over-cultivation: occurs when the land is used intensively and over a long period with a little or no rest so the soil structure is destroyed and soil fertility is lost

Oxbow lake: (also known as a horseshoe lake) a lake that is formed when a meander's neck is broken through and a new straight channel is created, cutting off the supply of water to the meander. The entrances and exits of the meander are sealed by deposition and the former meander is left as a still-water lake

Ozone: also known as tri-oxygen, is the triatomic form of oxygen (O_3). It differs from normal oxygen (O_2) in having three atoms in its molecule (O_3). It is a very pale blue gas with a distinctively pungent smell. In the troposphere it is created both naturally and by photochemical reactions involving gases resulting from human activities ('smog'). Tropospheric ozone acts as a greenhouse gas. In the stratosphere it is created by the interaction between solar ultraviolet radiation and molecular oxygen (O_2). Stratospheric ozone plays a decisive role in the stratospheric radiative balance. Its concentration is highest in the ozone layer

Ozone depletion: the reduction (depletion) of ozone gas in the Earth's stratosphere, caused by human created emissions of chlorine and bromine compounds. The main sources of depletion agents are refrigerants, solvents, propellants and foam-blowing agents

Ozone hole: see ozone layer

Ozone layer: the stratosphere contains a layer in which the concentration of ozone is greatest, the so called ozone layer. The Earth's ozone layer protects all life from the Sun's harmful radiation, absorbing 97–99 per cent of ultraviolet light (from about 200 nm to 315 nm wavelength), which otherwise would damage exposed life forms near the surface. This layer is being depleted by human emissions of chlorine and bromine compounds. Every year, during the southern hemisphere spring, a very strong depletion of the ozone layer takes place over the Antarctic region, also caused by human-made chlorine and bromine compounds in combination with the specific meteorological conditions of that region. This phenomenon is called the ozone hole

Pacific-type coastline: see concordant coastline

Peak discharge: highest point on the hydrograph when the rate of discharge is at its greatest

Peak rainfall: point on a flood hydrograph when rainfall is at its greatest

Pedology: study of soils, their factors and processes, soil characteristics and distribution

Percolation: downward movement of water from the surface through the soil and rocks. The nature of the rock is crucial to the percolation rate: when rock is permeable percolation may be rapid and when rock is impermeable, very little, if any, percolation is possible

Permafrost: ground (soil or rock and included ice or organic material) that remains at or below 0°C for at least two consecutive years. Most permafrost is located at high latitudes although some may be found at high altitudes in lower latitudes. See cryotic soil

Permeable: a type of soil which allows water to move through it easily

Permeable rock: allows water to percolate or pass through it, e.g. limestone, sandstone and chalk

Physical weathering: the processes of weathering by which physical actions (such as frost shattering) breakdown a rock into fragments

Piedmont glacier: a type of glaciation where steep valley glaciers meet at the foot of a glaciated area to form an almost stagnant sheet of ice. The valley glaciers spill into relatively flat plains, where they spread out and may form bulb-like lobes

Plate boundaries: locations where tectonic plates meet and the zones where the most active tectonic action is found (volcanoes and earthquakes). There are three different types of plate boundaries: divergent (plates moving apart from each other), convergent (plates moving towards each other) and transform (plates sliding past each other)

Plate margins: see also plate boundaries

Plates: see tectonic plates

Pleistocene: the previous geological epoch to the present Holocene in the Quaternary Period. It lasted from about 2.58 million to 11,700 BP. It covers a time of the planet's most recent extreme glaciation

Plucking: the action of a glacier as it moves ripping/pulling rocks from the bedrock/rock face. This is believed to be caused by the rock becoming frozen into the base or sides of the glacier and then being pulled out and carried away by the ice as it moves

Plunge pool: a deepened pool found at the base of a waterfall, caused by erosion from the falling water (hydraulic action) and abrasion

Plunging breakers: associated with beaches with steeper gradients, this is where wave energy is released suddenly as the crest curls and then descends violently

Podzol: a major soil type, associated with acidic soils, often found in areas of cold coniferous forest

Point bar: *see* slip-off slope

Polar cell: part of the Earth's atmospheric global circulation that assists in the transfer of thermal energy. In the three cell model of atmospheric circulation it is the most northerly cell in the northern hemisphere and the most southerly in the southern (hadley, Ferrel and Polar). Polar cells are the smallest and weakest cells and extend from between 60° and 70° North and South, to the poles

Polar easterlies: the polar easterlies (part of the Polar cells) are the dry, cold prevailing winds that blow out from the high-pressure areas of the polar regions at the north and south poles at surface level towards the lower latitudes

Population density: number of people living in a given area (usually a square kilometre). Density is calculated by dividing the total population of an area by the total area. The resultant information can be shown in a population density map

Population distribution: the pattern of where people live. World population distribution is uneven. Places which are described as sparsely populated contain few people while those places described as densely populated contain many people

Population pyramid: graphical representation of the age and gender distribution of a population. Numbers or proportions of males and females in each age group are plotted as horizontal bars with the males on the left and females on the right. Pyramids may be constructed to show single years of age or five-year age groups

Positive regime: in a glacial system where accumulation exceeds ablation (a positive mass balance) resulting in glacial growth and advance

Post-glacial rebound: see isostatic uplift/rebound

Pothole: a round- or oval-shaped hole in the bedrock of a river bed, which may be formed in one of two ways. 1) Sediment and other material carried by a river erode the bed. Turbulent flow causes pebbles to spin around in place and erode hollows into the river bed. 2) Flowing water encounters bedload and is forced over it, then down towards the bed, eroding behind the bedload and, where there are swirling eddies, small depressions. These can also be deepened by the actions in 1

Precipitation: any form of naturally occurring moisture (liquid or solid) falling from the sky. It includes rain, sleet, snow, hail and drizzle amongst others

Pressure release: a form of physical/mechanical weathering (disintegration) where overlying materials (not necessarily rocks) are removed (by erosion, or other processes), causing underlying rocks to expand and fracture (also known as unloading)

Prevailing wind: the most frequent wind direction a location experiences (the predominant wind direction)

Promontory: see headland

Pyramidal peak: an angular, sharply pointed mountain peak created by glacial erosion. The shape has resulted due to three or more corries eroding backwards from around the peak (also known as a glacial horn or horn)

Quaternary Period: a subdivision of geological time running from approximately 2,588 million years ago to the present time. It is divided into two epochs, the Pleistocene and the Holocene. The Pleistocene (2.588 million years ago to 11.7 thousand years ago) was generally a period of wide-scale glaciation and interglacials with cyclical growth and retreat of continental ice sheets (periods of planetary cooling and warming). The effects of these 'ice ages' resulted in large-scale changes to the landscapes and environments of the planet with continental glaciers reaching as far as 40° latitude. The Holocene (11.7 thousand years ago to today) is viewed by many as an interglacial and as being relatively warm within the context of the whole Quaternary period

Rain shadow: an area having very little precipitation due to a barrier, such as a mountain range, blocking the prevailing winds and causing moisture (precipitation) to be removed from the air before reaching the other side of the barrier

Rainsplash: the impact of raindrops on the soil can dislodge and move soil either outwards (flat land) or downhill (on a slope)

Raised beach: a former beach now located above sea level and no longer acting as a coastal beach. Its changed locations may be due to a lowering of sea level or to isostatic recovery

Range: the distance people are normally prepared to travel to use a service

Reclining (or falling) limb: shows the return of discharge to normal/base flow on a hydrograph

Recurved spit: where a coastal spit has developed an additional curve or a hook. This is usually caused by lengthy periods when the wind direction is changed or where a series of storms has altered the direction of sediment transport and deposition in relation to the original spit

Redevelopment: the rebuilding or renewal of parts of a city (usually the inner-city); this may involve totally clearing an area or just renewing the most damaged parts to retain the best features of the old alongside those of the new

Refugee: a stateless person who finds him/herself displaced and homeless, usually as a result of war, famine, religious/ethnic persecution or cleansing. A refugee is usually without documents, status or belongings

Regelation: a process of glacier movement found at the ice/rock interface beneath the glacier. Here the increased pressure found on the uphill side of a small object (less than 1 metre in width) causes the ice to melt, flow around the object as water and then refreeze on the downhill side where the pressure is less

Regime: difference in the discharge of a river throughout the year. For example, in the UK it would be expected that the discharge of most rivers would be greater in winter months than in the summer

Regolith: loose unconsolidated rock/debris that lies above the layer of solid bedrock

Rejuvenation: this happens when the river's base level falls (e.g. due to eustatic or isostatic sea level change or tectonic movement). The river

regains potential energy and rejuvenates (to exhibit characteristics found in the upper course) with vertical erosion becoming dominant. The river attempts to erode and re-establish a concave profile

Renewable resources: generated from sources which are not finite or exhaustible; wave and water power, solar and geothermal power are examples of renewable energy sources

Residual soil: soil that forms from the bedrock on which it resides or lies

Ria: a coastal inlet formed by the flooding of an unglaciated river valley following sea level rise

Riad: in Morocco, a riad is a large and very pleasant house contained within walls with a courtyard and gardens

Riffle: a rocky shallow section on the bed of a stream or river

Rill erosion: the creation, by heavy rain, of small (usually temporary) water channels, which over time can lead to larger gullies

Rising limb: rising portion of a hydrograph resulting from run-off of rainfall or snowmelt

River channel: the path followed by a river. It is the eroded depression in which the river flows. A channel is typically defined as the area confined within a river's bed and banks

River cliff: the outside bank of a river channel has been eroded and has been undercut resulting in bank collapse leaving a steep slope (the river cliff)

Roches moutonnées: bare outcrops of rock shaped by glacial erosion. The end facing the direction from which the ice moves is smoothed by abrasion but the other end is steeper, stepped, rough and irregular due to plucking

Rockfall: the falling of a newly detached mass of rock from a cliff or down a very steep slope. Rocks in a rockfall can be of any dimension

Rock flour: finely powdered rock formed by glacial or other erosion

Rossby waves: long, variable velocity, east to west moving waves (undulations) of air, found in the mid and upper troposphere, which travel around the globe. Recent studies are now suggesting that some forms of Rossby waves, those with the greatest amplitude, may reach into the stratosphere and may transport gases such as ozone into this level. This is suggested as being responsible for occurrences of warming within the stratosphere

Run-off: all the water that enters and flows out of a river system/basin. Can also be known as the river discharge and is usually measured in cumecs

Rural-urban fringe: the broad band that exists at the edge of a settlement, where urban land uses (e.g. housing, industry) make way for rural land uses (e.g. farming)

Sahel: a semi-arid to arid region to the southern edge of the Sahara Desert in Africa. It stretches across six countries from Senegal to Chad

Saltation: the most common movement occurs when soil particles, close to the ground, move in a series of jumps, bounces and rolls

Salt crystallisation: a form of physical/mechanical weathering (decomposition) caused by salt crystal growth exerting pressure on joints, forcing them to widen and rock to break off

Saltings: see salt marshes

Salt marshes: coastal areas of marshy ground intermittently inundated with saltwater. Usually with pools and rivulets of salt or brackish water and halophytic vegetation

Sand: a type of soil where the soil particle size is between 0.05 and 2.00 mm

Sand dune: a ridge of windblown sand found in deserts or near lakes and oceans. Coastal sand dunes are mounds or small hills of sand that form behind the parts of a beach affected by tides

Satellite: 1. a natural celestial body orbiting a planet e.g. the Moon. 2. a human-constructed device orbiting a planet, moon or other celestial body for investigation/observation, scientific study, military purposes and/or communications

Schist: a foliated medium-grade metamorphic rock formed by dynamic metamorphism at high pressure and temperature. Most schists have been formed from clays and muds which have passed through a series of changes into shale and slate before becoming schist itself; some schists have been derived from fine-grained igneous rocks such as basalt

Sea cave: a natural hollow, passage or chamber eroded into rock (e.g. cliff faces) by wave action at the coast

Sedimentary rocks: one of the three main rock types along with igneous and metamorphic. These have been formed from materials deposited at the Earth's surface. Minerals or organic particles accumulate and are compressed or minerals are precipitated following deposition. The weight of deposited sediments creates pressure on those previously deposited. During this process (compaction) loose sediments and grains are compressed and water expelled. Crystals of salts form and these act to bond the particles together (cementation) and so over time new layers of sedimentary rock are formed

Sex ratio at birth: ratio of male to female births

Shanty town: also known as a spontaneous settlement or squatter town, this is a settlement usually built using materials such as plywood, plastic and corrugated iron; often located in environmentally deficient sites within cities of the developing world

Sheet erosion: removal of the surface topsoil by heavy rain gently flowing down a slope

Short-wave solar (Sun) radiation: due to the Sun's heat it gives off radiation with a short wavelength that contains higher amounts of energy. Solar energy enters our atmosphere as short-wave radiation in the form of ultraviolet (UV) rays and visible light

Silt: a type of soil where the soil particle size is between 0.002 and 0.05 mm

Site: the place where a settlement is located

Site of Special Scientific Interest (SSSI): a conservation designation denoting a protected area in the United Kingdom

Situation: the position or location of a settlement in relation to the surrounding area, e.g. fertile soil, valleys, hills, the coast, river and routes

Slip-off slope: this is a gently sloping depositional landform that is formed on the inside of a river bend where the river slows, loses energy and deposits load

Slumping: a whole segment (soil or rock) of a cliff moving down-slope along a saturated shear-plane, often in a rotational movement

Snout: the end point of a glacier. The furthest point of a continuous glacier from its origin. Also known as the terminus

Snow line: the altitude in a particular place above which snow or ice remains on the ground throughout the year

Snowpack: an accumulation of layers of snow where the climate has extended periods of cold weather throughout the year (including at altitude)

Socio-economic conflict: a disagreement over values, methodology, environmental change/use, and economic exploitation of resources affecting occupation, education, income, wealth, place of residence and standard of living

Soft engineering strategies: projects that use natural resources and local knowledge to reduce the risk posed by a flood

Soil erosion: in agriculture, soil erosion refers to the wearing away of a field's topsoil by the natural physical forces of water, wind or through forces associated with farming activities

Soil profile: a vertical cross section of a soil, divided into a number of distinct layers, referred to as horizons

Solar constant: the rate at which energy reaches the Earth's surface from the sun. The value of the constant is approximately 1366 joules per second per square metre $(J/s \cdot m^2)$. Also referred to as around 1.366 kilowatts per square metre (kW/m^2)

Solar irradiation: see insolation

Solar radiation: the radiant energy emitted from nuclear fission reactions on the Sun. It is electromagnetic radiation including x-rays, ultraviolet and infrared radiation, radio emissions, as well as visible light

Solution: the process in which minerals are dissolved by water (also see corrosion)

Souks: found within the centre of many North African settlements, the souk is the market within the medina, or old city walls. The souk may also house small industries such as slipper and shoe making and iron working

South-Western Monsoon: a name given to the South West trade winds which bring heavy rainfall with the movement of the intertropical convergence zone (ITCZ)

Special Area of Conservation (SAC): a European Union designation denoting an area for the conservation of natural habitats and wild fauna and flora

Sphere of influence: the area served by a settlement or the area over which the settlement has an impact. The key relationship is between the population size and the number and range of services found. The larger the settlement the greater the number and range of services and the greater the 'sphere of influence'

Spilling breakers: waves in which the unstable top spills down the front of the wave-form as it advances into shallower water. Consequently it gradually diminishes in height until it moves up the beach as swash

Spit: an extended stretch of beach material that projects out to sea and is joined to the mainland at one end. Formed due to longshore drift continuing past where the coastline curves inward and away from its previous direction

Spring tide: when the Moon is either new or full, and the Sun, Moon and Earth are aligned. This results in their collective gravitational pull on the Earth's water strengthening and raising the height of the water beneath and thus increasing the tide's level

Spur: a narrow neck of high land extending into a river valley, often forming the divide between two tributaries

Stack: a column of rock standing detached from the tip of a headland and resulting from the collapse of a sea arch

Stadial: a period during glaciation when the temperature falls and more ice forms encouraging the extensive growth and re-advance of ice sheets and glaciers

Stem flow: occurs when water runs down a plant stem or a tree trunk

Stone lines: long rows of stones piled together to form barriers across a field, on either flat or gently sloping ground. They do not store water but slow its flow across the ground. The stone lines force the water to spread out across the soil, allowing it to seep slowly into the ground

Storage: within the hydrological cycle the term used to describe moisture contained within the system; in the soil, vegetation, lakes, ice, rivers and ground

Storm flow: storm run-off resulting from storm precipitation involving both surface flow and throughflow

Storm ridge: a steep-sided mound running along the rear of a coastal beach consisting of sand and/or pebbles built up by storm waves

Stoss: referring to the smooth slope of a roche moutonnée, it is the slope that faced the direction from which a glacier approached

Stratosphere: the layer of the atmosphere between the troposphere and the mesosphere. It is located at an altitude of between approximately 13 km (8 miles) and 50 km (30 miles)

Stream order: in classifying parts of arriver, the sizes range from the smallest – a 1st order stream – to the largest

Striations: scratches or gouges cut into bedrock or rock faces by glacial abrasion

Stump: a small low-lying rock island formed at the tip of a headland. Wave action erodes the area between the low and high water marks on a stack or needle to the point where the rock higher up cannot be supported. This collapses and leaves behind the stack/needle base as the low-lying rock island

Sub-aerial processes: this is a term used to describe events/methods that form features and take place on a land surface exposed to Earth's atmosphere

Sublimation: the process whereby a solid changes to a gas, or gas to a solid, without an intermediate liquid stage (without becoming a liquid first)

Submergent coastlines: where the sea has flooded a coastal area, e.g. rias and fjords (fiords)

Subsoil: the B horizon of a soil; the zone where iron oxides and clay minerals accumulate

Summer solstice: the time of the longest day, around 21 June in the northern hemisphere and 22 December in the southern hemisphere. It is experienced when the planet tilt for the hemisphere is most inclined towards the Sun. At noon the Sun is at its highest height above the horizon

Supraglacial moraine: deposits of rock debris that are found on the surface of glacial ice. This term can be used to describe lateral and medial moraine that has not reached beneath the surface of the ice, debris which falls from the valley sides to cover areas of the surface (e.g. rock falls and avalanches) as well as any rock debris or dust that settles in the top of the glacier

Surface creep: a very slow movement over the ground (usually larger particles of soil or stones) rolling and sliding

Surface current circulation: the horizontal movement of seawater in the oceans at, or near, the surface. It is driven by the circulation of wind above the surface, as friction between the wind and the ocean at the ocean/wind interface causes the water to move in the direction of the wind. The winds are created by atmospheric pressure so the currents can be seen as an interaction with the atmosphere. They are also a response to the flow of energy from the tropics to the polar regions, so surface current circulation is the 'surface' component of thermohaline circulation

Suspension: when fine soil is blown away suspended by strong winds in a dust storm

Sustainable resource: one that is used up at the same speed that it is renewed. For example, wood can be a sustainable resource if the trees are harvested at the same rate as new trees mature. Wind is a sustainable resource as it is not used up. Solar and hydroelectric power can be considered sustainable. Oil, natural gas and minerals taken from the earth do not regenerate and are non-sustainable. Fish stocks can be renewed and can be used in a sustainable fashion, but are presently being used at a greater rate than they are being renewed and are considered non-sustainable

Sustainable soil: a healthy soil that is in balance. Essential for the production of crops used to feed humans and livestock. In addition to providing a stable base to support plant roots, soil stores water and nutrients required for plant growth

Swash: the water that washes up on the beach after an incoming wave has broken

Swash-aligned coasts: coastlines oriented parallel or roughly parallel to the direction of the prevailing waves

Tarn: see corrie lochan

Tectonic plates: the lithosphere, the rigid outermost shell of the planet (the crust and upper mantle), is broken up into slabs called plates. On Earth, there are seven or eight major plates and many minor plates. Plate sizes range from a few hundred to thousands of kilometres wide. Plate thickness ranges from less than 15 km to around 200 km. The thinnest plates are inclined to be the youngest created and are found under the oceans. These are given the name oceanic plates. The thickest tend to be beneath the continents and are known as continental plates (also known as lithospheric plates or plates). Continental plates are mostly comprised of granitic rocks made up of relatively lightweight materials. Oceanic crust is much denser and heavier, composed mainly of basaltic rocks

Terminal moraine: all the debris scooped up and pushed by the front (snout) of glacial ice and deposited as a large mound of rocks, soil and sediments, marking the farthest extent of the advance of the ice

Terminus: the end point. In glaciation this is the end point of a glacier. The furthest point of a continuous glacier from its origin

Terrestrial radiation: long-wave electromagnetic radiation originating from Earth and its atmosphere

Thermal (heat) equator: the line which circumscribes the Earth and connects all points of highest mean annual temperature for their longitudes. The parallel of latitude 10°N has the highest mean temperature of any latitude (also known as the heat equator)

Thermally direct cells: in the atmosphere these are cells where the movement of air is as a direct consequence of the latitudinal differences in surface temperature. In the three cell model of atmospheric circulation both the Hadley cell and the Polar cell are thermally direct with higher temperatures at the surface driving convection

Thermally indirect cells: in the atmosphere these are cells which are dependent on the action of other cells to generate their movement of air. In the three cell model of atmospheric circulation this applies to the Ferrel cell which depends on the movement of air from both the Hadley and Polar cells. The upward leg of the Ferrel cell is dragged by the upward thermally direct movement of the Polar cell and the downward leg pulled downwards by the descending air from the thermally direct Hadley cell

Thermohaline circulation: a large-scale density-driven circulation in the ocean, caused by differences in temperature and salinity. 'Thermo' refers to temperature and 'haline' to salt content. In the North

Atlantic the thermohaline circulation consists of warm surface water flowing northward and cold deep water flowing southward, resulting in a net poleward transport of heat. The surface water sinks in highly restricted sinking regions located in high latitudes (also known as the Global Ocean Conveyor or Great Ocean Conveyor Belt)

Thermosphere: the outermost layer of the atmosphere lying between the mesosphere and the exosphere. It ranges from an altitude of approximately 80 km to around 450 km. Temperature increases with altitude reaching a maximum of 1,727°C

Threshold: the minimum number of people required to support a particular good, shop or office. Large stores may have a threshold population over 100,000, a shoe shop perhaps 25,000 and a small local convenience store 1,000

Throughfall: water dripping from one leaf or plant to another

Throughflow: water that continues to move downhill through the soil and ground and which may emerge into rivers, lakes or streams

Tidal flats: see mudflats

Tide: the alternate rising and falling of the sea, usually twice in each lunar day at a particular place, produced by the gravitational attraction of the Moon and Sun on the seas and oceans

Till: see glacial till

Tombolo: a sand or shingle bar linking an island to the mainland or another island

Topographic forcing: when moving air (wind) is forced to increase its altitude due to encountering hills or mountains

Topsoil: the A horizon of a soil; the most fertile layer of soil where humus, plant roots and living organisms are found

Total fertility rate: the average number of children that would be born per woman if all women lived to the end of their childbearing years and bore children according to a given set of age-specific fertility rates

Traction: the process whereby a current transports materials by rolling or sliding along the contact area where the current contacts with the land/rock at the base of the flow

Trade winds: the prevailing easterly surface winds in the tropics. They blow predominantly from the north-east in the northern hemisphere and from the south-east in the southern hemisphere

Translocation: movement of material in solution or suspension from one horizon to another

Transpiration: a biological process by which water is lost from a plant through the minute pores (stomata) in the leaves. Transpiration rates depend on the time of year (season), type and amount of vegetation

Transportation: the removal of weathered and eroded materials. This can involve gravity as well as the same agents as those of erosion

Tributary: a river or stream flowing into a larger river

Tributary glacier: a smaller glacier that joins onto a larger glacier

Tropical Continental (cT) air mass: a body of air formed in the lower latitudes over landmasses in subtropical zones. Temperatures range from warm to hot and having developed over a landmass the air is dry

Tropical Maritime (mT) air mass: a body of air formed over tropical and subtropical oceans. Temperatures range from warm to hot and having developed over oceans the air is moist

Tropical rain belt: a region of low pressure and rainfall which oscillates from the northern to the southern tropics over the course of the year, roughly following the thermal equator. Often referred to as a component of the intertropical convergence zone

Tropical storm: see cyclone

Troposphere: the lowest layer of Earth's atmosphere. This layer is the area suited to life as it exists on Earth. It contains the majority of atmosphere's mass (around 88 per cent) and around 99 per cent of its water vapour

Truncated spur: where a narrow neck of high land that extended into a river valley has been cut off and stunted by the erosion of a glacier as it occupied the river valley. This may result in a cliff face being the remains of the original spur. (Truncated spurs can also be created by wave erosion at coastlines)

Tsunami: a very large ocean wave caused by an underwater earthquake, or a volcanic eruption or landslide. It increases in height as it reaches shallower waters. Tsunamis can cause great destruction and loss of life in coastal areas

Tundra: a cold, treeless and usually lowland area in which the subsoil is permanently frozen. In warmer/summer periods where the top layer of soil thaws, mosses, lichens, grasses and small shrubs may grow

Ultraviolet (UV) radiation: electromagnetic radiation or light having a wavelength greater than 10 nm but less than 400 nm. These wavelengths are shorter than those for ordinary visible violet light but longer than those of x-rays. This is naturally emitted in sunlight and can burn the skin and cause skin cancer

Undercutting: erosion beneath an overlying structure/feature

UNESCO: the United Nations Educational, Scientific and Cultural Organisation

Upper beach: the area of dry beach above the average high tide mark and up to the primary dunes or sea cliffs. Although usually a dry, sandy area, it can be affected by storms or extremely high tides (also known as the backshore)

Upper course: this is the first stage of a river, the stage closest to its source. It has steep river gradients, and the river has a narrow channel. The river covers most of the valley floor. The dominant type of erosion is vertical and there are steep valley sides forming a V-shape. Interlocking spurs, rapids, waterfalls and gorges tend to be found here

Urban decay: refers to parts of the city that become run down and undesirable to live in; it causes economic, social and environmental problems

Urban decline: deterioration of the inner-city, usually caused by lack of investment and maintenance; often but not exclusively accompanied by a decline in population numbers, decreasing economic performance and unemployment

Urban deprivation: a standard of living below that of the majority in a particular sector of society that involves hardships and lack of access to resources. Places suffering from urban deprivation have visible differences in housing and economic opportunities for the poor compared to the rich

Urbanisation: the process by which an increasing percentage of a country's population moves to live in towns and cities

Urban regeneration/renewal: refers to a rebuilding of the physical, social and economic characteristics of run-down urban areas as part of a strategic plan to improve the area. In the UK, typical examples include housing, industrial locations and dockside developments in the inner-city. It goes beyond the redevelopment of just the physical area of a location and aims to tackle the social and economic problems of the area, such as poverty, poor health and unemployment. Urban regeneration projects are major interventions that require considerable financial contributions from both the public and private sectors

Urban sprawl: the spread of towns and cities into the surrounding countryside

U-shaped valley: a steep-sided valley with a wide, relatively flat base carved by glacial erosion. The term comes from the similarity between the valley cross section and the capital letter 'U'. May also be referred to as a glacial trough

Valley glacier: an extended mass of ice formed from snow falling and accumulating in mountain regions. The ice moves out from the area of accumulation within previously existing valleys which it erodes extensively both laterally and vertically

Vernal equinox: the point in the year when the Sun's position in the sky crosses the plane of the equator making day and night of equal length. This happens around 21 March in the northern hemisphere (the Sun tracking northwards) and 23 September in the southern hemisphere (the Sun tracking southwards)

Walker cell: named after the work of British physicist Sir Gilbert Thomas Walker (1868–1958), a model of air flow in the tropics in the troposphere. According to this model, parcels of air follow a closed circulation in the zonal and vertical directions (also known as Walker circulation)

Walker circulation: see Walker cell

Warm-based glacier: glaciers experiencing conditions where the base of the glacier is above the melting point of ice. There may also be meltwater throughout the glacier. The abundant meltwater assists in lubricating the glacier so that it moves relatively quickly

Water balance: worked out from inputs (precipitation) and outputs (basin discharge and evapotranspiration). The water balance affects how much water is stored in the river basin. The water balance of a basin/country can be studied using a water budget graph which shows the relationship between temperature, precipitation and evaporation rates over a year

Waterfall: water falling from a height, formed when a river or stream flows over a precipice or steep slope

Water table: the level below which the ground is saturated with water

Wave: an oscillating movement up and down of a body of water caused by the frictional drag of the wind at the wind water interface

Wave-cut notch: an indentation cut into a sea cliff at water level by wave action

Wave-cut platform: a gently sloping (5° or under) rock ledge that extends from the high-tide level at a cliff base to below the low-tide level. This has been formed by wave action eroding the base of the cliff, the cliff above collapsing and the material below then removed by waves or coastal currents. The cliff retreats and the rock platform is left

Wave pounding: the 'sledgehammer' effect of tonnes of water crashing against cliffs. It shakes and weakens the rocks leaving them open to attack from hydraulic action and abrasion

Weather: the state of the atmosphere at a particular location during a short period of time. Weather is made up of a number of elements including temperature, pressure, wind direction, wind speed, humidity, cloud type, cloud cover, visibility and precipitation

Weathering: refers to the breakdown and decomposition of rocks and minerals by the air, water, Sun and frost

West Wind Drift: see Antarctic Circumpolar Current (ACC)

Wetted perimeter: the parts of the cross section of a river or stream's channel in contact with the river water (usually river bed and banks)

Winter solstice: the time of the shortest day, around 22 December in the northern hemisphere and 21 June in the southern hemisphere. The time when the planet tilt is most inclined away from the Sun for the hemisphere in which it is experienced

World Heritage Site (WHS): a natural or man-made site, area, or structure recognised as being of outstanding international importance and deserving special protection. Nominated to, and designated by, the World Heritage Convention (part of UNESCO)

Xerophyte: any species of plant that has adapted to survive in an environment with little water

Zonal soils: mature soils that form under the influence of climate, vegetation and biota activity; they have formed over a long period of time and have reached a stable state

Zone of ablation: the area of a glacier with a net loss in ice mass due to processes such as melting, sublimation, evaporation and ice calving. This is found on the lower end of the glacier

Zone of accumulation: the area of a glacier, in its higher stages, where there is a net gain in ice mass and where the addition of ice is greater than the processes of ablation

Index

Page numbers in *italic* refer to glossary entries.